*The
Music of Herbert
Howells*

The Music of Herbert Howells

Edited by
Phillip A. Cooke and
David Maw

THE BOYDELL PRESS

© Contributors 2013

All rights reserved. Except as permitted under current legislation
no part of this work may be photocopied, stored in a retrieval system,
published, performed in public, adapted, broadcast,
transmitted, recorded or reproduced in any form or by any means,
without the prior permission of the copyright owner

First published 2013
The Boydell Press, Woodbridge

ISBN 978–1–84383–879–1

The Boydell Press is an imprint of Boydell & Brewer Ltd
PO Box 9, Woodbridge, Suffolk IP12 3DF, UK
and of Boydell & Brewer Inc,
668 Mt Hope Avenue, Rochester, NY 14620, USA
website: www.boydellandbrewer.com

A CIP catalogue record for this book is available
from the British Library

The publisher has no responsibility for the continued existence or accuracy
of URLs for external or third-party websites referred to in this book,
and does not guarantee that any content on such websites is,
or will remain, accurate or appropriate

This publication is printed on acid-free paper

A few people there are who regard attempted analysis as attempted murder. It is true that with words one can describe the shape of a tune, but not convey a sense of its practical emotional effect; that texture can be analysed to some extent, but its quality be known only through the living sounds. Yet there is a taint of humbug in the wholesale condemnation of attempts to examine the means by which a composer attains his ends. In the end all works are subjected to analysis; and not without real profit. But knowledge so gained is, or ought to be, only complementary.

Herbert Howells
('Vaughan Williams's "Pastoral" Symphony', 132)

Contents

List of Illustrations   ix
List of Musical Examples   x
List of Tables   xv
List of Contributors   xvi
Foreword   xviii
John Rutter
Acknowledgements   xix

Introduction: Paradox of an Establishment Composer   1
David Maw

PART I   Howells the Stylist

1   'In matters of art friendship should not count': Stanford and Howells   10
    Jonathan White
2   Howells and Counterpoint   22
    Lionel Pike
3   Window on a Complex Style: *Six Pieces for Organ*   37
    Diane Nolan Cooke

PART II   Howells the Vocal Composer

4   'Hidden Artifice': Howells as Song-Writer   62
    Jeremy Dibble
5   A 'Wholly New Chapter' in Service Music: *Collegium regale* and the *Gloucester Service*   86
    Phillip A. Cooke
6   Howells's Use of the Melisma: Word Setting in His Songs and Choral Music   100
    Paul Spicer

PART III   Howells the Instrumental Composer

7   'From "Merry-Eye" to Paradise': The Early Orchestral Music of Herbert Howells   118
    Lewis Foreman
8   Lost, Remembered, Mislaid, Rewritten: A Documentary Study of In Gloucestershire   139
    Paul Andrews
9   Style and Structure in the Oboe Sonata and Clarinet Sonata   153
    Fabian Huss

PART IV   Howells the Modern

10   'Tunes all the way'? Romantic Modernism and the Piano Concertos of Herbert Howells   170
    Jonathan Clinch
11   'I am a "modern" in this, but a Britisher too': Howells and the Phantasy   185
    David Maw

12 Austerity, Difficulty and Retrospection: The Late Style of Herbert Howells   222
    Phillip A. Cooke

PART V *Howells in Mourning*

13 *In modo elegiaco*: Howells and the Sarabande   240
    Graham Barber
14 On Hermeneutics in Howells: Some Thoughts on Interpreting His Cello Concerto   274
    Jonathan Clinch
15 Musical Cenotaph: Howells's *Hymnus paradisi* and Sites of Mourning   285
    Byron Adams

Appendix: Catalogue of the Works of Herbert Howells   309
Paul Andrews

Bibliography   347
Index of Works   353
General Index   356

Illustrations

Fig.

7.1	Howells's one-page sketch for a Symphony (from Notebook 2)	119
7.2	'Overture (to Bublum)', *The Bs*, Suite for Orchestra, Op. 13	122
7.3	Facsimile of the Diaghilev Ballet prospectus	130
7.4	*Sine nomine: A Phantasy*, Op. 37, opening page from piano score	134
7.5	*Paradise Rondel*, first page of manuscript in full score	137
13.1	'Eia mater', *Stabat Mater*, opening page of the complete ink draft, with pencil emendations	266
13.2	Autograph manuscript of 'Saraband', Sonatina for Piano	270
13.3	First page of an early draft of 'Sarabande', Partita for Organ	272
15.1	The Cenotaph in Whitehall, London. Armistice Day, 1920. Image courtesy of the Imperial War Museum	301
15.2	Memorial to the Missing of the Somme, Thiepval, Picardie, France. Photograph by Iain Kendall	305

Musical Examples

Chapter 2 (Lionel Pike)

Ex.

2.1	*Take Him, Earth, for Cherishing*, bars 1–9	25
2.2	*Take Him, Earth, for Cherishing*, bars 10–18	26
2.3	*Take Him, Earth, for Cherishing*, bars 19–23	28
2.4	*Take Him, Earth, for Cherishing*, bars 37–40	29
2.5	*Take Him, Earth, for Cherishing*, bars 58–66	31
2.6	*Take Him, Earth, for Cherishing*, bars 80–5	32
2.7	*Take Him, Earth, for Cherishing*, bars 92–6	32
2.8	*Take Him, Earth, for Cherishing*, bars 97–9	33
2.9	*Take Him, Earth, for Cherishing*, bars 109–11	34
2.10	*Take Him, Earth, for Cherishing*, bars 124–30	34

Chapter 3 (Diane Nolan Cooke)

3.1	'Fugue, Chorale and Epilogue', *Six Pieces for Organ*, bars 1–4	43
3.2	'Saraband (for the Morning of Easter)', *Six Pieces for Organ*, bars 79–82	44
3.3	'Master Tallis's Testament', *Six Pieces for Organ*, bars 23–6	45
3.4	'Saraband (for the Morning of Easter)', *Six Pieces for Organ*, bars 1–8	45
3.5	'Paean', *Six Pieces for Organ*, bars 56–7	46
3.6	'Saraband (*in modo elegiaco*)', *Six Pieces for Organ*, bars 51–2	47
3.7	'Paean', *Six Pieces for Organ*, bars 30–3	47
3.8	'Paean', *Six Pieces for Organ*, bars 106–12	48
3.9	'Saraband (*in modo elegiaco*)', *Six Pieces for Organ*, bars 38–46	48
3.10	'Saraband (for the Morning of Easter)', *Six Pieces for Organ*, bars 74–6	49
3.11	'Fugue, Chorale and Epilogue', *Six Pieces for Organ*, bars 76–85	49
3.12	'Preludio "sine nomine"', *Six Pieces for Organ*, bars 26–34	50
3.13	'Master Tallis's Testament', *Six Pieces for Organ*, bars 1–6	52
3.14	'Preludio "sine nomine"', *Six Pieces for Organ*, bars 1–4	53
3.15	'Saraband (for the Morning of Easter)', *Six Pieces for Organ*, bars 47–54	54
3.16	'Master Tallis's Testament', *Six Pieces for Organ*, bars 44–5	55
3.17	'Fugue, Chorale and Epilogue', *Six Pieces for Organ*, bars 54–5	56
3.18	'Saraband (for the Morning of Easter)', *Six Pieces for Organ*, bar 59	56

Chapter 4 (Jeremy Dibble)

4.1	'The Twilight People', *Five Songs*	65
4.2	'The Devotee', *Five Songs*	68
4.3	'Wanderer's Night Song', *In Green Ways*, Op. 43	70
4.4	*By the Waters of Babylon*	71
4.5	'The Goat Paths', *In Green Ways*, Op. 43	73
4.6	'Under the Greenwood Tree', *In Green Ways*, Op. 43	75
4.7	'Merry Margaret', *In Green Ways*, Op. 43	76

4.8	'An Old Man's Lullaby'	78
4.9	'The Restful Branches'	79
4.10	'Upon a Summer's Day'	80
4.11	'King David'	82

Chapter 5 (Phillip A. Cooke)

5.1	Magnificat, Evening Service in G major, bars 199–205	90
5.2	Magnificat, *Collegium regale*, bars 1–5	93
5.3	Nunc dimittis, *Collegium regale*, bars 5–10	94
5.4	Magnificat, *Gloucester Service*, bars 17–19	94
5.5	Magnificat, *Gloucester Service*, bars 63–4/79–81	95
5.6	Magnificat, *Collegium regale*, bars 28–30	96
5.7	Nunc dimittis, *Gloucester Service*, bars 55–7	97

Chapter 6 (Paul Spicer)

6.1	'Wanderers', *A Garland for de la Mare*, bars 6–13	103
6.2	'Wanderers', *A Garland for de la Mare*, bars 30–4	104
6.3	'The Lady Caroline', *A Garland for de la Mare*, bars 52–61	106
6.4	'Before Dawn', *A Garland for de la Mare*, bars 5–18	107
6.5	'Before Dawn', *A Garland for de la Mare*, bars 80–3	108
6.6	'The Old Stone House', *A Garland for de la Mare*, bars 47–51	108
6.7	'Andy Battle', *A Garland for de la Mare*, bars 79–83	109
6.8	*Te Deum* (St George's Chapel, Windsor), bars 37–46	112
6.9	*Te Deum* (St George's Chapel, Windsor), bars 52–6	113
6.10	*Te Deum* (St George's Chapel, Windsor), bars 161–5	113
6.11	*Te Deum* (St George's Chapel, Windsor), bars 164–73	114

Chapter 7 (Lewis Foreman)

7.1	'Scherzo (to Blissy)', *The Bs*, Suite for Orchestra, Op. 13	123
7.2	*Elegy*, Op. 15, opening viola line	125
7.3	*Sir Patrick Spens*, opening bars	129
7.4	*Procession*, Op. 36, climax	132

Chapter 8 (Paul Andrews)

8.1a	String Quartet no. 3, *In Gloucestershire*, Op. 34, 2nd version, 1st mvt, bars 1–6	147
8.1b	String Quartet no. 3, *In Gloucestershire*, Op. 34, 4th version, 1st mvt, bars 1–11	148
8.2a	String Quartet no. 3, *In Gloucestershire*, Op. 34, 2nd version, 3rd mvt, bars 1–9	149
8.2b	String Quartet no. 3, *In Gloucestershire*, Op. 34, 4th version, 1st mvt, bars 171–8	149

8.3	String Quartet no. 3, *In Gloucestershire*, Op. 34, 4th version, 3rd mvt, bars 1–16	150
8.4a	String Quartet no. 3, *In Gloucestershire*, Op. 34, 2nd version, 4th mvt, bars 1–9	151
8.4b	String Quartet no. 3, *In Gloucestershire*, Op. 34, 4th version, 4th mvt, figure 1 (bar 19)	152

Chapter 9 (Fabian Huss)

9.1	Sonata for Oboe and Piano, 1st mvt, bars 1–9	156
9.2	Sonata for Oboe and Piano, 1st mvt, bars 38–9	157
9.3	Sonata for Oboe and Piano, 1st mvt, bars 55–6	158
9.4	Sonata for Oboe and Piano, 1st mvt, bars 66–7	158
9.5	Sonata for Oboe and Piano, 1st mvt, bars 102–4	159
9.6	Sonata for Oboe and Piano, 1st mvt, bars 27–8/146–8/152–3	160
9.7	Sonata for Oboe and Piano, 2nd mvt, b. 26	161
9.8	Sonata for Oboe and Piano, 3rd mvt, bars 1–4	163
9.9	Sonata for Clarinet and Piano, 1st mvt, bars 1–4	166
9.10	Sonata for Clarinet and Piano, 2nd mvt, bars 194–5	167
9.11	Sonata for Clarinet and Piano, 2nd mvt, bars 272–3	167

Chapter 11 (David Maw)

11.1a	Sonata no. 1 in E major for Violin and Piano, 1st theme and motivic development in its exposition	197
11.1b	Sonata no. 1 in E major for Violin and Piano, climactic and developmental transformation of 1st theme	197
11.1c	Sonata no. 1 in E major for Violin and Piano, first theme transformed in 3rd mvt	197
11.2a	Sonata no. 1 in E major for Violin and Piano, enharmonic mutation in transition between 1st and 2nd mvts	198
11.2b	Sonata no. 1 in E major for Violin and Piano, enharmonic mutation avoided to achieve final closure	198
11.3a	Sonata no. 1 in E major for Violin and Piano, confusion of tonic and its relative undermining cadential direction	201
11.3b	Sonata no. 1 in E major for Violin and Piano, ostinato repetition undermining harmonic direction	201
11.4ab	*Fantasy String Quartet*, Op. 25, presentation and unfolding of motto theme. *Fantasy String Quartet*, Op. 25, transformation of motto theme in 1st episode	203
11.4c	*Fantasy String Quartet*, Op. 25, transformation of motto theme in 2nd episode	203
11.5	*Fantasy String Quartet*, Op. 25, abrupt key change through progression of half-diminished seventh chords	205
11.6a	*Fantasy String Quartet*, Op. 25, textural and harmonic rupture initiating closing section	206
11.6b	*Fantasy String Quartet*, Op. 25, harmony of closing section	207

11.7	*Rhapsodic Quintet*, Op. 31, unity and contrast in the principal themes	208
11.8	*Rhapsodic Quintet*, Op. 31, progressive transformation of 1st theme	209
11.9	*Rhapsodic Quintet*, Op. 31, textural and harmonic rupture at end of development	209
11.10a	*Rhapsodic Quintet*, Op. 31, harmonic and tonal architecture of exposition	210
11.10b	*Rhapsodic Quintet*, Op. 31, harmonic structure of 1st theme	210
11.10c	*Rhapsodic Quintet*, Op. 31, harmonic progressions by minor third in latter part of development	210
11.11	*Rhapsodic Quintet*, Op. 31, enharmonic duality in transition of recapitulation	212
11.12	*Rhapsodic Quintet*, Op. 31, harmonic process of closing section	212
11.13	*Phantasy*, Op. 29, no. 1, indebtedness to Ravel, *Jeux d'eau*	214
11.14	*Phantasy*, Op. 29, no.1, indebtedness to Debussy	215

Chapter 12 (Phillip A. Cooke)

12.1	*A Sequence for St Michael*, bars 4–7	225
12.2	Magnificat, *Chichester Service*, bars 150–5	228
12.3	'Interlude', Partita for Organ, bars 1–2	231
12.4	*Sweetest of Sweets*, bars 47–50	233
12.5	*The Fear of the Lord*, bars 88–91	234

Chapter 13 (Graham Barber)

13.1	Eight sarabande incipits (a) to (h)	241
13.2	Galiardo (Orlando Gibbons, *Parthenia*), bars 1–7	243
13.3	'Lambert's Fireside', *Lambert's Clavichord*, Op. 41, bars 1–8	244
13.4	'My Lord Sandwich's Dreame', *Lambert's Clavichord*, Op. 41, bars 1–8	245
13.5	Chacony in G minor (Henry Purcell), bars 102–9	245
13.6	'Wortham's Grounde', *Lambert's Clavichord*, Op. 41, bars 31–40	246
13.7	'Samuel's Air', *Lambert's Clavichord*, Op. 41, bars 14–23	247
13.8	'Saraband', *English Suite* (C. H. H. Parry), bars 1–14	248
13.9	'Sarabande', *Pour le piano* (Claude Debussy), bars 1–14	249
13.10	*Pastoral Symphony*, 4th mvt (Ralph Vaughan Williams), letter A, bars 4–10	250
13.11	'Saraband of the Sons of God', *Job, A Masque for Dancing* (Ralph Vaughan Williams), bars 1–8	250
13.12	'Agnus Dei', *Dona nobis pacem* (Ralph Vaughan Williams), bars 1–13	251
13.13	'King David', bars 1–10, rebarred in 3/2	252
13.14	'The Goat Paths', *In Green Ways*, Op. 43, bars 26–37	253
13.15	'To Music Bent', bars 1–18	254
13.16	Gloria, *An English Mass*, five bars before figure 52	255
13.17	Nunc dimittis, *Gloucester Service*, bars 1–17	256
13.18	'Master Tallis's Testament', *Six Pieces for Organ*, bars 1–8, barred in 3/4 instead of 6/8	257

13.19	'Scene VIII', *Job, A Masque for Dancing* (Ralph Vaughan Williams), letter Xx, bars 1–5	258
13.20	'Saraband (*in modo elegiaco*)', *Six Pieces for Organ*, bars 28–46	260
13.21	*Prelude: 'De profundis'*, bars 93–116	262
13.22	'Goff's Fireside', *Howells' Clavichord*, bars 1–8	263
13.23	'Rubbra's Soliloquy', *Howells' Clavichord*, bars 27–38	263
13.24	'Malcolm's Vision', *Howells' Clavichord*, recapitulation	264
13.25	'Cujus: (as a Saraband for the Morning of Crucifixion)', *Stabat mater*	265
13.26	'Eia mater', *Stabat mater*, bars 9–16 (continuing Ex. 13.1e)	265
13.27	'Iles's Interlude', *Three Figures*, bars 1–27	267
13.28	'Cujus animam gementem', *Stabat mater*, reduction of accompaniment from six bars before figure 18	268
13.29	'Virgo, virginum praeclara', *Stabat mater*, from one bar before figure 50	269
13.30	'Fac ut portem', *Stabat mater*, reduction of accompaniment only from seven bars before figure 55	269

Chapter 14 (Jonathan Clinch)

14.1	Opening of 'Sketches for a Finale', *Cello Concerto*, RCM, MS 8845c	279
14.2	An earlier sketch of the opening of the finale, *Cello Concerto*, RCM, MS 8845c	279
14.3	Psalm-Prelude, set 2, no. 3, bars 1–3	279

Chapter 15 (Byron Adams)

15.1a	*Elegy*, Op. 15, bars 1–4	297
15.1b	Psalm 23, Requiem, bars 1–2	297
15.2a	'Prelude', *The Dream of Gerontius* (Edward Elgar), bars 1–4	298
15.2b	'Preludio', *Hymnus paradisi*, bars 1–4	298

Tables

Table

11.1	Form of *Fantasy String Quartet* (HH 71)	189
11.2	Form of Sonata no. 1 for Violin and Piano (HH 78)	191
11.3	Form of *Rhapsodic Quintet* (HH 107)	194
11.4	Overlay of formal levels in the Sonata no. 1 for Violin and Piano	200
11.5	Form of *Phantasy* for piano, Op. 29, no. 1 (HH 74)	217

Contributors

Byron Adams is a Professor of Musicology in the Department of Music at the University of California, Riverside. He was coeditor of *Vaughan Williams Essays* and acted as scholar-in-residence for the 2007 Bard Music Festival, "Elgar and His World"; a book connected to this festival, *Edward Elgar and His World*, was published that year by Princeton University Press. He is an Associate Editor of *The Musical Quarterly*. He is joint series editor, with Rachel Cowgill and Peter Holman, of Boydell & Brewer's book series Music in Britain, 1600–2000.

Paul Andrews read Music and Library and Information Studies at Aberystwyth, and was awarded his Ph.D. for 'Herbert Howells: A Documentary and Bibliographical Study' in 1999. He worked in music libraries in Bedfordshire and at the Royal College of Music, and was the first project manager for 'Cecilia: Mapping the Music Resource of the UK and Ireland'. Paul was ordained a priest in the Church of England in 2000 and is a parish priest in the Diocese of Ely.

Graham Barber is Emeritus Professor at the University of Leeds and has contributed articles on church and organ music to numerous publications. He is well known as a concert organist in the UK, Europe and further afield.

Jonathan Clinch is a tutor in the Music and Foundation Departments at Durham University. His doctorate focused on the absolute music of Herbert Howells and featured a major completion of Howells's Cello Concerto, which is shortly to be published by Novello.

Phillip A. Cooke is primarily active as a composer, with many of his works performed by the country's leading choirs and ensembles. His compositions have won international prizes and have been broadcast across Europe. He is also active as a musicologist and has worked on the choral works of James MacMillan and Benjamin Britten in addition to Herbert Howells. He has held academic positions at Oxford University and Eton College and is currently University Lecturer in Composition at the University of Aberdeen.

Jeremy Dibble is Professor of Music at Durham University, specialising in British and Irish music of the nineteenth and early twentieth centuries. He has produced critical and analytical monographs on Parry, Stanford, Stainer, Esposito and Harty, and is presently working on a study of the musical style of Frederick Delius. He also maintains a major research interest in church music and hymnody and is Musical Editor of the forthcoming *Canterbury Dictionary of Hymnology*.

Lewis Foreman has published many books on music and musicians, including the standard biography of Arnold Bax (3rd edition, 2007) and *The John Ireland Companion* (2011) both published by Boydell & Brewer. His CD booklet and programme notes have been appearing for over forty years. He writes music and record industry obituaries for the *Independent*.

Fabian Huss is a part-time lecturer at the University of Bristol, where he completed his Ph.D. on Frank Bridge in 2010; he is currently working on a monograph on Bridge's music to be published by Boydell & Brewer. He has also published widely on E. J. Moeran.

David Maw is Tutor and Research Fellow in Music at Oriel College, Oxford, where he is also Director of Chapel Music; he is additionally Lecturer in Music at Christ Church, and The Queen's and Trinity Colleges in Oxford. His musicological interests are wide-ranging, from medieval to contemporary music; and he was coeditor of *Essays on the History of English Music* (Boydell & Brewer, 2010). He is also active as a composer and organist.

Diane Nolan Cooke, an organist and musicologist, holds degrees from the University of Bristol, Duquesne University, and the College of William and Mary. Her research has focused on the music of Elgar and Herbert Sumsion. She works at the Library of Congress in Washington, DC.

Lionel Pike is Professor of Music Emeritus at Royal Holloway (University of London), having been organist of the college chapel from 1969 to 2005 and, for four years, Dean of the Faculty of Music in the University of London. He was a chorister and assistant organist at Bristol Cathedral, and organ scholar of Pembroke College, Oxford, where his tutors were Sir David Lumsden and Dr H. K. Andrews. The research for his D.Phil. was in Renaissance music, though he has since published books on symphonic form, has edited church music by Henry Purcell for the Purcell Society and has written many articles on the works of the twentieth-century composer Robert Simpson.

Paul Spicer is a well-known choral conductor, composer, writer, lecturer, recording producer and conducting teacher. He was a composition student of Howells at the Royal College of Music and has written extensively about him, including the only biography to date. His most recent work is a biography of Sir George Dyson to be published by Boydell & Brewer.

Jonathan White read music at Oxford University, where he was also organ scholar at Lady Margaret Hall. Following a period as organ scholar at Canterbury Cathedral, he returned to Oxford to undertake doctoral research into the symphonies of Sir Charles Villiers Stanford and how these works tie in with his Anglo-Irish heritage. Having now completed his thesis, he is working on a more thorough exploration of Stanford's expressions of Irish identity as manifested through his wider musical output.

Foreword

I remember him so clearly: a sweet, silvery-haired gentleman, scarcely over five feet tall, still strikingly handsome in his eighties and always immaculately debonair in his attire, though you sensed that the beautifully cut suits had been made many years before and were carefully looked after. His speech was an elegant, expressive Oxford drawl; no trace remained of the west-country burr he must have had as a child. When a woman was present, his face would light up with a smile that had made many feminine hearts melt, and somehow his troubling deafness would disappear. He had charm, a now unfashionable quality, but it was so intrinsic to his personality that you never felt it was being switched on for effect.

I met him now and again in the 1970s, sometimes at the Royal College of Music, once at his home in Barnes, and memorably in Cambridge, a place of happy memories for him ever since his wartime stint as organist at St John's College – this had sparked off his second career as the composer who, more than any other, gave the Anglican Church its musical voice in the second half of the twentieth century. He loved to tell stories; in an earlier life perhaps he had been a Celtic bard, a weaver of dreams. Many of us heard his tales of a long-ago lunch with Ravel and Stravinsky, his encounter with Elgar, his excitement at the 1910 premiere of the Vaughan Williams *Tallis Fantasia* ... but his meeting with 'dear George' (he was referring to Gershwin) in America? Perhaps that one was just a dream.

I sensed that he always felt beholden to 'Uncle Ralph' – Vaughan Williams had the wider reputation and more illustrious career, and years earlier he had gifted Howells an annuity, probably from a mixture of sincere regard for Howells's work and guilt at his own more comfortable circumstances. Did that well-intentioned and generous act on the part of the senior composer perhaps inhibit Howells's never-very-well-developed instinct for self-promotion? Certainly, his reputation has remained overshadowed by Vaughan Williams, but in Phillip Cooke and David Maw's wonderful and wide-ranging book, he finally receives the critical and analytical attention he has always deserved, adding a major study to the valuable but all-too-slender Howells bibliography.

If you can loosely divide composers into novelists and poets, Howells was one of music's poets, but as the essays in this book reveal, this does not imply that his work was lacking in structural integrity or subtle compositional thought. Nor was his range narrow (though his style is instantly recognisable): for those of us who knew him best as a composer of exquisite cathedral music, it comes as a revelation to read about his work in so many other genres. And, as a composer so often pigeonholed as English, Howells is revealed as one whose non-English influences, not least Debussy, so powerfully shaped his style.

Howells the man, below the surface, was an enigma – the chapter on his spirituality explores this elusive aspect of him. The music, too, is not always easy to get to know, often yielding up its essence only gradually, but this book takes us closer to its heart and deserves a resounding welcome from all of us who love and value it.

John Rutter

Acknowledgements

THE first thing likely to strike a reader of this book is the superb photograph of Herbert Howells on its cover. Seated at the Broadwood grand piano in his habitual teaching quarters, Room 19 of the Royal College of Music, Howells is caught in a moment of reflection. As ever he is smartly dressed, and the setting is an institutional one, but the illumination from the window bathes him in a mystical light, accentuated by the evocative chiaroscuro; and so the photograph brings out a dichotomy of formality and poetry that is a prominent theme in the discussions of the book. Poignantly, he often referred to the piano as 'Mick's piano', thus touching on another of the book's themes, the influence on his creativity of his son's tragic, early death. The photograph was taken on 24 October 1972 by Joan Littlejohn, Howells's pupil and assistant during the final decades of his life. We are very grateful to her for enabling us to obtain the image and for granting us permission to use it.

The book would not exist at all had it not been for the support and enthusiasm of the Herbert Howells Trust. We are especially grateful to Andrew Millinger, the Honorary Secretary to the Herbert Howells Society, and to Miss Caroline Marks of St John's College, Cambridge, who facilitated our dealings with the Trust. Thanks are due also to Martin Neary, Chairman of the Herbert Howells Society for his interest in the project and to John Rutter for so readily agreeing to write the touching Foreword that heads the volume.

We have been most fortunate in our publishers. Michael Middeke and Megan Milan, our editors at Boydell & Brewer, have shown an inspiring commitment to the book and unceasingly encouraged us towards a production of the highest standards. In the later stages, we have benefitted from the consummate skills of Jo Bottrill and Robert Whitelock in the copy-editing and formatting of the text and contents. We are extremely grateful also to Florence Maw, for her fastidious and generously given assistance with the indexing, and to David Lee, for his tirelessly patient skill in realising certain musical examples of an unusual cast.

Lewis Foreman, Jeremy Dibble, Patrick Russill, Ronny Krippner and Jonathan Clinch all provided assistance of various kinds at crucial moments in the development of the project. Paul Andrews put in an enormous amount of time in assembling his comprehensive list of works, which will remain an essential tool to all future scholars of Howells's music, and to addressing questions arising in relation to it. The staff of the Royal College of Music Library, and especially Peter Horton and Michael Mullen, kindly facilitated our access to and use of the Howells archive that is kept there. We are grateful also to Adrian Partington and to all those involved in the Gloucester Three Choirs Festival, 2013 for their interest in the book.

Our editors agreed to the use of a large number of musical examples. This is especially important where the discussion concerns music that is less well known or unpublished, and the book is all the better for their inclusion. We are grateful to those who have granted us permission to cite works still under copyright. Our thanks are extended for the very generous permissions granted by the following.

The Herbert Howells Trust: excerpts from the unpublished songs 'The twilight people', 'The devotee' and 'Upon a summer's day'; from *The Bs* suite and *Paradise Rondel* for orchestra; and from the *Phantasy* for piano; and also from materials relating to early versions of the String Quartet, *In Gloucestershire*, sketches for the unfinished Symphony in D and Cello Concerto and manuscript drafts of sections of the *Stabat Mater*, Piano Sonatina and *Partita for Organ*.

Josef Weinberger Ltd: excerpt from *Three Figures: Triptych for Brass Band* (1960) reprinted by permission of Josef Weinberger Ltd.

Faber Music: *Procession* – music by Herbert Howells, © 1920 Ascherberg Hopwood & Crew Ltd, London W6 8BS, reproduced by permission of Faber Music Ltd; Symphony No. 3 ("*Pastoral*") – music by Ralph Vaughan Williams, © 1990 by Joan Ursula Vaughan Williams. All rights for the UK, Republic of Ireland, Canada, Australia, New Zealand, Israel, Jamaica and South Africa administered by Faber Music Ltd, London WC1B 3DA. Reproduced by permission. All rights reserved.

We are grateful also to the other music publishers who granted permission for the use of copyright materials.

Stainer & Bell Ltd: Herbert Howells: *Evening Service in G – Magnificat*, bars 199–205; Herbert Howells: *The Restful Branches – final cadence*; Herbert Howells: *Rhapsodic Quintet* – bb 1–5 (vln); bb 70–71 (clarinet); bb 148–149 and 257–264 (vln 1); plus various graphs of harmonic and tonal process of the work. All reproduced by permission of Stainer & Bell Ltd, London, England, www.stainer.co.uk.

Boosey & Hawkes Music Publishers Ltd: Herbert Howells: Elegy Op 15 (opening viola line, bars 1–4), © 1938 by Hawkes & Song (London) Ltd; Herbert Howells: 1st Sonata for violin and piano, © 1924 by Winthrop Rogers Ltd; Herbert Howells: King David (exx; bars 1–10, re-barred in 3/2), © 1923 by Winthrop Rogers Ltd. Reproduced by permission of Boosey & Hawkes Music Publishers Ltd.

The Associated Board of the Royal Schools of Music: Sonatina for piano by Herbert Howells, published extract, © 1976 by The Associated Board of the Royal Schools of Music. All rights reserved. Reproduced by permission of ABRSM. Manuscript extract: Reproduced by permission of ABRSM.

Alfred Music: *Take Him, Earth, for Cherishing* by Herbert Howells © 1964 The H.W. Gray Company. All rights assigned to and controlled by Alfred Music. All rights reserved. Used by permission.

Oxford University Press: 'Sweetest of Sweets' by Herbert Howells, © Oxford University Press 1978; 'The Fear of the Lord' by Herbert Howells, © Oxford University Press 1977; 'In Green Ways' by Herbert Howells, © Oxford University Press 1929; 'Lambert's Clavichord' by Herbert Howells, © Oxford University Press 1929; 'Job: A Masque for Dancing' by Ralph Vaughan Williams, © Oxford University Press 1934; 'Dona Nobis Pacem' by Ralph Vaughan Williams, © Oxford University Press 1936. Extracts reproduced by permission. All rights reserved.

Music Sales, which controls the works relating to the greatest number of the music examples and to which we are thus grateful for granting so substantial a bulk of permissions: An Old Man's Lullaby – Music by Herbert Howells, © 1947 Novello & Company Limited; To Music Bent – Music by Herbert Howells, © 1932 Novello & Company Limited; Fantasy String Quartet – Music by Herbert Howells, © Chester Music Limited trading as J Curwen and Sons; Quartet For Strings No. 3 '*In Gloucestershire*' – Music by Herbert Howells, © 1930 Novello & Company Limited; Sine Nomine (A Phantasy) Op.37 – Music by Herbert Howells edited by Paul Spicer, © 1922 Novello & Company Limited; Requiem – Words by Traditional Music by Herbert Howells, © 1936 Novello & Company Limited;

Chichester Magnificat and Nunc Dimittis – Music by Herbert Howells, © 1967 Novello & Company Limited; An English Mass – Music by Herbert Howells, © 1955 Novello & Company Limited; Evening Service – Music by Herbert Howells, © 1945 Novello & Company Limited; A Garland For De La Mare – Music by Herbert Howells, © Thames Publishing. Novello & Company Limited; The Gloucester Magnificat and Nunc Dimittis – Music by Herbert Howells, © 1946 Novello & Company Limited; Howells' Clavichord – Music by Herbert Howells, © 1961 Novello & Company Limited; Hymnus Paradisi – Music by Herbert Howells, © 1938 Novello & Company Limited; Partita For Organ – Music by Herbert Howells, © 1972 Novello & Company Limited; Prelude De Profundis – Music by Herbert Howells, © 1958 Novello & Company Limited; Sequence For St Michael – Music by Herbert Howells, © 1961 Novello & Company Limited; Preludio 'Sine Nomine' – Music by Herbert Howells © 1953 Novello & Company Limited; Saraband (For the Morning of Easter) – Music by Herbert Howells, © 1949 Novello & Company Limited; Master Tallis's Testament – Music by Herbert Howells, © 1953 Novello & Company Limited; Fugue, Chorale and Epilogue – Music by Herbert Howells, © 1953 Novello & Company Limited; Saraband (In Modo Elegiaco) – Music by Herbert Howells, © Copyright 1953 Novello & Company Limited; Paean – Music by Herbert Howells, © 1949 Novello & Company Limited; Sonata for Oboe and Piano – Music by Herbert Howells, © 1942 Novello & Company Limited; Stabat Mater – Music by Herbert Howells, © 1964 Novello & Company Limited;. Te Deum and Benedictus: Windsor – Music by Herbert Howells, © 1946 Novello & Company Limited; Three Psalm Prelude Set 2 – Music by Herbert Howells, © 1939 Novello & Company Limited. All Rights reserved. International copyright secured. Used by permission.

Finally, and most importantly, our heartfelt thanks go to Florence Maw and to Carolyn and Millie Cooke for their support and forbearance during the writing and production of this book.

The publication of this book has been made possible by the generous support of the Herbert Howells Trust.

Introduction: Paradox of an Establishment Composer

David Maw

THE Diamond Jubilee of Queen Elizabeth II is a fitting time to take stock of Herbert Howells's compositional achievement and legacy. He was one of the distinguished British composers commissioned to write for the coronation ceremony; and his work for this occasion, the Introit 'Behold, O God Our Defender'(HH 276)[1], composed by his account on Christmas Day in 1952,[2] seemingly epitomises his position. Aged sixty, he was a doyen of the English musical establishment. A professor at the Royal College of Music (RCM) since 1920, he was an accomplished and highly respected composer of church music who could be counted on to write something that would fit a state ceremonial occasion: music that would reflect national pride and identity before the world; music that would blend with the ceremonial, being part of it and not raising its voice beyond the pageantry.

If the muted tone and warm sound-world of the piece seem on the surface to manifest the respectability that would be expected for such an occasion, they sit oddly with the ecstatic turn the music continually takes.[3] There are just three clauses in the text (one and a half verses of Psalm 84), yet by taking each as the basis of a separate section of music, Howells stretches them into a piece of almost four minutes' duration. In a way scarcely prompted by either the words or the occasion, each of the three sections builds from a soft initial dynamic to an effulgent climax before dying down again. Each one depends on an unexpected twist in the harmony: the first, at 'Behold' in the first section, arrives on the anticipated supertonic, not in the root position of the harmonic sequence but on an unstable second-inversion chord; the second, at 'anointed' in the second, substitutes a first-inversion C major chord for the expected E major in progressing from and back to A; and the third, at 'better', releases a vocal stretto on the dominant of the supertonic, not into the anticipated F♯ minor but into B minor. The last of these winds down with a cadence progressing between first inversions of G and F majors (both with added minor sevenths and major ninths) before settling on the tonic E, exercising a gift for cadences that its composer had revealed as early as 1919, with his carol 'A spotless rose' (HH 109), in the same key. Yet such technical cataloguing seems to render the music in terms that could have been penned by any composer, when the effects they describe could only have come from one.

---

[1] Throughout this book, Howells's compositions are referred to by HH numbers, indicating their designation in Paul Andrews's catalogue of works given in the Appendix.

[2] Andrews, 'A Documentary and Bibliographical Study', Vol. I, 410–11. The vocal score is dated Christmas Day 1952, the orchestrated version is inscribed 31 March 1953.

[3] See also the account of this piece in Spicer, *Herbert Howells*, 153–4.

What is striking about the sensuality of this music is that it manages not to jar: it does not fight against the formality of the occasion and of its liturgical setting but blends perfectly with it. Yet what it blends into the stiff formality of a public ceremony is something highly personal and emotionally raw; and the fact of it constitutes a central and characterising paradox of its composer. Howells spent his whole career under the protection of the country's most prestigious institutions, yet he was the product of a poor, lower-middle-class family from rural Gloucestershire, which was a cause of psychological insecurity to him throughout his life. Gifted with a prodigious compositional technique, he nonetheless left many pieces unfinished or in variant forms and took little trouble to maintain his output in any kind of order. Achieving early renown as a composer, circumstances deflected him from this in the middle of his career, and it was teaching that constituted the backbone of his professional life. He composed extensively in all genres except the symphony and opera (though at one time entertaining ambitions for both of these), yet he became best known in the relatively peripheral sphere of church and organ music, even though this accounts for little more than a third of his output.[4] On one level, Howells successfully and self-consciously allied himself with the British musical establishment; on another level, everything about him – his background, psychology and musicality – resisted this.

Approaching Howells's Music

Study of Howells's music today builds on major foundational works by Peter Hodgson, Christopher Palmer, Paul Spicer and Paul Andrews.[5] These have dealt in particular detail with Howells's life (Hodgson, Palmer and particularly Spicer), the cataloguing of his views (Palmer and Andrews) and the surveying of his compositional output (Hodgson, Palmer and particularly Andrews). Discussion of the music itself has tended to consist of broad assessments of the composer's musical language and style (Hodgson and Palmer) and surveys of his achievement within different genres (Palmer). Inevitably, detailed consideration of specific pieces is not possible when the intention is to keep the whole oeuvre in view within relatively constrained space.

The principal object of the present volume, then, is to move towards a more nuanced understanding of these broader areas and issues through closer contact with individual works or with specific aspects that unite several works. It is not intended to be a comprehensive or synoptic account of Howells's musical output; and although attention is distributed widely across the composer's substantial and varied oeuvre, there are many works that are perforce neglected. We hope to stimulate interest and further study of this fascinating and complex figure in

---

[4] In the list of 381 works provided by Paul Andrews for this volume, church music accounts for 108 items and organ music for 28 more. An examination of his output up to 1945 would show such work to have been only a sideline.

[5] Hodgson, 'The Music of Herbert Howells' (1970); Palmer, *Herbert Howells: A Study* (1978) and *A Centenary Celebration* (1992); Spicer, *Herbert Howells* (1998); Andrews, 'A Documentary and Bibliographical Study' (1999).

the history of twentieth-century music. So whilst the church and organ music for which Howells is currently best known have a place here, the weight of interest lies elsewhere.

The contributors have followed a range of different approaches to bringing the detail of Howells's music into focus. Lewis Foreman has undertaken a thorough genre-survey of the orchestral music, showing what this type of writing can uncover about the richness of the music it addresses when pursued in depth. Style analysis and criticism form the basis of several of the chapters. Graham Barber, Phillip Cooke and Lionel Pike isolate specific characteristics or groups of works as a starting point for considering the question of style in a detailed way, whilst Diane Nolan Cooke deploys an innovative dialectic between aesthetic response and technical dissection to a similar end. Jonathan White shows how a biographical orientation can bring aspects of style into a fresh perspective. Source studies inform Paul Andrews's examination of the complexity of Howells's working methods as exemplified by the Third String Quartet, and reception history offers Jonathan Clinch a perspective on the problematic interaction between compositional intention and critical response that undermined the impact of Howells's most ambitious early compositions. Consideration of the aesthetic goals of Howells's music is achieved through analysis of compositional technique, by Jeremy Dibble and Paul Spicer, and of tonal and formal process, by Fabian Huss and the present author. Byron Adams and Jonathan Clinch in their chapters move beyond the sounding immediacy of the musical work in performance to explore its hermeneutics.

Each approach brings a different Howells into focus; but the subject does not dissolve into this multiplicity of perspectives. These studies are united through concern for five broad areas of Howells's work: his style, his writing for voices, his writing for instruments, his claims to being a modern and the impact of his mourning the death of his son.

Howells the Stylist

As was recognised early in his career, Howells's music is marked by a strongly individual voice that is nonetheless the product of assimilated characteristics from various sources (Tudor music, English folk-song, French impressionism). The section on style thus picks up on and develops one of the most striking and frequently discussed aspects of Howells's music.

Probably the most significant influence on the formation of Howells's musical language is also perhaps the most difficult one to hear – that of his composition professor, Sir Charles Villiers Stanford. Jonathan White's chapter argues for a complex relationship between the aging composer and his brilliant young student. Stanford was nearly sixty when he became Howells's professor, and his powers and influence were beginning to wane. His overbearing, if well-intentioned, tutelage was leading to a backlash from composers who had felt injured by it. Almost uniquely, Howells escaped the worst of his teacher's censure, but as White argues, this is not because Howells simply adopted Stanford's style and values; he had his own compositional enthusiasms and convictions to pursue, ones that would ultimately take him beyond the limits of Stanford's tastes. However, his need to succeed and, given his precarious family background, to be accepted, combined with his already impressive facility, led him during the period of his studies to create a style that carefully balanced Stanford's influence against his own emergent interests.

Lionel Pike considers the ubiquity of counterpoint in Howells's stylistic makeup, through close analysis of a single work. *Take Him, Earth, for Cherishing* (HH 307) is not notable for contrapuntal display, so the unassuming presence of a variety of different contrapuntal techniques in the work shows how firmly assimilated this approach to writing music was in Howells's compositional process. Moreover, the characterisation of each section by a different contrapuntal texture reveals a plan that seems to echo Roy Harris's Third Symphony.

It is well know that Howells drew on a wide range of stylistic sources in moulding his own musical language: the late Romantic style of the English music with which he grew up, the intense chromaticism of Rachmaninoff, the colouristic harmony of Debussy, the textural refinement of Ravel. Diane Nolan Cooke pursues the many dimensions of Howells's mature style in a detailed analysis of the *Six Pieces for Organ* (HH 226). Following through a dichotomy in existing responses to the style, between imprecise, general aesthetic descriptions on the one hand, and detailed, but dry, technical dissections on the other – both of which, she suggests, are liable to miss their target – she proposes a dialectical interplay of the two as a way of getting under the skin of Howells's particular synthesis.

Howells the Vocal Composer

Writing for the human voice was at the heart of Howells's compositional activities throughout his career. Solo songs dominated this work in his earlier years. Jeremy Dibble's chapter follows through Jonathan White's discussion by showing how much Howells owed to Stanford for his mastery of the concise yet intricate art of song. Of particular significance is his identification of the importance to Howells of concealing the compositional process in the finished work, a characteristic he suggests stems from his love of the Tudor musical ancestry.

Paul Spicer turns the focus on to a small but telling detail of technique in Howells's vocal writing: his use of melisma. As comparison with Finzi shows, melisma was not a necessity of vocal writing in English music at the time, as he wrote perfectly without it. Howells, though, made frequent and resourceful use of it in the service of various effects – most notably the enhancement of a quality of ecstasy.

Phillip Cooke examines the qualities that made Howells's emergence in the 1940s as a front-ranking composer of church music such a significant event. Into a world characterised by stylistic rigidity or bombast, Howells injected a striking note of sensuality and mysticism, drawing on the harmonic resources of French 'impressionist' composers. The new note that Howells's music struck in the world of church music was, as Eric Milner-White observed, 'of spiritual moment'.

Howells the Instrumental Composer

It was in the field of instrumental music that Howells first made his mark. He composed a substantial corpus of orchestral music up to the early 1930s, and Lewis Foreman shows how diverse this was. There were works of large-scale concert music and delightful miniatures to court public popularity, works with a narrative dimension and works of an abstract caste; there were also works without a clear generic precedent, such as the *Pastoral Rhapsody* (HH 134) and the experimental *Sine nomine* 'phantasy' (HH 126). Howells developed a voice with a clearly British accent, but he was deeply concerned with the new music of Stravinsky and Ravel, as his orchestration in particular demonstrates.

Chamber music was the other field of Howells's early excellence. The Piano Quartet (HH 66) was his first major publication. His music had a technical brilliance second to none amongst his peers; yet as he himself was quick to point out in an interview with Katharine Eggar: 'there's a legend abroad that I have a technique which enables me to write easily. That's not true.'[6] This is borne out by Paul Andrews's study of the sources of the Third String Quartet, *In Gloucestershire* (HH 62). He shows that one of the composer's most significant works emerged in three different versions before arriving at its final form. Technical facility, which Howells undoubtedly had, did not necessarily make the business of serious composition easy: when several solutions to a given challenge could be conceived, it might take a while to arrive at the right one.

Excepting the unfinished Cello Concerto (HH 205–7), no later work had quite the complex genesis of the Third String Quartet. Yet the seeming spontaneity of Howells's music on the surface conceals significant compositional thinking, planning and often rethinking underneath. As Fabian Huss shows, the two later sonatas, for oboe and clarinet (HH 239, HH 251), seem to exist in a kind of palimpsest relationship, the latter being a response to the experimentation of the former.

Howells the Modern

Howells's music is widely perceived as conservative, in large measure through his strong postwar association with church music. Yet, as Ralph Downes related, he was even thought of in the 1920s as an '*enfant terrible*';[7] and as the contributions here by Clinch, Foreman, Huss, Diane Nolan Cooke and the present author testify, his works of this time were firmly rooted in the new music of Debussy, Ravel and Stravinsky. He was explicitly concerned with establishing himself as a 'modern'.

Piano concertos (HH 31, HH 152) frame Howells's first period: the first written in 1913 whilst the composer was still a student at the RCM, the second in the early 1920s at the height of his first success. Jonathan Clinch places these pivotal works firmly in an emergent vein of 'Romantic Modernism', arguing that the dualism implicit in this label created the problem they posed for their contemporaneous reception: they were too Romantic to seem truly modern, and too modern to please a public keen to see a perpetuation of the Romantic tradition. In his desire to remain the darling of the public, Howells tried to portray his forthcoming Second Concerto, a terse and at times brittle work, as an easy-going essay in tune-mongering. As Clinch shows, this was an unsuccessful tactic for introducing a new and challenging work of art to the public.

---

[6] Eggar, 'Herbert Howells', 214.
[7] Palmer, *Centenary Celebration*, 224.

The present author's chapter examines the role of Cobbett's phantasy genre in Howells's progress towards a style that was both modern and British. Following up the composer's own commentary on his work, it argues that the phantasy was an ideal vehicle for the 'experiments in form' that he saw as prerequisite for modern composition. They enabled him to articulate 'complexity of mood', another of his modern desiderata; but the genre also seemed to connote a more literal vein of phantasy, reflecting his mystical leanings. If folk-song style gives the *Fantasy String Quartet* (HH 71) its Britishness, Howells's own comments show that he preferred to conceive this quality in more abstract terms – ones that are better represented by the *Rhapsodic Quintet* (HH 107).

The premiere of the Second Piano Concerto in 1925 is conventionally taken as a watershed in the composer's career and fortunes:[8] met with criticism he was unaccustomed to, he retreated into teaching and examining, his compositional activities focusing on smaller genres and losing much of the momentum built up in the preceding decade. This was not the end of his engagement with modernity, however. The large-scale setting of the *Stabat mater* (HH 309) defined the final stage of his career in the same way that *Hymnus paradisi* (HH 220) had defined its maturity. Phillip Cooke identifies a turning away from the lushness and sensuality of his mid-period towards a bleaker and more austere sound-world. The music of *Stabat mater* and of the pieces that followed it returns to the modernity clearly staked out in the early works and from which the middle period had seemed to retreat. The style is dissonant and difficult; the works have yet to find the place in repertory of his best known compositions.

Howells in Mourning

The shadow cast by the premiere of the Second Piano Concerto was to pale into insignificance when, a decade later, Howells's son Michael died, just nine years old, of polio. As Byron Adams notes, part of the tragedy was its avoidability. The effect of it on Howells was shattering, and it is no exaggeration to say that the rest of his life was lived in its memory. The significance of mourning and elegy in his work is explored in the final three essays of the book. Graham Barber traces the recurrence of the style of the sarabande in Howells's music. Although something like it can be found in *Lambert's Clavichord* (HH 165), it was only in the wake of Michael's death that it emerged fully fledged, in the *Six Pieces for Organ*. Its presence is not confined to pieces in which the sarabande idea is in the foreground. The Nunc dimittis of the *Gloucester Service* (HH 249) is underpinned by a sarabande rhythm that serves to emphasise the text's valedictory note.

Jonathan Clinch argues that Howells's protracted involvement with the uncompleted Cello Concerto project functioned as a kind of mourning ritual through his life, one in which he wrote himself into the solo cello part. Byron Adams relates the tragic circumstances of Michael's death and explores the role of Howells's masterpiece, *Hymnus paradisi*, in the composer's coming to terms with this loss. The work

---

[8] Meirion Hughes and Robert Stradling record the event in characteristically vivid terms; Hughes and Stradling, *The English Musical Renaissance*, 183.

was for Howells a cenotaph: his personal memorial transfigured into a memorial for all the departed. In this way, it relates directly to Edwin Lutyens's memorial for the dead of the First World War, the Cenotaph in Whitehall. Adams thus writes Howells firmly into the heart of British Modernism of the interwar period.

The chapters of this book seek to balance the view of Howells: to set the church and organ music in the perspective of his other compositional achievements and ambitions; to view the setbacks of his career against the successes and understand how he was able to derive creative impetus from them; to see the seeming facility and freedom of the music against the prevarications and labours of the compositional process; and to move consideration of these towards the centre-ground of musicological thinking. Yet the paradox remains. Through these chapters, we are repeatedly confronted by a composer working on at least two levels: from the faithful pupil of Stanford whose inclinations lay well outside his teacher's sympathies, to the bereaved parent who expressed his grief within the formalities of the sarabande. The 'knowledge so gained is … only complementary'.[9]

---

[9] Howells, 'Vaughan Williams's "Pastoral" Symphony', 132.

PART I

Howells the Stylist

CHAPTER 1

'In matters of art friendship should not count': Stanford and Howells

Jonathan White

Where Stanford the teacher is due for discussion time is not pressing. The paramountcy that was his so fitfully, but often so brilliantly and in so many fields was, in one sphere of his genius, unquestioned, undimmed, and (in our own history) unrivalled. One could so easily devote a whole address to the teacher: and for acknowledgement by any man lucky enough to have known him as such, a life-time would seem too little.[1]

ALTHOUGH his reputation as a composer is still the subject of continuing scholarly exploration, the position of Charles Villiers Stanford as one of the most notable musical educators in Britain in the late nineteenth and early twentieth centuries has been well documented both officially and in numerous anecdotal memories. Through his positions at the University of Cambridge and the Royal College of Music (RCM), Stanford had unprecedented access to much of Britain's emerging musical talent, and the list of students who passed through his teaching rooms in both establishments could double as a 'Who's Who' of British music of the early twentieth century. While the quotation contained within the title of this chapter is drawn from correspondence between Stanford and the violinist/composer Joseph Joachim,[2] it may serve as an interesting pause for thought on the nature of the relationship between this professor and his many students. Stanford was well known for his arch-conservative musical opinions, especially in later life, and much of his music reinforces his insistence that an adherence to Classical and early-Romantic principles was the only style in which any sensible composer could wish to write. However, the musical language that many of his students would develop, including Howells, departed markedly from that of their tutor and mentor, and although many of them would later dismiss Stanford's effectiveness as a teacher to some degree or another, others, notably Howells and Vaughan Williams, continued to extol his virtues as a composer and tutor decades after his death, and surely in the knowledge that their own music would have met with outright rejection from their former professor.

First Impressions

I knew nothing of Stanford until Ivor Gurney fired me, in 1911, with the idea that one's salvation lay in South Kensington. For there, Gurney alleged, was

[1] Howells, 'Charles Villiers Stanford.'
[2] Letters from Joseph Joachim to Charles Villiers Stanford, 7 February 1886, in Bickley 'Letters to and from Joseph Joachim'.

a man teaching composition at a place called the Royal College of Music. A further year of scriptorial struggle elapsed before I laid my life-and-death efforts on the great man's table.[3]

Whether or not Howells genuinely knew nothing of Stanford, save for singing the Service in B♭ major, is perhaps open to question. With Howells an articled pupil from 1909 of Herbert Brewer at Gloucester Cathedral, himself a pupil of Stanford's at the RCM, it seems unlikely that this doyen of the British musical establishment would have completely passed Howells by. However, as Howells himself points out in the same address, he only knew Stanford for the last twelve years of the older composer's life, a period that represented a rapid decline in his popularity and stature in the then radically changing musical landscape of early-twentieth-century Europe. Perhaps an aspiring composer and musician like Howells, while deeply embedded in the choral world of England of the time, and especially in a Three Choirs cathedral, which had seen many a performance of the Irishman's music, really could have managed to make it to this point without encountering Stanford in any meaningful or influential way.

Whatever the reality, the relationship between Howells and Stanford is probably one of the most extraordinary ones in recent British music history. Considering Stanford's opinions of contemporary trends in music of the early twentieth century, in which he despised the crushing chromaticism of Wagner and failed to come close to understanding anything that Richard Strauss had produced, to hail the composer of the 1965 setting of the *Stabat mater* (HH 309) as his 'son in music' might seem like a rather strange honour to bestow, not least when one considers the number of composers who passed through the halls of the RCM to Stanford's office, many of whom left somewhat the worse for wear. Stories of students being torn apart by the elder composer can be found in the diaries and memoirs of many of Britain's leading composers of the twentieth century, along with numerous articles, addresses and other anecdotes. However, one thing that emerges for Howells is that, as Paul Spicer has observed, he never experienced the 'loveable Irishman['s] ... notorious temper'.[4]

The reasons why Stanford favoured Howells so much above the many other students that he taught at both the RCM and Cambridge University remain unclear; indeed, to try to distil this to one or two reasons would be a futile endeavour. Furthermore, in spite of Stanford's damning criticism of many of his students' works for their tendency to pander to more recent tastes at the expense of the more conservative principles that he held, his success as a teacher was surely in the way his pupils helped to shape a new era for British music, rather than maintaining the style and tradition that Stanford and his direct contemporaries had worked so hard to establish in the later Victorian era. Whilst Howells, like so many of Stanford's other pupils, would develop a musical style that their teacher almost certainly would have dismissed had he lived long enough to hear it, Howells's earlier musical style shows a much more obvious debt to the Romantic style of Parry and Stanford, fused with more recent influences such as Elgar and Vaughan Williams,

[3] *Ibid.*
[4] Spicer, *Herbert Howells*, 32.

the latter's *Fantasia on a Theme by Thomas Tallis* making such a lasting impression on the young Howells when he heard its premiere at Gloucester Cathedral in 1910.[5] Focusing on some of Howells's earlier works, this chapter will examine the nature of the musical link between Stanford and Howells as expressed through these youthful endeavours.

Stanford the Professor

Whatever Stanford's success as a composer, a quick glance at the list of composers that he taught would, at least initially, suggest that he must have succeeded in this role. However, the reality seems to be that the Irishman's relationship with his various students was enormously varied, being extremely supportive of Howells, dismissive of Vaughan Williams's perceived overuse of modality[6] and cursory in his consideration of Arthur Benjamin's talents by virtue of his Jewish heritage,[7] to give but three examples. However, in spite of his often visceral criticisms, few of his students denied the man's ability to guide them through their early stages of compositional exploration.

> For his students, learning at his feet was a blending of Paradise and Purgatory, Heaven and Hell. For the weak and timorous it was early death; for the fellow who had lost his way, Ariadne's thread. It had no high-sounding method, no sacrosanct principles. It was guidance, penance and defiance coming from a man who solved few of his own problems but was passionately concerned to solve those of his pupils. On the day of his death his pupil, Holst, said to me: 'The one man who could get any one of us out of technical mess is now gone from us.' One agreed: recalling the hovering pencil, the caustic commentary, the surgeon-like dexterity with which the keen mind cut through to the seat of trouble, and the seraphic smile and childlike pride when the operation was over.[8]

George Dyson, another of Stanford's pupils, mused that 'of his particular approach to the art of teaching, the subject with which I am here to deal, it is not easy to write.'[9] Dyson continued:

> I remember a good many of his characteristic explosions. I happened once to bring into his room a book or a paper in which he came upon a photograph of Gladstone. He leapt at it. 'Look at his face, my boy! Sinister, sinister in every line. Ugh!' Thus Stanford the Orangeman. Another day I heard

---

[5] *Ibid.*, 22–3.
[6] Stanford is reported to have encouraged his students to experiment with modal composition, although clearly he felt that Vaughan Williams had gone too far. Dibble, *Charles Villiers Stanford*, 267–8.
[7] 'You Jews can't write long tunes. Always two-bar and four-bar phrases, repeated! Look at Mendelssohn, look at Meyerbeer, look at Wagner!' Benjamin, 'A Student in Kensington', 202.
[8] Howells, 'Charles Villiers Stanford'.
[9] Dyson, 'Charles Villiers Stanford by Some of His Pupils', 196.

part of a lesson given to a student who has since become famous. 'Blank', he said, 'your music comes from hell. From hell, my boy; H E double L'. Thus Stanford the purist ... Was Stanford a great teacher? In the sense in which it is customary to understand the term, I think Stanford's teaching had most of the major defects that teachers are usually counselled to avoid. The careful expression of principles, the weighing and collating of detail, the conscientious or laboured endeavour to understand or appreciate an alien or repellent point of view; these faculties had no sure place within his temperament. He could give first-rate technical advice ... But in matters more elusive, in questions of personal expression, of poetic or dramatic mood, of all the more modern devices of emphasis or atmosphere, he seemed to some of us to be a bundle of prejudices.[10]

While Stanford certainly held unwavering opinions on a wide range of matters, both musical and non-musical, Dyson's observations of the man would probably benefit from some contextualisation. It seems fair to say that Stanford as a composer himself was technically very gifted. Indeed, the overwhelming majority of his works demonstrate a gifted and able craftsman, who was capable of developing musical material and form, at times with flair and ease. A work like his Service in B♭, Op. 10 (1879), is a prime example of the composer's ability to manipulate thematic ideas over not only single movements, but, in this case, an entire liturgical setting. The first movement of his Symphony no. 3 in F minor, the 'Irish', Op. 28 (1887) also shows how Stanford managed to assimilate and rework the Brahmsian model of organic development, fashioning an entire symphonic movement out of a tiny thematic cell. However, in spite of his extraordinary ability to handle musical material, he was often criticised for doing so from too academic a perspective, one where musical craftsmanship appeared to overshadow individual creativity and inspiration. George Bernard Shaw, himself with an agenda to propagate, criticised Stanford's 'Irish' Symphony for its overly academic nature.[11]

Stanford's musical views were also very conservative and seem to have become increasingly so in his later life. By the turn of the twentieth century, Stanford and his music had begun the gradual slip into musical oblivion. So much so that it was only a last-minute addition that saw music by him included in the 1901 coronation of Edward VII in the form of a scored version of his setting of the *Te Deum* from the Service in B♭.[12] Many works dating from this period demonstrate Stanford's conservative and, at times, increasingly outdated compositional view. His seventh and final symphony, for example, stands as in interesting work within the context of early-twentieth-century music and, within that, of the composer's musical output. Notable for its brevity and its structural innovation, its almost unashamed Classical leanings question the purpose of such a work in this period. With a musical style closer to early Romantic composers like Schubert, Mendelssohn and Schumann, it seemingly bypasses almost a century of developments in symphonic writing. Thomas Dunhill recalled that Stanford was 'more particularly pleased with the fact

[10] *Ibid.*
[11] Shaw, 'Going Fantee'.
[12] Dibble, *Charles Villiers Stanford*, 339.

that in the seventh, and last, he succeeded in writing a full-blown Symphony which took less than twenty-five minutes to perform! It was a clever concession to modern requirements, but he did not concede a particle of his classical convictions.'[13] Stanford expressed many of his views on more recent trends in composition in his 1911 publication *Musical Composition: A Short Treatise for Students*, along with a handful of articles including 'Sanity (?) in Composition' published in the *Musical Herald* in 1917, and 'Some Recent Tendencies in Composition' in the *Proceedings of the Musical Association* (1920–1). This last began: 'Let me begin by saying that I am, and always have been, essentially a Progressivist, and welcome every innovation, however unfamiliar, provided that it makes for the enhancement of beauty as I consider it.'[14] Dyson almost certainly would have disagreed with Stanford's opinion that he was somehow progressive in his approach to music, and indeed I am sure that many of us would have difficulty in accepting Stanford's assessment of himself in this respect. However, while Dyson may have been correct in his assessment of Stanford's technical abilities, and no doubt many of his contemporaries would also have echoed his other observations, Dyson's comments should also be contextualised within his own musical opinions of the time. Although a student of Stanford's at the RCM, Dyson, like so many of his colleagues, would continue his studies abroad, and received considerable support and encouragement from Vincent Novello's daughter, Clara Gigliucci. He was also well acquainted with a number of leading European musical figures of the early twentieth century and met Strauss on at least one occasion. Dyson's own musical tendencies, as expressed in his publication *The New Music*, released in 1924, the same year as Stanford's death, appear to have favoured a Straussian approach to composition. Given that Stanford was outspoken in his criticism of Strauss, it is perhaps unsurprising that Dyson, like many of Stanford's other pupils, would later come to reject his former teacher in such a manner.

Stanford and Howells

So I knew Stanford vitally and only directly only for twelve short years – his last twelve ... I knew him, indeed, in the days of his increasing neglect, a neglect he continually felt. It hurt him. So that the man I worked with then, was, in a way, the shadow of the paramount figure that for forty years had been a major driving force in the creative and interpretive life of the nation's music. His paramountcy as a composer was, as it were, only a sort of legend to me. It was almost as if the active, dominating, indispensable, magisterial, seemingly unconquerable composer and conductor was unknown to me.[15]

Although it is well documented that Howells and Stanford had a great deal of respect for one another, both while in the professor–student relationship and subsequently, the nature of this relationship and how, if at all, it became manifest in the music of either composer is less clear. Although writing some forty years after

---

[13] Dunhill, 'Charles Villiers Stanford'.
[14] Stanford, 'Some Recent Tendencies in Composition'.
[15] Howells, 'Charles Villiers Stanford', 21.

their first meeting, Howells seems to imply that he never fully knew the greatness of the man. Of course, although Stanford may well have provided Howells with his first formal tuition in the sense of that received at the RCM, the Irishman was by no means the only influence on the young composer, either in his early career or subsequently. We already know of the profound influence that Vaughan Williams had had on Howells before his RCM days, along with Elgar and a host of other composers that he would almost inevitably have encountered while at Gloucester. In London, Howells had access to a wealth of other musical influences, including Ravel and Stravinsky, both of whose music had an impact on his compositional style. Stanford also suggested that Howells work with R. R. Terry, who instilled a fascination for Tudor music in the still impressionable young man – an influence that pervaded much of his musical style. Although many of these influences can be found in Howells's earlier works, especially those dating from his time at the RCM, there appears to be a much more Romantic strand weaving its way through some of his compositions from this period. Stanford praised Howells for his development of a musical style that he described as 'tempered modernism', a style that Dibble notes Bliss fought hard against.[16]

The first major work to fall into this category was Howells's Concerto in C minor for Piano and Orchestra, Op. 4 (HH 31), composed in 1913. As Paul Spicer has noted, the concerto demonstrates that Howells must have been familiar with the orchestral music of composers including Debussy, Ravel, Brahms and Rachmaninoff, and possibly even Stravinsky.[17] As a student of Stanford, Howells would have been unable to avoid the music of Brahms; and, as will be explored shortly, there is a clear link with Rachmaninoff in the case of this specific work. Ravel visited London a number of times in the early twentieth century; and so it is highly probable that Howells was familiar with his music, and may even have attended his concert in December 1913. It is known also that he was acquainted with at least some of Stravinsky's music, even at this early stage in his career and in spite of the fact that Stanford would almost certainly not have recommended it to his students.[18]

Alongside these influences, many of which have already been examined in the brief but extant studies of the concerto, one further work presents itself as a likely stimulus, at least, for the young Howells. Only a matter of years before Howells began work on his C minor concerto, Stanford himself penned a piano concerto in the same key. Work on his Piano Concerto no. 2 in C minor, Op. 126, commenced in 1911, and was completed on 28 July that year. As with many of his large-scale orchestral works, it demonstrates a stylistic debt to Mendelssohn and Brahms, two composers that Stanford held in high esteem throughout his life. However, the work also appears to have been influenced by the more epic style of concerto popular in the later nineteenth and early twentieth centuries as epitomised by Rachmaninoff. Indeed, the influence of the Russian composer appears to be deeply embedded within Stanford's own work from the outset, notably the Russian's own second, C minor Piano Concerto, a work that Stanford himself had conducted at the RCM in

---

[16] Dibble, *Charles Villiers Stanford*, 417.
[17] Spicer, liner notes to CHAN 9874.
[18] *Ibid.*

1908. Of even greater significance, however, is surely his performance of the work at the 1910 Leeds Festival with Rachmaninoff himself as the soloist. From the very beginning of Stanford's concerto, the parallels with Rachmaninoff's are evident. The rippling accompaniment figure in the piano solo juxtaposed against the long, sustained presentation of the primary subject material in the orchestra is surely derived from the corresponding section in Rachmaninoff's own concerto. The sensitive and emotionally charged second subject shares much with the equivalent subject in the Russian's concerto, and also with many of his Op. 23 Preludes. The result of these devices, however, is not a work devoid of any originality. Instead, Stanford combines them, and the other more Germanic influences, with his own unique style of composition, by now highly perfected, to create a work that retains a sense of compositional integrity and originality. Indeed, the sudden and unexpected shift to the enharmonic Neapolitan (E major) shortly after the presentation of the second subject in the relative major and its subsequent harmonic return to E♭, is a trait that can more readily be attributed to Stanford, along with the importance of semitone shifts in the development section. Stanford's masterful treatment of the orchestra and love of chamber music also shine through at several points in the concerto, notably his use of chamber groupings of instruments, something seen in the slow movement of his Symphony no. 6 in E♭ major, Op. 94 (1905). The concerto's slow movement again shares features with Rachmaninoff's second movement, although these are generally superficial in nature, and perhaps more accurately demonstrate Stanford's ability to write euphonious slow movements, charged with emotions, yet that still somehow convey the poise and reserve of the Victorian society of which he was very much a product. The dramatic opening of the final Allegro molto, largamente e sostenuto is also gesturally similar to many of Rachmaninoff's own concerto finales, with a strong, strident theme that dominates the movement, juxtaposed against a more lyrical second subject.

The Second Piano Concerto was originally written for pianist Moritz Rosenthal, whom Stanford had hoped would perform the work at its premiere. However, securing the first performance of the work proved to be more challenging than the composer might have wished. It was originally hoped that Rosenthal would take the work to the United States of America in 1913, but in the end this came to nothing. Leonard Borwick, to whom Stanford's previous concerto had been dedicated, had himself hoped to perform the work, something that presented itself as a possibility when Stanford received an invitation from Professor Horatio Parker of the University of Yale to receive an honorary doctorate at a ceremony in 1915. Stanford also received an invitation from Carl Stoeckel of the Norfolk Festival to conduct a concert of his own works in the spring of that same year, a programme that would include the concerto, along with his by then enormously popular 'Irish' Symphony. Stanford would then travel to Boston to conduct a performance of his Symphony no. 7 in D minor, Op. 124, before travelling on to Yale for the ceremony. Unfortunately for Stanford, his passage to America was booked on the *Lusitania* for a sailing on 15 May, and when the ship was torpedoed by the Germans off the coast of Ireland on 7 May, his hopes of making it across the Atlantic were dashed. The performance at Norfolk, however, did go ahead, although without the other works originally programmed, giving the concerto its first public airing. Following the concert, Stanford received word from Stoeckel that the performance had been a great success, and Cecil Forsyth, a close friend of Stanford's who himself attended the Norfolk concert, reported that 'Harold Bauer processed back and forth from the artists' room for about a quarter-of-an-hour.' The work was published by Stainer and Bell in 1915 and bore the dedication 'To two friends on either side of the Atlantic: Carl Stoeckel of Norfolk, Conn. USA, and Robert Finnie McEwen of Bardrochat', although the autograph score reads: 'To Carl Stoeckel Esq. In memory of the Norfolk Festival June 1915 from the absent composer. London, Nov. 22 1915.' Stanford himself had the opportunity of hearing a performance of the concerto at the RCM, in advance of the Norfolk performance, on 19 February 1915, and it was originally announced that the work would be performed under the direction of Sir Henry Wood at the Queen's Hall Promenade Concerts in October of that year with Murdoch as the soloist. This performance, however, was eventually cancelled, with the British premiere taking place in Bournemouth on 7 December 1916, under the direction of the composer and with Benno Moiseiwitsch as soloist, who subsequently championed the work.

Howells's Piano Concerto no. 1, his first major orchestral work, was written while he was still a student at the RCM, and dedicated to pianist Arthur Benjamin, who would perform the solo in the work's premiere in 1914 at the Queen's Hall under Stanford's direction. While it is clear that a variety of influences can be traced in Howells's work, notably those whose musical outlook was forward-looking, there are curious similarities with Stanford's own concerto that must be considered. Stanford's could easily be read as a direct response, or even a homage, to Rachmaninoff's work; and while there is nothing to suggest that Howells's work can be read in a similar way to either or both of these composers, the parallels with both works and the link with Stanford raise the question whether the younger composer's concerto suggests that he might have at least sympathised with Stanford's musical perspective to some degree in his early career.

First, of course, we must assess whether or not Howells actually knew Stanford's work, not least as some of the similarities that exist between Howells's and Stanford's concertos equally exist between Howells's and Rachmaninoff's, so we cannot discount the possibility that the influence from the Russian was rather direct than mediated through Stanford. Although Stanford's work was composed in 1911, it did not receive its first public performance until 1915, and then was not published until the following year. Beyond anecdotes from former pupils, it is unclear whether or not Stanford ever used his own works in compositional tutorials. Certainly few of his publications on composition refer to his own works, favouring references to the composers he himself held up as being masters of their art. This does not, of course, mean that Howells was not familiar with Stanford's own concerto, simply that we must bear in mind that this uncertainty exists when considering what parallels there might be between the two works.

The first parallel, while superficial, that should be considered is the very nature of Howells's concerto and its similarity to both Stanford and Rachmaninoff in this sense. The concerto is cast in what Dibble describes as the 'heroic' style, one in which pianist and orchestra are locked in an epic battle between forces.[19] This is a

---

[19] Dibble, *Charles Villiers Stanford*, 425.

tradition that can be traced right the way through the nineteenth century, back to works such as Beethoven's 'Emperor' Concerto. While it might be fair to say that Howells's choosing a concerto style similar to that of Stanford or Rachmaninoff need not be read as anything overly significant, in tackling the concerto genre, Howells, consciously or otherwise, engaged with over a century not only of tradition but also expectation. The style that Stanford chose to adopt was very much one of the nineteenth century. However, Stanford, by the early twentieth century, had become synonymous with musical conservatism, at times in the extreme. It probably mattered little to him whether or not his music was seen as being archaic. Indeed, in many ways he strived to create a musical style that hearkened back to what he might have described as a golden age of Romantic composition. Howells, on the other hand, as a new and emerging composer, would surely have been more cautious of adopting an overall musical style that was more akin to his forebears than his contemporaries. Indeed, when we consider how many of his RCM colleagues consciously rejected the vestiges of the older school of British composers, it is curious that this first major orchestral work by Howells would adopt a style that was very similar in nature to that of Stanford, even though it would also encompass a host of additional influences possibly giving it a more forward-looking nature.

Another feature that both concertos share is the use of chamber-like passages. Through much of his career, Stanford's large-scale music made references to smaller genres through his use of chamber scoring, as has already been noted. Howells too made use of such scoring in his own concerto. For example, his use of the solo violin with piano superimposed against the fuller ensemble towards the end of the development section of the first movement bears a striking similarity to Stanford's own concerto. Indeed, the latter composer used a similar device at almost exactly the same point. While Rachmaninoff's concerto alludes to chamber textures, for example in the second movement, with his use of violas against muted strings, it does not in fact revert to actual chamber groupings within a larger orchestral setting, as happens in both Howells's and Stanford's works. This is but one of a number of small yet potentially significant similarities that can be found in the concertos of both Howells and Stanford; and, while these are perhaps not overly important on their own, coupled with the overall nature of Howells's concerto, its proximity in composition to Stanford's, and the fact that it was the latter who attempted to champion the work in spite of press reports, surely we have to accept that there must be a link between the two works.

The real problem with these two works is that it still remains uncertain whether or not Howells actually knew Stanford's concerto. However, it is for this reason that the more general similarities are in fact all the more significant. It is not the more subtle details that are the key to understanding the relationship between the two concertos, although in some ways it would perhaps be even more remarkable if Howells did not know Stanford's work. That Howells wrote a work that, while in many ways radically different from Stanford's through its incorporation of a host of other more recent influences, still encompasses a sense of Romantic heroism that Stanford himself advocated, provides a direct musical link between professor and student that becomes all the more remarkable when we consider that this was Howells's first major orchestral work. It should be borne in mind that there were many other more contemporary examples of piano concerto writing in existence when Howells was composing his own work – Prokofiev, for example – to whom he could have turned. Given that Howells was clearly assimilating a great deal of music with enthusiasm in his early days in London, it seems he made a more conscious decision to embrace a more Romantic outlook in this work.

While I believe that Howells's First Piano Concerto does provide a direct aesthetic link with Stanford, to prove that the former's early style demonstrates a more general affinity with the latter's musical style requires more than one work. A brief overview of some of Howells's other compositions from the second decade of the twentieth century reveals some interesting observations. Another significant orchestral work from the period, his Suite for Orchestra, *The Bs*, Op. 13 (HH 42) – a collection of character pieces dedicated to and/or depicting in some way friends from the RCM at the time – is similarly 'Romantic', or maybe even post-Romantic, in its outlook; but with a musical language that seems to owe considerably more to the music of Vaughan Williams and Holst than it does to Stanford, it conjures up a sort of English pastoral musical landscape, foreshadowing his later 1923 *Pastoral Rhapsody*, Op. 38 (HH 134). This is not to say that Howells's suite is totally devoid of flashes of Stanfordian inspiration and technique. The emotionally charged 'Lament' dedicated to 'Bartholomew' (more familiarly Ivor Gurney) has the same 'euphonious' quality that Peter Brown identifies as a more original aspect of Stanford's orchestral writing.[20] Nor indeed is it to suggest that Stanford's own musical style would not chart a similar course. His *Fourth Irish Rhapsody* (1914), a work that Howells himself knew well, employs a similarly evocative musical landscape, far removed from the heavily Teutonic influences of his earlier works. Yet it comes at a point in Stanford's musical career when his own 'innovations' and changes in style parallel those of some of his current and more recent students, notably Vaughan Williams in this respect, and it raises the question of who was being influenced by whom.[21] Stanford had an ability to assimilate music and musical techniques with great ease and efficiency, subsequently employing them in his own music with little difficulty. Indeed, writing in an earlier edition of the *Grove Dictionary of Music and Musicians*, Stanford's friend Fuller Maitland commented that Stanford composed with such speed and enthusiasm that he did not always check that melodies of his creation were indeed his own.[22]

Howells's *Three Dances for Violin and Orchestra*, Op. 7 (HH 48), presents another possible Stanfordian parallel, this time with the elder's *Suite for Violin*, Op. 32 (1888), dedicated to Joseph Joachim and performed by the violinist at the Grosser Saal der Philharmonie, Berlin, at an all-Stanford concert the following year. Stanford's work presents what can only be described as a nineteenth-century

---

[20] Brown, *The Symphonic Repertoire*, Vol. 3b, 95.
[21] While there are striking stylistic similarities between some of Stanford's later orchestral works, notably the *Fourth Irish Rhapsody*, and those of former pupils like Vaughan Williams and Holst, these later works are also bound up in a much more complicated socio-political struggle; so these additional aspects would also have to be taken into consideration when assessing the extremely emotional and evocative musical language employed by Stanford. However, such an undertaking falls well outside the boundaries of this chapter.
[22] Fuller Maitland, 'Stanford', 120.

Anglo-Irish take on the Baroque suite, presenting a concertante work infused with Brahmsian and Hibernian traits. Although written several decades later, Howells's own work is remarkably similar in its general overview and approach, even though it might be more accurately described as a violin concerto in disguise, albeit possibly not a very good disguise. Perhaps most interesting are the 'Celtic' inflections in the solo part, notably in the second and third movements, again surely not a coincidence. Coupled with a musical language of which Stanford would almost certainly have approved, and that he could arguably have even written, this is yet another large-scale orchestral work in which Howells appears to be affirming the musical ideals of his teacher, and interestingly at a point at which Howells arguably no longer needed to impress Stanford in the way that he might have been keen to do in his early days at the RCM.

What, then, can we draw from this very brief overview of some of Howells's early compositions, mostly drawn from his time at the RCM? Paul Andrews has remarked that through his combination of 'languid romanticism' with 'chromatic seriousness' Howells created an 'ecclesiastical style for the 20th century as Stanford had done for the 19th'.[23] Whilst this is certainly the case in Howells's later music – and indeed it is his later choral works to which Andrews is referring in this observation – the composer's earlier works, as evinced by those stemming from his student days at the RCM, appear to embody considerably more of the 'languid romanticism' than they do his later innovations. Furthermore, not only do we find the 'Romantic' rather than more Modernist Howells in these early works, we also find a Howells whose musical language, for one reason or another, shows a clear and obvious debt to his teacher, and later friend, Stanford. It should be borne in mind that we are talking about a more general stylistic debt and similarity rather than being able to identify specific features in works by both men that demonstrate a common link. However, whilst this is very general it is also very telling. As the product of an established composer set in his ways, Stanford's musical language had changed very little from the point at which he reached his zenith in the 1880s. Howells, on the other hand, was approaching the musical world from a very different perspective. He had the benefit of a host of new ideas and musical styles to draw upon without the age and cynicism that his tutor had.

We might think little of this, though. All the anecdotes of Stanford and his approach to teaching suggest a man with a personality so strong, and at times even oppressive, that a still relatively naive and inexperienced Howells fresh from the Gloucestershire countryside might well have struggled to stand up to such a formidable character. However, although our perceptions of Stanford's teaching tend to be somewhat one-sided in the absence of any meaningful sources in this respect from the composer, it seems unlikely that Stanford would have held Howells in such high esteem had he merely turned out to be a carbon copy of the elder Irishman. Whilst Stanford no doubt had a profound effect on the young Howells, he was by no means the only character of similar standing whom Howells encountered during his time at the RCM. Alongside Stanford, Howells received tuition from Parry, Walter Parratt and Charles Wood, and the music of Vaughan Williams clearly had

---

[23] Andrews, 'Howells, Herbert'.

a great impact at this time also. So how, therefore, do we account for some of these early works? In many cases we might conclude that it was inevitable that a young and presumably still impressionable composer could not help but be influenced to some degree by those who taught him. As already mentioned, it is unknown to what extent Stanford would have exposed his students to his own music; but Howells's address in 1952 at the centenary of Stanford's birth, while obviously from a much later period in his life, demonstrates his intimate knowledge of the music of his former tutor, and it seems highly likely that Howells would have encountered a great deal of the Irishman's music whilst a student at the RCM. Thus, in the case of some early works, notably *The Bs*, we can assume that any apparent hints at Stanford's music, his tastes and his style might be the product of a thorough student, possibly keen to impress his tutor, even if only subtly. Works such as the Piano Concerto, however, are more difficult to dismiss in this fashion. While it is still questionable whether or not Howells would have encountered this work before he composed his own concerto in 1913, two years before Stanford's received its premiere, the nature of Howells's approach to the concerto and his incorporation of chamber textures, in particular, suggest that there must have been a much greater bond between this teacher–student pair. We should also bear in mind that even Howells himself, as expressed in his 1952 address, seems to have been aware that the Stanford he knew was clearly not the same Stanford who had rocketed to fame while still a young man in the 1870s and 1880s, suggesting that perhaps this man's overbearing personality had softened somewhat in his old age.

Howells's music may well have eventually given way to Dyson's great student revolution, in which legions of Stanford pupils rejected the conservatism of their teacher in favour of a more progressive approach. But perhaps here, in these early works, we find a very different Howells: not a sycophant keen to pander to his teacher's musical archaism – after all, the adage 'In matters of art friendship should not count' would suggest that two friends could differ on matters artistic without jeopardising any personal relationships – but rather, a young man so immersed in, and possibly even overwhelmed by, the world of musical conservatism of his mentor, that he could not help but to contribute towards Stanford's final stand-off against the 'stream of modernity'.[24]

[24] 'The New Stanford Symphony', *The Observer* (25 February 1912), 7.

CHAPTER 2

Howells and Counterpoint

Lionel Pike

THE music of Herbert Howells is inseparable from counterpoint: indeed, he considered himself to belong to the Tudor period 'not only musically but in every way'.[1] That was an intensely polyphonic era, and he himself normally thought in counterpoint (a trait he shared with Vaughan Williams). Thus the underlying feeling of 'H. H. His Fancy' (written in 1927)[2] is of a meditative and dreamy fugue, the word 'Fancy' standing both for the Tudor idea of 'imitative fantasia' and for 'the kind of music most admired by H. H'. As it happens, 'Foss's Dump' (no. 6 in the same collection) is also a fugue, but it is perhaps surprising that the piece written for H. K. Andrews[3] (no. 6 in Book I of *Howells' Clavichord* – HH 237) – that expert on all things pertaining to Palestrina and Byrd – eschews imitative counterpoint in favour of a melodic line with clear roots in Tudor keyboard dances, though with flowing contrapuntal accompaniment. Indeed, Howells's interest in Tudor music appears to have veered more towards the dance and air than towards the imitative fantasia or motet: 'Master Tallis's Testament' (from the *Six Pieces for Organ* of 1939–45 – HH 226) provides a modal tune with modally inflected supporting harmony, but does not use imitative counterpoint (even though Tallis was an expert at writing it); and when Bartók had tea with him in London, Howells demonstrated Tudor keyboard music by playing Farnaby's 'His Rest' and 'Tower Hill', and two pieces by Byrd (a pavane and 'The Carman's Whistle') – but not any of the Tudor imitative fantasias.[4] The early descendants of 'HH His Fancy' (in that they open with dreamy fugue subjects) are the second movement of the Organ Sonata of 1932 (HH 189), and the 'Fugue, Chorale and Epilogue' from the *Six Pieces*, though one can find many later examples. The complete fugue – but not this time at all dream-laden – at 'Newman's Flight' in *Howells' Clavichord* is the subject of an article published elsewhere.[5] Fugue and fugato in fact play only a small part in Howells's output: it may be that the composer himself considered the form a special mark of 'academic' musicians – and he was not a member of any formal university community.

---

[1] Palmer, *Herbert Howells: A Study*, 11. I am grateful to Dr David Maw and Dr Phillip Cooke for their help in the writing of this chapter.
[2] Written on 4 August 1927 and published as no. 11 in *Lambert's Clavichord* (HH 165xi).
[3] Included in *Howells' Clavichord*, published in 1961. The dedicatee was Herbert Kennedy Andrews (1904 –65): it was for Andrews's choir at New College, Oxford (where he was organist from 1956 to 1959) that Howells wrote the *New College Service* (HH 253).
[4] Palmer, *A Centenary Celebration*, 407.
[5] Pike, 'Flights of Fancy', 11–18.

Thus on the whole Howells's liturgical choral music has only short imitative sections; but this may be partly because the acoustics of the buildings for which he was writing would cloud the text if the music were to be too contrapuntal. Often he contented himself with little touches of part-movement, like the I–♭III–I against a major triad at the end of the Nunc dimittis in the *Collegium regale* (HH 246); with rather freely imitative counterpoint, like that at 'Peace Be within Thy Walls' in *O Pray for the Peace of Jerusalem* (1941 – HH 230i); or with a unison tune with descant, as in the *da capo* of *Like as the Hart* (1941 – HH 230iii), *A Hymn for St Cecilia* (1960 – HH 296) and most stunningly of all in the 'Gloria' of the *Collegium regale* evening canticles (1945). The orchestral and large-scale choral works with orchestra bristle with counterpoint, and possibly none more so than the *Missa sabriensis* (1954 – HH 275). Perhaps more frivolously one might make out a case for 'counter-pointing' of the Latin text in *Hymnus paradisi* (HH 220) with the sections that use English text (an idea foreshadowed in Vaughan Williams's *Dona nobis pacem*, first performed in 1936).[6] But I choose as a case study – perhaps somewhat perversely – a piece that is not obviously contrapuntal, in order to investigate how Howells could not avoid the device even when the prevailing language was not overtly polyphonic (a trait he shares with J. S. Bach). It is also a piece small enough to be considered in detail, and that can stand as an example for this composer's compositional procedures elsewhere. The treatment can thus be more thorough than in an attempt to discuss the composer's complete oeuvre. It will be evident that the piece falls into a number of sections that might well be viewed as variations on the main melodic material: but that is properly the subject for a study of thematic material and form rather than of counterpoint. And yet any discussion of counterpoint is bound to consider elements other than individual lines, for there is always an interaction of the various technical devices. One cannot entirely isolate them. I shall consider the following elements: the single line, two-part counterpoint, tune with accompaniment, fugato, free counterpoint, heterophony and the pedal point.

Take Him, Earth, for Cherishing *(1964 – HH 307)*

This anthem was written in memory of President Kennedy (and is sometimes called 'Motet on the Death of President Kennedy'), though it seems that the composer was additionally thinking of the untimely death of his son Michael (he had contemplated setting this text much earlier, in memory of him). Perhaps, then, there is in the composer's mind a kind of counterpointing between the death of his beloved son and the assassination of a beloved American President. The anthem was written at about the same time as the end of his composition of the *Stabat mater* of 1965 (HH 309).[7] The text is a superb translation from the Latin by Helen Waddell,

---

[6] The gestation of the work is complex, but it can be followed in detail in Palmer, *A Centenary Celebration*, 91–127.

[7] *Ibid.*, 153. In the published version the anthem is headed 'To the honoured memory of John Fitzgerald Kennedy, President of the United States of America', and in the manuscript (RCM MS 4620) 'In memoriam John Fitzgerald Kennedy'. Michael had died on 6 September 1935.

from the *Hymnus circa exsequias defuncti* of Prudentius (CE 348–413). Some of the musical material may well have been in Howells's mind already, though the ground-plan (but not the material) of the 1964 piece possibly owes something to the Third Symphony of Roy Harris; this latter (written in 1937) was, to many people, the 'Great American Symphony', so there could be strong reasons for Howells to have it in mind as he wrote his memorial to a Great American Citizen.[8] Perhaps the anthem might be thought of as being 'counterpointed' against the symphony, the vastness of the American prairie in Harris being replaced on a smaller scale and for smaller forces in an English-sounding anthem. Even though I know of no evidence that Howells encountered the symphony, it was a sensation in the years following its composition and was admired worldwide.[9] The similarities should not be pressed too far; and yet both pieces open with a single melodic line to which other voices are later added, both contain a climactic fugue (or *fugato*) and a quieter pastoral episode (though the positioning differs in the two works), and both end with a funeral tread. I shall therefore draw parallels between the works when they occur.

It is clear that the anthem exhibits a number of different ways of treating counterpoint, and I will deal with them (including – again perversely – single-line writing) in the order in which they occur in the anthem.

Single-Line Writing and the Appoggiatura

The piece opens with an unaccompanied melody of four distinct phrases, on the text

[I] Take him, earth, for cherishing,
[II] To thy tender breast receive him.
[III] Body of a man I bring thee,
[IV] Noble even in its ruin.

This is not melodically like plainsong, though the mixture of duplets, triplets and dotted-note figures ending with the final note starting on a weak pulse all give a sense of rhythmic freedom such as is often associated with that form of chant. The opening is extremely tightly organised (in a manner that is not commonly found in plainsong), and to understand the remainder of the work it is essential to unravel the organisation of this tune (like all good composers, Howells does not waste his material). It is based on a three-note shape that is often described (in chess terms) as the 'knight's move' shape: a stepwise movement followed (or preceded) by a leap of a third (which might be either major or minor) in the same direction. This is one of the most common shapes in western music: the statements can overlap and interlock with one another. The order of these intervals (where 1–2 is a step and 2–3 is the leap above it) can be 1–2–3 or 3–2–1; but related also are the sequences using the fourth (1–3) resultant from the combination of the two intervals 1–3–2 or 2–3–1. When the step is higher than the leap (5–6 being the leap, 4–5 being the

---

[8] Butterworth, *The American Symphony*, 84–7.
[9] I offer my thanks to Paul Spicer, Paul Andrews and Andrew Millinger for helping me to investigate whether Howells knew of this symphony.

Ex. 2.1 *Take Him, Earth, for Cherishing*, bars 1–9

step and 4–6 being the fourth) the formations 6–5–4, 4–6–5 and 5–4–6 are found (Howells does not use 5–6–4 or 6–4–5 in this piece). The sequence 1–3–2 is used only as a 'dead' interval: that is, one spread across the break between two phrases (see Ex. 2.1).

Phrase [I] moves from d' to f'♯: the relationship of those two pitches[10] is often explored later in the anthem, and the opening statement is echoed at dominant pitch at the end of [I]. The first three phrases all end on the dominant (pitch, not tonality) of B minor: only phrase [IV] ends on its tonic. The notes of the B minor scale (with the seventh being a'♮ rather than a'♯) are all used except for the sixth degree: the listener is therefore unable to tell whether the music is in tonal B minor (which requires g♮) or modal B Dorian (with the major sixth, g♯). There are no chromatic pitches, and the only semitone is between c♯ and d (though that is not stated directly). Phrase [II] expands its predecessor, and [III] is based on [II], though with rhythmic changes. Phrase [III] (which avoids the 'knight's move' shape) lifts the initial note of [II] up an octave to provide the highest note of the opening tune on the word 'Body' – a note that is unprepared, so making that entry all the more impressive. Furthermore, the f'♯–e' ('man I ...') of this phrase is a free inversion of the preceding c"♯–b'.

It is by hindsight that the listener appreciates the point made by the high c"♯ at 'Body of' in [III]. Not only is this the highest note of the opening section, but it is considerably prolonged, and it stands outside the b–b' octave of the rest of the melodic line. If one could admit that an unaccompanied melodic line could have 'harmonic' appoggiaturas, this must surely qualify. Not only is it outside the prevailing b–b' scale, but it is outside the central pitches of that scale, since it is not tonic, dominant, subdominant or third. It almost sounds as if Howells had in mind an A major chord, used as an appoggiatura against the prevailing B minor. This high c'♯ sets in motion the countless other appoggiaturas in the piece: in a sense,

---

[10] One already explored in the canticles for Westminster Abbey in 1957 (HH 281).

Ex. 2.2 *Take Him, Earth, for Cherishing*, bars 10–18

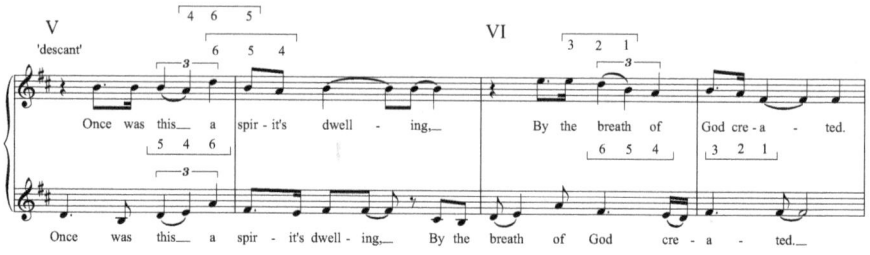

then, they could all be thought of as referring back to 'Body of a man' – a point of some significance in unifying both text and music. The descent from this high pitch (c″♯–b′–f′♯) is mirrored in the tonic to end [IV], so reversing the tonic–dominant motion of the initial phrase.

Two-Part Writing

Having echoed Roy Harris's Third Symphony by starting with unaccompanied melody, Howells now further follows that model by adding a second part, some of it in an organum-like style against a varied repeat of the opening melody (Harris then adds other voices; but one would scarcely expect Howells to follow Harris – if that is indeed what he was doing – precisely in every detail). This repeat is subtly changed as to rhythm, and yet is recognisably a repeat. The text here is

[V] Once was this a spirit's dwelling,
[VI] By the breath of God created.
[VII] High the heart that here was beating,
[VIII] Christ the prince of all its living.

The added part is a 'descant' to the initial tune – a device Howells used frequently in his choral music elsewhere: it is not imitative in the normal sense (though [VI] derives from [IV]), but it is closely based on the 'knight's move' shape (see Ex. 2.2).

It is the occasional parallel fourths, derived from the melodic fourths of the opening, that give the 'organum' feel; and at the end of [VIII] there is a feeling of heterophony in that both parts have a similar line but different rhythm (except that the two coalesce at the cadence into B). There are many repetitions of d″–b′ in this 'descant', reminding one of the opening proposition. In all eight phrases there has only been one direct melodic semitone (on 'here'), and no use of the sixth degree at all (and thus no g natural or g♯).

The special weight given to the c″♯s on 'Body of' in the opening melodic line is paralleled at the corresponding point in the two-part version. On the word 'High' the c″♯ is transferred to the 'descant', where it is prolonged: it emphasises the text by being the highest point of the section. Moreover, that descant starts the phrase with e″–f″♯, the quaver e″ acting like an appoggiatura to the high dominant note, then being echoed at two lower pitches (c″♯–d″, providing the first use of a direct melodic semitone in the piece, and then a′–b′). Finally, a descending appoggiatura (f′♯–e′, during [VIII]) is heard in a variation of the original tune, at the point where the end of the section moves into heterophony.

Tune with Chordal Accompaniment

Howells takes the logical further step of writing a tune with chordal accompaniment, thus thickening the preceding two-part texture. The text here is

[IX] Guard him well, the dead I give thee,
[X] Not unmindful of His creature
[XI] Shall He ask it:
[XII] He who made it
[XIII] Symbol of His mystery.

Phrases [IX] and [X] are closely related: the tune makes considerable use of semitones (largely avoided before this point): indeed, they are chromatic ones, though still closely organised around the 'knight's move' shape. 'Guard him well' in addition juxtaposes the pitches d″ and b′ by using the major and minor thirds of D followed by the major (enharmonically spelled) and minor thirds over B. This is a clear derivation from the first two notes of the anthem. The chordal accompaniment at last makes use of the sixth degree, the f′♯–g′♮–f′♯ movement resulting in an expanded Phrygian progression (B minor–C with minor seventh–B major); the middle chord of that progression evokes the so-called 'Howells scale', a feature not unlike Scriabin's 'mystic chord'. This passage is rounded out with a D minor chord, perhaps drawing on the b–d relationship set up by the first two notes of the piece (see Ex. 2.3).

The interval of a third is often an important factor in Howells's music: it is a feature that dates back to his fascination with Vaughan Williams's *Fantasia on a Theme by Thomas Tallis*, and a similar progression to b–d underlies the cadence that rounds off the whole section.[11] This is D minor–F♯, the f♮ of the first of these

---

[11] Pike, 'Tallis – Vaughan Williams – Howells'.

Ex. 2.3 *Take Him, Earth, for Cherishing*, bars 19–23

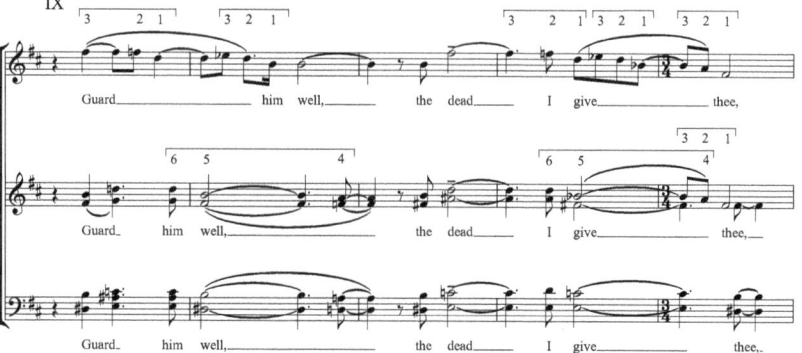

chords acting (enharmonically) as the leading-note of the final F♯ major chord. That ending has also been prepared at 'not unmindful of His creature', where the C major-plus-minor-seventh chord that harmonises the ♯4 (so beloved of Howells) moves directly to the F♯ major chord (even though there is an e' present as well). It has also been prepared by the melodic insistence on f♯s throughout this third section. The ruminative repeat of the opening words sung by the altos against the final chord of this section makes two points: at last g♯ is sounded (if incidentally and briefly), as if to provide a species of *tierce de Picardie* to the upper (rather than the lower) part of the scale; and Howells moves through the tritone (b♮) melodically, as he so often does in other works (notably at the end of *Hymnus paradisi*).

In this section the appoggiaturas become much more evident, since there is a background of harmony. At 'mindful' ([x]) f'♯ in the treble part is sounded against a C-major-plus-minor-seventh chord (prefiguring the tritone element of [xiii]); then a whole series occurs at 'ask it': [xii] and [xiii] give c''♯–b', c''♯–b', e''–d', e''–d'' and c''♯–b' (the last resolving via a'). This whole string of appoggiaturas does much to help set up the cadence in F♯ major at 'mystery'.

Fugato

The fourth texture (at [xiv]) is fugue; or, rather, it is *fugato*. Once again the plan of Roy Harris's Third Symphony is in the background, though the effect of the fugue in that piece is quite different, being triumphant and life-affirming. In Howells's anthem the text is about the coming of death:

[xiv]   Comes the hour God hath appointed
 [xv]   To fulfil the hope of men,
[xvi]   Then must thou, in very fashion
[xvii] What I give return again.

The vocal entries are not regularly spaced, and not on the tonic and dominant (though the first two are on d'' and a'), thus avoiding the predictability that one sometimes finds in the form. (If Howells had adhered too rigorously to Classical

Ex. 2.4 *Take Him, Earth, for Cherishing*, bars 37–40

fugal procedures the music might have taken on a Bachian aura: hence there is no countersubject, and no concentration on tonics and dominants.) It is in fact only the first three notes – which make the 'knight's move' shape – that are regularly imitated, so linking this section to those that surround it (see Ex 2.4).

The bitonal feel of these entries creates an uneasiness that illustrates the advent of death. Yet the background is D minor, with a g♯ that provides a touch of the tritone (suggested by the ruminating alto end of the preceding section) as well as sounding a pitch avoided at the opening. The D minor background also refers back to the penultimate sound of the previous cadence, and to the first note of the whole piece. Entries subsequent to the first four stretch the 'knight's move' shape, and D minor yet again cadences into F♯ major, this time with a touch of heterophony: there is a ruminative recollection of the opening (in the tenor) with another tritone. This is b♯, and when spelled enharmonically it helps move the tonality into A minor for the next section. As in the previous section, a series of appoggiaturas does much to set up the final F♯ major cadence.[12]

Central 'Pastoral' Section: Free Counterpoint

Not all of this section is 'pastoral', though that is its general nature, a nature suggested by 'wandering winds', 'empty sky', 'shining road' and 'woods'. Roy Harris had also introduced a 'pastoral' section,[13] though in his Third Symphony it had preceded the fugue. The text in Howells's anthem is as follows:

---

[12] A series of c″♯s in treble and alto (at [XVI]) eventually resolve down to b′, only to be replaced by another c″♯ that migrates to the bass and moves (via d′) to c♮ and b♭: then c′♯ is respelled as d′♭, and finally e′ and c♯ are used as appoggiaturas together.

[13] Roy Harris himself describes the sections as 'Pastoral'; see Butterworth, *The American Symphony*, 85.

[XVIII] Not though ancient time decaying
[XIX] Wear away these bones to sand,
[XX] Ashes that a man might measure
[XXI] In the hollow of his hand:
[XXII] Not though wandering winds and idle
[XXIII] Drifting through the empty sky,
[XXIV] Scatter dust was nerve and sinew
[XXV] Is it given to man to die.
[XXVI] Once again the shining road
[XXVII] Leads to ample paradise;
[XXVIII] Open are the woods again
[XXIX] That the serpent lost for men.

The section is largely based on A minor/A Dorian, which emphasises the note at the top of the first phrase of the whole piece, just as D minor [in XVII] had emphasised the first note and F♯, its last note. An open fifth drone (a–e) – a pastoral element – is heard at the beginning and ending of this fairly large section, and the tonality wanders off through B♭ minor and C♯/E major. The opening phrase picks up the *fugato*'s theme by using e–d♯–c, but there is not much use of the tritone here.

At the Phrygian shift to B♭ minor the tune apparently moves into the bass. Here the texture is of free (non-imitative) counterpoint, making much use of the 'knight's move' shape (see Ex 2.5). This is interrupted by a homophonic fanfare in C♯ minor [XXVI]: tonal movement from A to C♯ is a dominant version of the d–f♯ of which Howells has made much elsewhere, the point being emphasised by the C♯–A minor (with f♮)–C♯ of the fanfare itself. An exultant leaping figure in unison ('the shining ...') has elements of E major about it [XXVI], and it sets up a picture of woods [XXVIII] for which this sharp key area feels appropriate. It is a key that makes much of g♯, the sixth degree which was avoided at the beginning of the piece, now announced with great force at the top of the treble part. The freshness of the sound here owes much to the fact that this pitch was avoided for so long earlier on. The section starts with imitation in two parts, and has a little heterophony between the end of the first entry and the start of the second.

'The serpent ...' ([XXIX]) interrupts this idyllic pastoral quite abruptly: there is a return to A minor with pastoral a–e drones as at the opening of the section. The duetting trebles above this use the Dorian f♯ as well as d♯, creating a sense of bitonality, as if the upper parts are in E minor. But A wins the day briefly, before the whole large central section closes on a long dissonant chord that mixes A minor with the dominant seventh of B (omitting c♯). This bitonal chord could be laid out as three 'knight's move' shapes (see Ex. 2.6); furthermore, the mixture of B and A perhaps refers back to the opening monody with its (unheard) A background. Appoggiaturas yet again help to set up the cadence. At [XXVIII] and [XXIX] the treble parts use a whole series that do not resolve, b' eventually dragging the tonality up to a chord of B minor, and the alto rounds out the section with an upward d'–e' appoggiatura.

Ex. 2.5 *Take Him, Earth, for Cherishing*, bars 58–66

Climax and Funeral March: Heterophony and Pedal Point

The text of this final section is as follows:

[xxx] Take, O take him, mighty leader,
[xxxi] Take again thy servant's soul.
[xxxii] Grave his name and pour the fragrant
[xxxiii] Balm upon the icy stone.
[xxxiv] Take him, earth, for cherishing,
[xxxv] To thy tender breast receive him.
[xxxvi] Body of a man I bring thee,
[xxxvii] Noble even in its ruin.
[xxxviii] By the breath of God created
[xxxix] Christ the prince of living.
[xl] Take, O take him, earth, for cherishing.

Ex. 2.6 *Take Him, Earth, for Cherishing*, bars 80–5

Ex. 2.7 *Take Him, Earth, for Cherishing*, bars 92–6

The climax of the piece, at [XXX], is emphasised by the use of the tonic major, underscored by a shift from B to D♯ that draws attention to the major third (by building a chord on it) and by shifting the d–f♯ axis down to b–d♯. The d♯ helps to counter all the D minor chords heard earlier, and g♯ at last makes a considerable impact, as

Ex. 2.8 *Take Him, Earth, for Cherishing*, bars 97–9

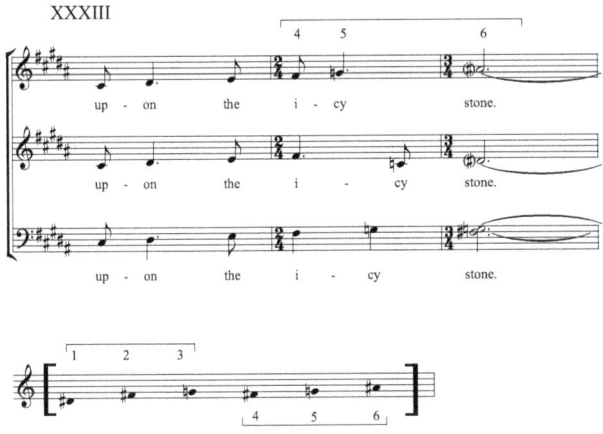

it had done during [XXVI] (in particular it is a vital element in the lyrical, arching soprano line at [XXXI]).

This climax makes powerful use of appoggiaturas. 'Mighty leader' sets them up with a♯–g♯ in the bass and c″♯–b′ in the second treble, then a multiple series on 'name' has a number of them in triads in the upper voices against a set in parallel thirds in the lower voices, moving at a slower speed (see Ex. 2.7). The idea is repeated three bars later, but without parallel thickening.

Example 2.7 shows how the influence of A (though now major rather than minor) returns, sounding against continuing elements of B major to prolong the effect of bitonality set up at the end of the preceding section. Heterophony is also heard again, with parallel triads – some of them augmented – moving at a different speed in the upper voices from that in the lower ones. In order to prepare for the recapitulation Howells annuls the sound of B major by countering g♯ with g♮ (helping to annul the powerful effect of the g♯s heard in the 'pastoral' section). This culminates – at [XXXIII] – in an icy held chord (illustrating 'icy stone') which basically interlocks two 'knight's move' shapes (see Ex. 2.8). The result is a dominant preparation for B minor with an extraneous d♯ – though some might hear it as a D♯ chord with both the major and minor third sounding; indeed, one might hear that d♯ as another appoggiatura, but not – on this occasion – dissonant.

The ending is an enhanced rewriting of the opening with a vital new element: this element is a tonic pedal like the slow beat of muffled drums in a funeral procession. The effect of loosened snares is achieved by the repetition of the consonants 't' or 'ch', which are elements of many of the words. Roy Harris's Third Symphony also ends with a funeral march over a repeated pedal with a relentless pounding rhythm.[14]

---

[14] The composer himself referred to this final section as 'Dramatic Tragic'; *ibid.*

Ex. 2.9 *Take Him, Earth, for Cherishing*, bars 109–11

Ex. 2.10 *Take Him, Earth, for Cherishing*, bars 124–30

The repetition of the opening line is made with some rhythmical variations: in particular, the voices stating it are not quite in unison, but give their own versions in a heterophony that picks up many of those devices heard earlier in the piece. At the end of the second phrase g♯ – avoided at the opening – is introduced so as to lead to a quite luminous statement of the third phrase, 'Body of a man I give thee'; and from here to the end the tonality is B major that is full of what, in Vaughan Williams's music, is known as 'blessedness' (though there are still some notes outside the tonic major).

Appoggiaturas are thickened into a chord at [XXXVI], C♯ from the opening line of the piece becoming a C♯ minor chord over the B pedal – a large-scale and distant recalling of that setting of 'Body' early in the piece (see Ex. 2.9). Two bars later this is echoed in a thinner form. At [XXXVIII] a♮–g♯ and c″–b′ are used, and then a whole string of d′♯–c′♯s occur in the alto.

Towards the end the use of counterpoint gradually fades away, and it eventually vanishes. Phrase [XXXIX] has a firm concentration on g♯, quite in contrast to the opening section. The alto part provides a tune to place against the chords in the other voices, and the rocking back and forth between c♯ and d♯ might be a miniature lullaby, such as is found (on a large scale) in the closing choruses of Bach's Passions.

The last two chordal phrases use appoggiaturas as almost the only contrapuntal device. The dissonant c″♯ in the alto is not immediately resolved, but is transferred to the treble, which resolves it to b′ in the final recall of the c♯ appoggiatura of the opening single-line phrase – though not before the treble voices have used a′♯–g′♯ and f′♯–e′ in parallel thirds. The penultimate chord has b–a♮ in the alto. In [XL] d♮s (enharmonically spelled) give a reminder of the opening tonality, and the downward-sweeping alto part links three 'knight's move' shapes, with some concentration on g♯ (see Ex. 2.10).

The treble part, in a final gentle benediction, sounds the initial 1–2–3 in the tonic major. In harmonic terms the cadence uses a mixture of G major/minor and B major/minor (which could be considered as a chord that sounds the 'knight's move' shapes, b–d–d♯ and a♮–b–d). The final chord – as so often before – is repeated on a weak pulse. This is a more 'blessed' end than the somewhat minatory one in Roy Harris's Third Symphony.

Conclusion

One does not have to demonstrate one's prowess in fugue to be thought contrapuntal; even such small things as appoggiaturas can enliven or add spice to the music. To the understandable objection that the appoggiatura is a harmonic rather than a contrapuntal device I point out that the result of good harmony is good counterpoint, and vice versa. It has been said that Howells is 'the master of the long line';[15] perhaps one might add that he is also the master of the appoggiatura. The device comes in short and long form, chromatic or diatonic (even, perhaps, consonant) form, in a single voice and in multiple voices, and overall it helps to control the emotional temperature of the music. This is not to say that every chord, every bar, is given its appoggiatura; but the uses of the device are legion, the resolutions from them – especially at cadences – very satisfying. This is a factor derived (perhaps subconsciously) from the Tudors, for whom a treatment of suspensions was a vital part of the fabric of music. The Tudors prepared their suspensions; Howells does not. The Tudors usually resolved their suspensions by a step down on the following weak beat; Howells does not.

Yet what is not in any way 'Tudor' is the sense of close, virtually symphonic, argument in the motet as a whole. The balancing of keys, the holding back of g♯ until it helps to make for an enhanced major effect, the growth of the appoggiaturas

---

[15] Sir Thomas Armstrong, in private conversation.

and the concentration on 'knight's move' shapes are all part of this way of thinking. Howells may perhaps have counterpointed his piece against Roy Harris's Third Symphony (though this remains unproven), but in its small way the English motet is also 'symphonic' in its construction. The anthem may exhibit close attention to detail, and be most carefully constructed; but that is not evident to the casual listener, and the overall effect is of overwhelming emotion, partly but by no means wholly occasioned by the particular circumstances prompting its composition – the assassination of an American President.

CHAPTER 3

Window on a Complex Style: *Six Pieces for Organ*

Diane Nolan Cooke

THE compositional style of Herbert Howells, the essence of which is admittedly difficult to articulate, seems to generate scholarly descriptions that fall into two categories. The first may be illustrated by some phrases of Christopher Palmer, taken from his discussion of Howells's impressionistic tendencies: '... the lines indeterminate and soft-drawn, the sum-total of texture a complex seen mistily through a haze of water or light ... effortless interweaving of myriad coloured strands, fluid, self-generating, kaleidoscopic ...'.[1] Such lofty and picturesque language, with an emphasis on visual metaphor, is common in attempts to describe a sound-world that can be mystifying even to the most astute listener. Then there is the contrasting clinical assessment, exemplified by a report of Howells's 'basic style' as 'tonal ... but with modal incursions, diatonic dissonance, cross-relations, pedal points and suspensions, as well as asymmetrical phrases, rhythmic vitality, and confident melodies'.[2] Assured that the devil is in the details, proponents of this perspective dissect and parse the music note by note, chord by chord, phrase by phrase, anticipating an epiphany. But neither the 'laundry list' of techniques nor Palmer's abstract portrait fully succeeds in capturing Howells's stylistic identity or explicating his achievements. A synthesis of these contrasting methodologies is necessary, and collections like the *Six Pieces for Organ* (HH 226) provide fertile ground for study of Howells's own integration of macrocosmic and microcosmic approaches to composition. These pieces offer an excellent window into Howells's style, with all the complexity that such a style embraces, yet without the intimidating vastness of a larger-scale work. The *Six Pieces* are Howells presented in manageable portions and should indeed be seen as a valuable offering to the persevering scholar.

Although Howells's output for the organ was sporadic, his two sets of Psalm Preludes and the three Rhapsodies had already established themselves in the repertoire by the time the *Six Pieces* were published in 1953. Having trained as an organist under Herbert Brewer at Gloucester Cathedral and Walter Parratt at the Royal College of Music, Howells's desire to write for the organ is not surprising; his well-known affinity for cathedral spaces also made the genre naturally appealing to him. Howells himself said that he was inspired by his 'brilliant set' of organist friends to compose for the instrument, and in the case of the *Six Pieces* it was Herbert Sumsion, Brewer's successor at Gloucester, who received the dedication.[3]

---

[1] Palmer, *Impressionism in Music*, 176n4.
[2] Hardwick, *British Organ Music*, 129.
[3] Howells, Introduction to broadcast of 'Paean', 2 May 1967, in Palmer, *A Centenary Celebration*, 435. It is not unreasonable to speculate that Howells had the acoustical space of Gloucester Cathedral in mind when writing the *Six Pieces*.

Howells spoke self-deprecatingly about his own playing,[4] but Palmer points out that descriptions of his improvising at St John's College, Cambridge are notable for the way in which they apply rather accurately to the written-down compositions: 'free, rhapsodic, difficult-to-grasp formally in a conventional analytic way but enormously satisfying emotionally and in terms of a broad, spacious, long-spanned design'.[5] (Such accounts also hint at the challenges faced by those who would study Howells's style.) Although the *Six Pieces* reflect this account to a degree, they are predominantly far from improvisational, displaying the care and refinement that has placed them among the important works comprising Howells's 'creative resurgence'[6] following the death of his son Michael in 1935.

The genesis of the project as a set is somewhat obscure; it seems that Howells completed five of the pieces between 1939 and 1940, and the sixth in 1945, with publication by Novello finally occurring another eight years later. According to Howells's own characteristically unreliable recollections, he focused on their composition while recovering from a long illness in April–May 1940,[7] but we know that he showed Sumsion versions of 'Master Tallis's Testament' and the 'Fugue, Chorale and Epilogue' as early as January of 1940.[8] In any case, the *Six Pieces* date approximately from the same period as *Hymnus paradisi* (HH 220) and anthems such as *Like as the Hart* (HH 230iii) and *O Pray for the Peace of Jerusalem* (HH 230i), and it is generally agreed that the set 'represents Howells at his most wide-ranging and original'[9] for the organ, in addition to revealing the composer's expert handling of modality. Three of the pieces – the two 'Sarabands' and 'Master Tallis's Testament' – illustrate Howells's long-standing fascination with Tudor music and Renaissance dance forms, and the tone of the collection as a whole reveals the inspiration of another age and time;[10] Howells is not seeking to be overtly progressive or contemporary, as we usually define such terms. More significant for this discussion, however, is the extent to which each piece achieves, or strives to achieve, a unique character that exhibits 'unity of mood', generally acknowledged as one of Howells's 'cherished ideal[s]'.[11]

The *Six Pieces* are an interesting test of the validity of the 'impressionist' label as applied to Howells. Shortly after the collection's publication, a reviewer wrote that 'the style is best described as a sort of Anglicized impressionism – all of the familiar impressionistic devices are used but in moderation and with a fine understanding of their application to the organ'.[12] As this exploration intends to demonstrate, one should refer to Howells's music as 'impressionistic' with some caution. Certainly, Howells is not an impressionist in the sense of depicting an impression of landscape or some aspect of the physical world, in the way that a Monet painting does, or even

---

[4] *Ibid.*
[5] Palmer, *A Centenary Celebration*, 173.
[6] Spicer, *Herbert Howells*, 115.
[7] Howells, Introduction to broadcast of 'Paean'.
[8] Spicer, *Herbert Howells*, 116.
[9] *Ibid.*, 140.
[10] The author acknowledges Paul Spicer for suggesting this second point; Paul Spicer, email communication to the author, 12 November 2012.
[11] Palmer, *A Centenary Celebration*, 173.
[12] Noss, 'Review: *Six Pieces for Organ*', 152.

in the manner of a Vaughan Williams *Norfolk Rhapsody*. Rather, Howells frequently exhibits 'impressionism' in the simpler sense of 'leaving an impression' on the listener – that impression being one of atmosphere or intangible feeling or spirit. The impression is perhaps inspired by an external source (another piece of music, such as Vaughan Williams's *Fantasia on a Theme by Thomas Tallis* in 'Master Tallis's Testament') or an extra-musical idea or emotion (the joy of Easter morning in the first 'Saraband'). This sort of impressionism is Howells's intentional 'unity of mood', his keen focus on expressing a particular artistic vision, and is arguably to blame for the typical forays into elevated language that permeate writings about Howells. But to fixate on the impression is to overlook the skill and technical means of achieving it, as the insufficiency of such extravagant descriptions of Howells's music bears witness. One's visceral response to Howells is partly an effect of his mastery of harmonic tension and release. The overarching structure of many of Howells's pieces (and one nearly ubiquitous in the works of English organ composers) is the gradual *crescendo* leading to a climax, followed by a *decrescendo* and fading away. Of the *Six Pieces*, the 'Preludio "sine nomine"', 'Master Tallis's Testament' and the 'Fugue, Chorale and Epilogue' all follow this trajectory. Within that larger form, Howells creates brief episodes of tension and conflict that may or may not resolve, building on one another cumulatively as the piece unfolds. Devices such as non-functional sevenths and ninths, along with suspensions and appoggiaturas on strong beats, are common features of Howells's unsettling harmonic plan. Rhythmically, too, Howells denies the listener equilibrium by favouring syncopation and complex subdivision of pulse – obvious with even the briefest glance at the score of 'Master Tallis's Testament'. Despite the sometimes gnarled and twisted path, however, Howells's arrival points can be moments of absolute, even shocking, clarity. The placement of the basic and familiar triad in an unfamiliar context could in fact be described as a particularly Howellsian hallmark, and calls to mind Vaughan Williams's belief that 'true originality' lay 'in the ability to make the simplest and most ordinary chord sound totally individual'.[13] Yet again the questions arise: what might be Howells's purpose in landing periodically on 'clean' triads, and what is the nature of the Howellsian context that allows his harmonies to speak so vividly? As we are obliged to rewiden the analytical lens, overall mood and 'impression' bid again for primacy of import. And herein lies the paradox and source for this discussion: the identification of specific technical tendencies turns out to be equally insufficient, and leads us inevitably back to a consideration of the more aesthetic qualities of context, ambience and emotional evocation. As this study of the *Six Pieces* will reveal, in Howells the dialectic of technique and aesthetic is greatly magnified, and perhaps by accepting this realisation one may begin to make humble progress towards a more substantial understanding of his style.

The dilemma, of course, is how to proceed in a way that does not undermine the acknowledgement of this dichotomy. Rather than merely starting with the details and working outwards, or beginning with the larger picture and deconstructing it (both of which are problematic and ultimately frustrating), one useful approach is to make acquaintance with the pieces in a way that might reflect the experience of

---

[13] Quoted in Layton, *Sibelius and His World*, 34.

the player who sets out to learn them – not in practical or mechanical terms, but in the more internal sense of progressing from one level of understanding to the next. This experience generally divides into three parts, supposing that in most cases the player hears a piece before deciding to learn it. In the first phase – listening – an overall notion of the piece takes root in the player's mind, while the ear catches here and there an intriguing detail of harmony, melody or rhythm. This is followed by access to a printed score, entailing play-through and study, during which the first 'impression' often fades to the background while specific building blocks become starkly manifest. Finally, as the piece is practised and learned, and the player's technical mastery and artistic sensibility begin to work in tandem, the overarching idea resurfaces with an added freshness. In this final stage, isolated techniques and components tend to reveal their place in the larger architecture, and yet the whole coalesces into more than the sum of the parts, sometimes reinforcing and other times altering the initial impression. The *Six Pieces* lend themselves to a study following this outline, as such an approach demonstrates that neither the technical nor the aesthetic concerns can ultimately take precedence, emphasising rather their mutual dependence and common goals. Moreover, it allows us to observe Howells's particular genius: the extent to which he continually surprises with a wide variety of emotional and aesthetic results sustained by the same characteristic devices.

Upon first acquaintance, three of the *Six Pieces* stand out for their striking emotional or atmospheric impact: the 'Preludio "sine nomine"', the 'Saraband (for the Morning of Easter)', and the 'Saraband (*in modo elegiaco*)'. These are arguably the most evocative and captivating for the listener, with an immediate appeal borne out of a seeming clarity of intent on the composer's part. The 'Preludio "sine nomine"' is the most obvious example of traditional impressionism in the *Six Pieces*, despite its brevity and non-descriptive title.[14] It projects an aura of brooding mystery; indeed an admirer once wrote to Howells that the work 'gives me the feeling I get from Thomas Hardy when he is taking us across a bleak moor in the twilight'.[15] The listener perceives an arc, from this bleakness to a more gentle warmth and then back again, which proceeds in an introverted and hushed manner while engaging in what Paul Spicer has described as 'simply outstanding impressionistic colouring'.[16] Spicer has noted in Howells's music the parallels with 'arch-impressionist' Maurice Duruflé,[17] and in the 'Preludio' an organist might be reminded of the shadowy opening of the 'Prélude' from Duruflé's *Suite* (1932), or the serene harmonies underlying the litany theme in the *Prélude et fugue sur le nom d'Alain* (1942). There is also something of the craftsmanship of Louis Vierne, a Romantic impressionist of sorts, in Howells's harmonic colours and motivic contours in the 'Preludio'. And yet, though the work is entrancing, it is not so much so that the ear fails to note prominent details such as

---

[14] It appears that Howells had a fondness for this 'non-title'. The *Missa sine nomine* (1912 – HH 28) and *Sine nomine: A Phantasy* (1922 – HH 126) are both unrelated to the organ piece.
[15] Charles Peaker, in Palmer, *A Centenary Celebration*, 435.
[16] Spicer, *Herbert Howells*, 116.
[17] Ibid., 47.

a falling melodic motif and a sparse texture that expands and contracts; the reverie is also broken by a rather startling final cadence.

While the lack of a real title perhaps enhances the mysteriousness of the 'Preludio', the titles of the two 'Sarabands' indicate much about the nature of the music to follow – structurally and rhythmically, but also thematically. Furthermore, they set forth expectations and proceed to fulfil them on first hearing, even while Howells's underlying procedures remain obscure. The 'Saraband (for the Morning of Easter)' communicates its Resurrection theme with various manifestations of genuine happiness: stately majesty at the opening, followed by poignant blissfulness in the central section, and then raucous ecstasy at the first theme's recapitulation. One is reminded of the rapturous exclamations of 'Holy is the true light' in *Hymnus paradisi*, a work that shares a similar spirit with this 'Saraband'. Howells's interpretation of the sarabande rhythm, with its stress on the second beat of the bar, unfolds in grand gestures, while one is simultaneously aware of a continuous streaming of smaller flourishes and ornamental fluttering. There is a sense of not straying far from the tonal centre, and yet harmonic interest is not lacking, especially in the conspicuous colour chords that Howells rhythmically punctuates. It is a piece that is instantaneously effective because it exudes joy, rather than merely depicting it. Likewise, its partner in the collection, the 'Saraband (*in modo elegiaco*)', is equally striking for its projection of mood, albeit one that is diametrically opposite. Admittedly, on first hearing the listener would not likely be aware that the piece was originally subtitled 'for Good Friday',[18] or that it was the last of the collection to be completed, Howells having written it over two days in September 1945, just after the tenth anniversary of Michael's death. Previous attempts to identify in the work such potent subjects as the Second World War, Michael's death or the Crucifixion have been at best inconclusive,[19] but in any case the piece's vivid mournfulness, whatever its source of inspiration, does not fail to impress. It is the shortest piece in the collection, straightforward and swift in impact. The sarabande rhythm is less obvious, overwhelmed by ever-building intensity and volume paired with melodic lines that sink down, claw their way up the scale, and then fall again. Perhaps the single most memorable aspect of the work is the way Howells ends it – not with quiet sorrow or gentle reassurance, but with an unrelenting *crescendo* leading to an astounding major chord. (A similarly intense conclusion appears in another Howells work centred on striving and supplication: the anthem *My Eyes for Beauty Pine* – HH 158). Whether it is true, as has been asserted, that 'there is in all of Howells's best music an underlying, elegiac sense of transience and loss',[20] the second 'Saraband' provides strong supporting evidence for such a view.

---

[18] Palmer, *A Centenary Celebration*, 150n20. The reason Howells changed the title is not known, but one supposes that, for an actual Good Friday liturgy, the appropriateness and utility of a piece with a loud C major conclusion may have been called into question. It is also possible that the placement of this 'Saraband' after, rather than before, the Easter-themed 'Saraband' in the order of pieces made the 'Good Friday' designation seem nonsensical. For whatever reason, however, Howells chose to retain the 'Easter' reference.

[19] Spicer, *Herbert Howells*, 140.

[20] Andrews, 'Howells, Herbert'.

Although the two 'Sarabands' and the 'Preludio "sine nomine"' demonstrate the degree to which Howells can impress upon first hearing, this does not imply an inferiority in the remaining three pieces; but they are rather more indeterminate in atmosphere, initially, and less emotionally charged. If any could arguably be grouped with the first three, it would be 'Master Tallis's Testament', which has a symbolic place in Howells's creative life and development. The composer said famously that 'Master Tallis's Testament' was a 'footnote'[21] to Vaughan Williams's *Fantasia on a Theme by Thomas Tallis*, a work that had a profound musical and spiritual impact on the young Howells. Although close familiarity with the earlier masterpiece is not essential, Howells's work noticeably shares some of its Tudor harmonic inflections and melancholy beauty. Certainly the name 'Tallis' alone reveals something of Howells's inspiration, and the word 'Testament' portends an aura of solemnity. Yet, there is a pervasive coolness that distinguishes this piece from the visceral immediacy of the two 'Sarabands' and the 'Preludio'. On first hearing one is conscious of a melody that does not travel far, which is repeated in various guises as it builds to a climax and then dies away again. In its tidy phrasing and dark harmonic colouring, 'Master Tallis's Testament' seems introspective more than evocative, keeping the listener at a distance even as fiery flashes occasionally break out of the texture (and visual metaphor irresistibly beckons). That the 'Fugue, Chorale and Epilogue' also keeps the listener at arm's length is less surprising, given its formal nature and explicit, somewhat rigid tripartite structure, which remain the most prominent aspects on initial hearing. It follows the conventional *crescendo*–climax–*decrescendo* pattern as well, and being nearly twice as long (when performed) as the other pieces, the work perhaps offers fodder for the not infrequent criticism that Howells engages in 'note-spinning when inspiration has slackened'.[22] The first fugue subject appears promising, as one perceives an inherent sense of pathos in the rising and falling contours (Ex. 3.1), while the second fugue subject has chant-like qualities and features a triplet. But the listener is certain to notice a tediousness in the material both leading up to and following the chorale, which is the piece's high point; further, the moment of clarity offered by the chorale seems too fleeting, in spite of its internal effectiveness and robust presentation. Howells puts his propensity for 'note-spinning' to better use in 'Paean', and with this title he at least lays out a straightforward goal: to evoke joy, thanksgiving and exultation, as in an ode. But 'Paean' is the lightest in emotional substance of the set, even while maintaining a superficial and improvisatory exuberance, and one senses from the composer less commitment at the deepest levels. From the outset the listener is expecting a toccata, and receives what might better be characterised as an *interrupted* toccata, in which the chordal fanfares seize the focus away from the toccata figuration. It is a vibrant and buoyant work, likely recognisable to the organist as one that would be entertaining to perform, and Howells's distinctive voice is not entirely

---

[21] Spicer, *Herbert Howells*, 23. Howells was present at the premiere of Vaughan Williams's work at the Three Choirs Festival in Gloucester Cathedral in 1910.
[22] Finzi, 'Herbert Howells', 181.

Ex. 3.1 'Fugue, Chorale and Epilogue', *Six Pieces for Organ*, bars 1–4

lost in the wash, but it does not leave the same kind of soul-searing impression on first hearing that other pieces in the collection do.

Having gauged, theoretically, the player-as-listener's first speculative response to each piece, the next natural step is to attempt to draw back the curtain and delve into the components of Howells's technique, from which the initial impressions may (or may not) spring. The player has the opportunity, in the learning-and-practice stage, to examine the details that stood out on first hearing, but he must also allow for the pieces to undergo a process of partial demystification; such should be the case in our analysis here. Of course, sometimes Howells's methods are not so enigmatic: after considering the score of the 'Preludio', for example, it is rather obvious how the unsettling Phrygian mode, combined with the solitude of a single note, octave, prolonged rest or lengthy pedal point, could evoke a sense of vast space – perhaps even the admirer's lonely moor. And in studying the scores of all of the *Six Pieces*, one soon discovers that is also true that Howells was inclined to overuse certain gestures and techniques – an admission that does, at least temporarily, tend to diminish the sense of mystique. To regard Howells as 'manneristic' is not entirely unreasonable, especially if one employs the term in a descriptive rather than accusatory way (as an example of the latter, Gerald Finzi derided Howells's use of pedal points as 'a tired slap-dash mannerism').[23] Some of Howells's mannerisms might seem artificial, such as the fluttering demisemiquavers that serve as ornamental passing tones and trills, which are prominent in the two 'Sarabands' and 'Master Tallis's Testament'; but like the preponderance of false relations in these pieces, these affected gestures are requisite when incorporating stylistic elements of earlier periods, especially elements derived from dance. These ornaments may also be remnants of Howells's improvisatory organ-playing. Other ostensible mannerisms, such as the aforementioned pedal points, do appear repeatedly in various guises: they may be the literal kind, as found in the 'Preludio' and 'Paean', or the kind that merely hold the harmony hostage to create a static canvas, as does the pedal ostinato of the epilogue section of the 'Fugue, Chorale and Epilogue'. Interestingly, Howells noted in a 1936 lecture outline that the pedal point could serve for the listener as a 'point of contact' between the 'old' sound-world and the new realm of modern music,[24] suggesting that his use of the device was partly motivated by its 'user-friendly' aspect. Perhaps the mannerism most apparent to the player studying the *Six Pieces* is Howells's insistence

---

[23] *Ibid.*
[24] Howells, in Foreman, *From Parry to Britten*, 196.

Ex. 3.2 'Saraband (for the Morning of Easter)', *Six Pieces for Organ*, bars 79–82

on thick-textured, crashing chords that border on indulgent. Spicer has noted that Howells did not refrain from 'trying to cram as many notes as possible into his chords',[25] and nowhere is this more evident than in the ninth chord and surrounding harmonies at the rowdy moment of recapitulation in the Easter 'Saraband' (Ex. 3.2). 'More is more', Howells so often seems to be saying.

Beyond such mannerisms, however, one recognizes some broader compositional processes at work, especially pertaining to the self-imposed limits Howells places on the pieces by choosing to follow a particular form, and how harmony, melody and rhythm work together within those limitations. Initially, the educated listener would be vaguely aware, in 'Master Tallis's Testament' and the Easter 'Saraband', of the melodic and harmonic constraints of the four-bar phrase characteristic of the Tudor forms Howells employs in those pieces. When examining Howells's phrases more closely, however, one notices that, while the melodies and harmonies do not necessarily *seem* to go far, Howells manages to venture to considerable extremes internally. He maintains the illusion by staying close to the tonal centre, returning to the 'home' of a standard triad or the melodic pitch from whence a particular line began, but there is often a flurry of activity in the inner voices, as exemplified by 'Master Tallis's Testament'. In this piece, which turns out to be a theme and two variations, Howells follows late-sixteenth- and early-seventeenth-century practice in building up from variation to variation without altering the basic form, harmony or melody.[26] Yet passages such as that shown in Ex 3.3 illustrate Howells's ability to develop aural interest and convey very little sense of restriction. In the Easter 'Saraband', the prevailing diatonicism and comfortable familiarity of C major do not prevent Howells from landing, at the very first stressed second beat of the piece, on a bold ninth chord (Ex. 3.4). Rhythm, in particular, becomes Howells's ally in situations where the harmony and melody are less flexible; again, this is on view in 'Master Tallis's Testament', where Howells exploits syncopated contrapuntal textures, fraught with appoggiaturas and suspensions (Ex 3.3). He can in fact be quite exacting when it comes to rhythm and note values, as in the penultimate bars,

---

[25] Spicer, 'Partita', 882.
[26] Hardwick, *British Organ Music*, 136.

Ex. 3.3 'Master Tallis's Testament', *Six Pieces for Organ*, bars 23–6

Ex. 3.4 'Saraband (for the Morning of Easter)', *Six Pieces for Organ*, bars 1–8

where an Adagio marking is followed by *perdendosi* (dying away), layered over the rhythmic augmentation of the theme's final phrase – all of which might otherwise have been approximated by a simple rallentando marking. Internal rhythmic complexity plays a role in other pieces as well, such as in the counterpoint of the 'Fugue, Chorale and Epilogue', where the first fugue subject and its countersubject feature some syncopation, while in 'Paean', the accents thrust on top of the toccata figuration create syncopations and signature appoggiaturas that keep the music from settling into the three-beats-per-bar metre that is prescribed. The rhythm of the chordal fanfares in 'Paean' also wreaks havoc on the metre, even as, harmonically, these colourful, attention-grabbing modules essentially circle back to where they

Ex. 3.5 'Paean', *Six Pieces for Organ*, bars 56–7

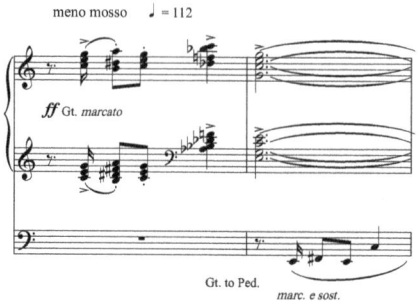

began (Ex. 3.5). Howells once lamented that the average listener was disposed to 'search for rhythmic excitements that are merely metric',[27] so it is logical to find Howells exploring alternatives.

Some of Howells's harmonic and melodic practices do merit a closer look, especially those that are pervasive in the *Six Pieces*, and those that appear to have affected the initial impression or, as the player learning them might suspect, are growing in significance as part of an optimal aesthetic presentation taking shape. Generally speaking, Howells's harmonic notions fall within the larger category of diatonic dissonance that encompasses much music of the so-called 'English musical renaissance' of the early twentieth century. In the *Six Pieces*, however, familiar triadic harmony juxtaposed with deliberate twists of convention results in some Howellsian fingerprints, including progressions and cadential movement by the interval of a third, and the use of non-functional seventh chords (and ninths to an extent), often in succession. By insisting so frequently on moving by the interval of a third, rather than a fourth or fifth (not that the latter are entirely absent), Howells introduces a slight sense of disorientation even when the individual chords themselves are clear. Sometimes these progressions pivot on a common tone, but just as often do not. Example 3.6 from the 'Saraband (*in modo elegiaco*)' illustrates a series of these progressions, moving from C major, to E♭ minor, back to C major and then to A major. In 'Paean' one finds an example that extends over several bars (Ex. 3.7) and emphasises the common tone A, while bars 110–11 in Ex 3.8 display the progression (F major to D major) in abrupt form. The importance of this progression for Howells is perhaps most manifest in the fact that two of the pieces end with a cadence that moves by a third: the 'Preludio' (A minor to F♯ major, which is arresting even upon first hearing), and the Easter 'Saraband' (E major to C major). The Easter 'Saraband' contains some of the strongest traditional cadences in the collection, yet Howells concludes with this unusual cadence and intersperses the peculiar progression throughout the piece. In a structural sense, too, the Easter 'Saraband' exhibits this harmonic idiosyncrasy, with a central section in A♭ framed by the main thematic material in C major on either side. Similarly, substantial portions of the 'Saraband

---

[27] Howells, letter to George Barnes, in Foreman, *From Parry to Britten*, 195.

Ex. 3.6 'Saraband (*in modo elegiaco*)', *Six Pieces for Organ*, bars 51–2

Ex. 3.7 'Paean', *Six Pieces for Organ*, bars 30–3

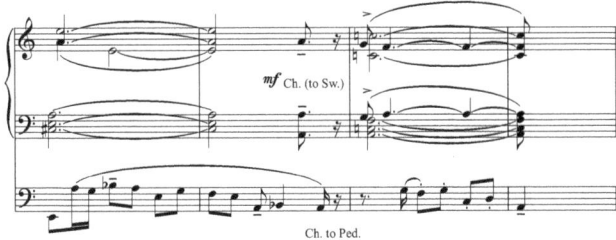

(*in modo elegiaco*)' seem occupied by a conversation between C major and A major (and occasionally minor), including the forceful alternation between these chords at the recapitulation of the theme (Ex. 3.9).

Seventh chords, meanwhile, appear throughout the *Six Pieces* and are partly responsible for the 'colourful' quality so often associated with Howells's style, but they are most prevalent in the pieces with lengthy passages of high density, emerging at climactic moments and instances of rhythmic accent. One particular sequence of two punctuated sevenths occurs several times in the Easter 'Saraband', accentuating the second beat of the sarabande rhythm (Ex. 3.10, bar 74), while the sevenths in 'Paean' tend to appear on the first beat of a bar, featuring extensively in the coda over the tonic pedal point until eventually giving way to the D major triad. In the 'Fugue, Chorale and Epilogue', an important C major seventh (accompanied by accents, *tenuto* markings and a *crescendo*) is the breaking point of the development section leading up to the chorale statement, forming a plagal cadence that rather overshadows the tonic first inversion harmony at the entrance of the chorale. The sevenths then infiltrate the chorale, expanding into occasional ninths and even elevenths (Ex. 3.11); Howells seems to encourage the player to bask in conspicuous progressions such as that in bar 80, where a ninth built on E crashes into a massive A major seventh in second inversion. Sevenths play a lesser role in the Tudor-inflected 'Master Tallis's Testament', though they are occasionally interwoven into the texture, and in the triad-heavy 'Saraband (*in modo elegiaco*)', where they serve in a more transitional capacity. And surprisingly, what

Ex. 3.8 'Paean', *Six Pieces for Organ*, bars 106–12

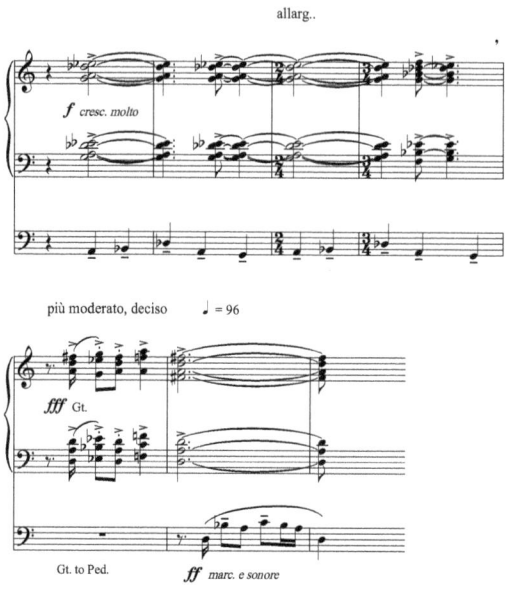

Ex. 3.9 'Saraband (*in modo elegiaco*)', *Six Pieces for Organ*, bars 38–46

we have previously identified as the conventionally impressionistic 'Preludio' does not depend on sevenths either, though the first solid appearance of F♯ major as the tonic comes in cadential movement from a C♯ minor seventh (see Ex. 3.12, bars 33–4), presaging the final harmony of the piece.

Ex. 3.10 'Saraband (for the Morning of Easter)', *Six Pieces for Organ*, bars 74–6

Ex. 3.11 'Fugue, Chorale and Epilogue', *Six Pieces for Organ*, bars 76–85

A note about Howells's general use of key relationships and harmonic plans is worth making at this point. Scrutiny of the more technical elements of these pieces has shed light on the composer's method of moving back and forth between contrasting harmonic means, both in a larger structural sense, and at the microcosmic level from one chord to the next. This includes alternation between modality and tonality as well as the major and minor forms of a chord. Howells's use of modes is frequently mentioned as one of his preferred archaisms, and in the *Six Pieces* he employs the Dorian mode in 'Paean' and 'Master Tallis's Testament', and the Phrygian in the 'Preludio'; but in all three cases the modes are not strictly adhered to. Even in 'Master Tallis's Testament', the most harmonically conservative in the set, Howells moves freely between the Dorian mode on G and G minor (not to mention the theme's resolution to G major), often lowering the E natural

Ex. 3.12 'Preludio "sine nomine"', *Six Pieces for Organ*, bars 26–34

to E♭ and raising the F natural to F♯. This results not only in false relations, a characteristic of the Tudor style, but in the piquant presence of the raised fourth scale degree (C♯) in the tonicisations of the dominant D, creating some periodic brightness in the otherwise shadowy sound-world of the piece. In 'Paean' the key contrasts are more sectional, with the Dorian mode used for the toccata portions, reflecting a Duruflé-like diatonicism, while the chordal fanfares centre on block triads moving by thirds or in retrogressions in the direction of various major keys, enhanced by the ubiquitous colour chords and even tritone clusters (Ex. 3.8). The modal scale is most explicit in the 'Preludio', exposed by the thin texture, but again Howells relieves the Phrygian 'bleakness' with changes of key along with texture and registration.[28] In addition, Howells occasionally dabbles with the

---

[28] As per the English style of organ registration, Howells rarely prescribes specific organ stops in the *Six Pieces*, but notably calls for a change to strings (from diapasons) at bar 26 of the 'Preludio'.

whole tone scale and, to a lesser extent, chromaticism, when he plays with shifting harmonic schemes. The touches of chromaticism are primarily attached to the changing of keys in rapid succession, used almost predictably by Howells for development or exploratory purposes, while the whole tone scale (or hints of it) functions as one of his concluding devices, as seen at the ends of the 'Fugue, Chorale and Epilogue' and especially the Easter 'Saraband', where it is quite blatant. It is certainly fair to say that, in the *Six Pieces*, Howells does not shy away from the means available to him for both showcasing *and* undermining the harmonic relationships determined by the tonal and modal systems he has selected for each piece.

Howells's melodies and melodic techniques receive perhaps less attention than his harmonic schemes, neglected by the player and analyst alike, but this is not due to a lack in tunefulness; rather, they are sometimes simply less exotic than his harmonies or, as noted above, limited in scope. Howells wrote that he considered the 'immemorial habit of "top part" listening' to be one of the 'universal difficulties' for music listeners in the modern era,[29] and his music does challenge that tendency by focusing more on 'interior' aspects. In the *Six Pieces*, melodies are usually found floating or creeping along, up and down the scale, in a manner suggesting that their purpose is more decorative than integral to the composition; or, put differently, that for Howells melodies are principally just necessary embellishments of harmony. Such a theory is debatable; but nevertheless, ordinary stepwise melodic movement indeed abounds, evident throughout 'Master Tallis's Testament', 'Paean' and the two 'Sarabands'. In 'Paean' the stepwise melodic fragments are chant-like, which is a natural outgrowth of the modality.[30] The theme in 'Master Tallis's Testament' is much longer but also extremely narrow in compass in some parts (Ex. 3.13), essentially spanning only a fourth in the first section and always circling back to G. In the 'Saraband (*in modo elegiaco*)', the stepwise melodic movement is even picked up by the pedal as the 'walking bass' provides propulsion towards the triple-*forte* climax. But stepwise movement does not translate into monotony, nor does it preclude creativity, especially when Howells wraps his melodies in ornamentation. The opening semiquavers of the Easter 'Saraband' (Ex. 3.4) constitute a written-out ornament, and though they merely pivot around the primary note G, this swirling motif becomes a hallmark of the piece alongside the demisemiquaver embellishments (the theme of 'Master Tallis's Testament' can be seen as an extended reshaping of the 'Saraband' motif, even using the same pitches).

Although appoggiaturas and appoggiatura-like figures are among the devices that seem somewhat manneristic in Howells, these small ornaments work in tandem with the underlying harmony to give Howells's melodies vitality and dramatic flair. Appoggiaturas and suspensions serve to delay the inevitable, especially

---

[29] Howells, letter to George Barnes, in Foreman, *From Parry to Britten*.
[30] Howells acknowledged on occasion the plainsong contours of his melodies. He wrote that the main theme of his choral-orchestral work *Sine nomine* 'savours of plainsong', and that plainsong 'can roughly be regarded as the folk-music of the Church'; Palmer, *A Centenary Celebration*, 437.

Ex. 3.13 'Master Tallis's Testament', *Six Pieces for Organ*, bars 1–6

in the $\hat{2}$–$\hat{1}$ configuration, and are therefore natural tension-builders. In 'Paean' a prominent melodic appoggiatura at the *poco largamente* (bar 133) becomes the seed of material in the coda, inspiring a carillon figure and an emphatic, accented melodic statement in the pedal. In the Easter 'Saraband', the appoggiaturas can take on a rebellious quality, creating sharp clashes of a minor second before resolving down (Ex. 3.10, bars 75–6). Howells also uses the technique in a more fundamental way, as in the 'Saraband (*in modo elegiaco*)', where the appoggiaturas are a key feature of the slow-moving melody and heavy atmosphere. Here one finds full chords in suspension relationships, functioning as appoggiaturas in ways that only melody notes normally do. However, the chief instance where Howells must take extra special care in his handling of melody comes in the 'Fugue, Chorale and Epilogue'. In the case of fugue, the subjects are the focus – they are, in fact, the only material with which the composer has to work. Not unexpectedly, there is a good amount of stepwise movement in Howells's fugue subjects, but, as the listener ascertains on first hearing, the first subject in this piece contains a distinctive drop of a fifth in the second phrase (Ex. 3.1). It is a potentially powerful motif, seemingly constructed for conveying an intensity of feeling. We do see a similar descending figure elsewhere – in the 'Preludio', for example (Ex. 3.14), and in the Easter 'Saraband', where the melody habitually drops off by a third or fourth at the ends of phrases – but the consequences are ultimately greater in a fugue. Howells adds a triplet in the second fugue subject – a device that, though it appears in a decorative fashion in 'Master Tallis's Testament' and the Easter 'Saraband', appears as a melodic motif only here in the *Six Pieces*. The full significance, and conceivable success, of the melodic contours Howells has chosen are not realised until the chorale, where the fugue subjects are combined and transformed into melodies in the truest sense.

Various elements and facets of Howells's compositional procedures reveal themselves upon closer inspection (and for the player, through the repetition of practice), but the processes of clarification and demystification are still only part of the

Ex. 3.14 'Preludio "sine nomine"', *Six Pieces for Organ*, bars 1–4

analytical journey. It is not difficult to become tied up in the details of voice leading, complex rhythms and key relationships, and likewise, synthesising Howells's means with his moods, so to speak, is not an easy task. Yet akin to the player who is approaching performance, attempting to integrate accuracy of technique with artistry, we must seek to be secure and cognisant of the intricacies of the score, rather than overwhelmed by them. Although certain elements manifest themselves repeatedly in Howells, these gestures and devices do not have a prescribed meaning. This is the hazard of analysing his style incrementally, or solely in piecemeal units of melody, harmony and rhythm, whether that unit is a single chord or an entire section: as soon as one attempts to ascribe 'meaning' to a specific component, or define its impact, Howells refutes that attempt. The *Six Pieces* teach this time and again; Howells refashions his techniques to suit a particular musical vision, manifesting mastery of detail with the broader picture – often, the 'impression' – always in mind. One reads much of the compositional ability of 'thematic transformation', in reference to Howells and many other composers, but his achievement in the *Six Pieces* might be more aptly described as 'elemental transformation': a process of manipulating, fine-tuning and adapting musical devices to context. Even Howells's alleged mannerisms can be included in this process and serve as vehicles for conveying his artistic ideas. It is a consummate flexibility that is enviable in the art of composition, and for the scholar, one that accounts for the appealing diversity of character in Howells's works, but which is also not incompatible with critical judgements and the acknowledgment of possible weaknesses.

In examining the mutability of technical elements for a larger aesthetic purpose, the Easter 'Saraband' is an especially useful source, as so many of Howells's preferred techniques are embedded in it, and because it projects such a highly personal conception of a particular emotion (joy). Consider, for example, the effective comparison of certain aspects of the Easter 'Saraband' and the 'Preludio', pieces that conjure distinctly different moods. If the 'Preludio' represents Howells the introvert, the 'Saraband' finds Howells engaging his most self-consciously extroverted compositional voice. Yet the two pieces contain passages that have remarkably similar contours, as in Ex. 3.12 and Ex. 3.15. In structural context, each passage appears as, or within, a central section of the piece that contrasts in key and atmosphere with the surrounding material. Note that the passages are of approximately the

Ex. 3.15 'Saraband (for the Morning of Easter)', *Six Pieces for Organ*, bars 47–54

same length, with long-held chords over a static harmony (stylised pedal points), and that the main melodic motif is an appoggiatura figure accompanied by scale movement. In both cases the pedal point is embellished by this appoggiatura figure also. In the 'Preludio', despite the dominant F♯ pedal point (of the current B major key), the gently oscillating chords hover on the mediant and the subdominant with an added second: these are harmonies that do not lead the ear strongly in any particular direction, allowing Howells to alleviate the austere mystery of the prelude's opening with a sensation of pleasant, improvisatory, almost timeless suspension. This establishes a sense of calm that is vaguely reassuring, rather than unnerving or disorienting, and the feeling of anticipation usually created by a dominant pedal point is not present. As becomes clear, Howells never intended to move towards B major as the tonic, but uses this passage as a slow and dreamy drift towards F♯ major. In the Easter 'Saraband', meanwhile, the sonorities found in Example 3.15 are part of a section seemingly intended to evoke tranquility, in contrast to the unruly intensity that surrounds it. The music is imbued with a prayerful, almost pleading quality, accomplished with textures featuring clusters of seconds and thirds, not unlike those in the corresponding passage in the 'Preludio'. Here, however, aided by a few flickering demisemiquavers, Howells is manipulating the stepwise movement and appoggiaturas into more swirling motifs, serving to increase the intensity rather than relax it; he manages this over a supertonic pedal point, which, somewhat improbably, heightens the anticipation more than the dominant pedal point in the 'Preludio'. This is Howells's skill in elemental transformation, which permits him to converse in a language of chosen techniques, both broad and specific, in order to articulate an 'ecstatic vision'[31] in one context and an impressionistic haze in the other.

[31] Sutton, 'The Organ Music of Herbert Howells', 177.

Ex. 3.16 'Master Tallis's Testament', *Six Pieces for Organ*, bars 44–5

In one smaller detail of comparison already observed, that of final cadential movement by a third at the ends of the 'Preludio' and Easter 'Saraband', the differences in ambience and dynamic are obvious; but it is still remarkable how, in the first instance, this arresting harmonic movement provides natural closure to the piece's lingering eeriness through *lack* of a common tone, while in the second instance, the presence of the major third (E) of the tonic C as the common tone, underscored as the root in the penultimate chord, bestows a conspicuous elegance on the progression that befits Howells's objectives for the piece.

Elemental transformation is evident throughout the *Six Pieces* in myriad ways, but one of Howells's favourite 'mannerisms', the demisemiquaver embellishment, offers another opportunity to demonstrate the point. In the Easter 'Saraband' these flourishes have a strumming or percussive effect, reminiscent of a festive, cacophonous procession in which the participants might be playing instruments. The same ornaments translate to entirely different effect in 'Master Tallis's Testament', no longer portraying rippling exuberance but instead suggesting exhalations or inhalations, such as sighs of resignation in downward motion (Ex. 3.3, end of bar 25) or gasps of hopefulness reaching up to the main note (Ex. 3.16). The tempo here is of course much slower, but the figuration is the same. Howells adapts the embellishment to suit the serious atmosphere, while simultaneously and paradoxically employing it to further his aesthetic purpose. Another variation of the device appears in the 'Fugue, Chorale and Epilogue', in which the flickering figures make their first appearance in the developmental material leading up to the chorale. Again one cannot help but notice the superficially similar patterns in bar 55 in this piece (Ex. 3.17) and bar 59 in the Easter 'Saraband' (Ex. 3.18). But in the former the demisemiquavers hasten the increasing tension, particularly because the rhythms have been relatively fluid up until this section, while in the latter they have a feeling of spontaneity, erupting from the stream of quavers as in an overflow of emotion. Although the chordal 'Saraband (*in modo elegiaco*)' focuses chiefly on alternating moments of clarity and restless contemplation, even the solid triads are tweaked by judiciously placed flutterings, which exacerbate the sense of nervousness and agitation. And such examples of Howells's aptitude for this transformative procedure are not exhaustive: where seventh chords, appoggiaturas and the raised fourth scale degree have an energising effect in one work, similar devices bring a subdued, internal tension to the other; or where massive colourful harmonic progressions suggest euphoric shouts in one context, they become anguished cries in another;

Ex. 3.17 'Fugue, Chorale and Epilogue', *Six Pieces for Organ*, bars 54–5

Ex. 3.18 'Saraband (for the Morning of Easter)', *Six Pieces for Organ*, bar 59

or where a stepwise melody functions as driving force in one passage, it conveys repose elsewhere. Rather than choose a new palette for each piece, Howells pursues the more efficient course of taking the cache of tools at his disposal to conjure the picture that has formed in his mind; the revelation of the *Six Pieces* is that it is not a limitation for the composer, but a challenge that, when met, results in ever greater variety.

While the esteemed ideal of 'unity of mood' is undoubtedly integral to Howells's compositional process, the scope of the *Six Pieces*, as the player-cum-analyst comes to appreciate, potentially allows for broader objectives in certain works. We have observed how, in their general impression, the 'Fugue, Chorale and Epilogue' and 'Paean' seem to lack the emotional depth present in the other pieces in the set. The admission we must make, however, is not that this initial impression is necessarily inaccurate, but that there may be other more relevant questions to consider. The 'Fugue, Chorale and Epilogue' is the only work in the collection in which Howells wrestles primarily with problems of form, and if it ostensibly lacks intimations of atmosphere or an external association on which to fixate, must the impact of the piece rest solely on Howells's innate technical cleverness? Howells has always been admired for his formal and contrapuntal technique – what Finzi described as his 'diamond-cut brilliance'[32] – so one is likely to be disappointed with the murmuring and meandering quality of much of the material in the piece. The fugue has

---

[32] Finzi, 'Herbert Howells', 181.

a delicate texture similar to that in parts of the 'Preludio', but unlike the languid abstraction of that piece, Howells's fugal passages display more of a dry rootlessness. Finzi cuttingly remarked that 'the "Fugue, Chorale and Epilogue" from which at first one expects much, leads to the question why Howells's fugal expositions are sometimes so dead'.[33] If the dissonances lack richness, one should first remember that the number of voices in fugue is rigidly prescribed. As primarily a technical exercise, the nature of it is perhaps averse to a tendency in Howells to avoid precise repetition of any sort, be it the layout of a melody, the configuration of a chord or (as we have seen) the emotional connotation of a gesture.

Finzi's comment is not entirely unjust, but preoccupation with this point places burdensome expectations on aspects that Howells may have moved beyond, aesthetically, when designing the piece. In fact, Howells seems to assert with the 'Fugue, Chorale and Epilogue' that a masterful command of musical architecture is an aspiration equally worthy to 'unity of mood'. The pattern of gradual *crescendo*, climax and *decrescendo* may be a formulaic concept, but Howells demonstrates that this structure does not find satisfaction alone in the clichéd notion of 'triumph over adversity'. True, the fugue and its development do suggest a struggle, which is finally overcome in the triumphant declamations of the chorale and then pondered as an echo in the *tranquillo* epilogue. But consider the chorale, with its signature Howells sonorities (see Ex. 3.11), the joining end-to-end of parts of the two fugue subjects to form a single clear melody, and the bold pedal statement of the first subject at the transition to the epilogue. The clarity of these gestures does much to offset the deficiencies of warmth and finesse in the outer sections; if anything, the chorale is too brief, but even if the perfect balance is not achieved, this does not render the work an aesthetic failure. Howells manages to deny that the formality imposes too strict a limit on his imaginative powers, and he actually illustrates something more significant – that the tripartite structure is deserving of respect when the composer seeks creative ways to connect the material of each section and reinvent it, infusing it with vitality. The 'Fugue, Chorale and Epilogue' shows Howells's efforts to work within the most conventional trappings of English organ composition, and he has produced a commendable model.

Likewise regarding 'Paean', a consideration of form may hold the key. That 'Paean' lacks the multi-layered intricacies found in some of the other *Six Pieces* is partly due to the nature of a toccata, in which note-spinning is the modus operandi. Peter Hardwick goes so far as to describe 'Paean' as 'one of the great twentieth-century British essays in the genre'.[34] At the same time, however, the piece does not sustain the apparatus of perpetual motion, and might be more properly viewed as a study in rhythmic and harmonic contrasts: smooth semiquavers versus jagged chords, syncopation versus on-the-beat rhythms, transparent modal harmonies versus non-functional triads, sevenths and ninths. To pursue 'unity of mood' in performance or analysis becomes nearly a contradictory aim, when Howells's intention seems to be creating and revelling in these contrasts. Closer examination suggests Howells took a decisive and successful approach to the piece's composition:

[33] *Ibid.*, 183.
[34] Hardwick, *British Organ Music*, 136.

identifying the distinctions that intrigue him, choosing and assembling the suitable means for their expression, and then executing his intentions with enviable ease. It may be neither a subtle nor a passionate work, but it still celebrates the sheer force of Howells's compositional personality.

Although the dialectic between technique and aesthetic sometimes remains stubbornly obscure, despite the spotlight focused on it, it is interesting to note how a number of common compositional goals in the *Six Pieces* seem to have emerged. These are objectives that assist one in getting beyond the indefinable aspects of Howells's methods, even though these goals are not thoroughly met in every piece. They also provide valuable insights for the hypothetical player, whose ideal learning experience we have sought to replicate as a means of achieving a deeper comprehension. The first goal is Howells's emphasis on dynamism. We have just reviewed how Howells delights in contrasts in 'Paean', but in the Easter 'Saraband' and the 'Fugue, Chorale and Epilogue' as well Howells insists on mutability of expression and forceful changes of character. At the recapitulation of the main theme in the Easter 'Saraband' (Ex. 3.2), for example, Howells does not merely 'resurrect' the first melody in its original form, but takes the second, slightly more ornamented incarnation and enlivens it with full-fisted chords, octaves, accents and a triple-*forte* marking. It is a fierce gesture, and by comparison the touch of colour in the ninth chord in the piece's first bar seems almost quaint. Even in the works with more consistent moods and lesser extremes of means, smaller juxtapositions and conflicts materialise to relieve any sense of stagnancy; 'moderation' is simply not a term that applies comfortably to Howells.

The second goal was once suggested by Christopher Palmer, who wrote: 'In Howells there is no foaming at the mouth. How to restrain but not inhibit – how many composers truly master *that* art? Howells did.'[35] Restraining when necessary without inhibiting is about precision, not control, and does not have to be at odds with Howells's aspirations towards dynamism just discussed. In an animated piece such as 'Paean', one perceives this restraint in moments like the transition to the final return of the toccata figuration over a dominant pedal point, where Howells characteristically reins in the exuberant progressions of the climactic fanfare section. Moreover, in works like 'Master Tallis's Testament', which is remarkable for what Howells achieves with minimal material, the music persuades not by undisciplined ostentation but by resolute commitment to a thoroughly defined vision. That elegant restraint is a major part of the Howells mystique. The 'Saraband (*in modo elegiaco*)' also shares this conservative precision; the elegiac quality of the piece is meticulously but clearly developed by the composer's choosing of a handful of suggestive devices and dark triadic harmonies in unusual relationships. If such self-conscious procedures occasionally lead to charges of mannerism, Howells at least cannot be accused of arbitrariness.

The third objective of tension and release has surfaced previously in this study and is worth stressing again. Howells intuitively pursues this goal from the smallest details up to the largest considerations, from one chord to another and from one extended passage or section to the next. The many examples of this include when, in the

---

[35] Palmer, *A Centenary Celebration*, 212.

Easter 'Saraband', he punctuates dissonances in succession and then lands fleetingly on a solid triad, repeating the process to heighten the tension and, equally, the sense of relief when the progression finally rests. As structural examples of this goal, consider the 'Fugue, Chorale and Epilogue', which finds footing as it churns, builds and releases tension, even if it does so dispassionately; or witness the tension of striving desperately for something not quite attainable in the 'Saraband (*in modo elegiaco*)', which is all the more compelling when that which comes is not relief, but only the insinuation of infinite *crescendo*. This goal of creating tension is in many ways the ultimate objective of all of Howells's compositional ideas, both aesthetic and technical, and leads us to the final, related aim of encouraging technique and artistry to be mutually dependent on each other in speaking to the listener. The composer's intentions and techniques are synthesised at an extraordinary depth in the transparent 'Preludio', where the fragile musical threads blur the lines between mood and means, making it more difficult to make such distinctions. Yet all of the *Six Pieces* display Howells's expert fusion of atmosphere and technical elements in some way, drawing attention to the composer's skill and technical dexterity in a given moment, but likewise allowing the overarching impression to transcend the use of any identifiable device as the music proceeds. The hope of any composer is to inspire, and Howells seeks to do so by realising a style in which methods and artistic expression are fully integrated.

What, then, of the initial impressions? Have they been reinforced, or altered in some way, and does it even matter? Would a player who has thoroughly learned a piece ever understand it the way he did when he first heard it? To this last question we suppose not, but one can still genuinely regard Howells as a modified impressionist when it comes to the 'Preludio', the Easter 'Saraband', and the 'Saraband (*in modo elegiaco*)', for which the first impression seems to have adhered most faithfully following our scrutiny. (Despite the title of the second 'Saraband', one never suspected that Howells's interpretation of the elegy was of the 'country churchyard' sort.) 'Master Tallis's Testament', however, now seems less cold, and more deeply rooted in a sensibility that is much more passionate than its careful construction suggests, while the 'Fugue, Chorale and Epilogue' has shown itself to be a worthy, if flawed, work in Howells's canon that has much to teach about structure in English organ music. And in 'Paean', it turns out that Howells shows no lack of commitment to artistic goals, rather indulging in them with gusto. But as to whether the initial impression matters much: on this only Howells the man, with his personal insecurities, might take much time to dwell.

Vaughan Williams wrote that 'no man can make a living body out of dead clay unless he has first stolen some of the heavenly fire';[36] for the scholar, Howells's possession of this fire is not in doubt. The quandary, however, is explaining how the unique glow of the fire derives from burning without charring all the basic materials in its path. This leaves little time for practicalities, including the aspects of the *Six Pieces* that pertain specifically to the instrument for which they were written. The pieces do merit a closer look from the performer's perspective, as they present numerous technical challenges, including awkward stretches, control of dynamic expression and articulation of the various types of accents on a non-percussive

[36] R. Vaughan Williams, 'Good Taste', 28.

instrument. We have, in fact, landed on another paradox: in considering how an organist becomes acquainted with the pieces as a parallel for our analytical approach, the question of whether Howells writes idiomatically for the organ never seems to pose itself with much conviction. The *Six Pieces* attract attention as much for their status as essays facilitating a study of Howells's style as they do for their high regard in the organ repertoire. One might say more appropriately that Howells writes idiomatically for *himself*, and that his musical persona tends to subordinate the medium through which it speaks. Collectively the *Six Pieces* offer varying glimpses of that multifaceted compositional personality, but also reveal identifiable common threads and a composer fully engaged with the fundamental artistic struggle of what one wants to say versus how one manages to say it. For Howells, technique and aesthetic are two sides of the same coin, and in works such as the *Six Pieces*, the coin often seems to hover indefinitely in the air, spinning like a sphere with no 'sides' at all. Robin Wells has written that 'the closer one comes to understanding Howells's style, the more conscious one is that … the idiom and in particular the handling of contrapuntal lines and dissonances becomes so personal as to be almost elusive'.[37] Discerning Howells's gift for the development of striking ideas in countless variations, and acknowledging that gift as the foundation of his grander musical vision, are helpful first strides at the very least. That a style so recognisable and individual would also be so difficult to define is a great irony, but an examination of the Six Pieces shows that the Howellsian veil is not impenetrable.

---

[37] Wells, 'Howells's Unpublished Organ Works', 459.

PART II

Howells the Vocal Composer

CHAPTER 4

'Hidden Artifice': Howells as Song-Writer

Jeremy Dibble

THROUGH the legacy of a song tradition kindled with such fertile imagination by his revered masters, Parry and Stanford, and the powerful ambience of a new, nationally conscious art, fired on the one hand by the co-option of Elizabethan and Jacobean verse and on the other by the prevalent contemporary aesthetic of both Housman and the emerging Georgian poets, it was perhaps inevitable for a neo-Elizabethan lyricist such as Herbert Howells, a lover of literature, prose and the spoken word, to turn the idiom of song into an expression of his own particular fastidious chemistry of melody and harmony. More to the point, however, the genre of solo song, as the ultimate miniature gestalt – a sum of more than the constituent parts of words, music, voice and accompaniment – was for Howells the opportunity to enshrine in music, on an intimate scale, those values of intricacy and involution. For him such values represented a deep artistic need for musical integrity on multiple architectonic levels, a mentality exemplified by the processual thinking of late-nineteenth-century German musical intellectualism and, above all, of Brahms. Such a mentality was of course especially prevalent in Brahms's instrumental essays, but it was also no less evident in his vocal works and especially in his many songs This predilection for Brahmsian artifice had, on the one hand, been instilled into Howells by Stanford (himself a supreme architect of songs), but the desire to express those most personal and private aspirations ultimately emanated from an atavistic emulation of the Tudor masters' artistic relationship between composer and his maker. Detail, device and unity were attributes special to Howells's sensibility – he often sketched but failed to finish a song – and they inhabit his art of song-writing on many levels.[1]

Although Walter de la Mare and Wilfrid Wilson Gibson, both prominent Georgians, have been regularly cited as literary refuges for Howells – and it is undeniable that he set their verse more often than that of other authors – the truth is that Howells was largely catholic in his choice of poetry. A survey shows that he was equally happy in medieval, Elizabethan and Jacobean idioms as he was in the early twentieth century with English writers such as Maurice Baring and F. W. Harvey, and there are also various examples of him working with Irish authors of the so-called 'Celtic Twilight' (Seamus O'Sullivan, James Joyce and William Byrne), and French and Afrikaans texts, as well as German and Chinese translations. Formally he is perhaps more conservative in that many of his songs reflect a

---

[1] Howells's output of songs, relatively slender in quantity, occupies in the main an earlier period of his creative life between 1911 and 1928, with a particular concentration of works between 1915 (when he was working under Stanford's watchful eye) and 1920. Even *A Garland for de la Mare* (HH 111), published posthumously in 1995, was the result of revisions to songs composed in 1919 and 1920.

preference for lyric poetry, and his preferred emotional world, with its inclination towards 'atmosphere' and contemplation, reveals a penchant for texts that explore themes of tranquillity, beauty (both physical and spiritual), quietude and the pastoral, with all its connotations of (childhood) innocence, naivety, awe and timelessness, overlaid not infrequently with melancholy and introspection. It is no accident, therefore, that style forms such as the lullaby (or cradle song) are common to Howells's catalogue of songs, as are the themes of rest; sleep; prayer; lament; nature's idyll; and the erotic, sensual joy of female beauty. And we should not forget that, although he did not associate himself with the folk-song movement in the way that contemporaries such as Holst, Vaughan Williams, Butterworth and Moeran did before and after the First World War, he was nevertheless drawn to traditional melody, particularly in the *Four French Chansons* (HH 98) with the structural possibilities they offered.[2] Yet, among his output of published songs, there are some instances of more exploratory forms in which the intricacies of his instrumental works are brought to bear in fascinating and unique ways. Moreover, Howells's Elizabethan proclivities – reflected perhaps most readily in the organ works and *Lambert's Clavichord* (HH165) – ensured the presence of the 'dance' as a potent influence in many of the song forms and styles. These elements together contribute to an art form of pointillistic precision, a fact revealed in the care with which Howells approached the matter of syllabic stress; the scansion of poetic line; and the contour, shape and tessitura of musical gesture. But key to a deeper understanding of Howells's skill as a song-writer is the relation of poetical meaning to musical form.

Of course, Stanford's own dicta, of which Howells would have been well aware from his teacher's *Musical Composition* of 1911, stipulated that a song, as a miniature, needs to be 'so perfect in every detail that it [would] bear examination under a magnifying glass'.[3] Such advice Howells swallowed whole. Detail, mechanism, the relationship between textural function and musical function, and perfection of structure combined to form an equation that was sine qua non to him. Stanford's attitude to the setting of poetry was also clear: 'Another is that the poetry to which it is set is (or should be) the chief consideration, and that music should be co-ordinate or subordinate to it without ever being *super*-ordinate.'[4] This is also true of Howells's aesthetic, though increasingly, as his art of song-writing developed, the relationship of voice and accompaniment became more and more 'co-ordinate' and interdependent. But adding to his teacher's guidance, Howells asserted an important dictum of his own. As a composition teacher, he would often direct his pupils, eager to find a suitable text for a song, to Palgrave's *Golden Treasury*,[5] a rich anthological source for many an English song-writer since its publication in 1861. Howells's advice was not only motivated by a love of English lyric verse, but

---

[2] Howells also arranged three folk-melodies – 'I Will Give My Love an Apple', 'The Brisk Young Widow' and 'Cendrillon' (HH 181) – which were published posthumously in 1996.
[3] Stanford, *Musical Composition*, 129.
[4] *Ibid.*
[5] In conversation with Joan Littlejohn (a former pupil of Howells), April 2012.

also by that verse's intrinsic properties. As Palgrave suggested in the preface to his collection:

> The Editor is acquainted with no strict and exhaustive definition of lyrical poetry, but he has found the task of practical decision increase in clearness and in facility as he advanced with the work, whilst keeping in view a few simple principles. Lyrical has been here held essentially to imply that each poem shall turn on some single thought, feeling, or situation. In accordance with this, narrative, descriptive, and didactic poems – unless accompanied by rapidity of movement, brevity, and the colouring of human passion – have been excluded.[6]

This was, however, not only Howells's dictum to his own students but one by which he increasingly approached the art of song composition himself. In other words, in selecting shorter, rather than longer, poems for song – which were eminently more suitable for the genre – the interpretation of 'a single thought, feeling, or situation' – would not only be crucial to the gestation of appropriate musical ideas, but more importantly to the formation of the musical form and argument. In many instances, Howells's songs depend largely on the treatment of a single, monothematic idea, where the poetic, indeed *emotional*, 'turn' is often signalled by a deft musical function or transformation, and where this occurs, one often senses a powerful feeling of *anagnorisis* (discovery) and *peripeteia* (reversal of fortune). Such events, simple in meaning yet executed by complex means, may also be experienced in all manner of structural locations, perhaps in the altered musical gestures of a repeated strophe, in the deft manipulation of tonality or in the fleeting rhetoric of the coda.

There are abundant indications of Howells's meticulously calculated attitude to song in the early *Five Songs for Low Voice*, Op. 2 (HH 26), which he wrote between August and November 1911 and dedicated to his future wife, Dorothy Dawe. Consisting entirely of settings of Irish poets,[7] the set discloses Howells's obsession with poetry of the 'Celtic Twilight', and particularly the successors to Yeats such as Seamus O'Sullivan, which, at the time, commanded enormous popularity and esteem. The songs were also part of the portfolio he submitted to the Royal College of Music (RCM) for his scholarship application in which, no doubt, Stanford detected prodigious signs of facility and technique. The first song of this set, a setting of Seamus O'Sullivan's 'Twilight People' (HH 26i) reveals, perhaps typically for a young aspiring student composer, a sense of over-ambition, notably in the epic piano part (which reeks of Rachmaninoff); but already one can observe the process of a more complex structure. O'Sullivan's three verses, which depict a familiarly bleak Irish landscape of lament and exile, receive a novel, sonata-like interpretation. Verses one and two, which present two differing thematic ideas (Exx. 4.1a

---

[6] Palgrave, *The Golden Treasury*, i.
[7] Howells may well have gleaned his interest in Irish poetry from his early friendship with Ivor Gurney. It is particularly telling that, in his tribute to Gurney for *Music and Letters* in January 1938, Howells quoted those very poets (such as O'Sullivan and Gore-Booth) that appeared in his 1911 songs; Howells, 'Ivor Gurney', 14.

Ex. 4.1 'The Twilight People', *Five Songs*

and 4.1b), are cast in contrasting keys, while verse three attempts to conflate both ideas in the tonic, as if, in their synthesis, to capture a sense of political and cultural reawakening. A further interesting mechanism in Howells's secondary idea is the fluid nature of its tonality, which embarks from F♯. This upward shift from the tonic of E♭ minor establishes a pattern for the whole of the verse, which ascends through A minor and C minor before, somewhat prematurely, arriving back in E♭ minor. The pattern is subsequently repeated in the reprise of verse three, and its influence on the tonal behaviour of the song is underlined by a telling progression from the prevailing E♭ minor (with its tolling pedal point) to a chord of G minor in the concluding bars (Ex. 4.1c), highlighting the 'transformation' of the minor-third shift to the major.

One factor that is baldly apparent from Howells's *Five Songs*, Op. 2 is that the music of Wagner was a potent influence in the early phase of Howells's development, as it had been on Holst and Vaughan Williams before him. The melancholy, slow-paced, chromatic harmony of *Tristan und Isolde* (and especially the earlier manifestation of 'Träume' from the *Wesendonck Lieder*) provided the most palpable of models for the anguished parts of Thomas Keohler's 'The Devotee' (HH 26ii); yet, for the conclusion to each verse, more resolute in tone, Howells opted for a more resolute diatonic voice, in which the Parry of *Blest Pair of Sirens* (whose own E♭ tonality is plainly resonant here) – itself a Wagnerian work in which English diatonicism mingles with that of *Die Meistersinger* – was a fertile resource. The

Ex. 4.1 continued

remaining three songs – 'The Waves of Breffny' (HH 26iii, Eva Gore-Booth), 'The Sorrow of Love' (HH 26iv, Seamus O'Sullivan) and 'The Call' (HH 26v, George Roberts) – continue to explore this same mood of introspection; indeed, it is a fatal weakness of the set that a livelier tempo or more buoyant sensibility is not included to relieve the prevailing air of gloom.

The same might be said of a further set of five 'Celtic Twilight' *Songs for Low Voice*, Op. 7 (HH 38), written in June and July of 1913 entirely to poems from Fiona Macleod's *Poems and Dramas*, three of which are marked 'lento', the other two 'tranquillo'. The same Wagnerian threnody is unmistakable in the wilting chromaticism and anguished dominant minor thirteenths of 'The Valley of Silence' (HH

38i), while the spell of *Tristan* is compellingly communicated in 'When the Dew Is Falling' (HH 38ii) – which has much in common with 'The Devotee' – and 'When There Is Peace' (HH 38v) through the symbolic choice of B major – though in the case of the latter, its strongly monothematic accompanimental design and lush, atmospheric harmonic content suggest perhaps that Wagner had been filtered through the more recent, *Tristan*-inspired finale of Delius's *A Mass of Life*, which had received its first London performance in 1909 and was a work Howells surely knew by 1913.

Although Howells chose to put his *Songs for Low Voice* aside – he reassigned Op. 7 to the later *Three Dances* for violin and orchestra (HH 48) – there are a number of significant points of interest in this collection and in the earlier *Cycle of Five Songs for Low Voice* that point to more mature tendencies in his later songs. One unmistakable feature is Howells's attention to motivic detail, and how melodic lines, combined with a fastidious attention to vocal rhythm and scansion, have a rhythmical freedom that moves flexibly between arioso and recitative. In the case of 'The Sorrow of Love', Howells even went as far as to mark the opening tempo 'Poco lento e quasi recit', and the entire rationale of the song is one of dialogue between expansive vocal phrases and accompanimental interjections (not unlike Parry's 'Through the Ivory Gate' from *English Lyrics*, Set III, which Howells undoubtedly knew well).[8] Another, arguably more fascinating, facet of Howells's songs at this early juncture is his manipulation of key. His use of chromaticism has already been mentioned, but Howells deploys a fluid sense of tonality in various ways to assist the illustration of text. In 'The Devotee', for instance, the song begins tangentially, with a series of progressions that, eight bars later, settles on the dominant of C minor (Ex. 4.2). This technique of tonal 'obliquity' he clearly retained in his later vocal works; moreover, songs such as 'The Waves of Breffny' and 'The Sorrow of Love' demonstrate a liking for 'progressive tonality' where, from one established key centre, we arrive, at the conclusion, in another. In both these songs, which travel between F♯ minor and A major, Howells seems to have the intention of conveying a sense of inner catharsis ('The Waves of Breffny') or reconciliation in the face of unrequited love ('The Sorrow of Love'). Furthermore, with the unusual tonal behaviour of these two songs, one is conscious of their transitional role within the larger set of songs, which is itself anticipated in microcosm by the minor-third progressions of the first song (see above):

'The Twilight People'	E♭ minor
'The Devotee'	E♭ major
'The Waves of Breffny'	F♯ minor–A major
'The Sorrow of Love'	F♯ minor–A major
'The Call'	A major

Indeed, this key scheme compellingly outlines a meta-structure to the *Cycle of Five Songs* (which is, of course, implicit in Howells's title), in which the songs suggest a larger cycle implied not only by their tonal interconnectivity but by their textual programme of inner stirring, anguish, catharsis and departure.

---

[8] Howells, 'Hubert Parry', 228.

Ex. 4.2 'The Devotee', *Five Songs*

The meta-key scheme of the later *Five Songs* of 1913 is less clear, but there is no shortage of tonal experiment among the individual structures. Moreover, a predominance of through-composed designs (only 'St Bride's Song' (HH 38iv) is stanzaic, and even then considerably elaborated) suggests that Howells was keen to pursue his Wagnerian musings with even greater alacrity. The hushed, enigmatic landscape of 'The Valley of Silence', based essentially on one falling chromatic motif from C to G, sets out in A minor (the resonances of *Tristan* being especially pungent in the accompanimental departure in bar 8), though in a true late-nineteenth-century manner, the key is only ever defined by its imperfect cadence in bar 17, an event that also marks the close of the first verse. For Macleod's second, more ethereal verse, Howells's conclusion in E major (concording with the final line's numinous sentiment, 'Eddies of prayer') emerges after a considerable divergence to the Neapolitan (F) and its subdominant B♭, with the effect that its crystallisation in the last four bars, with plagal cadence and whispered close, is all the more telling. For 'When the Dew is Falling', Howells made use of an interesting G♯ minor–B major dialectic to project a sentiment of lost love. The key of G♯ minor remains the principal tonal agent for the 'lament' of the first three verses, but with the last verse, the effect of transformation is inventively enacted by an oblique approach to B major, initiated by a striking reprise of the opening material in the very foreign area of D minor. In a similar, but even more radical manner, the stanzaic 'St Bride's Song' concludes, not in the E♭ minor of the song's main corpus, but in C minor, where Howells no doubt intended to inject a sense of foreboding. But arguably most dramatic of the set, 'By the Grey Stones' (HH 38iii) represents an intensification of the declamatory style of 'The Sorrow of Love', though here Howells's assimilation of Wagner is considerably overlaid with a heady dose of Debussy, fully suggesting a close acquaintance with *Pelléas et Mélisande*. Casting the song ultimately in C major, Howells's oblique approach to the tonality through its extended *Tristan-esque* introduction is striking, as is its ultimate return after the extrovert gestures of the more animated central section.

Although Howells's approach to song, and his stylistic language, underwent considerable change in the years directly after 1913 – where his assimilation of Vaughan Williams, modality and French colour is conspicuous – the declamatory and through-composed style adopted in the *Songs for Low Voice* of 1913 was not altogether abandoned. It is no accident that Gurney's 'war' songs, written in the theatre of the Western Front, without the aid of a piano, appealed to him where his friend's later songs were often the subject of criticism.[9] This small corpus of Gurney's 'war' songs evinced a similar through-composed sensibility, and, with their more disciplined motivic fabric, impelled Howells to orchestrate two of them.[10] Stanford too, was thrilled with them; proudly showed them to his colleague, Charles Wood; and conducted them at the RCM in 1917. In 'A Wanderer's Night Song' (HH 60i), the first of the original set *In Green Ways* of 1915,[11] where Howells used his own translation of Goethe's poem 'Wanderers Nachtlied II', its link with Howells's earlier Wagnerian songs is much in evidence in the through-composed structure, based heavily on a set of extended phraseological repetitions, each from a contrasting tonal beginning. The rationale of Howells's method, in this instance, is executed with quiet yet disturbing eloquence, as the F♯ minor of the opening yields to a chilling C minor (Ex. 4.3). But in accordance with Goethe's simple lyric, the song ends serenely in A major with the promise of rest at journey's end.

Shortly after the completion of the first version of *In Green Ways*, Howells produced arguably his most hybrid solo vocal work, *By the Waters of Babylon* (HH 68), a chamber work for baritone, violin, cello and organ, in 1917, setting words from Psalm 137 (later made famous in the opening chorus of Walton's *Belshazzar's Feast*). In its quasi-symphonic conception – Howells called it a 'Rhapsody' – it shares much with the similarly hybrid *Bible Songs* of Stanford written in 1909,

---

[9] Howells, 'Ivor Gurney', 16–17.
[10] The two songs were 'In Flanders' (F. W. Harvey) and 'By a Bierside' (John Masefield), which Stanford conducted at the RCM on 23 March 1917 and 1 July 1919. Howells was in fact no stranger to the orchestration of songs. Also included at the premiere of *In Green Ways*, Op. 10 (HH 60) in 1916 were three orchestrations of Sterndale Bennett's 'May Dew', 'To Chloe' and 'Gentle Zephyr', and that same year he also provided an instrumentation of Haydn's duet 'Saper vorrei se m'ami' (14 July 1916).
[11] Howells's *In Green Ways* was composed in 1915. It was first performed in an orchestration by Ethel McLelland for flute, clarinet, string quartet and strings at the RCM on 25 February 1916. The manuscript of the set is now missing. In 1928, to satisfy a commission from the 1928 Gloucester Three Choirs Festival, Howells sought to revise the entire set and assigned it a new opus number, 43 (HH 172). The setting of Theodor Storm was excised and replaced by 'The Goat Paths' (James Stephens). The order of songs was also revised. A slightly larger orchestra of two flutes, oboe, two clarinets, bassoon, timpani, percussion, harp, piano and strings was employed, and a version for piano and voice was published the same year. *In Green Ways* was first produced in London at the 1929 Promenade Concerts with Dorothy Silk, and was given a second time at the Gloucester Festival (with Isobel Baillie) in 1931. All were conducted by the composer.

Ex. 4.3 'Wanderer's Night Song', *In Green Ways*, Op. 43

which gravitate between lieder and solo cantata. Howells's conception, with the 'obbligato' role of the solo strings and the unremitting elegiac disposition (which it shares with *Elegy for Strings* of the same year – HH70) also brings to mind the pathos of the Passion genre, and may well have been an expression of the appalling sacrifice of the trenches. Once again, Howells's expressive 'environment' is one of 'Quasi Lento', though in this more extended context, the structure is multithematic rather than monothematic, and helps articulate the central, vocal ternary structure and the outer instrumental frame. The frame itself recalls the rhapsodic manner of the Parry-influenced first organ rhapsody (HH 57i) of 1915, though its language looks forward to the more advanced second and third rhapsodies of 1918 (HH 57ii, iii). Significantly, Howells achieves a sense of impact through the juxtaposition of the frame's initial limpid F♯ minor and the strident vocal entry in C minor ('By the waters of Babylon'), a tonal experiment initially essayed in 'Wanderer's Night Song' (Ex. 4.4). The organ's rhapsodic musings return in a more sonorous secondary paragraph in E♭ to suggest the reluctant 'song of exile' ('How shall we sing the Lord's song in a strange land?'), though this fragile tonal area is constantly in conflict with C minor, which is eager to assert the work's broader mournful demeanour. This is achieved with considerable climactic effect at the reprise ('O daughter of Babylon'),

Ex. 4.4 *By the Waters of Babylon*

where the main vocal material returns in the organ and strings, while Howells's placing of this thematic recapitulation above a dominant pedal – adroitly intensifying the sense of irresolution – allows for a semitonal shift downwards (from the dominant of C) to F♯ minor. This return to F♯ naturally recalls the opening tonality, though Howells subtly uses this tonal event as an instrumental postlude to the vocal threnody, and when the invocation of the initial organ frame is effected, F♯ functions as part of a plagal cadence to C♯ minor, the key (symmetrically a semitone *above* C) in which the rhapsody ends in a mist of gloom. Concluding in a new tonality was a technique Howells, who was far from being bound to the old convention of beginning and ending in the same key, had already practised in his earlier Irish songs as both a structural and illustrative tool. Here, however, one senses a new awareness of tonal integration in which the resulting tonality formed the culmination of a calculated, goal-directed argument. Such a technique is evident in many of his later songs, one of which, 'King David' (HH 102), evinces a masterly use of long-term tonal thinking, discussed below.

One other song, composed some eleven years later for the revised version of *In Green Ways*, was a setting of James Stephens's 'The Goat Paths' (HH 172ii), a thoroughly Georgian manifestation in its portrayal of a pastoral idyll. Most effective, like all the songs of the set, in its orchestral garb, the song is perhaps unique in Howells's output for its vocal elasticity and economy, much if which is quintessentially derived from Stephens's short, unequal, asymmetrical prose (which, as Banfield has noted, plays skilfully on repetitions of words and rhymed assonance),[12] conceived as an evocative narrative of goats, randomly foraging back and forth along mountain paths:

> The crooked paths
> Go every way
> Upon the hill
> They wind about
> Through the heather,
> In and out
> Of a quiet sunniness.

Howells's musical response is one of free fantasy in which a single musical motif (Ex. 4.5a), developed contrapuntally (a metaphor, Banfield suggests, of the 'intertwining' paths), acts as the principal cement to each of the eight stanzas, and a secondary one is used as a transitional 'comment' between stanzas. Key to Howells's sense of fantasy is the extemporary nature of the vocal freedom and the metrical emancipation of the counterpoint below (one, incidentally, enhanced by the orchestral polyphony). Yet, underlying the idyll is a compelling motivic and tonal design, as well as one that plays on a larger architectural level of tempo and harmonic rhythm – further examples of hidden artifice that are not obvious from the freer, quasi-improvisatory foreground. From the modal E minor of the first stanza, Howells moves to G for the second, and from this point the voice is left virtually alone for what seems like a vocal cadenza for the third. Yet, even here, at what seems like the point of greatest metrical freedom, Howells deftly draws

---

[12] Banfield, *Sensibility and English Song*, 218. Howells was to note, after hearing Stephens's extraordinarily rapid recitation of the poem, that he had conceived it quite differently (see Palmer, *Herbert Howells: A Study*, 16).

Ex. 4.5 'The Goat Paths', *In Green Ways*, Op. 43

together those quintessential modal features of the movement so far, notably the Phrygian F of the voice's opening statement and the F♯ and D of the flattened-seventh triad, before re-establishing E minor at the close ('In the sunny Solitude'). For the sixth stanza, the longest of all, Howells's texture becomes at once more contrapuntally complex, motivically saturated and rhythmically animated, while tonally the canvas moves sharpwise as the poet's more urgent quest for inner stillness is symbolised by the rich, multilayered, polyphonic climax in A major, replete with high extended A for the voice ('and bound / To the deeper Quietude') and concentration (Ex. 4.5b). Then, by degrees, Howells effects his recovery to E through a second vocal cadenza ('In that airy Quietness'), in which the modal and Phrygian components are heard finally against a fading tonic pedal in the orchestra – as Banfield aptly states, 'an inspired calculation'[13] – though in the enigmatic final bars, where the voice rises entirely alone to B (the fifth of the triad), Howells surely leaves us with the serene implication of a *tierce de Picardie*, as if the poet ultimately finds resolution in contemplation ('Something Lying on the ground, / In the bottom of my mind').

While at the RCM under Stanford, Howells's production of songs noticeably intensified, especially during 1915 and 1916. What is more perceptible, however, is that, no doubt under Stanford's influence, his approach to song underwent a process of simplification in which shorter lyrics were clearly favoured above longer narrative poems. His interest in the Irish poets, at least as suitable vehicles for song, had also waned, as he explained in his article 'Words for Musical Settings' for the *Athenaeum* in December 1916:

> Their work, as poetry, is on a high level. But the music of words is in it so evidently, so sonorously, so delicately, that the addition of music proper is in most cases wrong because it is superfluous. And such an imposition of one essentially musical expression on another which is itself already unmistakably musical leads to that sort of essence of beauty which, commendable enough as an oasis of beauty in a desert of ugliness, is out of place and unnecessary in modern British settings ...[14]

The upshot of this retreat into simplicity was, for songs with observably less complex structures, a greater emphasis on vocal lyricism, and a more refined focus on the 'message' of the poem, thereby embodying that fundamental dictum that the song should 'turn on some single thought, feeling, or situation'. There was, however, to be no compromise in terms of artifice, except that it would become more calculating, and more adept in light of the essential interpretation of the text and the sense of musical unity; indeed, in this regard, Howells's method would evince an increased sympathy for *absolute music* that would resonate equally in the fertile productivity of his chamber works written at much the same time.

Howells's setting of Goethe's 'Nachtlied' was one such example of a shorter, more concise lyric, and other songs of *In Green Ways* also exemplified this desire for a single focus. In his setting of Shakespeare's 'Under the Greenwood Tree' (HH 6oiv), Howells's emphasis is on the idea of free, unfettered living in the outdoors, with only winter's cold as the 'enemy'. Such a bucolic picture is readily provided by the background of consecutive, 'unsophisticated' triads; but the bite of the cold weather, at the heart of the two refrains ('Come hither, come hither'), is symbolised by the arresting semitonal shift from the triad of C to C♯ (Ex. 4.6), a progression already foreshadowed in the major–minor tonic harmonies of the first two bars, the semitonal triadic movement from F to F♯ in bars 4 and 5 (as well as those from A♭ to A) and the beguiling motif that slithers down chromatically from F to E♭ in bars 3 and 4. In Skelton's capricious lyric 'To Mistress Margaret Hussey' (characterised

---

[13] Banfield, *Sensibility and English Song*, 218.
[14] Howells, 'Words for Musical Settings', 614–5.

Ex. 4.6 'Under the Greenwood Tree', *In Green Ways*, Op. 43

by the short, clipped lines), Howells conceived a scherzo, 'Merry Margaret' (HH 60ii), in which the two-verse structure is punctuated by the opening words ('Merry Margaret /As Midsummer flower, / Gentle as falcon / Or hawk of the tower'). As a key factor of this punctuative textual 'ritornello' is the flattened seventh (E♭) of F, which Howells accentuates time and again in the first seven bars, clearly as an illustration of the character's gentle caprice. In bars 1 and 4, it appears as part of a dominant minor chord, in bars 2 and 6 as part of a sonorous ninth (dominant substitute) and in bar 3 as a melodic component that is later assimilated by the opening vocal lines (Ex. 4.7a). As a false relation (one of Howells's many allusions to a latter-day *musica ficta*), this then features extensively in the seductive development of verse one and, transposed to D, in verse two. Even more significant, however, is Howells's luxuriant use of E♭ at the climax to each verse. Here, cleverly, Howells manufactured a refrain from Skelton's words by assigning significance to the meaning and assonance of the word 'far', which, as a hyperbole ('Far, far, passing'), is accompanied by a succession of luxuriant harmonic 'sound moments' on E♭ and G (very much reflecting the composer's predilection for French music), and a high A for the voice (Ex. 4.7b). But this is not all, for E♭ also influences the strong sense of subdominant harmony that colours the deliciously sensuous close to each verse and helps generate the high, anticlimactic B♭ ('Gentle as *fal*con') at the close of verse two.

This attention to detail proved to be archetypical of Howells's song composition thereafter. Charles Camp Tarelli's rondel form in 'Roses' (HH 59i – from *Three Rondeaux* of 1915), albeit freely interpreted, gave rise to a beautifully crafted through-composed structure in which, complying with the rondel spirit (the first word of the poem is also the last), the opening motif (a falling fifth) with its tonality of D is withheld until the very end, while the rest of the song, Gurney-like in its transparent diatonicism, is a controlled rationalisation of the falling fifth by way of the flatwise modulations through F, B♭ and E♭. Similarly, the second song, 'A Rondel of Rest' (HH 59ii), enunciates Arthur Symons's moral imperative of 'sweet rest through honest toil' by way of a series of carefully paced, tranquil pedal points that begin inverted but, with resolution, are placed more normatively in the bass. The role of the pedal is also important in Shelley's bleak 'The Widow Bird' (HH 55iii – from *Four Songs*, Op. 22 of 1915–16) where Howells creates a fascinating

Ex. 4.7 'Merry Margaret', *In Green Ways*, Op. 43

(a)

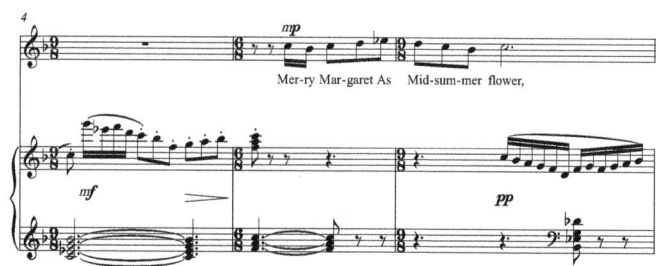

(b)

interplay between the imagery of the mill-wheel, itself an internal bass pedal, and the motionless pedal of grief and its wintry projection.

Howells's liking for pedal points largely reflected his love of the lullaby genre and songs on the theme of rest, and there is no shortage in 'An Old Man's Lullaby' (HH 73) from *Three Songs* of 1917[15] – an exquisite interpretation of Thomas Dekker's famous 'Golden Slumbers'. Howells no doubt knew Stanford's fine setting of this text with its well-defined 'charm' and subtle injection of fretfulness at the words 'Sleep, pretty wanton, do not cry' (where the hemiola disrupts the regular triple metre). Howells's 'charm' is another internal pedal point, which, oscillating between G and F, is significant for the manner in which the tonality seems to fluctuate ever more insistently between G minor and B♭. Two apparently decisive moments, in the third line of each verse ('And I will sing a *lullaby*') seem to confirm the dominance of G – in the first verse the progression to a D minor (minor v of G) and in the second to a wonderfully transformative D major triad (the genuine v of G), but each time the uncertainty returns, until, in the coda, G minor tenderly yields to B♭ (Ex. 4.8).

'The Restful Branches' of 1918 (HH 94), on a theme of grief and the catharsis of solitude and tranquillity, presents a comparable tonal duality of B♭ minor and D♭ – one that is encapsulated in the final cadence, which seems initially to gravitate plagally to B♭ but, with Howells's typical sleight of hand, resolves by step to D♭ (Ex. 4.9). But one of the most striking and affecting of Howells's songs written between 1915 and 1917 must be the inspired setting 'Upon a Summer's Day' (HH81), taken from Maurice Baring's short story 'The Hunchback, the Pool and the Magic Ring' (from *The Blue Rose Fairy Book*, published in 1911). A simple lyric in three verses, its short narrative of a love suit emphasises the value of true love over material possessions. Howells captured this in a deliberate assimilation of the folk idiom not only by opting for a simple, modal melody, but by retaining the same melody for each verse. However, within this simple framework, the initial rejection of the lover's show of riches (gold, silver, horses) is subtly portrayed by an insistent return to F♯ minor in the first two verses, even though there are hints – the dominant ninth of A in the first verse for instance – that he has already been accepted (Ex. 4.10). And this acceptance is finally embodied at the end of the last verse with a cadence in A major, while the moral of Baring's lines ('For a sigh, a song and a tale half-told, and for a wisp of hay') is enshrined in the simplest of accompanimental textures.

Howells continued to bring this fastidious sense of artifice to his later songs. The *Four French Chansons* (HH 98), arrangements of existing monophonic songs, reveal a highly developed technique of stanzaic variation for all their overt simplicity and mantra-like repetition, aided by Howells's enhanced harmonic language. His setting of Wilfrid Gibson's 'Blaweary' (HH 100v) of 1921, though of his own melodic creation, uses the same type of variegational technique and is a particularly dexterous example of Howells's play on asymmetrical phraseology. Perhaps his most sophisticated stanzaic structure is his setting of the medieval carol 'Come Sing and Dance' of 1927 (HH 164o), which, with its contemporary metrical interpretation

---

[15] From the autograph at the RCM. Howells's title for this song was originally 'Golden Slumbers Kiss Your Eyes', but it was excised and the present title written below in another hand.

Ex. 4.8 'An Old Man's Lullaby'

of a Renaissance 'basse danse' – in this case 3/2 (hemiola) in the verses and 3/4 in the refrains – and a colourful use of key, makes for an intricate combination of through-composition and strophic variation. The song is rich in motivic development – the relationship between the opening idea for piano and the ecstatic utterance 'Eia' is an obvious instance – but the larger scheme is also highly original. After the first verse in A♭, the refrain ('Come sing and dance, Alleluia'), replete with dominant pedal, carries us to E♭. A transition, a further variation on the preludial bars, brings us back to A♭ for a much embellished version of the music of the first verse, but with the arrival of the 'Alleluia' of the refrain, Howells uses the opportunity to intensify the sense of ecstasy by moving to v of D (the voice's shift up to E♮ rather than the customary F is especially striking). By contrast, the third verse, which commences on the dominant of D, becomes a developmental paragraph where the use of 'Eia' is palpably more insistent, as is the sense of heightened elation through the disruption of the established two-bar hemiola pattern. In addition the euphoric mood is accentuated by the recovery from D to A♭, with which, when the dominant of A♭ is reached, we experience the arrival of the refrain. However, in the manner of the second verse, the greatest moment of rapture is reserved for the

Ex. 4.9 'The Restful Branches'

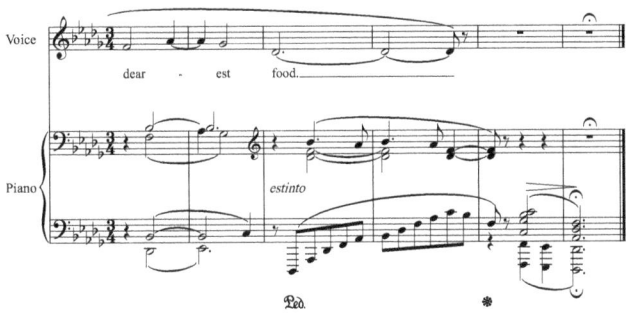

'Alleluia', which is underpinned by the tonicisation of A♭, the return of the opening motif and the regularity of the original hemiola phraseological pattern. The presence of other details, such as the heterophony of the 'Eia' material, shared between piano and voice, and the heart-warming subdominant colouring of the final refrain, sums up a work of considerable mastery.

The alliance of dance and song was a phenomenon to which Howells returned on several occasions. His setting of Henry Newbolt's 'Gavotte' (HH 108iii), also published in 1927, is a deft assimilation of the French dance's poise and metrical character. Another, 'Lady Caroline' (HH 111ii), which was eventually included in *A Garland for de la Mare* – published posthumously in 1995 – but dates back to its original composition for Howells's setting in 1919–20 of poems from de la Mare's *Peacock Pie: A Book of Rhymes* (1913), is a sedate and highly sensual minuet. Palmer and Banfield have written of the close artistic affinity between Howells and de la Mare, and how the poet's intrinsically musical verse (he was a musical poet with a musical background as a chorister of St Paul's Cathedral) and its diminutive scale and Georgian pastoralism appealed to the song aesthetic that Howells had developed in the years after his study at the RCM.[16] Indeed, many of the songs for *Peacock Pie*, Op. 33 (published in 1923), such as 'Mrs MacQueen' (HH 104iii), 'The Dunce' (HH 104iv) and 'Miss T.' (HH 104vi) reveal Howells's affinity for aphorism. There is no doubt, too, that de la Mare's prowess for children's verse was a skill that Howells also found entirely amenable to the composition of song. Yet there are numerous examples of de la Mare's verse, notably in *A Garland for de la Mare*, where, for all their outwardly childlike images and the ability to tell stories, the properties of simplicity of construction, clarity and economy of language inhabit a much more adult world of darkness and irony. In this regard, 'King David',[17] also taken from de la

---

[16] Palmer, *A Centenary Celebration*, 177ff.; Banfield, *Sensibility and English Song*, 208–32; see also Chapter 6 of the present volume.

[17] 'King David' was completed, according to the autograph manuscript, on 7 August 1919, though a surviving letter from de la Mare to Howells relates that it was already finished, presumably in draft, by February of that year (Palmer, *A Centenary Celebration*, 184). It was originally published by Winthrop Rogers in 1923. By the late 1960s Howells made it known that he had designs on completing

Ex. 4.10 'Upon a Summer's Day'

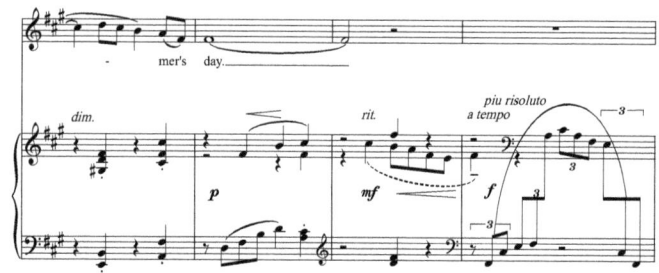

Mare's *Peacock Pie*, marked a confluence of these sensibilities that, for good reason, Howells himself considered to be one of his finest works; moreover, so taken was de la Mare with the setting that he hoped no other composer would set it.[18]

Besides the auspicious rhetorical language that de la Mare uses throughout the poem – as Banfield has commented, 'quite beyond the expectations of its metric dimensions'[19] – one of the most striking elements of de la Mare's poem, a rich, symbolic narrative in five short verses, is its opening – 'King David was a sorrowful man: / No cause for his sorrow had he'. To a child this may have communicated a simple message of a sad king, a figure of legend; but an adult knowledge of the Bible would readily suggest more disturbing sources for David's guilty conscience – adultery with Bathsheba, the death of Uriah on the battlefield – and his grief at the death of Absalom. Indeed, so great was David's 'haunted' melancholy, that the 'hundred harps' (referring, of course, to David's own musical mastery of the instrument) could not ease his sorrow. The symbol of the nightingale invokes several interpretations: first, the old classical notion of the nightingale's song as a lament; later, that the nightingale was revered as nature's most spontaneous poet, and one

A Garland for de la Mare and that 'King David' had to be a part of the collection. Yet, because the song was already published, he made no effort to publish the other songs during his lifetime (Palmer, *A Centenary Celebration*, 177).

[18] Palmer, *Herbert Howells: A Study*, 16.
[19] Banfield, *Sensibility and English Song*, 226.

that human poets, notably those of the Romantic period such as Keats and Shelley, aspired to equal. But, in essence, de la Mare's use of the nightingale is for the purpose of catharsis, and to this end he was probably making reference to the spirit of Hans Christian Andersen's tale, *The Nightingale*, of 1844 (where the nightingale charms away the evils from the dying king).

In keeping with the grandeur of de la Mare's language, Howells's song is on an equally impressive scale – indeed, it might be argued that the song is more a miniature *scena* in its length, manner and drama – and in providing a suitable musical vehicle for the poetical narrative, the composer created a structure of considerable motivic tautness, polyphonic complexity and tonal involution, unequalled in his other songs. Although, on one level, 'King David' should be considered as one integrated structure, the construction of de la Mare's poem, where the emotional 'turn' (almost sonnet-like) at the beginning of the third verse ('He rose') marks off the first two verses from the remaining three, is also suggestive of two sections. In accordance with this delineation, Howells couched the first elegiac part in E♭ minor, the second, charged with catharsis and transformation, in the Neapolitan, E major.

The notation of E major in Howells's tonal structure obscures an important significance of the larger scheme, in that E forms the goal of a broader tonal descent to its enharmonic equivalent, F♭. Although Howells's first section is firmly couched in E♭ minor, the presence of the subdominant, A♭ minor, is too prominent to be ignored. Its prolonged presence as a ninth chord at the opening (bars 1–5) is striking enough as a representation of David's inner anguish, but the chord ultimately dominates the harmony for the first stanza (bars 7–8, 12 and 14–17), and it is no accident that it is also conspicuous at the transition in bars 31–5, a persistent presence that surely signifies the sense of inner torment within the first part of the song. What is even more intriguing is that the opening statement on the subdominant also corresponds with the establishing of the local tonic of the second stanza, G♭, and the arrival of E major – enharmonically speaking, F♭ – producing a stepwise descent from A♭ through G♭. A further significant factor is that the original ninth chord on A♭ provides an important pivot between E♭ minor and G♭ major and the final arrival of F♭, but once F♭ has been established, the chord returns no more, as if to signify the sense of catharsis.

Howells's motivic interrelationships are copious and do much to interplay with the tonal scheme outlined above. The opening gesture presents two important embryonic ideas – a progression iv^9–i–iv^9, in which the dissonant subdominant ninth, as a gesture of sorrow, is given special emphasis, and a melodic motif B♭–G♭–B♭ ('a'). The vocal part itself, almost plainsong-like in its stepwise orientation around E♭, embarks with an inversion of 'a' (E♭–G♭–E♭; see Ex.4.11a). With each further phrase, the tessitura expands upwards, until it reaches a peak with D♭, spelling out the triad of G♭ before descending through a second triad of E♭ minor ('b'; see Ex. 4.11b). This idea, moreover, is contrapuntally concealed in the tenor range of the piano. As if to emphasise David's melancholy, the first verse ends inconclusively with the opening progression and motif, and leads more urgently to verse two. Here, the same pitches of the initial melodic motif are retained but harmonised with a *reversal* in G♭ major – i.e. I–IV–I – as the spread arpeggios of the harps attempt to ease his unrelenting sadness (Ex. 4.11c). Yet, for all the luxuriant sonority, David's gloom cannot be assuaged, and this is illustrated with the introduction of a further

Ex. 4.11a–h 'King David'

(a)
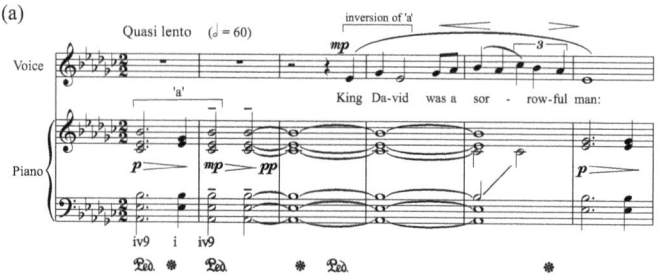

(b)

(c)

motivic figure ('c'), based on a conflation of 'a' and 'b', and presented canonically in the piano as a counterpoint against the rhapsodic voice (Ex. 4.11d). Here Howells's polyphonic invention is profuse, not only by way of the canonic writing, but also the imitation between voice and piano. Verse two, like verse one, concludes on the subdominant, and the two gestures of the piano and voice that follow (and here Howells deftly allows the first words of verse three to act as a bridge) condense those quintessential elements of the first section ('a' and 'c') leaving the subdominant suspended (Ex. 4.11e).

Verse three, marked 'Placido', enharmonically reinterprets A♭ as G♯ in E major. This sublime effect is enhanced by the reiteration of the opening material of verse two, but now in a transformed tonal environment. In addition, the nightingale's

Ex. 4.11a–h *continued*

Ex. 4.11a–h *continued*

song (consisting of the pitches $\hat{5}$–$\hat{6}$–$\hat{3}$) is itself based on an intervallic rearrangement of 'c' and the bridge from verse two (Ex. 4.11f), a motivic relationship that becomes more obvious as a recurrence of 'c', concealed once again in the piano, is subsequently introduced. This recurrence of 'c' no doubt represents something of David's *anagnorisis*, but this is even more skilfully symbolised by the vocal line, where 'c' gradually assimilates the nightingale's motif. Verse four, in accordance with de la Mare's poem, provides the climax, and does so by a move to the dominant, B, and a development of the nightingale's motif, which is increasingly adopted by the voice. The drama of Howells's climax is sufficiently *Tristan*-esque with its anguished 4–3 suspension on the submediant, though more significantly it is the motivic element (B–D–E) of the nightingale's song, reinforced by the D–E trill, that signals the catharsis of David's sorrow (Ex. 4.11g). Arguably even more deft, however, is the pause on the subdominant (E minor – surely a reference to the first section), recalling the unresolved nature of verses one and two and the opening motif of 'a' in the voice ('And the bird in no-wise heeded'). The subdominant of verse four leads, of course, effortlessly to the tonic E major in verse five, where, initially, we hear a reprise of verse three, but this is a feint, for superseding this material is the 'harp' music of verse two, replete with nightingale's song. David's catharsis is complete, a *peripeteia* confirmed by the more profuse polyphonic manipulation of 'c', by the final line of text ('Till all his own was gone'), which fuses the nightingale motif and (at its close) 'a', and the short but concise postlude that, replete with plagal cadence, summarises all the important motivic components (Ex. 4.11h).

The complex, intricate matrix of motivic and tonal interplay in 'King David' serves to reinforce Howells's modus operandi of 'hidden artifice', for much of the subtle musical calculation is concealed. Indeed, though the larger narrative structure of the song on one level may be bipartite, the E♭ minor section functioning as an introduction to the main body (ostensibly tripartite in design) of the song in E major, it is evident that the thematic co-relations are much more complex. In fact, one could argue for the presence of a highly modified sonata structure, given the recapitulation of the music of verse two (heard initially in the context of a 'second subject', the relative major) in verse five (in the 'tonic'), and that verse four is persuasively analogous to a developmental phase. It is a level of intellectual sophistication that points to Brahms and that Stanford evinced in his later works. As for Howells, 'King David' was the summit of his achievements as a song-writer and, with Warlock's *The Curlew*, remains one of the finest masterpieces of English song in the first half of the twentieth century, as well as one of the composer's most characteristic and representative works.

Furthermore, the involution of ideas that 'King David' and, indeed, many of Howells's songs reveal is a desire to create an art form that endeavoured to reconcile a message of simplicity (which the listener could understand without difficulty) with one of hidden complexity. In one sense, as already stated, the importance of Brahms, filtered through Stanford, was a vital ingredient, but one suspects that, though Howells rejected the existence of God, he nevertheless cleaved to the values of his beloved Elizabethans, such as Byrd and Tallis. Theirs was a desire to create an art form of excellence (not least for their patron, Elizabeth) that might, on one level, please the sensibilities of the human ear yet, on another, far more profound, was one between composer and Creator, where hidden intricacy and artifice were the stuff of private veneration.

CHAPTER 5

A 'Wholly New Chapter' in Service Music: *Collegium regale* and the *Gloucester Service*

Phillip A. Cooke

> If I made the setting of the Magnificat, the mighty should be put down from their seat without a brute force that would deny this canticle's feminine association. Equally, that in the Nunc dimittis, the tenor's domination should characterise the gentle Simeon. Only the 'Gloria' should raise its voice.[1]

THESE words were written by the composer in 1967 as the sleeve note for a recording of *Herbert Howells' Church Music* that was released on the Argo record label.[2] As well as providing useful information to the listener, it also acts as a blueprint for Howells's aesthetic when composing music for the evening service, the largest and most performed part of his oeuvre. This quotation not only sets out Howells's compositional agenda but also suggests that the composer felt there were deficiencies in the extant settings that could no doubt be remedied by his unique and idiosyncratic compositional voice. This blueprint would apply to the vast majority of Howells's mature settings (1945–75) and is especially pertinent in the two most celebrated settings: *Collegium regale* (HH 246 – 1945) and the *Gloucester Service* (HH 249–1946). The word 'revolution' may be a touch strong for the changes made to the music for evening worship under Howells's aegis, but there are certainly some striking but subtle developments that Howells brought to these canticles.

The evening canticles – Magnificat and Nunc dimittis – are as old as the Church of England itself, and steeped in tradition and conservatism. The daily tread of these two canticles defines the evening worship of the Anglican Church, and they are familiar to generations of churchgoers. Evensong is arguably not the place for experimentation, or for the progressive. However, by the late 1940s a noticeable change was evident in Anglican music: the functional had been replaced by the atmospheric, the respectable by the mystical, and beneath the traditional surface was music of an other-worldly and impressionistic quality. The words may have remained the same, but much else had inextricably changed. It would be in the hands of Herbert Howells that this change solidified, building upon subtle and discreet developments that had brought Anglican music from its nadir in the early part of the nineteenth century to its arguable zenith in the middle of the twentieth century; it would be Howells that codified a 'wholly new chapter' in service music, the legacy of which is still present today.

Howells's relationship with the evening canticles was enhanced during the Second World War, when he had the good fortune of securing the position of temporary organist at St John's College, Cambridge, deputising for the war-bound Robin Orr.

---

[1] Palmer, *A Centenary Celebration*, 400.
[2] Herbert Howells, sleeve note to *Herbert Howells' Church Music*, vinyl LP (Decca, 1967), Argo RG507.

It was here that a chance conversation and an unusual challenge occurred, sparking the creative fire in the composer that would produce the *Collegium regale* settings (both morning and evening canticles) of 1944–5. This challenge involved the Dean of King's College, Cambridge, Eric Milner-White (later to become Dean of York); the organist Boris Ord; the composer Patrick Hadley; and Howells. Milner-White suggested, for the sum of one guinea, the composition of a new *Te Deum* for the King's College Choir: something that Howells duly fulfilled with the *Collegium regale Te Deum* (HH 245), performed in 1944. This work was the start of Howells's substantial work within the Anglican Church and brought about a new era of liturgical music, both for the composer and for the Church.

Milner-White would stress the important contribution Howells was to make in a letter a few years later when he stated: 'By these last two services of yours [*Collegium regale* and *Gloucester Service*], I personally feel that you have opened a wholly new chapter in Service, perhaps in Church, music. Of spiritual moment rather than liturgical. It is so much more than music-making; it is experiencing deep things in the only medium that can do it.'[3] Milner-White's use of words such as 'spiritual' and 'deep' are integral to Howells's aesthetic in writing music for the Anglican liturgy – again and again words such as these return with increasing regularity and repeated conviction. In order for the composer to rewrite music for the Church, he had first to rethink and restyle his position as a composer both inside and outside the church music world.

By the time of his appointment at St John's, Howells was a diminished figure in the mainstream musical scene – he was no longer the great white hope of his early years that had seen him proclaimed Stanford's favourite and most promising pupil.[4] Much of this was due to his lack of mainstream orchestral and chamber music in recent years; by 1941 it had been over twenty years since his early successes of 'Puck's Minuet' (HH 83) and the *Rhapsodic Quintet* (HH 107). It can also be traced to the death of his son, Michael, in 1935 and the compositional paralysis that followed. By the early 1940s Howells was arguably known more as a teacher and adjudicator than as a leading composer. It is perhaps no surprise that he sought some comfort within the relative safety of church music, a genre where his compositional voice could be heard and respected. It was in many ways his first love, from his time as an articled pupil at Gloucester Cathedral, through the Westminster Cathedral years to being Assistant Organist at Salisbury Cathedral, to his tenure at St John's College; he had never really strayed far from the protection of the Church (whether Anglican or Catholic). Essentially, one could view the legacy of Anglican (and, to a lesser extent, Catholic) music that Howells bequeathed the Church as payment in kind for the support and inspiration he had been offered throughout his career.

In order to understand the departure that the *Collegium regale* and the *Gloucester Service* represent it is necessary to discuss the state of church music in the generations prior to Howells. Howells himself had little time or sympathy for Victorian

---

[3] Palmer, *A Centenary Celebration*, 168.
[4] Howells benefited greatly from support from the likes of Hubert Parry and Stanford, who referred to the composer as 'my son in music' (*ibid.*, 51). Stanford also referred to Howells as 'one of the most striking and brilliant brains I have ever come across' (as quoted in Dibble, *Charles Villiers Stanford*, 417).

church music; in a letter he wrote to Harold Darke (organist of St Michael's Cornhill and conductor of the St Michael's Singers) shortly after beginning at Salisbury Cathedral (1917) he stated: 'I have talked to you often enough of the sort of repugnance which even some of the best church music kindled in me – merely because it all filtered through that nasty mood which has been part of my musical mentality since Gloucester.'[5] The performance of music for church worship in the first half of the nineteenth century was so different from our contemporary experience as to be almost unrecognisable: choirs were ad hoc, performances were slipshod, and the repertoire was tired and narrow. As George Guest notes, "The choir in Hereford Cathedral on Easter Day 1833 consisted of boys and one man (the Dean's butler) who sang bass. Bangor Cathedral had no choir in 1802 (though the stipend of the Bishop was £6000 a year), and it is recorded that the only musical instrument in Llandaff Cathedral in 1850 was a bass viol."[6] The Oxford Movement began to improve conditions for the performance of choral services in the mid nineteenth century; and reformers such as Sir John Stainer (1840–1901) and Sir John Goss (1800–80) at St Paul's Cathedral began the process of giving credibility to the composing and performance of liturgical choral music.[7] But that is not to say that the quality of the music composed matched the intentions of the reforming zeal; Stainer (recognisable to many through his enduringly popular *The Crucifixion* of 1887) was a highly prolific composer and respected organist and academic (alongside his position at St Paul's, he held positions at Magdalen College, Oxford and was Professor of Music at the Faculty of Music at Oxford University) but much of his work lacks artistic merit and has failed to stand the test of time. The musicologist and educational reformer Sir Henry Hadow referred to Stainer's music as 'deplorably easy to write',[8] and Edmund Fellowes in his seminal book *English Cathedral Music* states that 'almost all of Stainer's anthems suffer primarily from a failure to match with music the magnificence of his verbal texts.'[9] Stainer's contemporary, the much more renowned and worldly Sir Arthur Sullivan (1842–1900), also found time when he was not writing operetta to write a large body of church music, but he fares little better. Fellowes states that 'too often the idiom of his [Sullivan's] anthems is out of keeping with the splendour of the words';[10] Arthur Hutchings in his book *Church Music in the Nineteenth Century* goes even further to declare 'Sullivan's church music is best forgotten; from it we can but illustrate only the nadir of sanctimonious vulgarity.'[11]

---

[5] As quoted in Spicer, *Herbert Howells*, 126.
[6] Guest, Introduction to *The Treasury of English Church Music*, Vol. IV: *1760–1900*, xii.
[7] The Oxford Movement was an affiliation of High Church Anglicans, many of whom were members of the University of Oxford. They sought to demonstrate that the Church of England was a direct descendant of the Church established by the apostles. Notable members of the movement included John Henry Newman, John Keble and Gerard Manley Hopkins.
[8] Hadow, *Church Music*, 24.
[9] Fellowes, *English Cathedral Music*, 244.
[10] Ibid., 248.
[11] Hutchings, *Church Music in the Nineteenth Century*, 109.

Certainly the standard of music written for the Church, and the standard of composer writing for the Church, was not as high as it would be in Howells's time; there is an overriding sense of the 'amateur' regarding church composers of the mid-to-late nineteenth century – well-regarded organists and choir directors trying their hand at the medium rather than fully professional practitioners of their art. Many of the most performed canticle settings of the Victorian era would still be in circulation at the time of Howells's appointment at St John's, but have since fallen into obscurity. In John Patton's illuminating survey *A Century of Cathedral Music: 1898–1998* we can see that popular settings by the likes of Stainer and Mendelssohn (alongside lesser-known names such as George Muswell Garrett and Stephen Elvey) that were performed in over 60 per cent of choral foundations in 1898 were performed 20 per cent less in 1938 (three years before Howells began at St John's) and were unperformed in 1998.[12] Tastes changed; and as better crafted and more sympathetic settings were written, so these vestiges of Victoriana disappeared. That is not to say that there are not some fine settings and inspired music (one need not look much further than Thomas Attwood Walmisley's groundbreaking Evening Service in D minor of 1855) from this period, but there should be the realisation that they are uncomplicated and functional settings and are cut from a very different cloth than Howells's. They represent compositions written with the primary aim of providing music for worship – they are not sophisticated, autonomous pieces, but rather well-crafted (in the main) settings for the purpose of musical accompaniment to worship.

It is the settings of Charles Villiers Stanford (1852–1924) that provide the antecedent for Howells, the subtlety of craft, technique and sympathy to text that is characteristic of Stanford's work can all be found in Howells's canticle settings. It would be fair to suggest that the level of sophistication in canticle settings increased as much in the hands of Stanford as it would in his highly thought-of pupil. It would be Stanford's two most celebrated settings, the Evening Service in G (1902) and the Evening Service in C (1909) that influenced the younger composer most and seem to pave a way for the aesthetic developments that Howells made in the 1940s. Stanford is arguably the first British composer since Purcell to bring the sophistication of the secular music genres to church music composition and to be a composer respected across the whole musical spectrum. His five settings of the services were in general use by the time of Howells's tenure at St John's and still remain the cornerstone of Anglican service music in the current day.[13] The main area of development that influences Howells's settings is the 'symphonic' design of Stanford's work: the composer envisages each canticle as a coherent whole rather than as a succession of unrelated musical events that one might often find in earlier settings. He emphasises this by having melodic figures or motifs that reoccur throughout the

---

[12] Patton, *A Century of Cathedral Music*, 15. Patton's book is a survey of service music lists of all the country's choral foundations taken during five snap-shot years over the century: 1898, 1938, 1958, 1986 and 1998. It provides very interesting statistical information regarding the changes in taste and repertoire over a turbulent century.

[13] For more information see Patton, *ibid*.

Ex. 5.1 Magnificat, Evening Service in G major, bars 199–205

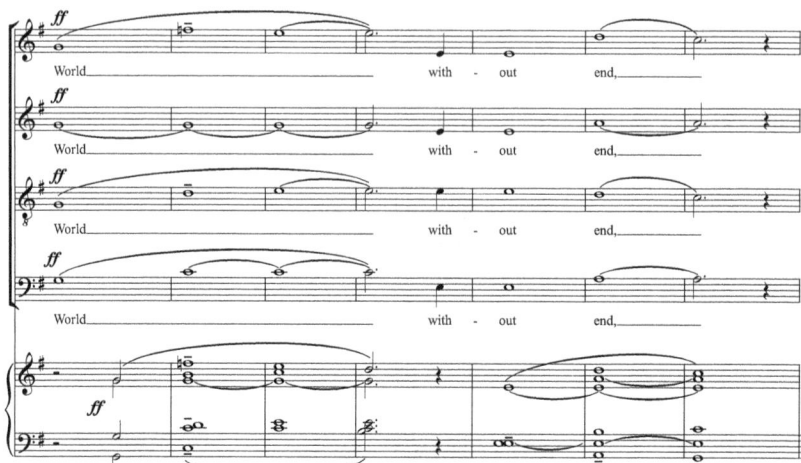

setting, binding the work together and adding to the subtlety, sophistication and coherence of the piece. Stanford can be viewed as the true reforming character in Anglican music, for the 'first-rate craftsmanship and sincerity of purpose'[14] in all his output invigorated church music and influenced a new generation of composers.

The work of Howells that most fell under the spell of Stanford was the early Evening Service in G major of 1919 (HH 91). Although Howells is primarily known for his post-1944 settings, his first forays into the genre began much earlier, with his first setting of the Nunc dimittis (in Latin) being composed in 1914 whilst in thrall of the Renaissance polyphony he was exposed to by Dr Richard Runciman Terry at Westminster Cathedral. The Evening Service in G, his first full evening service, appeared five years later.[15] Three further settings were composed in the intervening years: a setting for unison voices in 1924 and two settings for men's voices in 1935 and 1941. The Evening Service in G major is indebted to Stanford, both musically and in its mood and atmosphere. It is a straightforward and largely homophonic setting showing little of the sensuousness and melismatic polyphony that characterise the later settings. However, there are moments that suggest the impressionistic qualities of King's and Gloucester: notably the harmonies that accompany 'World without end' in the 'Gloria' of the Magnificat (see Ex. 5.1).

[14] Fellowes, *English Cathedral Music*, 254.
[15] Terry's pioneering work with the Westminster Cathedral Choir would not only bear fruit in Howells's early Latin pieces, but would include performances of works by many of the leading composers of the day, including Gustav Holst and Ralph Vaughan Williams. He was also instrumental in the liturgical revival of Renaissance polyphonic music from the likes of Thomas Tallis and William Byrd.

There are other hallmarks of Howells's mature style: the sectional soprano solo on 'For He hath regarded the lowliness of His handmaiden', the characteristic ♭IV–I cadence on 'His Name' and the rhapsodic melisma (one of the few) on the word 'Glory', amongst others. It is no surprise that Howells would choose to take influence from Stanford for this setting, his first for full choir and organ in English; and the work is more influenced by Stanford's C major setting (which had been written ten years earlier) than the one in the same key. It follows the same formal scheme as the Stanford work, with similar climaxes, modulations and changes of texture (the opening melody of 'My spirit doth magnify the Lord, and my spirit hath rejoiced in God my saviour' follows a very similar contour to the same passage in Stanford's). Although Howells employs greater harmonic, metrical and textural freedom than Stanford, the work never strays too far from the traditions espoused by his mentor.

The influence of Stanford on Howells would be present throughout his career (indeed the *Collegium regale* takes influence from Stanford's Evening Service in G in terms of texture and the succession of musical events) but what makes the later work very different from the 1919 setting is the tone, or the mood. As Paul Andrews notes, 'There is a straight-forwardness to Stanford's music that suggests a more confident age then our own.'[16] Certainly Stanford's settings are confident and assured: from the opening rising fourth of Mary's rejoicing in the Magnificat of the G major setting to the powerful unison of 'World without end' in the same work's 'Gloria', Stanford does not suggest the introspection and reticence of the *Collegium regale*. If the prevailing mood of Stanford's settings is that of unswerving faith and belief, the mood in Howells's could be described as doubt, or perhaps religious reserve. Stanford's settings belong to an age of religious truisms – the Victorian and Edwardian doctrine of Christian obedience; Howells's settings belong to an age of suspicion and questioning, wearied by two world wars and a changing society. They also reflect the respective composers: Stanford assured and confident; Howells, no less assured of his technique, but introspective and sensitive nonetheless.

It is not as simple as to suggest that the task of 'developing' and 'revolutionising' music for church worship was passed straight from Stanford to Howells. Twenty years passed between the death of the former and the composition of *Collegium regale*, and much music was composed in between. The vast majority of the music composed for the Church during this period was of a well-crafted, well-intentioned, post-Stanford style – much more sophisticated and well constructed then that composed by the Victorian precursors, but still lacking the individuality and originality of Stanford. Much of the repertoire stemmed from men who had first practised their art during the late Victorian and Edwardian periods, or from composers who wore the mantle of the older composers with little thought for progression or vitality. In his book *Twentieth Century Church Music*, Erik Routley (who refers to these composers as 'conservative craftsmen') states that 'although this music is entirely derivative, music of this standard was new to the English Church at the time of composition.'[17] Orthodoxy is a key word in describing Anglican music in the

---

[16] Andrews, liner notes to Herbert Howells, *The Complete Morning and Evening Canticles*, Vol. I.
[17] Routley, *Twentieth Century Church Music*, 38.

first three decades of the twentieth century, and there are few dissenting voices to be heard above the crowd.

One dissenting voice that had a real impact on Howells and his compositional aesthetic was that of Ralph Vaughan Williams (1872–1958), a composer of a similar reforming character to Stanford, though one who's influence did not permeate church music quite as much as did that of the older composer. In spite of this, his influence in the interwar years was paramount, and his challenge to the accepted orthodoxy prepared the ground for *Collegium regale* and Howells's 'wholly new chapter'. The key element that Vaughan Williams introduced was a retrospective awareness of musical history; as Routley puts it, 'it was the past to which they [Vaughan Williams and Gustav Holst] looked first … before they considered what imitations of the future they could convey'.[18] This was most evident in the wholesale introduction of modal elements into church music: not just the long, plainchant-like melodies of works such as *Benedicite* (1930) or *Sancta civitas* (1925) but the erosion of traditional cadences and tonic–dominant progressions in favour of a freer, more linear language. Vaughan Williams also introduced proto-Howells elements such as 'mood-creation' and 'other cunning devices to provide atmosphere surrounding argument'[19] that would bear fruit in Howells's canticle settings of the 1940s onwards. Although Vaughan Williams was a pupil of Stanford, the differences between the outlooks of the two men could be stark: Vaughan Williams 'reaching out towards an unknown future, but in the reviving of an unknown past',[20] Stanford not indulging in 'folksy sham-antiques' or attempting to 'do what Byrd and Gibbons had already done better'.[21] It is somewhere in the combination of Stanford's orthodoxy and traditionalism and Vaughan Williams's dissention and progressiveness that we find the canticle settings of Herbert Howells. The groundwork had been set for a new chapter in service music.

So what was this 'revolution' in Anglican music? What were the defining traits of Howells's aesthetic that brought about this 'wholly new chapter in Service music'? What are the musical characteristics of Howells's canticle settings that suggest such a departure from previous generations?

First it is the composer's response to the text (inherited from Stanford): his sensitivity to and sympathy with these two age-old poems. Howells was well aware of the cultural and traditional role the evening service plays in Christian society, but he was also fully aware of the ethos of the service, the progression from 'introversion to proclamation'[22] as Paul Andrews notes. He was also aware that these are not just religious dogma, or sermons; they are very beautiful poems that deserve the same amount of care and compositional attention that a composer might give to Hardy, Owen or, in Howells's case, Walter de la Mare.

Another facet of Howells's sensitivity to the text is the use of word painting. This is an awkward term that is often used in a derogatory sense to denote mannerist

---

[18] *Ibid.*, 23.
[19] *Ibid.*, 27.
[20] *Ibid.*
[21] Hutchings, *Church Music in the Nineteenth Century*, 114.
[22] Andrews, liner notes to *The Complete Morning and Evening Canticles*, Vol. III.

Ex. 5.2 Magnificat, *Collegium regale*, bars 1–5

and gestural tendencies in works, but it is used in a more subtle, mood-creating way by Howells and is one of the key weapons in his compositional armoury. If we take the opening lines of the Magnificat as an example – 'My soul doth magnify the Lord, and my spirit hath rejoiced in God my saviour' – these are deeply felt words spoken by a young woman who, although overjoyed at her calling, is dazed by the enormity and wonderment of the situation. In the hands of certain Victorian composers (even in the celebrated setting by Walmisley), this could be a bombastic, *forte* opening for unison male voices and organ in a powerful, declamatory fashion. For Howells it is something much more uncertain and reticent – not an unhappy moment, but something more contemplative befitting the major change to this woman's life (see Ex. 5.2).

Howells's choice of solo trebles for the opening of the *Collegium regale* shows a very simple but subtle response to the text, and one very different from that often found in Victorian settings – why begin the song of a young woman with loud men's voices? Gone is the powerful, male-dominated 'magnify the Lord', replaced with the treble voices, their purity suggesting the celestial virginity of Mary and the miracle of her conception. The opening five bars of the Magnificat set the mood for the whole work: the plangent modality, slow rate of harmonic change and prominent tritone, and the recitative, chant-like entry of the trebles all feel a long way from pre-Stanford settings. The opening reticence of Mary's song conjures the most beautiful and atmospheric opening by the composer, responding as much to the perceived 'feeling' behind the text as to the words themselves.

Howells responds in a similar fashion in the opening of the Nunc dimittis, the song of Simeon, in which the old man prepares for heaven having seen the infant Christ. Again, simplicity and subtlety are the prominent features: a long, diatonic and conjunct tenor solo gently intones the opening lines of the text. In this solo voice, Howells again stresses the mood and atmosphere behind Simeon's words – there is a weary yet contented feel to this melody, the simple modal line having a somewhat earthy, human quality to it (see Ex. 5.3).

Again, words such as 'atmosphere' and 'mood' are useful when discussing Howells's thought processes behind the canticle settings – 'mood-creation' is a term that seems somewhat fitting when describing these works, and 'mood' is a term Howells often used in relation to his compositions. Howells was a mystic, a spiritualist and a sensualist; he was fully aware of the atmospheric qualities that his music, combined with the correct ambience and acoustic, could bring to

Ex. 5.3 Nunc dimittis, *Collegium regale*, bars 5–10

Ex. 5.4 Magnificat, *Gloucester Service*, bars 17–19

the listener. He is often referred to as an 'impressionist', and this is an apposite term when describing the King's and Gloucester settings, which are shrouded in a light-infused halo that seems to magnify the mystery and the majesty of the texts. The opening of the *Gloucester Service* is as much an essay in mood-creation as the opening of *Collegium regale*: here reticence and contemplation are replaced by effervescence and verve (see Ex. 5.4).

The divided trebles move in and out of each other's melodic lines, reflecting and shimmering as they pass each other, enhanced by the third contrapuntal line in the organ (playing a Dorian mode on B); the effect is purely impressionistic with the gentle dissonances becoming lost in the huge acoustic of Gloucester Cathedral. Paul Spicer refers to the 'trance-like ecstasy'[23] of this melismatic writing, and ecstasy is a word that succinctly sums up the *Gloucester Service* – from the opening rising fifth in the trebles, through the astonishing polyphonic dexterity of the Magnificat to the final passionate declaration in the 'Gloria' of the Nunc dimittis, ecstatic utterances abound. It becomes an even more pertinent term when one understands that Howells wrote himself of 'the ecstasy he felt at seeing light flood through the great east window of Gloucester Cathedral'[24] – light is the ecstatic quality in this setting and it increases the impressionistic qualities. Christopher Palmer summed it up neatly when he stated: 'It *sounds* like what Gloucester's east

---

[23] See Chapter 6 and Spicer, *Herbert Howells*, 136.
[24] Andrews, liner notes to *The Complete Morning and Evening Canticles*, Vol. III.

Ex. 5.5 Magnificat, *Gloucester Service*, bars 63–4/79–81

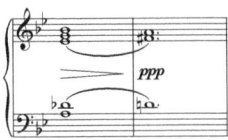

window *looks* like.'[25] Light is present throughout the setting created by Howells's unique combination of texture, polyphony and harmony: the simple homophony of the opening of the Magnificat creates a bright, open space for light to enter: the three-part polyphony of Ex. 5.4 suggesting light reflecting and refracting though a window, and the powerful chords that herald the 'Gloria' suggesting the blazing glow of direct sunlight.

To qualify the use of the word 'ecstasy', it should perhaps more rightly be 'ecstasy' and 'agony', for these two opposed feelings are never far away in any of Howells's works. For Howells, ecstasy *is* agony and agony *is* ecstasy – as Palmer states, there is a 'sense of loss on one hand, Beatific Vision on the other'.[26] These two terms sum up Howells's canticle settings, from *Collegium regale* right through to the stark later settings of his final years. This schizophrenic quality is best represented by Howells's use of harmony, his most potent and sensuous compositional tool and the most expressive representation of his personality. On a purely musical level his harmony can be reduced to a series of added chords, false relations and piquant 'blue' notes, but this goes no way to explaining the expressive qualities behind the music. For it is in the harmony that we find ecstasy and agony often transmuted into a series of 'pleasure/pain' chords that are strewn throughout the canticles. These take many different shapes, though Howells repeatedly returns to two favoured chords: a bitonal interlocking of seemingly unrelated triads, and the simultaneous false relation in inner parts for purely dramatic effect (see Ex. 5.5).

The first of these two examples has interlocking E♭ and A major triads creating a bitonal chord (and thus a form of extended dominant) that accompanies the words 'Abraham and his seed'. This opaque harmony adds to the tension of the passage, which is made all the more important by the striking resolution to D major for the words 'for ever' – Howells chooses to cloud the uncertainty of Abraham's lineage until the final moment where he focuses on the notion of eternity in a radiant major chord.[27] The second example is typical of Howells's love of chromatic inflections with false relations and simultaneous false relations occurring in quick succession. This strident use of the minor second was favoured by Howells throughout his canticles and can be found in many of the settings from *Collegium regale* right through to the final set, the *Dallas Canticles* (HH 345) of 1975. 'Pleasure/pain' is an

---

[25] Palmer, *A Centenary Celebration*, 147.
[26] *Ibid.*, 153.
[27] He does the same thing at the same point in the *Gloucester Service*, here a bitonal combination of B and F major resolved onto E major – the dominant of the work.

Ex. 5.6 Magnificat, *Collegium regale*, bars 28–30

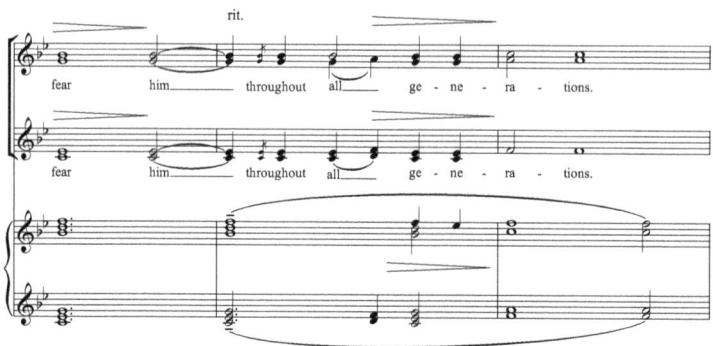

appropriate term for these chords: the harsh dissonances of the tritone and minor second are bitter flavours, but it is precisely this bitterness that makes us realise how sweet the sweetness of Howells's resolutions can be. There is perhaps something sexual about these moments: there is a teasing and a toying to Howells's harmonic progressions, often delaying the expected moment of resolution and our feeling of reconciliation.

Not all of Howells's harmony is quite so impassioned, though even the most prosaic passages are tinged with the sensual and the evocative. If we were to describe Howells's use of harmony in a succinct term, we might describe him as a master of 'soft dissonance',[28] for this succinctly sums up the composer's expressive harmony. Much of this soft dissonance comes from Howells's use of added chords – they are an integral part of his harmonic language. As one might expect, minor and major sevenths are used regularly, but it is the ninths, elevenths and thirteenths that characterise his harmonic palette. Though there is nothing particularly new about the inclusion of these chords in a modern harmonic language (French composers had been using them regularly for many years) it is often the way that Howells uses this harmony that distinguishes them. Many of these chords are formed as passing harmonies over the pedal points that Howells favoured, though often they are used purely for their sonorous, colouristic qualities. A good example is in the Magnificat of *Collegium regale*, where a startling minor-eleventh chord accompanies the words 'fear him throughout all generations'. Howells subsequently dissolves the tension by resolving the chord to F major, but the effect of this chord (especially as an organ accompaniment) is striking (see Ex. 5.6).

A lot of the dissonances in these works result from the highly contrapuntal, polyphonic nature of Howells's vocal music: the linear flow of the music, the highly melismatic word-setting (especially in the *Gloucester Service*) and the ambiguous dissonances created by the collision of these polyphonic lines help to enhance in the quality of 'otherness': it is challenging music (aurally and practically) but it somehow manages to be both traditional yet progressive – there is plenty of dissonant

[28] Ottaway, 'Herbert Howells and the English Revival', 898.

Ex. 5.7 Nunc dimittis, *Gloucester Service*, bars 55–7

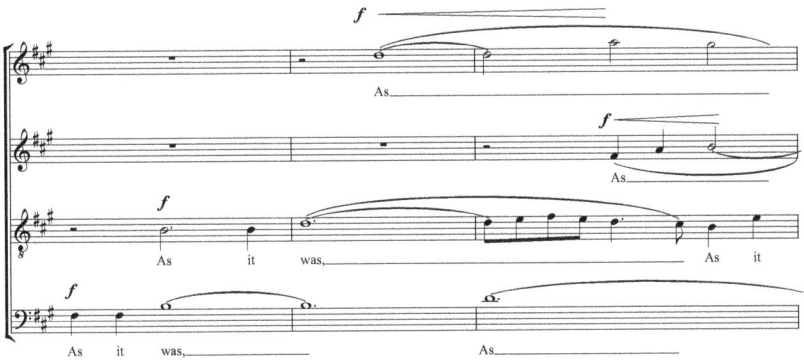

music, but it is never *too* dissonant to disrupt the continuum of tradition to which Howells felt very much connected.

Perhaps the most expressive moment in all of Howells's canticle settings occurs in the Nunc dimittis of the *Gloucester Service*; for in one simple amendment, one subtle flick of the composer's pen, we have arguably the most sublime and radiant moment that Howells would ever create. This happens in the 'Gloria' of the Nunc dimittis – its simplicity is profound and its effect is breathtaking. The seeds of this moment are sown in the 'Gloria' of the Magnificat, where the basses and tenors leap up a perfect fifth (the dominant interval of the work) to D, thus providing the trebles with a platform for their own leap to a rapturous top A for the beginning of the line 'As it was in the beginning'. This moment is spine-tingling and pure Howellsian mood-creation. However, he somehow manages to make the same moment in the Nunc dimittis even more rapturous and ecstatic; 'he twists the knife'[29] in the most subtle way at this moment to the greatest effect. Instead of rising a perfect fifth together the basses and tenors rise independently, but by a fourth and a third respectively, changing the harmonic and intervallic content of the section and increasing the tension. The trebles enter on the same note and rise the same perfect fifth; however, they crucially spend much longer on their opening D, delaying and suspending the euphoric moment until it becomes unbearable – the arrival at the top A is wildly ecstatic and becomes the emotional climax of the entire service (see Ex. 5.7).

The effect of this passage is truly spell-binding, and it is one of the great moments in the Anglican musical canon. This is a representation of 'Christ in his glory and majesty, rather than Jesus friend and Brother';[30] it is Howells at his most powerful

---

[29] Spicer, *Herbert Howells*, 137.
[30] *Ibid.*, 132.

and transcendental, though it arguably represents much of what he had been striving for throughout his career – the moulding together of disparate influences to create a meaningful expression of the composer's inner thoughts and beliefs. It would also represent the end of Howells's more rhapsodic and impressionistic canticle settings, for he would never try to replicate the ecstatic utterances of the *Gloucester Service*. His first major period of canticle settings ended with the *St John's Service* of 1957 (HH 282), and although this period includes the powerful and expressive *St Paul's Service* (HH 264 – 1951), the settings became progressively less rapturous and more inward-looking. His second major period of canticle settings (from 1966 to 1975) highlighted a very different side of the composer's persona: they are often austere, angular and dissonant. They are also very difficult to perform and to understand, which has led to their not gaining a place in regular church worship like the earlier settings. That is not to suggest that they are lacking in musical merit – the *Sarum Service* (HH 312–1966) is warmly diatonic and intimate; the *Hereford Service* (HH 327–1969) shows Howells experimenting with form and texture; the *York Service* (HH 340–1973) is dramatic and amusingly flamboyant, and the *Dallas Canticles* show the increasing importance of the text of the Nunc dimittis in the composer's thoughts. Perhaps the service that most deserves a place in the repertoire is the *Chichester Service* (HH 317; see Chapter 12).

It is my opinion that Herbert Howells's evening canticle settings do represent a 'wholly new chapter in Service music'; they constitute a quiet revolution in Anglican worship that took church music away from the traditional and orthodox music of the post-Victorian period to something more relevant for the wearied and questioning post-Second World War generation. Howells's inclusion of elements of a more sensual and spiritual persuasion represented a major change in the service music for the daily worship of the Church, and the importance of well-crafted music for these events. In many ways the changes brought about in Howells's settings mirrored the changing relationship between society and religion – the move away from collective, congregational worship to a more individual form that is rather about introspection than proclamation. His aesthetics also find resonance in western Christian society's gradual move away from religion and the rise of 'spirituality' as a dominant trait. As Erik Routley notes, 'sacred and secular are nowadays so thoroughly mixed up in church art';[31] and the music and aesthetic of Howells seem to fit uncannily into this description.

The over-familiarity of these two great canticle settings has contrived to dull the luminous intensity of the *Collegium regale* and the *Gloucester Service*.[32] In an age

---

[31] Routley, *Twentieth Century Church Music*, 211.
[32] In 1998 the *Collegium regale* was performed in 67 per cent of choral foundations making it one of the twenty most performed canticle settings (four of Stanford's settings made it into this list). The *Gloucester Service* was performed in 58 per cent of foundations. For more information see Patton, *A Century of Cathedral Music*.

where the weekly music lists of cathedrals run from Gregorian chant to the contemporary, it is hard to imagine how different these works must have sounded in the postwar austerity of 1945–6. However, Howells's settings represented a necessary progression in church music – they reflected a new postwar age where everything, slowly and subtly, had changed forever.

CHAPTER 6

Howells's Use of the Melisma: Word Setting in His Songs and Choral Music

Paul Spicer

MELISMA (the writing of a number of notes to one syllable) is a fundamental element in Howells's compositional style. We will examine its varied use, his motivation for using it, and its effectiveness. Saint Augustine famously wrote of singing without words as expressing feelings too deep for words. He was referring to the ecstasy of, for instance, a melismatic 'Alleluia' sung to Gregorian chant where the word is suspended mid-syllable and pure melody takes over. This is something Howells understood instinctively and often emulated. Melisma[1] is a very common compositional tool and it may seem odd to focus on such a well-used feature in this chapter, but if the contrast is made with the word setting of Gerald Finzi (1901–56), a direct contemporary of Howells and another distinguished song-writer, it may help to clarify Howells's approach to word setting in general. Melismas have been divided into two types that set them apart from purely syllabic setting. These indicate scale: 'neumatic' having only a few notes to the syllable and 'melismatic' being a longer flourish.

Finzi consciously avoided melismas. It is hard to find a single example in either his choral music or his entire output of songs. The two exceptions are the word 'weep' at the end of 'Come Away, Death' from *Let Us Garlands Bring* and the famous eight-part contrapuntal 'Amen' in *Lo, the Full Final Sacrifice*. Apart from these there is just one single pairing of two notes (neumatic) hidden away in the middle of eighteen minutes of expansive, rhapsodic music in this much loved anthem. Melisma was consciously rejected by Finzi in favour of syllabic word setting, which he felt helped clarity of expression and reflected his view of the supremacy of the word. For Howells, by contrast, the melisma was a musical tool that helped him to express ecstasy. The dividing line between spirituality and sensuality in his music is so blurred as to make them almost synonyms, and both to some degree define Howells's music. He also felt, unlike Finzi, that the device both clarified (in a different way) and gave descriptive emphasis to a word.

Howells was passionate about words and it is important first to understand what fired the engine of his creativity before picking apart his method. He read widely, wrote beautifully, annotated many of the books he read extensively in the margins, and chose texts for setting to music from a wide variety of authors old and new. His favourite poet was Walter de la Mare (1873–1956), who was popular with many composers of this period partly because he was musical (he had been a chorister at St Paul's Cathedral in his youth) but mostly because his poems were either richly descriptive or lived in a kind of fantasy world that seemed to lend itself to musical

---

[1] See Crocker, 'Melisma' for more detailed information.

treatment. This kindled Howells's imagination uniquely and is the principal reason for focusing on these poems for our examination of his text setting.

Howells loved de la Mare's mystery and wonder: the wide-eyed child being told a story, fairies and hobgoblins, birds and animals. De la Mare was a consummate story-teller and his imagination drew readers into his world as if into the other side of Alice's looking-glass. But this was no comfortable world shielding the reader from the harsh realities of daily existence. De la Mare often used fantasy to reflect the dark side of the world under the cover of what might seem to be an innocuous agent – a fairy, or an animal. Certain images surfaced again and again in de la Mare's poetry. One was the robin, and we will come across an important example in Howells's song setting (HH 111iii) of de la Mare's 'Before Dawn' (*'The Veil' and Other Poems*). But in another poem, 'A Robin' (*'The Fleeting' and Other Poems*), de la Mare painted this uncompromisingly bleak image:

> Lurking where shadows steal,
> Perched in his coat of blood,
> Man's homestead at his heel,
> Death-still the wood.

The dawn was another subject that fired de la Mare's imagination: that cusp of the moment when night gives way to day; the moment of balance between worlds, the world of fantasy and dreams, which evaporates with the dew into the realities of day. Here is part of a poem called 'Dawn' from the same collection (verses one, three and six). Note the appearance of the robin again:

> Near, far, unearthly, break the birds
> From spectral bush and tree,
> Into a strange and drowsy praise,
> The flush of dawn to see.
>
> The restless robin – like a brook
> Tinkling in frozen snow –
> Shakes his clear, sudden, piercing bells,
> Flits elf-like to and fro.
>
> The milk-white mists of night wreathe up
> From meadows greenly grey –
> Their every blade of grass ablaze
> With dewdrops drenched in day.

Already we can see a pattern emerging and what it is about this imagery likely to fire the imagination of a sensibility like Howells's. Other images appear and reappear in de la Mare's poems: old and empty houses, ghosts and fantastic fairy-tale figures, woods, dream-worlds, birds (not just the robin), beautiful ladies and the transitory nature of life, though he doesn't let this become the obsession of Hardy or Finzi. Of the eighty-odd songs that Howells wrote there are some thirty-five settings of poems by de la Mare. Some of these are missing and some incomplete, but it still shows how fundamental this affinity with the older man was. Howells also turned to de la Mare for the perfect text for a part-song, 'The Scribe' (HH 285), in honour of Vaughan Williams's eightieth birthday: 'What lovely things thy hand hath made'. In the flyleaf of Howells's copy of Faber's *Tribute to Walter de la Mare on His Seventy-Fifth Birthday* [2] de la Mare inscribed a poem called 'Echoes', which he had put in a collection entitled *Poems for Children*:

> The sea laments
> The livelong day,
> Fringing its waste of sand;
> Cries back the wind from the whispering shore –
> No words I understand:
>
> Yet echoes in my heart a voice,
> As far, as near, as these –
> The wind that weeps
> The solemn surge
> Of strange and lonely seas.

And he inscribed it 'Walter, with love to Herbert: January 20 1951'. De la Mare is known to have felt Howells's setting of 'King David' (HH 102) to be so perfect that he did not want anyone else to set it. And surely the line in 'Echoes' that prompted the dedicatory inscription is that start of verse two: 'Yet echoes in my heart a voice, / As far, as near, as these'. Howells's musical voice chimes in uncanny sympathy with de la Mare's inner musical ear. Howells told Christopher Palmer: 'I always enjoyed talking music to de la Mare; he was one of the few poets I've known who really *understood* music – one always felt he was on one's wavelength, that for instance his concept of "rhythm" was identical with one's own.'[3]

The strength of the connection between these two men is demonstrated by Howells's own *A Garland for de la Mare* (HH 111), which was written over a very long period of time, roughly between 1919 and 1973. A number of songs apparently destined for a second group of Howells's *Peacock Pie* settings (HH 104) found their way into this set. It is interesting that in his diary for 1936, following his son Michael's death, when he was 'frozen' with grief, Howells notes that while staying with the Sumsions at Gloucester he worked on a setting of 'The Lady Caroline' (HH 111ii) – one of his 'beautiful lady' songs. He often found writing these small-scale pieces, like the piano music, to be a kind of 'relaxation'. They were something he could enjoy writing that did not have the enormous effort of an orchestral score. The *Garland* collection was only identified as such by Howells in 1969 (a diary entry for 2 August states that he was 'sorting ideas for the de la Mare "Garland"').[4] However, he could not see it into print because he would not allow a collection to be published as a tribute to his friend without *the* song acknowledged as his masterpiece in the genre, 'King David'. That had already been published separately. The collection was published posthumously by Thames in 1995 with 'King David'.

---

[2] Bett, *Tribute to Walter de la Mare*.
[3] Palmer, *Herbert Howells: A Study*, 16.
[4] Ibid., 177.

Ex. 6.1 'Wanderers', *A Garland for de la Mare*, bars 6–13

This then sets the scene for looking in more detail at the way in which Howells approached his setting of the words and images that were such a powerful motivation to his musical creativity. Howells's natural sense of melodic expansionism found the melisma to be a perfect tool to perform various functions: word painting, the creation of an ecstatic lyrical outpouring (ref. St Augustine), pure word reflection (but not painting) and word emphasis. De la Mare's poem 'Wanderers' (*Peacock Pie*) was set by Howells in 1968 (HH 111i) and begins with the mystical image of the night sky. This will have had a particular resonance for Howells, whose father had used to wake him up at 5 a.m. on clear and starry mornings to talk to the boy about 'stars, planets and distances'.[5] The poem begins:

> Wide are the meadows of the night,
> And daisies are shining there,
> Tossing their lovely dews,
> Lustrous and fair.

Three melismas occur in these first four lines, on the words 'daisies', 'Tossing' and 'lovely' (Ex. 6.1). The first two are obvious word-painting devices where he creates the feeling of the endless string of distant stars and the 'tossing' of 'their lovely dews'. The effect of this second melisma is heightened by the syncopation where the end of the word lands as if the tossed dew is suspended momentarily. The third melisma on the word 'lovely' is a simple and generous gesture to reflect the adjective (word reflection).

Later in the song the words 'move', 'circling' and 'fair' are also given characteristic melismatic treatment (Ex. 6.2). The short (neumatic) melisma on 'move' prepares for the shape of the melodic line, which almost mirrors the word 'circling'. The word 'fair' is a climactic moment underlined by Howells's marking *espress. molto*. Note here the use of the falling minor third and rising perfect fourth, which became well known as the opening motif in the 'Gloria' of the *Collegium regale* (HH 246) evening canticles. Howells used this motif extensively, especially at moments of climax or rising intensity. Questioning him about it (*c.* 1972), the present author found him to be unusually reticent where he was normally forthcoming regarding such

---

[5] Hodgson, 'The Music of Herbert Howells', 5.

Ex. 6.2 'Wanderers', *A Garland for de la Mare*, bars 30–4

points. It seemed as if the figure held a personal significance for him that he was not prepared to discuss. The manner of his evasion that day remains a particularly strong impression. For Howells, then, at the opposite end of the syllabic spectrum from Finzi, these moments were far more than indulgent lyrical flourishes but gave time for reflection or appropriate expression on a chosen word.

It is instructive to note de la Mare's free construction in 'Wanderers', each line having a different number of syllables: 7, 7, 6, 4, 6, 5 (which Howells makes 7 by setting all the syllables of the word 'wanderers'), 10, 6 (made into 7 by adding the word 'and'), 7, 7, 10, 4. Howells makes musical sense of this freedom partly by setting up a repeated pattern in the piano part at the start before the voice enters, creating an impression of rhythmic regularity, and by concentrating on the essential simplicity of de la Mare's regular word stresses: three in the six- and seven-syllable lines, two in the four-syllable lines and four in the ten-syllable lines. Howells changes the metre to enhance flow, to allow for melismatic elongation of the phrase (as in bars 5–8 of Ex. 6.1), or to deal with the effect of different movement to and from word stresses.

Certain words and images fired Howells's imagination and recurred in numerous songs. We feel him revelling in his ability to create a sensuous moment, heightening the sense of fantasy that de la Mare laid open for him. In the poem 'Lovelocks' from his first published collection, *Songs of Childhood* (1902), de la Mare describes a child's (presumably, given the collection's title) observation of the Lady Caroline's obsession with her hair. This intensely sensual poem (which becomes a very adult response to the lady's beauty in Howells's hands) will have instantly appealed to Howells, whose love of beautiful ladies was a driving force in his life and a powerful aid to his creativity. This song, like all his 'beautiful lady' songs, is set in a gentle but stately triple metre (perhaps a minuet) that somehow enhances the feeling of the girl's poise and lift of her head.

Howells was passionate about stylised dance forms and used them often in his songs, recreating the spirit of the dance in a contemporary form that gave him licence to alter the format as it suited him. In 'The Three Cherry Trees' (HH 111v), for instance – a siciliana – he moves effortlessly between 9/8 and 6/8 (between three and two in a bar) where the dance is normally in a constant three. Here is the supremacy of the word, and if all those 6/8 bars are syllabically set for reasons of textual rhythm, the 9/8 bars, as we will see shortly, can be alluringly melismatic when appropriate.

In 'The Lady Caroline', however, Howells's model was W. Denis Browne's 'To Gratiana Dancing and Singing', a song that he told Stephen Banfield was 'one of the dozen or so tunes that had been present in his mind all his life',[6] although he points out that the melody was taken from an anonymous 'Allmayne' in Elizabeth Rogers's Virginal Book. Browne's approach to melisma in his vocal line is wholly different from Howells's and seems to arise from a variety of stimuli, including an archaic emphasis on unimportant words ('See! *with what* constant motion ...') and filling in when there are too few syllables for his pre-existent melody, as occurs on the word 'steers' in line three of verse one. This could be regarded as word painting, except that the melisma is so long that the word is almost obscured and any such musical point therefore lost. In fact, the melody was more than likely memorable to Howells because of Browne's original treatment of the piano accompaniment, which Howells mimics in 'The Lady Caroline'. It was the texture with which he so strongly connected. There are fundamental differences, most notably in the time signatures: Browne's is in 4/4 (a pavane) where Howells's is in 3/4, but it is the gracefully stepping bass line (perhaps 'jumping' might be a better word) that is so characteristic, together with the wholly independent piano part used in both songs. In fact, so separate and complete a lyrical entity is the right hand of the piano part in Howells's song that it is almost a two-part song for voice and piano. It is perhaps interesting to think of this right-hand piano melody as being one long melisma expressing feelings 'too deep for words'. Additionally, Browne's wonderfully imaginative use of tenths in the left hand of 'To Gratiana', which creates some magical sonorities, is replaced in Howells's song by lute-like arpeggiando starts to each bar in verse two and at points in verse three. This is Howells the recreator of early dance forms in a contemporary idiom.

How, then, does Howells deal with musical line and word setting in 'The Lady Caroline'? The first verse is remarkably syllabic, with just two lyrical melismas found unsurprisingly on the words 'Lady' and 'beauteous'. The first is ecstatic and the second descriptive. The first verse reads:

> I watched the Lady Caroline
> Bind up her dark and beauteous hair;
> Her face was rosy in the glass,
> And 'twixt the coils her hands would pass,
> White in the candleshine.

Following the song through, the other significant melismas occur on the words 'sweet', 'lightly', 'sing', 'song' and '*tossed* her *beauteous hair* about'. Of these the word 'tossed' is a clear example of word painting where the musical figure mirrors the upward throw of the hair (not dissimilar to the same use of the word in Ex. 6.1). It is in the final, climactic verse where the most passionately extravagant (ecstatic)

---

[6] Banfield, *Sensibility and English Song*, 154.

Ex. 6.3 'The Lady Caroline', *A Garland for de la Mare*, bars 52–61

melismas occur, as in Ex. 6.3. It is as if the different levels of melisma are built up through the song to culminate in ecstasy.

In seeing how Howells responds to individual words as they encourage his melodic expansion it is interesting to contrast his setting of de la Mare's poem 'Before Dawn', from the collection called *The Veil and Other Poems*, to 'The Lady Caroline'. Spirituality; a sense of 'other', mystery, vision; and the sense of distance engendered by inspiration taken from music of a much earlier period are all elements in the chemical makeup of much music of this period by a wide variety of composers. It is perhaps surprising, therefore, to think how many composers of this time regarded themselves as, if not atheists, then certainly agnostics, and yet many wrote deeply searching church music, Howells principal among them. Sacred and secular so often rub shoulders via the medium of words, and a song might be as deeply affecting, spiritually, as any canticle or anthem. Howells's setting of 'Before Dawn' is just such an example. De la Mare's imagery powerfully evokes the pre-dawn greyness, the cold and stillness of winter, and uses the birth of Jesus to intensify the image.

Howells uses far-spaced piano textures to create a very particular atmosphere: the painting of extreme cold, of starry skies at 'Now night's astir with burning stars' (this is very similar to the opening of 'Wanderers' quoted above), the bringing in of the Archangel Gabriel as the heavenly protector of the baby Jesus – the intermediary between God and the child's earthly mother, quietening the robin (again) whose red breast is perhaps a portent of the end of Jesus' life right here at the start. Then, furthering this dual imagery the poem ends with the triumph of spring over winter, which is also, of course, a metaphor for the triumph of God in putting His son on earth to save mankind. Howells feels this imagery so deeply, and here is a classic example of that sense of remoteness or distance painted in sound. In a perceptive article in *The Music Teacher*, Katharine Eggar pointed out that 'Some might say that the "remoteness" in Howells's music is due to his looking back to the past in music; others, nearer to the point, might say that the quality of the music to which he looks back is also "remoteness".'[7] There is a rare word-setting error in this song. Occasionally words may be left out. That happens

---

[7] Eggar, 'An English Composer'.

Ex. 6.4 'Before Dawn', *A Garland for de la Mare*, bars 5–18

where Howells omits the word 'hath' in the fifth line of verse three. It suits his purposes much better to make this change. However, the placing of the highly significant word 'Lo!', occurring at the end of de la Mare's verse four and at the start of Howells's final verse, so that it joins with the words 'No snowdrop yet ...', makes a completely different emphasis in drawing of our attention to the snowdrop rather than to the magically dim lamp burning faintly at the end of the previous verse. It is a strange anomaly.

> ... And gold the Strangers go
> Into a dusk where one dim lamp
> Burns faintly, Lo!
>
> No snow-drop yet its small head nods,
> In winds of winter drear.

Whether this might be a result of Howells setting from memory is questionable but certainly possible. Gurney often made errors of memory, especially when in the trenches with no access to his books.

The word setting in 'Before Dawn' is more syllabic than 'The Lady Caroline' and helps to highlight those words that Howells instinctively singles out for melismatic treatment. In verse one, for instance, only the words 'smoulders' and 'sleeps' have melismas (Ex. 6.4). These appear to be more emphatic than descriptive melismas. The whole of the song continues in this manner with comparatively reticent melismas on words that colour key moments of the poem. So, in verse four it is now obvious that there will be expansions on the words 'burning' and 'darkness' but nowhere else. The most expansive melisma of all is reserved for the climactic word 'Spring' in the final verse to which the whole poem has been leading. It is an ecstatic outpouring (Ex. 6.5). Thus far we can see Howells consistently colouring particular words in different settings but taking an overall approach that differs with the tenor of a poem. Thus, an unashamedly descriptive poem like 'The Lady Caroline' will evoke a different response from 'Before Dawn', which conveys a deeper, more complex message.

Ex. 6.5 'Before Dawn', *A Garland for de la Mare*, bars 80–3

Ex. 6.6 'The Old Stone House', *A Garland for de la Mare*, bars 47–51

'The Three Cherry Trees' (written in 1969) comes from de la Mare's set of poems called *The Listeners* (1912). It is another 'beautiful lady' song and is interesting to compare with 'The Lady Caroline'. We have seen that it is a siciliana, where dotted rhythms abound; and the whole song has, like 'The Lady Caroline', a poise that reflects a light heart watching pure beauty. The lady in this poem is very different, however, from the narcissistic Lady Caroline. It is obvious that she is very young when we first encounter her, and it is only when she grows to maturity ('but blossoms to berries do come') that she is stolen away by a lover, and her dreams ('dreamed a most beautiful lady') come true. This lady is seemingly quite unaware of her powers of attraction, and yet de la Mare compares her with the beautiful blossom of cherry trees, with varieties of beautiful birds all with lovely songs, but she transcends them all. Howells's sensuality is nowhere more apparent than in these two lovely songs. It is interesting how much sadness there is in his representation of the poem in music. This might reflect the deserted garden that she once frequented (the last verse) or the distant image in his mind of something that was unutterably beautiful but hopelessly unattainable.

In Howells's setting there seems a greater demand for clarity in the telling of the story. Melismas are few and far between. The syllabic structure of the poem is not as simple as it might appear at first glance. The verse pattern is similar: two shorter lines, one longer and two shorter. However, the longer line varies between verses from ten to twelve syllables, and the shorter lines also vary, creating interesting problems for the composer. He treats the first two verses similarly by introducing a 6/8 bar at the midpoint of the phrase and writing a long note for the voice under which the piano has what might be thought of as a transferred melisma carrying its own melodic line forward. Verses three and four have the largest number of syllables in the long line (twelve), and Howells changes tack by writing dotted quavers across the beat in a phrase that consists almost completely of neumatic melismas and that, in verse three, seems to paint the picture of 'one long summer's day'. As in 'Before Dawn' his climactic melisma is reserved for the final phrase: 'That happy and beautiful lady', the final two words having familiar expansive treatment (Ex. 6.6).

Ex. 6.7 'Andy Battle', *A Garland for de la Mare*, bars 79–83

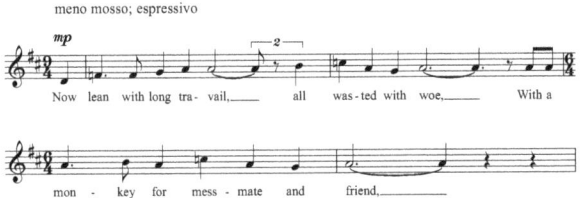

This cumulative treatment accords with what we have seen in other songs, where the most expansive (ecstatic) melismas are reserved for the song's culmination.

We have focused thus far on songs of a particular mood and subject matter that is generally reflective and encourages the use of expansive melodic lines through images of emotional intensity, or that describe the mystical or wondrous. It is therefore instructive to note that in other moods Howells could eschew the melisma almost altogether. 'Andy Battle' (HH 111x) from *A Garland for de la Mare*, a poem from *Peacock Pie*, is a good example. There are five pairings of notes to a single syllable in this song but no point where there is a word that Howells feels needs more extensive melodic expansion. Part of this is because of the essentially strophic nature of the setting, not that this would normally rule out a variation if Howells had felt so moved. The last verse, for instance, has these words: 'Now lean with long travail, all wasted with woe …'. In other circumstances the words 'lean', 'long travail', 'wasted' and 'woe' might all have been candidates for melismatic treatment, but not here. Instead, a slower tempo and a lengthening of the time spent on 'travail' and 'woe' are substituted for a lyrical expansion (Ex. 6.7).

'The Old Stone House' (HH 111iv), also from *Peacock Pie*, is even more syllabic than 'Andy Battle'. Here there are not even pairings of notes to a syllable. This is interesting, too, as the 'Lento, tranquillo (quasi negativo)' marking at the head of the song leans towards Howells's reflective mode and a natural expansiveness. However, there is a sense of minimalism – an approach, in fact, that might take its cue from the line 'Only a little greening where the *rain drips down*'. The feeling is of desolation and an unsettling nervousness in the eeriness of the place. Howells separates phrases as if the onlooker is listening between observations: 'Nothing on the grey roof … nothing on the brown … Nobody at the window … nobody at the door …' etc. It is an instinctive picking up of a de la Mare atmosphere.

But we can turn to another song, this time to a poem by Wilfred Wilson Gibson (1878–1962), a poet whose work Howells set a number of times, and see in *Old Meg* (HH 133) from 1923 another 'Quasi lento' setting with not a hint of a melisma. The difference surely lies in the ancient old crone who sings of her despair at having to travel alone with no man to help her pick cherries, carry her pack and, most tellingly, 'kindle her pipe' – a nice double entendre to show that no-one is too old for love. Howells's setting is remarkable partly for its economy, but mostly because the first two verses sit on a tonic pedal point (E♭) that, in the manner of another sarabande, has a constant second-beat placing in a 3/2 time signature. Even when the last verse moves to A♭ major, which Howells contrives to imply is a dominant–tonic relationship, and the A♭ becomes a new pedal point, we are fooled until the last three words of the song, and a shift to a *real* dominant seventh (with a flattened third) and a return to E♭ major, with one last second-beat placing of the bass. Above all this contrivance moves a perfectly syllabic setting, the implication of which is that the old woman is past the extravagant lyrical stage of life, the pedal points seeming to suggest by their very insistence her dogged determination to overcome her physical disabilities.

Within the limited space of this chapter these examples will have to stand representative of Howells's output of songs, but we should turn our attention also to his choral music. Howells wrote choral music throughout his life. His earliest works in the genre were written for Westminster Cathedral, where Stanford had sent him to hear 'polyphony for a penny m'boy', the price of the bus fare from South Kensington (Royal College of Music) to Victoria Street where Richard Terry was performing groundbreaking performances of Renaissance and Tudor music with his choir at the new Roman Catholic cathedral. Howells's reaction was immediate, and his *Missa sine nomine* (HH 28 – later renamed *Mass in the Dorian Mode*) was his first professionally performed work. Many other Latin motets followed, and we can trace the development of his style and his passion for polyphonic writing from these remarkable early works. Howells's devotion to early music stems from these youthful years and his 'road to Damascus conversion' moment in September 1910, when he heard Vaughan Williams's *Fantasia on a Theme by Thomas Tallis* for the first time in Gloucester Cathedral as a youth of only seventeen. The implications of Vaughan Williams's work would take a number of years to work their way into Howells's system, but he admitted that 'if I had to isolate from the rest any one impression of a purely musical sort that mattered most to me in the whole of my life as a musician, it would be the hearing of that work not knowing at all what I was going to hear but knowing what I had heard I should never forget.'[8]

Other works followed these, notably two lovely madrigal settings, *In Youth Is Pleasure* (HH 49 – 1915) and *Before Me Careless Lying* (HH 84 – 1918, and dedicated to Terry). Both these settings, though showing signs of his own developing musical personality, are still essentially reflections of the madrigal style he learned from classic composers of the genre, an offshoot of his similar experience with church music at Westminster Cathedral. It was not until remarkably late in his career that he found what was essentially his life's vocation in writing a huge canon of works for the Anglican Church (see Chapter 5).

Howells's success in this genre really comes through his atmosphere creation, his impressionistic colouring and his instinctive feel for place. The reverberant acoustic in which his choral music is ideally heard somehow has his long, soaring phrases mirroring the shape of the interplay of ribs in stone-vaulted roofs. In his article on Vaughan Williams's *Pastoral Symphony* for *Music and Letters* he wrote that the composer 'builds up a great mood, insistent to an unusual degree'.[9] This accurately describes Howells's own approach to song and choral composition, and how

---

[8] *Echoes of a Lifetime*, BBC Radio 3, compiled and presented by Robert Prizeman (1981).

[9] The passage is cited in Chapter 11, pp. 197–8.

his setting of words gives him an opportunity to create moods where he 'neither depicts nor describes' but creates an aural atmosphere in which melisma becomes an essential stylistic tool as well as a necessary means of making text fit in contrapuntal flow. Melisma, consciously chosen for appropriate textual enhancement as described earlier, becomes, in Howells's hands, a considerable force in his technical armoury. This is emphasised as much by those points – even whole songs – where the device is not used at all.

Aural atmosphere also raises issues of liturgical environment. Howells is dealing with mystery (as we saw often in the songs). He is painting pictures of a remote (that word again) but benign God whose image is shrouded and to whom we look upwards to the heavens. This music does not fit with 'horizontal' evangelical worship, where a touchy-feely God is an almost visible presence. Howells envelops us with a harmonic style rich in soft dissonance and sometimes sensual to the point of inappropriateness. But Howells talked always of 'fitness', and if his music connects with some of our most basic instincts at key points, we recognise that rush of warmth as a reflection of a deep-seated *human* response to faith. He wrote once that 'It may be that the future of English Church-and-Cathedral music is hedged with difficulties and doubts. I fear the gross threat of a "pepping-up", the cheap surrender to popularity ... these are inherent dangers. They must be countered by men of genius who from time to time shall offer the Church works of supreme fitness.'[10]

In a chapter such as this it is only possible to take a representative work to stand as typical of his approach. Much has been written about the *Collegium regale* settings and many of his other often-performed works. Howells wrote a number of settings of the *Te Deum*, and each setting is notably different in its approach, while sharing familial trademarks. The three most significant settings in this author's view are those written for St Mary Redcliffe, Bristol (HH 310); King's College, Cambridge (HH 245); and St George's Chapel, Windsor Castle (HH 269). We will therefore look at the one written in 1952 for Windsor, as it is an outstanding setting and so rarely performed.

Almost all Howells's *Te Deum* settings begin with a unison phrase. The text for this canticle is long and involved, and it is instructive to see what motivates his approach to the different forms of musical setting he uses. After the unison opening ending at 'the Father everlasting' Howells breaks the texture open for tenors and sopranos to take 'To thee all angels cry aloud', underneath the end of which altos and basses continue with the words 'the heavens and all the powers therein'. But where another composer might use this method as a means of economy, Howells repeats the words so that all parts can sing them. This, then, is another facet of his word setting that has not yet occurred in this survey – his freedom in repeating words and whole phrases. It is a feature of his choral settings that differs markedly from his songs, where word repetition is very rare. It often happens through the necessity of making words fit between vocal parts in a contrapuntal progress. Another common approach to the early pages of his *Te Deum* settings is the essentially syllabic setting

---

[10] Howells, 'The Music of Charles Wood', quoted in Palmer, *A Centenary Celebration*, 305–7 (307).

Ex. 6.8 *Te Deum* (St George's Chapel, Windsor), bars 37–46

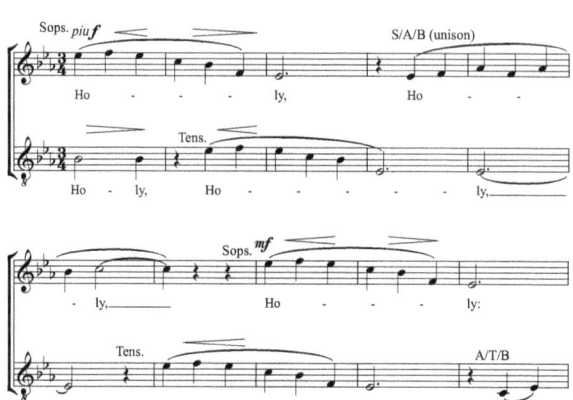

of words. Windsor also has this purposeful start, and it is not until we reach the words 'Holy, Holy, Holy' that not only do we see the expected melodic expansion but also the first contrapuntal interplay. In relation to the point about word repetition just made, this creates five 'Holy's, and the effect is, of course, to underline the ecstatic devotional characteristic of the word (Ex. 6.8).

In fact, this is the only one of Howells's settings of these words that is treated like this, with all the others either still being in unison (like *Collegium regale*) or having three separate and comparatively simple statements. But moving on we discover that this first melismatic display is only a preparation for the shorter but more melodically powerful phrase for 'Heaven and earth are full of the majesty of thy glory'. Only the word 'Heaven' is treated melismatically; but where the phrase in Ex. 6.7 moves only by step upwards at its start, the word 'Heaven' is given a rising minor third, a classic method of raising vocal intensity (Ex. 6.9).

A list follows of all the groups of devout people who praise God. This is dealt with in a new 'Un poco più moto' section by giving each a different vocal grouping: tenors and basses for the 'glorious company of Apostles', sopranos for the 'fellowship of Prophets', canonically treated basses and sopranos for the 'noble army of Martyrs' and tutti for 'The holy Church throughout all the world'. Throughout this section, the word 'praise' has been melismatically treated making it the focal point of each phrase. This is very similar to Howells's approach in both the Bristol and Cambridge settings, where it is singled out in an expansive (ecstatic) gesture.

With the exception of predictable melismas on the words 'infinite' and 'everlasting' (as much word painting as ecstatic), the next section is almost entirely syllabic. There is a hushed awe for the bass solo at 'When thou took'st upon thee to deliver man', and the low voices sing of the 'sharpness of death' leading to the dark unison phrase 'We believe that thou shalt come to be our judge'. What follows is, in this writer's view, one of Howells's most beautiful choral creations. The 'più tranquillo' section at 'We therefore pray thee help thy servants' is also strongly reminiscent of Howells's approach to this kind of passage in the opening pages of *The House of the*

Ex. 6.9 *Te Deum* (St George's Chapel, Windsor), bars 52–6

Ex. 6.10 *Te Deum* (St George's Chapel, Windsor), bars 161–5

Mind (HH 274).[11] If any passage could be singled out to stand for Howells's unique approach to choral word setting which so moved Dean Milner-White it would be this (not uniquely, of course, but especially representative); and it is partly the melisma that, although we might not realise it in casual listening, gives the passage its extraordinary emotional power. The corresponding passages in the Bristol and Cambridge settings are also notable and powerfully emotive. These words seem to have made a real impression on Howells and each is clearly different from the other. Where Windsor's is so distinctive is in its apparent suspension of time, which is partly achieved by lengthy pedal points while the voices interact above.

The passage begins innocuously but simply, with the organ setting up a chord of F major, which moves from F to an E♭ in its top part over which the upper three choral parts begin a contrary-motion syllabic phrase. All this over a long pedal point. The basses join when the tenors reach a middle C and descend the scale to a low C. The phrase ends with the F major seventh chord, which the organ had set up for them. The next phrase ('whom thou hast redeemed with thy precious blood') is equally simple and syllabic. But now Howells begins to prepare the ground for the major melismas to come but uses long notes tied over bar lines to give singers expressive lines in the phrase 'Make them to be numbered with thy Saints' (Ex. 6.10). This leads naturally to the words 'glory everlasting', which take on the tied-over note characteristics of Ex. 6.10 but now expand them into glowing melismas in one of the most magical linear and harmonic wind-downs of his output. All this sits on another much longer pedal point on E♭. A few bars serve to show the interplay of vocal parts (Ex. 6.11).

Was there ever a more generous interplay of vocal lines than here? Certain features add to the emotional intensity and expression of spiritual ecstasy of this

---

[11] Motet for chorus and organ (also scored for strings) to words by Joseph Beaumont, composed in October 1954.

Ex. 6.11 *Te Deum* (St George's Chapel, Windsor), bars 164–73

passage: the long lines against crotchet movement; the rising thirds (noted elsewhere) in vocal lines, as in the tenors in bar 4, the sopranos in bars 4–5, the altos in bar 5 and, most expressively of all, the tenors in bar 8 leading up to their tied-over A♭; and, also previously noted, the tied notes everywhere, which create expressive tension as they move into the next strong beat of their line. No other composer writes quite like this, or with such an instinctive feeling for the pure musicality of the experience and knowledge of what a singer will find emotionally powerful to express. It is this ability to give *every* part a singing line in the truest contrapuntal sense that underscores Howells's genius in this genre. And it is here where the solo song meets the choral music. Howells once said 'I have composed out of sheer love of trying to make nice sounds',[12] and nowhere is this more apparent than here.

Howells was a remarkable composer with a real flair for word setting. Partly because of his love of melisma, the expansive lyrical gesture, his music is often challenging to sing but ultimately rewarding. The depth of his feeling for words, his real understanding of shape and structure, his instinctive musicianship and his deeply embedded sensuality – as much harmonic as melodic – all contribute to the creation of a style that draws people into a mystical world of half lights and shade, of the other side of the looking-glass. In this the melisma in all its forms and implications has a major role to play in Howells's armoury of techniques, as we have seen. It is a remarkable legacy.

[12] Prizeman, *Echoes of a Lifetime*.

PART III

Howells the Instrumental Composer

CHAPTER 7

'From "Merry-Eye" to Paradise': The Early Orchestral Music of Herbert Howells

Lewis Foreman

MANY years ago, in the 1960s, when even Howells's chamber music was little known, the present author attended a rehearsal of the Piano Quartet (HH 66), which bears the dedication 'To the Hill at Chosen and to Ivor Gurney who knows it'. The music was unfamiliar to the performers, and the pianist read this dedication out to his colleagues and they all smirked in a condescending way before going on to play the music quite beautifully. Certainly there was a time when such an association by a composer would not be treated seriously, yet landscape had a profound impression on Howells's early music and we need to consider quite what he meant by such statements in respect of these evocative scores. Writing to his brother in 1922 he asserted that he could translate a feature of landscape 'into musical terms, and be so expressed'.[1] In an article on Howells in 1920 the critic Edwin Evans wrote about his music: 'the Gloucestershire countryside is a better school than any academy', finding a 'sense of open-airishness combined with a feeling for distance that engenders a strain of mysticism'.[2]

Howells himself evoked the country of the River Severn in several works. It was his friend Ivor Gurney who, writing to Howells during the First World War, asked him to 'Show us Tintern and sunset across the Malvern and Welsh Hills. Make us see the one evening star among the trees.' 'What', Gurney asked, 'of the Forest of Dean Symphony? What of the opening pages of the sight from Newnham-on-Severn looking across the valley to the hills. An A major beginning surely.'[3]

Howells's pre-September 1935 orchestral works are a diverse corpus of pieces: two piano concertos (HH 31 – 1914; HH 152 – 1925); three suites (for orchestra (HH 42 – 1914); for violin and orchestra (HH 48 – 1915; and for string orchestra (HH 80 – 1917)); a short ballet (HH 193 – 1933); a cantata (HH 77 – 1917); a set of orchestral songs (HH 172 – 1928); three longer pieces of sundry kinds (HH 70 – 1917; HH 134 – 1923; HH 159 – 1925); three miniatures (HH 83 – 1919/20; HH 125 – 1920/22); and a work for large orchestra, soloists and chorus that defies normal generic categories (HH 126 – 1922). Discussion of these works can most sensibly be done in chronological order.

Howells's Piano Concerto in C minor, Op. 4 (HH 31), to become the first of two, was a remarkable achievement for a twenty-year-old composer, a composer who had barely started his studies at the Royal College of Music (RCM). Howells's piano concertos are discussed in detail in Chapter 10, yet here we need briefly to note it and its successor in the 1920s, as they frame our discussion of the early orchestral

---

[1] Howells to his brother Leonard, 19 January 1917, quoted in Palmer, *A Centenary Celebration*, 49.
[2] Evans, 'Herbert Howells', 89.
[3] Foreman, *From Parry to Britten*, 90.

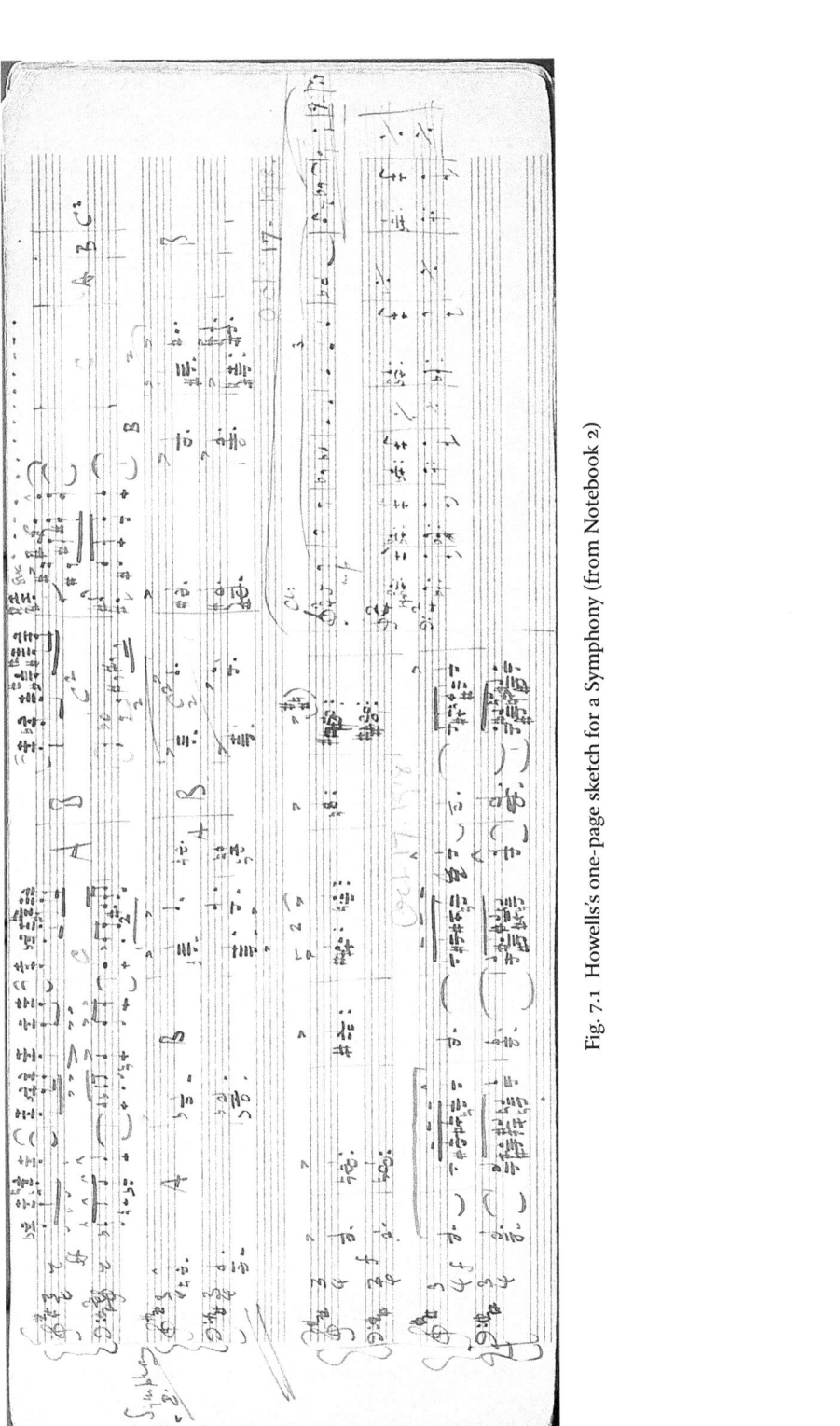

Fig. 7.1 Howells's one-page sketch for a Symphony (from Notebook 2)

music. With little history of composition on such a scale, Howells had produced a three-movement concerto playing nearly forty minutes. It was first performed at a Patron's Fund Concert at Queen's Hall on Friday 10 July 1914, with Howells's college friend, an equally young Arthur Benjamin, as soloist, and Stanford conducting.[4] It was not heard again in Howells's lifetime – the First World War intervened, Howells moved on stylistically, and for many years the score was said to be lost. Howells was reported as saying it was 'unduly pompous'.[5]

So, Howells was already an individual voice of striking personal vision and remarkable technical command, even if in his early work he reflected the influences of the time. In this brief pre-First World War period – what Arnold Bax referred to as 'that sinister carnival time, the London summer of 1914'[6] – Howells benefited as much as any musicians on the London scene. Not least of this was the music of the Diaghilev Ballet. We need to remember the impact the composers of the Diaghilev Ballet had on the music of Howells and his contemporaries; Howells was not alone in being dazzled by Stravinsky's treatment of the orchestra in works such as *Petrushka*, first seen in London on 4 February 1913. This can particularly be heard in Howells's Suite *The Bs* (HH 42), where responsibility for his fascination with orchestral piano in three of the five movements may be laid at Stravinsky's door. And yet here in many ways we might consider Howells to have already found a personal voice.

Howells's Suite *The Bs* (or *The Bees*, as one page of the manuscript would have it) is a remarkable achievement, for in it Howells finds much of his early mature orchestral language. It celebrates his friends at the RCM in the weeks immediately after war was declared in 1914.[7] This circle of talented young musicians included Arthur Benjamin ('Benjee'), Arthur Bliss ('Blissy'), Ivor Gurney ('Bartholomew'), Francis Warren ('Bunny') and Howells himself ('Bublum'). To them, by their nicknames, Howells dedicated the music 'with my love'. *The Bs* was heard in a student concert at the RCM in June 1915, but had to wait for a public performance until Dan Godfrey produced it with the Bournemouth Municipal Orchestra on 13 February 1919.[8] That same year the Diaghilev Ballet season at the Alhambra between 30 April and 22 July announced a 'Suite' by Howells as a 'symphonic interlude'. It was presumably the same suite, though when the present author asked Howells himself about it around 1980 he said he could not remember.[9] It seems highly probable that single movements were played on different occasions, and certainly at Bournemouth in

---

[4] Sir Arthur Bliss said 'badly conducted by Stanford'; Palmer, *A Centenary Celebration*, 373–4.

[5] Spicer, *Herbert Howells*, 37.

[6] Bax, *Farewell, My Youth*, 94.

[7] The manuscript is dated 'Oct–Nov 1914'.

[8] The programme note for the Bournemouth performance gives the second and third movements reversed, running in the sequence: Scherzo ('Blissy') – Lament ('Bartholomew').

[9] Since then Christopher Palmer has published Howells's 1919 notes on his own music, in which the composer writes: 'It is also being played at the Alhambra during the Russian season this summer'; Palmer, *A Centenary Celebration*, 71.

April 1923 the Scherzo ('Blissy') appeared on its own, while the movement for Bunny Warren, the only one of the group to die in the trenches, became a memorial piece. The overriding impression of this music is of Howells's astonishing self-confidence and sureness of touch in handling the orchestra in only his second orchestral work.

Howells's extended overture to this suite could well stand on its own. It presents an exuberant self-portrait, marked in the composer's words by 'the love of narrative and the sounds of wayside fairs' (Fig. 7.2).

Howells's second movement, 'Lament', his portrait of his great friend Ivor Gurney ('Bartholomew'), who of course also hailed from Gloucestershire, reflects Gurney's 'remoteness of mind and fascination of folk-lore'. Poet and composer, Gurney's creative life was short-lived, and after being gassed during the war he spent his last fifteen years in a mental institution. But when Howells wrote this affectionate portrait all that was in the future, and Gurney was a significant musical talent and a great admirer of Howells. Here Edwin Evans's remark about a 'sense of open-airishness combined with a feeling for distance' immediately comes to mind, Howells writing music of involving atmosphere that rises to a passionate and sustained climax.

'Blissy' is a brief Scherzo running less than three minutes. Howells's music perhaps conveys Bliss's impulsive energies more closely than the other portraits, with its mercurial, almost Mendelssohnian vivacity with sudden good-humoured outbursts and changes of direction (Ex. 7.1).

The elegiac fourth movement – well, perhaps not as elegiac as the Ivor Gurney piece – celebrates the only unknown name among the group, and in a strangely prophetic way. Howells's friend 'Bunny' was Francis Purcell Warren, reputedly a brilliant viola player, though destined to die at Mons. His name appears third from the foot of the RCM war memorial in the lobby of the college. Howells appears to have been very close to 'Bunny' Warren, and his death cut deep, the composer later commemorating him in his grieving, emotional *Elegy* for viola, string quartet and string orchestra (HH 70) first heard at the Mons Memorial Concert on 17 December 1917. Howells describes his four-minute portrait as a 'Mazurka alias Minuet'. While they might both be taken as indications for the metre used, here, amid classic Howells 'open air' music suggestive of country dancing, the alternation of woodwind and strings and the orchestral spacing tell us he had already found the idiom later to be made popular by 'Puck's Minuet' (HH 83i) and 'Merry-Eye' (HH 83ii). The short movement starts and ends with an elegiac feel – and it is hard to resist the temptation of finding in it an anticipation of a tragedy to come.

Finally we have 'Benjee', Arthur Benjamin, brilliant pianist and composer, recently arrived from Australia and already the soloist in Howells's First Piano Concerto. Benjamin, a wartime aviator, was shot down and became a prisoner of war.[10] A certain brashness is perhaps suggested in Howells's extrovert processional[11] evoking his friend. In the closing pages the two principal themes signalling Howells himself return from the opening movement, and we end with the composer seemingly

---

[10] Benjamin's First Violin Sonata was written in a German prisoner-of-war camp and significantly is not mentioned in Howells's article 'Arthur Benjamin' in *Cobbett's Cyclopaedic Survey of Chamber Music*.

[11] The programme note for the Bournemouth performance in February 1919 said: 'one seems to be marched through the quaint pandemonium of the fair again'.

122   *The Music of Herbert Howells*

Fig. 7.2 'Overture (to Bublum)', *The Bs*, Suite for Orchestra, Op. 13

unable to tear himself away from his friends. Much later, in 1948, Howells revisited the 'Bunny' and 'Blissy' movements as 'Corydon's Dance' and 'Scherzo in Arden' in *Music for a Prince* (HH 255).

Howells wrote his *Three Dances* for violin and orchestra (HH 48) for another college contemporary, George Whittaker, completing them in January 1915. They

Ex. 7.1 'Scherzo (to Blissy); *The Bs*, Suite for Orchestra, Op. 13

were first performed in a student concert soon afterwards, but were then forgotten until revived by Erich Gruenberg in a BBC broadcast in 1989. Whittaker was only thirteen when he first played this music. Although, like *The Bs*, the piece was written during wartime, Howells had clearly not yet been touched by tragedy when he wrote this serene music, and in the slow movement, 'Quasi lento, quieto', his glorious wide-spanning melodic line is worthy to be set beside such verdant evocations as Vaughan Williams's *The Lark Ascending*[12] and Julius Harrison's *Bredon Hill*, both of which postdate it. At this date the two earlier models of which Howells might have been aware were Mackenzie's *Benedictus* and Battison Haynes's *Romance* for violin and orchestra. Here Howells is touched with the untroubled 'Peace of Eden', a mood he never completely regains, before the brief virtuosic finale.

The Suite for String Orchestra of 1917 (HH 80), or rather for string quartet and strings, was never established as a coherent work but was plundered for its first two movements. The finale, 'Serenade', was only launched as an independent work in the 1990s, when Christopher Palmer found he needed a short filler to complete a Howells CD programme for Chandos and Richard Hickox in 1993. Written in Gloucestershire, the opening Prelude is dated 21 May 1917 and later reappears as the first movement of the Concerto for String Orchestra of 1938 (HH 215). The other movements followed quickly, the central 'Elegy' dated at Lydney on 24 May 1917 and the finale at Lydney in June of the same year. The whole thing was clearly conceived and written very quickly. The finale, 'Serenade for Strings', running around four and a half minutes, could well find a place in a light music programme, but our main interest is the heartfelt 'Elegy', apparently written in just four days, which when revised as the *Elegy* for viola, string quartet and strings, Op. 15, became his memorial to his friend 'Bunny Warren', dead at the Battle of Mons, and it featured in the Mons Memorial Concert at the Royal Albert Hall on 17 December 1917 when the London Symphony Orchestra was conducted by Sir Hugh Allen.

In this music for string orchestra Howells is in thrall to two great models of the time – Vaughan Williams's *Fantasia on a Theme by Thomas Tallis* and Elgar's

---

[12] Vaughan Williams's *The Lark Ascending* was actually written in 1914, but it was not orchestrated until 1920, and the orchestral version was not heard in London until June 1921.

Introduction and Allegro, both written for string quartet and tutti strings. In the *Elegy* we might feel Howells is making tribute to *Tallis*, though it is worth remembering that in this he was not alone and, for example, a year before, Howells would probably have heard F. S. Kelly's *Elegy for Rupert Brooke* for harp and strings, which is similarly influenced in a much more superficially obvious way. The Australian composer and pianist Kelly, who had been at Rupert Brooke's burial on the Greek Island of Skyros, had himself died on the Somme in November 1916. As we listen to the sustained solo writing for the viola in Howells's moving score with its lack of real contrast, one has to wonder to what extent Howells is evoking his friend through that instrument's contribution (Ex. 7.2).

Howells's music was not much recorded during his early career, but competing recordings of the *Elegy* were made immediately before the Second World War by the two leading British string orchestras of the day, the Boyd Neel String Orchestra and the Jacques String Orchestra, reviewed in the *Gramophone* for August and November 1939. The first to appear was the Jacques recording,[13] when a reviewer wrote:

> Herbert Howells is a quiet and retiring figure in English music and writes very little. But what he does write is of beautiful quality ... This *Elegy* ... is the expression of a single mood and no conventional contrast is provided. That mood is stated by the elegiac theme given out by the cello at the start and worked up to a sonorous and passionate climax ... Thus a true contrast is made within the one mood.[14]

Almost immediately the second version came out.[15]

'Puck's Minuet', Op. 20, no. 1, is dated November 1917. It was commissioned by Herbert Brewer and is dedicated to his daughter, Eileen. Howells tells us it was written in the waiting room at Reading station during a three-hour wait for a train to Gloucester.[16] It must have been vividly imagined because Howells tells us it went straight into full score, and indeed was published (by Goodwin and Tabb) before it was performed. The score was seen by Hamilton Harty and first performed by him at Queen's Hall on 4 March 1919 with the London Symphony Orchestra. Howells describes his forces as a 'small orchestra', and he writes for an ensemble without horns or heavy brass, but with orchestral piano. Although illness kept him from the hall, Howells tells us it was encored.[17] Probably because it was published and easily available it was widely played[18] and became a popular work of the time, for

---

[13] Herbert Howells, *Elegy for Strings*, Jacques String Orchestra, audio recording (Columbia, 1939), DX 922.

[14] *Gramophone* (August 1939), 17.

[15] Herbert Howells, *Elegy for Strings*, Max Gilbert (viola) and the Boyd Neel String Orchestra, audio recording (Decca, 1939), M 484/5.

[16] Palmer, *A Centenary Celebration*, 437. Elsewhere he said '... a single sitting of about four hours in the reading and reference room of Reading Public Library'; Palmer, *Herbert Howells: A Study*, 17.

[17] Ibid., 71.

[18] The pattern of repeated performances of orchestral works from the late nineteenth century to the 1930s was frequently driven by the practice at that time of having

Ex. 7.2 *Elegy*, Op. 15, opening viola line

example being performed four times at Bournemouth in the space of four years.[19] Even more, it became a favourite of Sir Henry Wood who programmed it at the Proms on eight occasions.[20]

'Puck's Minuet' and the later *Procession* (HH 125) were played consecutively at a promenade concert at Queen's Hall on 25 August 1932, when Howells contributed a totally different note that is also worth quoting:

> This Minuet – one of two pieces for small orchestra – was composed in October, 1917, and was designed expressly for the Gloucestershire Orchestral Society. Though written to an imaginary scene, it little matters what particular 'picture' is in the listener's mind, so long as there *be* a picture. It would seem, however, that airy Puck takes strange and ill-assorted companions for the dance – perhaps a Falstaff among them? It is scored for two flutes, two clarinets, a bass clarinet, a piano (used as an orchestral instrument), three separate violins, the usual strings, timpani, bass drum and triangle. Most of these instruments dance in the keys of B minor or D or C major – save the triangle and bass drum, whose privilege it ever is to dance or play in several keys at once.[21]

It was the only orchestral work by Howells to be recorded at the time, when Julian Clifford conducted it on one side of a twelve-inch seventy-eight[22] and the

> score *and* parts on sale, purchase giving the right of performance in perpetuity to the owner – thus works at that time that were on hire frequently failed to find repeated performance because it would be cheaper and easier to play those already held. Howells both suffered and benefited from this.

[19] 19 October 1922; 2 April 1923; 4 May 1924; 2 December 1926.
[20] 1919, 1920, 1924, 1925, 1927, 1930, 1932, 1943.
[21] Palmer, *A Centenary Celebration*, 436.
[22] Herbert Howells, 'Puck's Minuet', Julian Clifford (conductor), audio recording (Decca, 1932), K 522.

Gramophone critic found it 'one of the prettiest, most charming pieces for small orchestra',[23] which seems to summarise the view of Howells's admirers of the time.

The second piece for small orchestra was 'Merry-Eye', dating from 1920. Double the length of 'Puck's Minuet', it was written in August 1920 for Sir Henry Wood and the Proms, and was first performed at Queen's Hall on 20 September 1920 with the composer conducting. The composer contributed an ambiguous and unspecific note about 'Merry-Eye' for the programme at the first performance. He wrote:

> This piece has not necessarily a programme, but if an idea of such be entertained, it can be supposed that the listener meets with an average-type character out of the domain of folklore – called Merry-Eye – who reveals more about himself and his personality than folklore itself ever tells of him or his kind. Much that he relates is true to his name and to such part of his history as is common reading-public property; much else, on the other hand, contradicts this. Merry-Eye's name is – like most titles – only half suggestive of youth.[24]

Was he thinking of some character remembered from the Gloucestershire byways of his youth? It underlines the curious fact that Howells's early orchestral music – and indeed his chamber music – was, in fact, a hymn to Gloucestershire. In these colourful scores he is celebrating the country of his boyhood, and, indeed, the countryside, before the onset of the changes brought by the development of the motor car. Howells celebrates the spirit of place.

Howells tells us that 'I spent the greater part of my honeymoon writing *Merry-Eye*, because when my newly-wedded wife and I stepped on the train I opened my *Times* only to be reminded of the fact that I'd promised Sir Henry Wood an orchestral piece for that season of Summer Proms ... which left me about three weeks.'[25] This is a splendid story (Eric Fenby later told a similar one about his overture *Rossini on Ilkla Moor*) but surely to be taken with a pinch of salt – Howells rationalising that he had allowed himself to be so committed on his honeymoon!

The ballad cantata *Sir Patrick Spens* (HH 77), for baritone, chorus and orchestra, was first sketched in 1916 with string quartet accompaniment and was written in its final form in 1917–18. This was not the first choral setting of this well-known Scottish traditional ballad. In Victorian times there had been versions by Robert Lucas Pearsall, Arthur Murray Goodhart and W. Augustus Barratt. Howells probably knew the 1907 setting by his old teacher Herbert Brewer at Gloucester Cathedral, which had been performed at the Gloucester Three Choirs Festival in 1913. Curiously, at much the same time that Howells produced his version the Scottish composer David Stephen (1869–1946) set the text, published in Dunfermline in 1922.

It was Howells's first great compositional disappointment, for it failed to achieve performance, and despite the publication of the vocal score in 1928, it only achieved a single performance in his lifetime, in Newcastle, in 1930. The printed vocal score indicates that the option of performance with smaller forces ('strings, some wood

---

[23] *Gramophone* (July 1930), 20.
[24] Promenade concert programme, Queen's Hall, 30 September 1920.
[25] Palmer, *Herbert Howells: Study*, 17.

wind, three or four brass instruments and piano') might be followed, very much in emulation of Vaughan Williams's practice of cueing his choral works for smaller forces, but even so, no performance came. In fact the difficulty of the choral writing undoubtedly stood in its way. Howells had taken Stanford's *Revenge* as his model, but there the choral writing is constantly diatonic and tuneful, and fairly easy for a local choral society to master. This is not true of Howells's choral writing, and the present writer can report that several times in the 1970s and 1980s he tried to get this work revived, only to face refusal when one choral director after another actually saw the music. Indeed, the conductor of the first (and for long, only) performance, W. G. Whittaker, wrote of this in the programme note for the first performance: 'uncompromisingly modern, bristling with difficulties for the singers, which are almost as forbidding as the seas of which they sing'.[26] Yet curiously Howells said his intention was communication:

> I wanted to set *Sir Patrick* with the best possible attempt at this essential swiftness of action; obviously 'folk-y' music was the best possibility. All my tunes therefore have the directness of simple folk-tunes; the choral technique is founded on the need for swift action; there is no word repetition, and very little suggestion of anything approaching a contrapuntal treatment. The voices are concerned with directness and speed in conveying the narrative; the vividness and suggestions of more purely musical sorts are left to be conveyed by the orchestra.[27]

Howells tells us he intended his tunes to have the directness of folk-tunes, but in fact they are all original. He went on to say:

> For Sir Patrick – and to suit my intentions therein – one might almost have used a dozen or so of *actual* folk-song tunes, and have stated them with considerable downright baldness. But where only instruments are concerned, I loathe the folk-song pot-pourri sort of thing, where a given tune (a folk tune) is stated in entirety and then expatiated upon.[28]

Now that it has been recorded by a top-line team,[29] the power and effectiveness of the music can be heard by all with an interest.

From the point of view of our discussion of Howells's orchestral music, here we have a work quite notable for its orchestration. The setting for the orchestra is boldly conceived with virtuosic writing across the spectrum. As Edwin Evans wrote at the time, it is 'perhaps the most forceful work he has written, and it proves that although primarily a lyricist, he is quite alive to the fact that a robust subject is suitable material for lyrical treatment'.[30]

---

[26] Newcastle-upon-Tyne, 1 February 1930, quoted in Hodgson, 'The Music of Herbert Howells', 95
[27] Eggar, 'An English Composer', 129.
[28] Ibid.
[29] Herbert Howells, *Sir Patrick Spens*, Roderick Williams (baritone), The Bach Choir, Bournemouth Symphony Orchestra, David Hill (conductor), audio CD (Naxos, 2007), 8.570352.
[30] Evans, 'Herbert Howells', 87.

The structure of the cantata is underpinned by the orchestra. For such a piece written so soon after *A Sea Symphony*, we might expect Howells to be influenced by Vaughan Williams's remarkable achievement, and of course there are moments where Howells cannot hide that model. But overall it is notable for its independence of treatment.[31] The score is in two parts, separated by a pause and an evocative orchestral interlude. The first part presents a rumbustious seascape, telling the story of Sir Patrick Spens's disastrous mission to Norway to fetch the King of Norway's daughter, despite its being an unwise time of year to sail. The sweeping, onward-running triplets of the opening bars, over which the brass punch out the heroic motif in octaves, are confidently done and remarkably sustained (Ex. 7.3).

After succeeding at the first Carnegie Publication competition with his Piano Quartet, Howells submitted *Sir Patrick Spens* to the next competition but failed to be recommended for publication. In fact he came pretty close. His score was assessed by Donald Francis Tovey, Sir Granville Bantock and Hugh Allen, and while not recommended for publication it was adjudicated 'Class B' ('works important enough to merit serious consideration'). The manuscript was returned to the composer on 9 May 1919. Tovey set the tone when he wrote:

> A very remarkable work; but, in my opinion, a mistake. The question is, what is our duty towards mistakes on such a plane. I don't happen to believe in this method of setting a ballad: it's very interesting to young composers to devote their powers of illustration to the opportunities afforded by the way in which a primitive ballad describes regularly one incident in each story – but the larger the scale & the more elaborately the illustration is done the weaker the total impression becomes; & the whole resulting art-form is a debilitating experience for the composer. This man would, I am sure from what we have seen of his nobility of style both here and elsewhere, have produced a much greater (because timely) setting of this very ballad if he had made up his mind to supersede De Pearsall [i.e. Robert Lucas Pearsall (1795–1856)] with it as an unaccompanied chorus. At present it is little more than a 20th century Stanford's *Revenge* (a work for which I have considerable respect bien entendu) handicapped by many fidgety rhythmic difficulties for the chorus.[32]

Procession (HH 125) has some of the orchestral brio of *Sir Patrick Spens* and was first written in 1920 as a piano piece, and dedicated to Arthur Benjamin. It was subsequently scored for the Proms, the orchestration completed on 9 July 1922. Interviewed by the composer and journalist Katharine Eggar, Howells is quoted as saying:

> A composer has to do something to let off steam sometimes. One gets up in the morning with something going on in one's head – it isn't the work one ought to be doing, but it wants to be attended to. So one lets it off on the

---

[31] When, a dozen years on, George Dyson quotes *A Sea Symphony* in the orchestral accompaniment to 'The Knight' in his *Canterbury Pilgrims* he is, of course, doing so deliberately.

[32] Scottish Record Office, GD 281/41/57.

Ex. 7.3 *Sir Patrick Spens*, opening bars

piano, because that's the easiest way. It's rather dangerous for us, perhaps, but we do it.[33]

Critics compared *Procession* to Ravel's *Bolero*, even though it is very much shorter. The critic for *The Times*, reviewing the 1922 Prom performance, wrote:

> Mr Howells's idea has been to take a single theme and subject it to a treatment which, while not destroying its shape, develops it to a big orchestral climax. He trusts chiefly to the instrumental colouring to maintain the interest. The result is certainly a happy one, and it is principally due to the fact that the theme itself is quaint and full of character ... Mr Howells uses a large orchestra, calling in the aid of organ and pianoforte, and everything is used with surety and a good deal of originality of effect. We hope to hear it again.[34]

Like 'Puck's Minuet' it was taken up by Sir Henry Wood, who programmed it on six occasions in the 1930s, and altogether it has had eleven Proms performances.[35] Here Howells asks for large forces including triple wind (comprising all the extras: piccolo, cor anglais, bass clarinet, contrabassoon, and two cornets as well as two trumpets). Again he asks for orchestral piano with harp and adds the organ at the climax. Howells tells us that his inspiration came from a dream: the inexorable tread of marching feet as a crowd approaches from a distance and recedes. (Elgar would later adopt a similar shape in 'The Wagon Passes' in the *Nursery Suite*.) Christopher Palmer tells us the place was a Russian city, Howells perhaps again influenced by *Petrushka*.

When the Diaghilev Ballet opened at the Alhambra in 1919 the programme listed a large number of composers of 'symphonic interludes' to be played between the ballets (Fig. 7.3). Among young British composers was Howells, and in that cosmopolitan atmosphere he certainly learned a trick or two. As the relentless repeated motif of *Procession*, with its modal flavour, grows ever louder (Ex. 7.4), the orchestration, in the use of orchestral piano, with harp and xylophone colouration surely reflects his excitement with the then new.

The climax of Howells's early orchestral music comes in the visionary textures and ecstatic counterpoint of *Sine nomine* (HH 126), his response to a commission

---

[33] Eggar, 'An English Composer', 130.
[34] *The Times* (30 August 1922), 10.
[35] 1922, 1924, 1931, 1932, 1934, 1935, 1936, 1937, 1943, 1944, 1946.

Fig. 7.3 Facsimile of the Diaghilev Ballet prospectus

for Gloucester Cathedral and set very much in its time by its use of wordless voices, both solo and choral, treated as part of the orchestra. The 1920s saw various British composers use such vocalise to underline ecstatic moments of visionary power or emotional penetration, probably inspired by Debussy in 'Sirènes' and Ravel in *Daphnis et Chloë*, then still very new. For Howells the example of Holst's

Symphonic Interludes

1.	*" Jota Aragonesa "	Glinka
2.	*" Baba-Yaga "	Dargomijsky
3.	*Finnish Fantasia	Dargomijsky
4.	*Islamey (orchestrated by Alfredo Casella)	Balakireff
5.	*" Russia " (symphonic poem)	Balakireff
6.	Overture on Russian Themes	Balakireff
7.	*Unfinished Symphony (two movements)	Borodin
8.	*Finale of " Mlada "	Borodin
9.	*Scherzo	Borodin
10.	*Overture " The Fair at Sorotchinsk "	Moussorgsky
11.	*Scherzo in B	Moussorgsky
12.	*Intermezzo in C	Moussorgsky
13.	*" A Fairy Tale "	Rimsky-Korsakoff
14.	*Chanson Russe	Rimsky-Korsakoff
15.	Overture on Russian Themes	Rimsky-Korsakoff
16.	*Suite " The Maid of Pskoff "	Rimsky-Korsakoff
17.	Overture Solennelle (on Russian Themes)	Liapounoff
18.	*Mazurka " Près de la Guinguette "	Liadoff
19.	" Stenka Razin " symphonic poem	Glazounoff
20.	*Fête Villageoise	Zolotareff
21.	*Scherzo (from symphony)	Stravinsky
22.	*Clair de Lune (orchestrated by Eugene Goossens)	Debussy
23.	*Le Rouet	Ravel
24.	*Alborada del Gracioso	Ravel
25.	*La Peri	Dukas
26.	*Rhapsody-Valse	Florent Schmitt
27.	*Danse Désuète	Florent Schmitt
28.	*Suite " Le Festin de l'Araignée "	Albert Roussel
29.	*" La Ville Rose "	Albert Roussel
30.	*" Fête des Vendanges "	Déodat de Séverac
31.	*Gymnopédies (orchestrated by Claude Debussy)	Erik Satie
32.	*" Course aux flambeaux "	Roger-Ducasse
33.	Suite Brève	Louis Aubert
34.	*Triana (orchestrated by Arbos)	Albeniz
35.	*El Puerto („ „ „)	Albeniz
36.	*" Nocturnes," symphonic poem for piano and orchestra, *played by the composer*, M. de Falla
37.	*Russian Suite	Arnold Bax
38.	*" Four Conceits "	Eugene Goossens
39.	*Suite	Herbert Howells
40.	Three Pieces (Chinoiserie, Valse Sentimentale and Kosatchoque)	Lord Berners

First Performance in London.

The Russian works performed by arrangement with Messrs. J. & W. Chester, 11, Great Marlborough Street, W. 1.

2

Fig. 7.3 continued

Planets, Vaughan Williams's *Pastoral Symphony* and Delius's *Song of the High Hills* must have been even more powerful, while his contemporary Arthur Bliss (in his *Rhapsody*; early, lost piano concerto; and *Rout*) gave it a more domestic scale. Soon Vaughan Williams (in *Flos campi*) and Bax (in *Walsinghame*) would also adopt a similar palette.

Ex. 7.4 *Procession*, Op. 36, climax

In the polyphonic period composers of Masses named their music after the idea they took as the cantus firmus. So *Sine nomine* ('without name') denoted a Mass based upon an original rather than a borrowed theme. Howells called his *Mass in the Dorian Mode*, his first major work composed before he went to the RCM, the *Missa sine nomine*' (HH 28). *Sine nomine*, subtitled *A Phantasy*, for soprano and tenor soli, chorus, organ and orchestra, was composed for the 1922 Gloucester Three Choirs Festival. Possibly the title refers to the plainsong-like theme that is the music's principal motif. It was first performed on 5 September 1922 in Gloucester Cathedral as a curtain raiser to Mendelssohn's *Elijah* and was not well received. It was seen as a difficult new work by such a traditional Three Choirs audience to a morning concert starting at 11 a.m. Howells himself conducted. It was not heard again until it was revived at Gloucester on 25 August 1992, at that year's Three Choirs Festival. It was a particularly undeserved seventy-year silence, for now that we can assess it from performance not only is it is clearly revealed as the high point of his earlier music, but it also looks forward to *Hymnus paradisi* (HH 220). It is helpful being able to write about this music after hearing two contrasted live performances and a recording. We know from the composer himself that one of the great influences on him was being present at the first performance of Vaughan Williams's *Tallis Fantasia* in 1910. In 1992, here we were back in that same cathedral acoustic for the revival of *Sine nomine*, a work written specially for it.

The orchestra creates an impressionistic web of sound in which the soloists vocalise in a kind of reverie, their melisma perfectly judged to create an increasingly ecstatic mood; powerful climaxes are built, and the choir, also vocalising, provide a radiant coda. Howells did not intend words to be set to his vocal lines but at the first performance, as 'a last-minute imposition, a suggestion of Plunket Greene's',[36] a Latin text was added. Modern performances have adopted Howells's original intention, which clearly is preferable. The first vocal score of the Howells was of the choral ending (the last sixteen bars) published by Goodwin and Tabb in 1922. Its revival has been underpinned by the piano reduction of the whole work by Paul Spicer, published by Novello for the performance in 1992.

Is the composer still in the shadow of Vaughan Williams? Although there may be occasional sounds reminiscent of the more impassioned flights of the *Pastoral Symphony*, to this commentator at least, Howells has already moved on. It must

---

[36] Palmer, *A Centenary Celebration*, 418.

have seemed startlingly up to date in 1922. In one movement it has a ternary feel to it – a slow reverie that Howells said 'savours of Plainsong', leading to a middle section 'essentially rhythmic and strenuous' that rises to a passionate climax and is followed by a quiet closing section 'almost to a degree of remoteness'[37] – with the character of an epilogue. The impact of the music is of an orchestral work – with glorious extended passages without the voices. After the first orchestral climax, soaring writing for a solo violin reveals what a Howells Violin Concerto might have been like (far different from the enjoyable but untypical *Three Dances* of 1915).

The return of the solo voices in unison was very well done at Gloucester, and at the climax of the second long orchestral passage the organ reinforced the texture with spine-tingling grandeur before soloists, choir and finally orchestra faded out in a twilight close. I timed it at 13' 49 " (later Douglas Bostock's recording ran at 14' 44").[38]

One recounts these memories of performance because of the importance in this work of the sound and balance, especially of the solo voices. It is an issue, in remarkably similar writing and also for soprano and tenor soli, which we have also to consider when listening to the later masterpiece *Hymnus paradisi*, which we will not otherwise discuss here. The actual character of the voices is important in that they must be pure and not too robust, but equally need to be heard through the orchestral texture. The music's visionary character is never in doubt.

Howells was concerned to ensure that his textures remained open and clear. The effect of light in his music (which he finally brought to triumphal completion in *Hymnus paradisi*) turns on the music never becoming clotted. He told Katharine Eggar that 'I worked for many days after I thought I'd finished *Sine nomine* taking out superfluous notes. I thought I'd left out everything that possibly could be left out; but I found again that work as one will, the crowning difficulty is generally the getting rid of dead weight.'[39]

Sine nomine was recorded as part of a mixed choral programme by Royal Liverpool Philharmonic forces in the Philharmonic Hall, Liverpool, conducted by Douglas Bostock, in July 2002.[40] At the sessions the principal issue was the relative balance of the vocal soloists, and it is certainly true that upon them turns the successful realisation of Howells's vision. Not least is the tenor soloist's first entry (Fig. 7.4).

The orchestral *Pastoral Rhapsody* (HH 134) dates from the autumn of 1923. This glorious exercise in nature mysticism was first heard under the composer's baton at the Eastbourne Festival in November that year. Subsequently revised, it was conducted by him again at Bournemouth in March 1924, and it appeared with the Hallé Orchestra in Manchester in January 1925, before it was forgotten. At this time he wrote several evocative orchestral works in one movement. The one-movement

---

[37] Howells's comments about the work are taken from *ibid.*, 437.
[38] Herbert Howells, *Sine nomine*, in *Elgar and the English Choral Tradition*, Royal Liverpool Philharmonic Chorus and Orchestra, Douglas Bostock (conductor), audio CD (ClassicO, 2002), CLASSCD 456.
[39] Eggar, 'Herbert Howells', 214.
[40] See above, n. 35.

Fig. 7.4 *Sine nomine: A Phantasy*, Op. 37, opening page from piano score

form of *Sine nomine*, after the artistic success of the Gloucester performance, demonstrated to Howells that a single movement could work on so large a scale. This was, perhaps, the realisation on a larger canvas of the then fashionable one-movement phantasy shape of his earlier chamber music (see Chapter 11). The folk-inflected themes and the singing wind and violin solos are common both to this and to the *Paradise Rondel* which followed.[41] Why did Howells allow it to be forgotten? One possible explanation is that perhaps he felt it too close to Vaughan Williams so soon after his *Pastoral Symphony*. Yet now, at a distance of almost ninety years, one hears it as a distinctive personal voice, and its atmosphere is striking.

Vaughan Williams's *Pastoral Symphony* would have loomed large on Howells's horizon at this time (he wrote a long article on it when it was new[42]) because it shared the programme when Howells's Second Piano Concerto (HH 152) was promoted by the Royal Philharmonic Society at one of their Queen's Hall concerts in

---

[41] Indeed Jonathan Clinch argues that it was later transformed into *Paradise Rondel* (see p. 182).

[42] Howells, 'The Pastoral Symphony of Ralph Vaughan Williams'.

April 1925. This was billed as a significant occasion – one of the leading composers of the younger generation in a prestige event. Percy Scholes wrote it up in the *Observer* the day before, noting:

> The first performance of a new Piano Concerto by a native composer of serious aims, the solo part played by one of our foremost native pianists, the orchestral part by our finest native orchestra, under the direction of a talented young native conductor who has made a name for himself with phenomenal rapidity – surely we can call this combination an 'event'.[43]

In fact it was a disaster. Press coverage harped on the unusual happening of a commentator standing up at the end of the concerto and shouting 'Thank God that's over!'. The objector was Robert Lorenz.[44] Howells's reaction was bewildering and extreme – although the music was already in proof, he withdrew it and it was not heard again until after his death. Paul Spicer quotes his daughter Ursula's assessment of her father at this time: 'He was a mess, like so many people, underneath, and wasn't big enough to overcome that'.[45]

So his two major concert works that might have contributed to his long-term place in the concert repertoire, both piano concertos, were withdrawn by their composer for reasons it is difficult to fathom. A less insecure artistic figure might have been tempted to soldier on and find a champion for both. In fact the performance was the conclusion of a long-worked process intended to lead to publication and performance, for the Second Piano Concerto appears to have been completed by the end of 1922, as related by Katharine Eggar in her interview with Howells published in December 1922.[46] Howells claimed that 'my new Piano Concerto ... is more concerned with counterpoint (of a modern sort) than with harmonic colour, and it takes less than 20 minutes in performance'.[47] As soon as the first slow episode is reached it becomes apparent that what he has actually produced is a synthesis of his earlier programmatic orchestral works writ large. If he had given it some title such as 'Scenes from Gloucestershire' he would probably have had a good deal more success, and probably more accurately announced to his public what they were being offered.

Paradise Rondel (HH 159) was completed on 25 July 1925 and was first heard that year at the Three Choirs Festival on 9 September in the Shire Hall, Gloucester. Paradise is in fact the name of a village in the Cotswolds, near Painswick, and as Howells remarks in his notes for the first performance, any other village name might

---

[43] *Observer* (26 April 1925), 10.
[44] I am grateful to the late Patrick Piggott for the name of the objector. Lorenz (1891–1945), was known at the time as an odd-ball who would comment on works in Queen's Hall. His obituary appeared in the *Musical Times* (January 1946), 30, and observes: 'On several occasions he raised his voice – a strong and resonant one – against some work of which he disapproved.' An article by Lorenz, 'An Amateur on Critics', had appeared in the *Musical Times* (March 1923), 178, and others did so between the wars.
[45] Spicer, *Herbert Howells*, 82.
[46] Eggar, 'An English Composer', 130.
[47] Ibid., 130.

have done: 'Paradise is a good walking-place, full of tunes for those who can hear them.'[48] In this brilliantly scored movement Howells brings his early Ravelian orchestral style to its zenith – but 'Rondel'? Howells is referring to the fourteenth-century form of Roundelay – country songs or dances in which the opening lines constantly recur. Various composers at this time use the term for short pieces or songs, and Howells himself had already published his *Three Rondeaux* in 1918 (HH 59), the middle song being 'A Rondel of Rest'. Howells's orchestra is not particularly large, excluding the brass but with four horns, and includes orchestral piano, harp and celesta.

The harp and celesta both provide colour, but the piano is of interest as it has the unusual function of driving the fast music on, and is largely written as a relentlessly running line, sometimes doubled at the octave. This adds to the 'open-airishness' of the conception, to use Edwin Evans's term again. Broadly, Howells gives us a ternary shape: an 'Allegro, e Vivace' first section (Fig. 7.5), brilliant and colourful and rising to a romantic string-led climax, which is followed by a spectral quiet middle section in which various instrumental solos create a remarkably delicate and half-lit landscape, the solo viola (muted at first) setting the mood, and the strings divided. The fast music returns, but the sun is increasingly clouded now and the end is quiet.

Howells's exquisitely worked and characteristic early orchestral writing is also to be noted in his song cycle *In Green Ways* (HH 172), typically evident in the orchestral introduction to the first song, 'Under the Greenwood Tree'. All his life Howells wrote exquisite songs, but with the exception of his celebrated setting of 'King David' (HH 102) they have not been widely sung. The cycle *In Green Ways* was revised in 1928 from an earlier attempt, and was heard at that year's Three Choirs Festival, which was at Gloucester. There it was sung by Joan Elwes with Howells conducting the London Symphony Orchestra, and the following year it reappeared at a Promenade concert when Dorothy Silk was the soloist. Later it surfaced again at Gloucester sung by Isobel Baillie. It was one of two scores Howells submitted to Oxford for his doctorate in 1937, and it was then forgotten until revived by the late Tracey Chadwell in a broadcast in October 1986.

In Green Ways was his only orchestral score[49] written between the disastrous first performance of the Second Piano Concerto and *Penguinski* (HH 193), a four-minute *jeu d'esprit* written for a humorous ballet at the RCM in 1933.[50] *Penguinski* was long completely forgotten until recorded by Richard Hickox and the BBC Symphony Orchestra in 2000.[51] Much has been made of the influence of Stravinsky in this music, and certainly there are overtones of specific moments from contemporaneous music by Stravinsky, which was heard regularly and promptly at Queen's Hall in the 1930s. Yet apart from the almost obbligato use of orchestral piano, and a

---

[48] Programme note to Three Choirs Festival, Gloucester, 9 September 1925.

[49] Although the choral setting, *A Kent Yeoman's Wooing Song*, dates from 1930, it was not orchestrated until 1953.

[50] Penguins were a subject of considerable interest to Londoners in the 1930s because of Lubinsky's modernist Penguin Pool at the London Zoo, but we should note that Howells's score predates the construction of that by a year.

[51] Herbert Howells, Piano Concerto no. 1, Piano Concerto no. 2 and *Penguinski*, Howard Shelley (piano), BBC Symphony Orchestra, Richard Hickox (conductor), audio CD (Chandos, 2000), CHAN 9874.

Fig. 7.5 *Paradise Rondel*, first page of manuscript in full score

passing allusion to *Pulcinella* and the *Capriccio*,[52] what strikes one most about it is the way it exultantly crowns the world of his earlier short orchestral pieces.

[52] The *Pulcinella Suite* had been first heard in London, at Queen's Hall, on 24 October 1925, and *Capriccio* at the same venue on 21 March 1931, when Stravinsky himself was the piano soloist.

The extent and quality of Herbert Howells's early orchestral music was not apparent during his lifetime, even to his students. Only since his death in 1983 has this corpus been explored again; and now that we can write about it after experiencing it in performance, it is evidently the work of a very talented composer with an individual style from the outset. Yet it was not played again in his lifetime. Whether his suppression of this music was caused by technical or musical reservations during the rise of mid-century avant gardism, or was connected for some more personal reason with the death of his son in 1935, is difficult to assess. But in the light of Richard Hickox's recordings, it is clear to the author of this survey that here is a composer who had found his personal voice with a body of delightful and personable music that can speak to a wide audience.

CHAPTER 8

Lost, Remembered, Mislaid, Rewritten: A Documentary Study of *In Gloucestershire*

Paul Andrews

HOWELLS composed three essays for string quartet, all of them begun and two of them signed off early in his career. The first was the student piece *Lady Audrey's Suite* of 1915 (HH 50), then came *Fantasy String Quartet* of 1917 (HH 71), and lastly *In Gloucestershire*, posthumously published as String Quartet no. 3 in 1992 (HH 62). Together with the Piano Quartet (HH 66), *Rhapsodic Quintet* for clarinet and strings (HH 107), four sonatas for violin and piano, the postwar sonatas for oboe and clarinet, and a number of smaller pieces for various combinations, they make up Howells's entire output of chamber music, a small but very significant body of important and accomplished works mostly written before the Second World War and predating the later reflowering of his career as a composer of church music. But while the composition and publication history of *Lady Audrey's Suite* and the *Fantasy String Quartet* presents little in the way of difficulty to the commentator from a historical and documentary point of view, *In Gloucestershire* is an entirely different matter. This substantial, thirty-minute, four-movement sonata structure is in many ways an enigma. Originally one of Howells's earliest major works, *In Gloucestershire*, on the way to its final definitive version, underwent a process of revision and recomposition that occupied its composer on and off for twenty or more years and generated at least three discrete versions, two of which survive complete. It is a work that has twice been lost and subsequently rewritten. The ambiguity surrounding a date for the completion of the final version, probably in the 1930s, has led some commentators to suggest a link between the elegiac nature of the slow movement and the emotional trauma Howells suffered as a result of the death, at the age of nine, of his son Michael, though this cannot be proved. Unravelling the work's history is made difficult by the paucity and anecdotal nature of the documentary evidence, and by the lack of any definite dates, either for the work's final completion or for any performance in its published form during Howells's lifetime. This chapter attempts to map a path through a thicket of confusion and tentatively to outline a possible composition history for the work, consistent with the available evidence.

Howells first composed a string quartet with the descriptive title *In Gloucestershire* in the summer of 1916 (HH 62a). The score was lost very soon afterwards and no trace of this first version remains. A second version dates from 1920 and survived in the form of a non-autograph set of parts currently in private hands (HH 62b).[1] A third version is represented by cancelled movements in a set of non-autograph parts in the collection of the Royal College of Music (RCM) (HH 62c),[2] and the final

---

[1] Performing materials for this version, made for a centenary performance in 1992, are available for hire from Novello.
[2] RCM, MS 4646.

version (HH 62d) by two autograph manuscript scores (one of which is incomplete) and the same set of non-autograph parts.[3] Unusually for this composer, none of the surviving manuscript material is dated.[4] The definitive version is HH 62d, published in 1992 and subsequently recorded. It is titled String Quartet no. 3, *In Gloucestershire*, following the composer's own designation on the complete manuscript score. Some minor reconciliations between the manuscript score and parts were required in the preparation of the printed edition.[5]

There is some significant documentary evidence for the quartet's early history. In 1919, Howells compiled an annotated list[6] of his works for the critic Edwin Evans, who was engaged in writing a two-part article on the composer for the *Musical Times*.[7] This list has an entry for 'A string quartet (*In Gloucestershire*) written in 1916; now lost'. A student notebook[8] kept by Howells contains two lists of works, compiled *c.* 1917, which include an entry for a 'String Quartet in A minor'. These lists constitute the sole documentary evidence for such a work. No surviving version of *In Gloucestershire* and none of Howells's other works for string quartet are in the key of A minor, yet it is at least possible that these entries refer to the lost original version of this work, the key of which is unknown, particularly since the evidence suggests that the second version is effectively a new work, based on at least some new material. Howells's friend and colleague Marion Scott, writing presumably with the composer's permission and collaboration in the *Christian Science Monitor* for December 1920, tells the story of this seemingly catastrophic loss and the beginning of its recovery. The article is unsigned, but an entry in Howells's diary for 24 February 1919 identifies Marion Scott as the paper's 'special music correspondent':[9]

> Four years ago in the summer vacation of 1916, Howells who is a devoted lover of his county, composed a string quartet in its honour. He felt himself that it was one of the best things he had done and was 'real Gloucestershire'. Barely had the score been finished when it was lost on a train journey between Lydney and Gloucester. The presumption is that it was left in the carriage; anyhow all search failed to find it. The loss seemed absolute, no duplicate existed; the composer could not remember a note. Thus matters rested till the autumn of 1919 when quite unexpectedly, Howells began to recall fragments of the lost themes. He decided to rewrite the quartet and had indeed actually begun it when fresh inspiration suddenly came to him. The old themes were discarded, new material flooded his thoughts and in a fortnight of ceaseless work, he finished the quartet.[10]

---

[3] *Ibid.*

[4] Howells was usually meticulous in assigning dates to his manuscripts, frequently also indicating the place where the work was completed.

[5] Herbert Howells, String Quartet no. 3, *In Gloucestershire* (London, 1992).

[6] RCM, Herbert Howells Archive.

[7] Evans, 'Herbert Howells', 87–91, 156–9.

[8] Herbert Howells Archive.

[9] Palmer, *A Centenary Celebration*, 77.

[10] Scott, 'Herbert Howells: His "In Gloucestershire"', 12.

An arresting story, but should we take it unquestioningly at face value? The oddest aspect seems to be the composer's inability to recall anything of a substantial work on which he had just expended a good deal of concentrated creative effort. Many who knew Howells remember that he was fond of stories and he was not above embroidering the facts if they got in the way of a good one.[11] But it is also difficult to see why Howells should have completely invented such a tale, and for the purposes of this investigation, I shall accept that there was an early version of the quartet that somehow disappeared soon after its composition. In fact, the stirrings of Howells's creative imagination may have begun even earlier than autumn 1919. His diary entry for 31 January 1919 carries the heading 'An unborn string quartet' and continues 'Churchdown and Gloucester … This morning I saw string quartet tunes along the way.'[12]

In the absence of any other clues, Peter Hodgson, a former pupil of Howells who compiled the first catalogue of his works in 1970, dated the quartet to 1920, citing a performance scheduled by the Spencer Dyke Quartet on 30 April 1923.[13] Hodgson derived this date from an article by Katharine Eggar, where it was designated the first performance.[14] However, a report in the *London Times* newspaper for that date suggests that Howells withdrew the work from this recital, 'wishing to rewrite' part of it. *In Gloucestershire* had in fact received a private performance in 1920, at the home of Marion Scott and her parents. A printed invitation for this event is preserved in the composer's archive. It took place on 19 March at the home of Mr and Mrs Sydney Scott and Miss Marion Scott, 92 Westbourne Terrace, Hyde Park, and was called 'A Gloucestershire Evening'. In addition to *In Gloucestershire* and Ivor Gurney's song cycle *Ludlow and Teme*, the Gloucestershire poet F. W. Harvey read a selection of his verses. The musicians were the members of the Philharmonic Quartet, joined by the tenor Steuart Wilson in Gurney's song cycle. The performance of *In Gloucestershire* is specifically designated a premiere on the invitation. Marion Scott's description of this occasion, and of another like it, is quoted by Harry Plunket Greene, Stanford's son-in-law and first biographer:

> Miss Scott says: After the war I recall two happy evenings at our house when we gave big musical parties at which we produced Herbert Howells' quartet *In Gloucestershire* and Gurney's *Ludlow and Teme*. Sir Charles and Lady Stanford were there and many of his composers were among the guests. It was delightful to see how his old pupils gathered round him – Dunhill, Bliss, Harold Darke, Howells and Gurney among them – and he talked to them all in turn and seemed so happy as he held his little informal levée.[15]

---

[11] One of Howells's favourite stories – that he was compelled to compose the orchestral piece 'Merry-Eye' during his honeymoon in 1920 because the original commission had gone astray, and that he only realised that he had to do it quickly when he saw it announced in *The Times* en route – was shown to be a fabrication by the survival of the letter from Henry Wood commissioning the work among his papers after his death. As quoted in Palmer, *A Centenary Celebration*, 88–9.
[12] Herbert Howells Archive.
[13] Hodgson, 'The Music of Herbert Howells', 296.
[14] Eggar, 'An English Composer'.
[15] Plunket Greene, *Charles Villiers Stanford*, 113.

W. W. Cobbett, writing his regular 'Chamber Music Notes' column in the *Music Student*, noted that on 19 March 1920:

> at the home of one of the few London Hostesses who are interested in chamber music a delightful evening was spent ... listening to the first performances of works by two young Gloucestershire composers. A string quartet (minus the final) by Herbert Howell [sic] already distinguished by his work in this field and a song cycle *Ludlow Time* [sic] for tenor, string quartet and piano by Ivor Gurney.[16]

It is significant that the Howells quartet was played without its finale. Even at this early stage, he was clearly already subjecting the work to revision. On 20 March, Edwin Evans wrote informing Howells of an evening of chamber music that he and Eugene Goossens were organising

> at Madame Karsavina's house on Sunday evening April 11th, and I should very much like to hear a work of yours. I think we have a string quartet in the programme, so perhaps it would be an opportunity to play your *In Gloucestershire* or at least part of it, but if you have other suggestions to make, we will see what can be done with them.[17]

Evans was writing the day after the performance documented above. As a well-known critic sympathetic to modern British music, he may well have been present at the soirée. Howells wrote in his own diary on 9 May that he had been to a rehearsal of the work with the Philharmonic String Quartet in preparation for a performance at 'Murray Davey's'. It is probable that the work was still under revision in the late 1920s and early 1930s because Marion Scott's 1929 survey of Howells's chamber music (in *Cobbett's Cyclopaedic Survey of Chamber Music*) mentions it only to take note that, as the composer's 'most advanced and mature work in [the] form', it remained unpublished.[18] But did it remain unfinished? If *In Gloucestershire* had been in a complete state at this time might it not seem unusual for the author of the first published account of the work, a friend of the composer who had played host to its 'first performance' in 1920, to have excluded a more extended analysis from this otherwise exhaustive survey? Scott's contribution to the *Cyclopaedic Survey* must have been prepared well in advance of its publication date of 1929 and, in any case, Cobbett's preface explicitly states that 'with rare exceptions, MS. works are ignored',[19] thus precluding more detailed analysis. But if it was incomplete, would it have been admitted at all as one of Cobbett's 'rare exceptions'? Perhaps the version Scott referred to is the earlier one that she remembered from the performances at her home. Clearly matters were in a state of flux, and another commentator suggests that it was still not finished in 1930. Hubert Foss wrote in that year, in an article on Howells that seems to have been intended as a valiant attempt to revive

---

[16] Cobbett, 'Chamber Music Notes' (1920).
[17] Letter from Edwin Evans, 20 March 1920, in the Herbert Howells Archive.
[18] Scott, 'Herbert Howells'.
[19] Ibid.

a reputation as a composer that was already in decline, that *In Gloucestershire* 'reaches me in MS with no slow movement and an illegible finale, having suffered a number of critical onslaughts from its composer already'.[20]

This accurately describes one of the manuscript scores in the RCM (see below). By the late 1920s much of the real hope that had been invested in the young Howells that he might become one of the brightest stars of English music, perhaps at the same level as figures such as Vaughan Williams and Holst, was quickly evaporating. The big works simply had not materialised, and references in the musical press to Howells as a teacher and adjudicator were becoming as common as any to him as a composer. Foss's explicit aim in his piece was to draw public attention back to Howells the composer and to this end he had examined a number of unpublished manuscripts, including the incomplete *In Gloucestershire*.

This now draws us towards a summary of the manuscript sources for this elusive quartet. But first it is worth noting that neither Peter Hodgson nor Howells's later biographer Christopher Palmer drew any attention in their accounts to the fairly straightforward evidence presented by the material held in the RCM's collection of Howells's manuscripts that there might be more than one version of this work.

This material falls into three sections:

(1) A score, in ink, of the first and second movements largely as they appear in HH 62d, together with a pencil draft of the finale from the same version that contains numerous alterations and rubbings-out, and several paste-overs. The ending is inked in. This score lacks a slow movement and so represents work in progress. It fits the description given by Foss in the article quoted above.
(2) A later revised score on paper of more recent origin, entitled Third String Quartet (*In Gloucestershire*). The first of three gatherings contains the first two movements on twenty-one pages, the twenty-second being ruled for a third movement but otherwise left blank. A second gathering contains the third movement, and a third gathering the finale, which is simply headed 'last movement'. There are minor differences between the completed movements of scores 1 and 2.
(3) A set of parts, each part consisting of the first two movements on paper of the same older type as score 1. These gatherings also contain parts for two further movements, not represented in either of the scores. These have been crossed through, and occasionally marked 'Not this one'. The parts for these movements are complete as far as the second violin, viola and cello parts are concerned, but the first violin part lacks all but the first page of the slow movement. These two cancelled movements are substantially different from those found in the final version. The revised third and fourth movements, more or less matching the complete score, are on paper of newer origin.

From this evidence alone it is clear that Howells put the quartet through a process of revision from a version that included the cancelled parts, via the earlier score, to a completion represented by the later score and uncancelled movements in the

---

[20] Foss, 'Herbert Howells'.

parts. The lack of a slow movement in the earlier score, and its presence in a separate gathering in the later one, suggest that it might have been the last movement to be composed (and, as we shall see, encourages those who like to speculate about psychological or emotional explanations for the content of a composer's music). Yet until the rediscovery in 1985 of an earlier non-autograph set of parts (HH 62b) a reconciliation of all of this with Scott's original account presented certain difficulties. Neither of the versions represented by RCM, MS 4646 exactly matches the description of the work given in that article, particularly in relation to the tempo markings for the four movements, which Scott quotes in Italian (1. Allegro non troppo; 2. Scherzo – Allegro ma sempre ritmico; 3. Andante assai espressivo; 4. Presto). All the rubrics for performance in the material contained in RCM, MS 4646 are in English. Part of Scott's description of the work is also relevant: 'The second subject [of the first movement] is of the utmost significance. It is the theme of the slow movement.'[21] A vestige of the main theme of the slow movement (Ex. 8.2a), as it is represented by the cancelled parts, appears in the first movement of both scores, but not in a way that could be described as 'of the utmost significance', while in the new slow movement, this theme is itself relegated to a position of secondary importance, and the main idea of the new movement (Ex. 8.3) appears nowhere else in the quartet.

The discovery in private hands of a previously undocumented non-autograph set of parts of a string quartet entitled *In Gloucestershire* shed some light on this inconsistency. Richard Drakeford, a former pupil of Howells, had acquired the set from a private collector in Oxford in 1957; they came as a complete surprise when he told the composer about the find: 'The score and parts were lost years ago soon after the first performance. I'm intrigued. Would your friend be so kind as to let me see the relics he came by?'[22] It is curious, and perhaps says something about Howells's own rather laissez-faire attitude to his own music, that in his exchanges with Drakeford he did not make any mention of the early history of the quartet (other than to say that the very first version had been lost), nor of the possible existence of other versions, even though what we now consider to be the definitive score had almost certainly been completed some twenty years previously. Drakeford made a score from his newly acquired parts and Howells made a number of small revisions and cuts. A performance of this edition was given by the London String Quartet at the Little Missenden Festival on 15 October 1961, an occasion at which Howells was unable to be present, although he had attended at least one rehearsal (on 4 October), as his diary reveals. The performers retained the score and parts after the performance to play the work to the composer at a later date (though whether they actually did is not known) and the music was never returned either to Drakeford or to Howells, so this version passed out of circulation for a second time until its rediscovery in 1985. These parts are the sole source for HH 62b and it is perhaps not too fanciful to claim that they represent the 'missing link' in the work's convoluted history.

---

[21] Scott, 'Herbert Howells: His "In Gloucestershire"'.
[22] Letter from Howells to Richard Drakeford, 3 March 1957, in the possession of Richard Drakeford.

The parts were very clearly prepared by a professional copyist, and they are equally clearly of some age. The initial, fanciful though perhaps forgivable assumption on the part of the present writer that this was the lost 1916 original, was immediately called into question when they were compared with the definitive score in RCM, MS 4646, for while there are many differences, there are also passages where both versions are identical in so much detail as virtually to exclude the possibility that Howells, in his later revisions, was recalling a lost work from memory. In particular, the differences between the two versions of the Scherzo are so few and so confined to marginal details that to all intents and purposes the movement can be regarded in both versions, indeed in all the versions, as being the same.

A comparison of this set with the material in RCM, MS 4646 helps us to construct what inevitably must remain a conjectural composition history for *In Gloucestershire*. In particular it is almost certain that HH 62b represents the version reconstructed by Howells in 1919/20 after the loss of his 1916 original and is therefore the work seen and described by Marion Scott in her 1920 article. These may have been the parts prepared for the work's earliest performance or performances in Scott's home. The tempo indications are exactly as Scott transcribes them, and the second subject of the first movement, which is completely different from the equivalent passage in the published version, is indeed the principal theme of the slow movement.

Taking into account all the manuscript evidence, together with Scott's article, we can begin to piece together a sequence of events. The story that Howells told of how he composed the first version of *In Gloucestershire* in 1916 and almost immediately lost it on a train, never to be recovered and instantly forgotten, can be taken at face value or not. Since nothing tangible survives of this ghostly first attempt, we can enjoy Howells's account for the good story that it is and go along with his version of events that subsequently, in 1919 as Scott relates, he began to recall the work and, in writing it out afresh, effectively recomposed it. This second version, or some of it, was performed at least once during the early 1920s and has been reconstructed from the recently rediscovered set of parts.[23] Following this version's first performance or performances, Howells subjected *In Gloucestershire* to a process of extensive revision that extended over a number of years. The set of parts in RCM, MS 4646 including the cancelled movements represents an interim version for which Howells provided a completely new first movement while retaining the Scherzo from the 1919 score and making minor revisions to the slow movement and finale. He then discarded both of these latter two movements, replacing the finale first (the earlier, incomplete score in RCM, MS 4646) and finally writing a new slow movement (the complete score and uncancelled movements in the parts).

The dating of this sequence presents the most persistent difficulty of all, since no dates appear on any of the manuscript material. Assuming that the identification of HH 62b with the version described in the *Christian Science Monitor* article is correct, it dates from early 1920. The slow movement 'bears the date Christmas Eve 1919, the finale is marked Dec 31 and the work was completed a week later, the

---

[23] The version reconstructed from these parts has to take account of some changes made by Howells and pasted into the parts in 1957.

title page having the inscription "Jan 7, 1920 Lydney, Glos"'.[24] After this, the assigning of dates almost becomes anyone's guess, but it is highly probable that Howells was still working on the quartet into the 1930s. It is helpful that Howells's musical calligraphy underwent a complete and significant change from around 1930 as he adopted and perfected the beautiful italic hand for which his manuscripts are famed. His handwriting in the complete manuscript score is in this mannered italic style. This itself indicates a later date, and although it is extremely doubtful if the hand could be as late as 1957, the possibility of a final completion date after Howells's collaboration with Drakeford cannot be completely ruled out. But this seems to me to be unlikely. Perhaps Howells had his own reasons for forgetting or deliberately neglecting to draw Drakeford's attention to the complete score. In any case, the calligraphy is entirely consistent with works written in the mid-to-late 1930s, and is in fact very close in style to that of the Kyrie eleison, later incorporated into the *Missa sabrinensis* (HH 275–1954), but originally written as an independent work in the mid 1930s.

The tragic story of the death from polio in 1935 of Howells's son Michael must occupy a pivotal point in any account of the composer's biography. Howells never came to terms with his loss and it is at least arguable that Michael's shadow was cast over almost everything he subsequently wrote. Because we do not know exactly when in the 1930s *In Gloucestershire* was finished, it has to be a possibility that it was not completed until after Michael's death. It is at least possible therefore that the completion of *In Gloucestershire*, particularly of its slow movement, places it in that category of works that Howells wrote in the immediate aftermath of Michael's death and perhaps, like *Hymnus paradisi* (HH 220), consciously or unconsciously suppressed. This is where the link between life and work invites speculation: Michael became ill 'in Gloucestershire' and he is also buried there, so the title might, for its composer, take on more than a merely topographical significance. The slow movement certainly seems to inhabit the elegiac world that characterises Howells's other commemorative pieces, but this is a characteristic that is also inherent in works that have no such intensely personal stimulus. In his biography of Howells, Palmer wrote that 'The slow movement must be Howells's own anthem for doomed youth',[25] while acknowledging that memories of friends killed in the First World War and the protracted agony of Ivor Gurney's last years are also associated with his childhood and youthful memories of Gloucestershire. It needs to be emphasised that any attempt to make *In Gloucestershire* a 'Michael' piece remains the purest speculation. The lack of dates on the manuscript sources and the fragmentary and anecdotal nature of the documentation both encourage and frustrate such attempts at second-guessing the composer's extra-musical concerns. Too many uncertainties remain to allow us to connect *In Gloucestershire* unequivocally with the death of Howells's son. Why did Howells leave all the manuscripts undated when he was usually meticulous almost to the point of obsession in the matter of recording these details? How did he apparently in later life come

---

[24] Scott, 'Herbert Howells: His "In Gloucestershire"'.
[25] Palmer, *A Centenary Celebration*, 51.

Ex. 8.1a String Quartet no.3, *In Gloucestershire*, Op. 34, 2nd version, 1st mvt, bars 1–6

to forget about the existence of one of his most important instrumental works? Was he never happy with it and was it simply abandoned? That might go some way towards explaining why there seem to have been no documented performances. The RCM parts appear to be marked up for rehearsal at least, but no announcement or review of a performance later than 1923 has so far been found. However, it is never the composer's job to make life easy for his critics and commentators, so perhaps Howells is not be criticised too much for all the questions that remain, frustrating though they are.

However, it seems to me that one fact is incontrovertible. *In Gloucestershire* is not simply one work: as it survives its extraordinary evolution it leaves us with two linked but essentially separate and individual string quartets that date from two distinct periods in Howells's composing life. They are not of equal importance and weight. The later HH 62d is one of Howells's great works, a piece of considerable emotional, structural and compositional depth; HH 62b is a well-wrought piece that in the absence of the later completion would entirely justify perhaps a secondary place in Howells's catalogue. Both versions share a brief mercurial Scherzo, but there is a precedent even for this elsewhere in Howells's music. Howells withdrew his Second Violin Sonata of 1917 (HH 79) after a number of performances and recycled its Scherzo when he came to write his Third Sonata of 1925 (HH 136), including

Ex. 8.1b String Quartet no.3, *In Gloucestershire*, Op. 34, 4th version, 1st mvt, bars 1–11

it almost unchanged. It is now acknowledged that both are very fine works, both viable, and that the Second Sonata entirely justifies an independent place in the repertoire. I would like to suggest that the same is true for the two versions of *In Gloucestershire*, two separate string quartets that similarly share a Scherzo.

Example 1 shows the opening of both versions of the quartet. The tight rhythmic control of the 1920 score (Ex. 8.1a) gives way to a free rhapsodic style in the later version (Ex. 8.1.b).

Example 8.2 shows the motif that Scott refers to in her article as being of 'pivotal importance'. Example 8.2a is the opening of the earlier version's slow movement; the viola's theme in it has previously been heard as the first movement's second subject. Example 8.2b is the climactic point in the first movement of the revised score at which this theme, no longer so important to the work as a whole, nevertheless appears.

Example 8.3 is the opening of the slow movement in the later version. It too begins with a viola solo, but in contrast to the simple intervals and chords heard in Example 8.2a, this is a wistful, perhaps sorrowful, sinuously chromatic yearning melody that immediately begins to generate harmonically ambiguous counterpoint, building into a movement of great emotional intensity. The 'pivotal' motif of Example 8.2a is heard briefly in this movement (at figure 6), but its significance for the movement as a whole is much less than in its predecessor.

Example 8.4 is the opening of the two finales – Example 4b excludes eight introductory bars. The thematic material of both versions shows Howells using similarly

Ex. 8.2a String Quartet no.3, *In Gloucestershire*, Op. 34, 2nd version, 3rd mvt, bars 1–9

Ex. 8.2b String Quartet no.3, *In Gloucestershire*, Op. 34, 4th version, 1st mvt, bars 171–8

Ex. 8.3 String Quartet no.3, *In Gloucestershire*, Op. 34, 4th version, 3rd mvt, bars 1–16

shaped motifs in entirely different ways. At figure 2 in Example 8.4b, the first violin plays a theme that is perhaps derived from Example 2a.

In conclusion, the version of *In Gloucestershire* catalogued as HH 62b is a confident, well-constructed work in the folk-tune inspired modal idiom derived, perhaps over-derived, from the example of Vaughan Williams. It does not carry the same emotional weight and reach as its mature successor, nor does it represent an advance on the astonishingly precocious Piano Quartet, but it certainly adds to our knowledge of Howells's developing style at a time, around 1920, when he was beginning to make a name for himself. It stands up as a viable work in its own right and in this writer's view merits its place in Howells's catalogue and in the repertoire. HH 62d probably dates from fifteen or more years later and is without doubt one of Howells's greatest achievements: an important example of the composer at

Ex. 8.4a String Quartet no.3, *In Gloucestershire*, Op. 34, 2nd version, 4th mvt, bars 1–9

the height of his powers, a master of his craft. It is a powerful argument in favour of his mastery of instrumental forms, full of emotional complexity and depth – rhapsodic, yet finely balanced and controlled in form and structure. In its slow movement in particular, whether connected with Michael's death or not, we have an example of Howells writing in that elegiac mode that he made his own, to match anything he ever composed.

Ex. 8.4b String Quartet no.3, *In Gloucestershire*, Op. 34, 4th version, 4th mvt, figure 1 (bar 19)

CHAPTER 9

Style and Structure in the Oboe Sonata and Clarinet Sonata

Fabian Huss

THE Oboe Sonata (HH 239 – 1942) and Clarinet Sonata (HH 251– 1946) are the only substantial chamber works dating from Howells's later period, providing an opportunity to observe his mature musical language from an alternative perspective to that presented by the choral and orchestral works. The extended forms and limited textural range facilitate an examination of elements such as thematic working, harmonic procedures at all hierarchical levels and their articulation of structural relationships, as well as the aesthetic priorities they imply. The latter will be contextualised further through a consideration of wider trends in British music and culture, drawing on comments by Howells and several of his contemporaries.

The Oboe Sonata was written for Leon Goossens, but when the oboist raised some doubts about the work's structure, Howells recalled it, saying that he would 'have another go at it'.[1] This was the last that was heard of it until Christopher Palmer borrowed the manuscript while working on *Herbert Howells: A Centenary Celebration*; luckily he made a photocopy, as the manuscript later disappeared, and the work was not performed until 1984. The Clarinet Sonata was written four years after the oboe work, for Frederick Thurston, and it resumes some of the concerns of the earlier sonata. Superficially, the Clarinet Sonata seems tighter in construction than its predecessor, avoiding some of the earlier complexities in favour of more obvious structural divisions and relationships.[2] Simplified versions of some local complexities, notably rhythmic patterns in 7/8, can also be observed; Howells had already considered such a simplification in the Oboe Sonata, marking a 4/4 time signature in the margin of the Scherzo, but he evidently never mustered the energy (or time) to attempt a serious reworking. For that matter, the Clarinet Sonata may have appeared to him a more viable, more approachable alternative. There are a number of notable similarities between the works. The sonatas are of similar length, with similarities of basic structure: the first halves of both works are meditative and expository (in the Clarinet Sonata this is a single movement, in the Oboe Sonata it is a linked pair of movements that share thematic material); the second halves constitute substantial Scherzos, with first-movement material reappearing towards the end. The Scherzos themselves have a number of significant similarities, including the fragmented rhythmic figures of principal material, the use of 7/8 material and central sections featuring syncopated piano chords.

---

[1] According to Goossens, as quoted in Peter Dickinson's preface to the 1987 Novello score.
[2] In my discussion of structural features throughout this chapter, I am interested in the articulation of relationships both among and within sections, by a diverse array of features that are relevant to the sense of structural unfolding.

If the simplifications in presentation of material and structure suggest that Howells had developed doubts about the comprehensibility of the Oboe Sonata's complexities by the time he came to compose the later work, the choice of instrument may also be significant – perhaps he came to suspect that the intense, extended paragraphs of the Oboe Sonata were unsuited to the instrument. He commented on Vaughan Williams's Oboe Concerto in 1947 (i.e. the year after the Clarinet Sonata):

> The oboe is an instrument born to be brief, and to that circumstance the style of any work written for it should be accommodating. Even if you bring Mr Leon Goossens' limitless breathing powers and his unique tone-control to the playing of it, this instrument must still avoid the easy sin of outstaying its welcome. No other instrument can make one want more; none should more scrupulously leave one still unsated.[3]

While there are periods of respite in the Oboe Sonata, its sustained paragraphs are frequently demanding, and Paul Spicer has suggested that this may have been the real reason for Goossens's reservations.[4]

Both sonatas present opportunities to examine a number of prominent elements of the mature style, many of which can be approached through a consideration of what has been described as the 'ruminative' character of material, style or process.[5] The technical workings of this aspect have remained somewhat nebulous, despite being noted in some form by various commentators, being broadly defined by an eschewal of dramatic gesture and dynamic opposition in favour of fluidity of phrase structure, texture and harmony, often involving an elliptical treatment of material. There are a number of similarities with Vaughan Williams's 'contemplative' manner, which Howells discussed in relation to the *Pastoral Symphony* in an article of 1922, defending it from the charges of dullness and monotony that he knew (perhaps even at this early stage) could also be levelled against his own music.[6] By way

---

[3] Howells, review of Vaughan Williams, Concerto for Oboe and Strings, 89.
[4] Spicer, *Herbert Howells*, 128–9.
[5] Both Spicer and Dickinson apply this term to Howells's music.
[6] This charge was allowed even by his advocates, for instance Hubert Foss writing in 1930:

> His invention, however, does not run to arabesque or technical display, and shrinking in the English way from virtuosity, prefers drabness to vulgarity. He suffers, too, from the prevalence of the modal cadence in England at the time of his studentship, with its liking for a tune that wanders round one note. Finally, his harmony, strong as it often is, never leaves the English soil for a moment. It seems to fear the acid, or the dramatic, or the brutal. (Foss, 'Herbert Howells', 115)

Hugh Ottaway notes of the Organ Sonata: 'The kind of harmonic texture that was to reach fulfilment in *Hymnus Paradisi* and the works that followed is already formed here, and its dissolving, kaleidoscopic nature calls for a subtlety of colouring and definition beyond the resources of any organist. Without this subtlety there is a danger of monotony, and many passing details will tend to be submerged' (Ottaway,

of conclusion, he identifies the elements of the *Pastoral* that could be met with derision by its critics but identified as virtues by those in the appropriate frame of mind: 'According as we feel individually, reticence may be the gift of the devil or of the gods, folk-song origin a limitation or an expansion, "fifths" a thorn in the flesh or a blessed relief, common chords an intolerable platitude or a newly-discovered beauty, modal inflection mere mannerism or a world of colour. Vaughan Williams believes in these.'[7] Clearly Howells did too, and the article reveals his priorities as much as Vaughan Williams's.

While the ruminative treatment of material can make Howells's music seem rhapsodic, at least superficially, he was clearly fascinated with musical form, and the combination of fluidity of material and structural ingenuity is a significant hallmark of the mature style. As we shall see, the blending of these elements is fundamental to the effect of his music, the technical processes of each aspect informing those of the other (suggesting that they are in fact two sides of the same coin). Howells's fascination with form has been noted by several commentators and is conveniently supported by the 1919 diary entry about 'long, ponderous thoughts on problems of Musical Form'.[8] The wide range of formal arrangements explored in his music is noteworthy throughout his oeuvre, suggesting a more fundamentally experimental approach than that of most of his English contemporaries. A combination of clear divisions and blurred or overlapping outlines, applied to a wide range of formal schemes (from simple or additive forms to sonata variants and more complex, unorthodox arrangements), makes for varied, unpredictable structures. Ruminative or static elements can also create tension with more dynamic structural points very effectively.

As in the music of the French impressionists (who were of course a significant formative influence on his language),[9] there are periods of apparent stasis in Howells's music: for instance, through the avoidance of obvious teleological progress, in the use of relatively discrete harmonic areas rather than continuous functional progression; or simply through unorthodox foreground and middle-ground harmony, such as through the manipulation of mode and use of colouristic or elliptical progressions. A retreat from chromatic excess can be identified in the music both of the French impressionists and of their English admirers, who rely instead on a balance of colours drawing on modality; non-traditional collections such as whole tone and octatonic scales; and the colouristic deployment of diatonic formations, whether simple triads or chords with added degrees. While such

---

'Herbert Howells and the English Revival', 898–9). I will discuss the 'dissolving, kaleidoscopic' harmonic language with its 'danger of monotony' below.

[7] Howells, 'Vaughan Williams's "Pastoral" Symphony', 132.

[8] Diary entry, 1 March 1919, quoted in Spicer, *Herbert Howells*, 65. It may also be worth recalling his comment, made in connection with the Second Violin Sonata, that 'we youngsters must approach symphonic and sonata forms from new directions'; quoted in Palmer, *A Centenary Celebration*, 72.

[9] Classic impressionist examples of unconventional prolongation and stasis may be found in the whole tone expanses of Debussy's 'Voiles' (*Préludes*, Book I), the sudden shifts of 'Mouvement' (*Images*, Book I) and indeed the combination of the two in 'Cloches à travers les feuilles' (*Images*, Book II).

Ex. 9.1 Sonata for Oboe and Piano, 1st mvt, bars 1–9

devices can result in periods of stasis, they often contribute to the articulation of non-traditional structural devices, whether suggestive of tension and resolution, or reflecting some other dynamic. The song *King David* (HH 102), considered by Christopher Palmer to encapsulate the essence of Howells's compositional style, uses movement between static planes to reflect de la Mare's poem;[10] more usual is a manipulation of elements such as mode to suggest transformation within a grounded framework, for instance in *The Little Boy Lost* (HH 120). This procedure suggests, somewhat paradoxically, a simultaneous sense of stasis and motion, and is a result of the integration of static or elliptical elements into a dynamic formal framework: stasis, or an illusion of stasis, is emphasised while subtle transformations take place, or structurally meaningful relationships are forged, within clear formal outlines. Thematic treatment often reflects this technique, suggesting a free unfolding and exploration of motivic elements in sustained, varied melodic paragraphs. This process again tends to be very carefully controlled, emphasising and developing significant thematic elements in a manner that fosters a sense of structural coherence and integration.

The Oboe Sonata provides opportunities to examine both the static/elliptical and dynamic/structural elements of Howells's mature language, and the manner in which they interact. The harmony of the first movement is emblematic, with a key centre of A being prioritised amid various deflections, typically introducing sharps. The initial deflection to G♯ (as the oboe enters) is prophetic of the many chord

---

[10] Palmer, *A Centenary Celebration*, 130.

Ex. 9.2 Sonata for Oboe and Piano, 1st mvt, bars 38–9

progressions emphasising semitone relationships (Ex. 9.1). Motif *a* is particularly pervasive throughout the first section, appearing in various forms, but often outlining a fourth, augmented fourth or fifth. While the motif often involves two adjacent notes and one that is more remote (for instance the 'leap and step' outline of the first instance), variants of this scheme also occur widely, and the derivation outlining a triad (*a'*) is used repeatedly.

After some abrupt movement between keys, the section concludes with a return of the A pedal note, the approach from G♯ balancing the initial deflection (bar 31); the prominent B♭ and E♭ from bar 34 onwards hint at a Locrian mode. The abrupt fluctuations in harmony dividing these areas give an unsettled, 'suspended' effect, the prioritisation of F♯ and harmonic reference to A minor/C major in bars 26–7 (with a prominent B pedal in the bass, looking ahead to the recurring Locrian element) making it seem elliptical rather than progressive in harmony. A constant motion through ever-fresh areas would be sensuously colourful yet aimless; Howells's harmony is neither, which is precisely why it seems elliptical. In other words, the variation of integrated harmonic elements is ruminative in effect, aided by the progressive treatment of motivic material. Such procedures can be observed in many of his larger works, an excellent example being the first section of the *Cello Fantasia* (HH 205), whose meandering harmony provides a sense of superficial harmonic motion that is brought into focus at the return of the opening E minor chord after figure 2; given the variety of harmonic fluctuation over the previous thirty bars, that is an impressive feat. The subtle shift from tonic to subdominant colouring (through the addition of C♯) manages to conflate the suggestions of both harmonic reference and motion. Perhaps the most impressive example of this process on a large scale is the Third Violin Sonata, particularly the first movement, where local fluctuation is almost entirely constrained within a basic framework that seems to explore primary harmonic centres and areas (whether key notes or collections) from a number of different angles, gradually establishing subtle relationships and hierarchies, often involving careful variation of key and mode.

A second section (Ex. 9.2) recreates the progression from 'suspended' harmony on the sharp side to a Locrian A, with the latter being established more emphatically (Ex. 9.3); while *a* is still used widely, *b* is now particularly prominent, the two

Ex. 9.3 Sonata for Oboe and Piano, 1st mvt, bars 55–6

Ex. 9.4 Sonata for Oboe and Piano, 1st mvt, bars 66–7

final notes being but one example of the many melodic constellations suggestive of suspension and resolution. The impressionistic parallel fifths and dominant formations of bars 66–7 (Ex. 9.4) look ahead to parts of the slow movement, as do some of the semiquaver accompaniment patterns from this point onwards. Howells sometimes uses local disturbances of harmony such as that observed in bars 66–7 to break up periods of stasis or more gradual harmonic motion.

A period of accumulating momentum follows, leading towards a Locrian mode on E. The arrival at this harmonic/modal area is emphatic, the oboe's climactic high F in bar 90 being repeated at the outset of the next section (Ex. 9.5). Locrian harmony/modality is pervasive, as E is clearly prioritised, persisting until bar 112, when a typical deflection ushers in motion towards E minor. Again the effect is a suggestion of simultaneous motion and stasis. There is also, from a functional point of view, an increase in tension. It is of course potentially dangerous to read too much into possible functional implications of modal harmony (for instance, is a Locrian E simultaneously at a lower and higher level of harmonic tension than A minor?), but it should not be discounted as one option in Howells's palette.[11] Perhaps manipulation of mode can be used to suggest destabilisation (rather than harmonic tension per se), and he frequently uses it to build up considerable dissonance within a fundamentally simple harmonic framework.

---

[11] Howells is not the only British composer of his generation to use mode in a quasi-functional manner; see, for instance, my discussion of E. J. Moeran's Sonata for Two Violins and String Trio, 'Technical Focus and "Stylistic Cleansing"'.

Ex. 9.5 Sonata for Oboe and Piano, 1st mvt, bars 102–4

Much-needed textural contrast is provided by an outburst following the abandonment of the oscillating crotchet bass pattern (bar 131), leading to a subdued closing section prioritising E♭ major, whose flattened sixth and seventh degrees (and briefest of raised fourths in bar 155) look ahead to the closing paragraphs of both the slow movement and epilogue. This is an interesting scale (that is, a major scale with sharpened fourth and flattened sixth and seventh degrees), consisting of a complete whole tone scale with one added note; because of the high whole tone content, it is a potentially ambiguous and destabilising collection, but Howells is careful to ground it emphatically on a tonic note. It is furthermore consistently related to an integrating motivic device, a semiquaver figure related to similar patterns earlier in the movement and based on *a* (Ex. 9.6).

The arrival at E♭ is also telling in a number of other ways, first in that it suggests a rather paradoxical resolution of key, absorbing the 'flat tendencies' of the Locrian E and A, and (at least briefly) stabilising the mode, while simultaneously being harmonically remote from the original tonic. Second, E♭ is a key of some significance in Howells's output, being the key of resolution in both *Hymnus paradisi* (HH 220) and the *Missa sabrinensis* (HH 275). In neither case is it the opening key, emerging rather as a key capable of bringing stabilisation and rest. Its use here suggests that he may indeed have viewed it as a temporary stabilisation in the Oboe Sonata, an interpretation supported by the retrospective links to the end of the slow movement and epilogue (more of this below). In *Hymnus* the concluding segment is Lydian, sharing the sharpened fourth of the Oboe Sonata; the *Missa* goes further, also using the flattened sixth and seventh degrees. The endings of the Oboe Sonata and *Missa* are in fact remarkably similar, and the mood of the latter may give an indication of Howells's expressive aims in the closing paragraphs of the Sonata, suggesting transcendence as well as resolution: thus the restless explorations of the central sections are not simply cancelled by the return of primary thematic material and the original tonic, but the final bars suggest a further integration, accepting rather than marginalising the remoter regions.

It may be worth commenting briefly on Howells's approach to texture at this point, as it works in tandem with the elliptical treatment of harmony and motif; much of the effect of his music relies on the accumulation of momentum (or perhaps 'substance' would be an appropriate description) through textural elaboration. This is particularly significant in the choral-orchestral works, but also applies to

Ex. 9.6 Sonata for Oboe and Piano, 1st mvt, bars 27–8/146–8/152–3

passages of smaller works such as the sonatas under consideration here. The passage between bars 79 and 101 is representative, creating space between the Locrian modes on A and E while also accumulating momentum. The constitution of texture is essential to the effect of 'ruminative' harmonic and motivic elements, and the accumulation of intensity or creation of what might be described as an 'expanse of intense material' is a recurring feature of Howells's music. Finzi noted a 'brilliance [that] has led to note-spinning when inspiration has slackened and to the excessive complication, not of the fumbler, but of a mind which really seems unaware of technical difficulties'.[12] While it is understandable that this type of elaboration would have seemed regrettable to Finzi, his evaluation perhaps misunderstands the intended effect, or simply fails to recognise it.[13] In a rather impressionistic procedure, Howells uses the accumulation of textural and dynamic intensity as one among several local devices suggesting increasing tension or momentum; this is particularly useful where the rate of underlying harmonic motion is relatively slow. Once again, the appearance can be static, while the intensification of sound mass is actually dynamic.

The first movement of the Oboe Sonata is expository, establishing primary harmonic and thematic elements as a point of departure. References to conventional sonata structuring are ambiguous, and the possible interpretation as a sonata exposition with two discrete subjects (those pervaded primarily by *a* and *b*, respectively) is not borne out by later treatment of material. Rather, the resumption of *b* in the Scherzo contributes to the overall outline of a continuous arch, with the end of the slow movement being the most remote point from the framing sections in A. The slow movement follows on continuously from the first, recycling material from a much earlier song, 'O Garlands, Hanging by the Door (HH 121 – 1921). The initial section is characterised by a rich, saturated diatonicism, transposed down a semitone from the song's C major, but reharmonised slightly to centre on G♯ minor rather than B major. The parallel ascending triads found in the original are reserved for the intrusion of chromatic chords, first in bar 13, then from bar 26 onwards, when the song's rolling semiquaver accompaniment pattern is introduced (Ex. 9.7). At this point, both texture and harmony refer back to features of the opening movement, especially bars 66–89, suggesting that these similarities may have recalled

[12] Finzi, 'Herbert Howells', 181.

[13] Howells was not surprised by Finzi's reservations, writing to him after the publication of the article: 'I could have listed beforehand the features of my works that w^d have given you the more or less satisfaction' (11 April 1954). This did not deter Finzi from making a similar remark about the *Missa sabrinensis*: 'one found the complication of texture a bit exhausting to take in for the first time' (10 September 1954). Finzi–Howells correspondence, courtesy of Stephen Banfield and the Gerald Finzi Trust.

Ex. 9.7 Sonata for Oboe and Piano, 2nd mvt, b. 26

the song to his mind when contemplating the Oboe Sonata's slow movement. More fundamentally, the use of pre-existing material suggests that he wanted to incorporate an idyllic, innocent serenity that differs sharply from the half-lights of the first movement; perhaps he felt that the style of the song would suit his expressive purposes at least as well as any new material he could provide. The contrasts of mood, key and texture certainly aid the sense of remoteness, which is further emphasised by the final harmonic dissolution.

After some harmonic fluctuation, an *assai tranquillo* coda reinstates the original (slow movement) key signature, now explicitly embracing B major (rather than the Aeolian G♯ minor of the opening), although, as already noted, this is coloured in the final gesture by flattened sixth and seventh degrees and a sharpened fourth degree, a feature repeated at the end of the work (where it is centred on A). The resulting whole tone flavour suggests dissolution or suspension, but at the end of the work the effect is nevertheless one of resolution – a dispersal of tension, perhaps. The collection anchored on B is of course almost identical to the one that closes the work (and indeed the E♭ version leading to the slow movement), suggesting an ultimate absorption of the slow movement's key into the stable outer areas.

The conspicuous harmonic anchoring in the tonic at the outset, meanwhile, resembles the outer movements of the Organ Sonata (HH 25) and the final movement of *Hymnus paradisi*. The latter contrasts sharply with the movements that precede it, where oblique approaches to tonicised areas, varied use of mode and chromaticism destabilise any strong sense of a primary key, with a number of recurring key areas or axes emerging throughout the work. The final part, 'Holy Is the True Light', is stabilised by the emphatic articulation of E♭ in the outer sections (minor and major, respectively – as in the Oboe Sonata), after a predominance of 'sharp' keys in the earlier movements. In the Oboe Sonata, the emphatic establishment of the tonic key suggests an analogous impulse to 'ground' the extended, complex form harmonically before deviating into less stable areas. This surely also reflects generic convention, as English composers of Howells's generation continued to see chamber music as an abstract and technical genre; Bliss's experiments of the 1920s are exceptions that prove the rule, making use of unorthodox ensembles and overtly rhapsodic generic/formal schemes, in contrast to the serious tone and complex forms of his later chamber works in established, historically prestigious chamber genres.[14]

---

[14] Other pertinent examples include Frank Bridge's continued search for formal-structural complexity articulated by his radical post-tonal language from the

The large-scale A minor–B major–A major progression across the entire Oboe Sonata provides an overarching harmonic framework, focusing the local disturbances. The initial deflections prefigure the later progressions to 'sharp' keys, both remote (B major) and stabilising (A major). It is likely that Howells would have felt such emphatic harmonic solidity and logic to be a necessary component in chamber music composition on a large scale. Motivic treatment ties in with this aesthetic, with continuous development of motifs creating fluidity without obscuring the structural significance of primary motivic elements. Such procedures are of course typical of Howells more generally, enhancing the ruminative effect, and strengthening the impression of a freely unfolding form, while in fact exercising an advanced level of control. Thus the illusion of rhapsody is created, implying a duality that perfectly sums up his later style, suggesting unconstrained expression within the parameters of rigorously controlled technical elements. There is more than a hint of rotational processes, operating on several levels. In particular, the resumption of first-movement material in the slow movement, and the links between the end of the latter and the epilogue, create a complex network of relationships that once again balance static and developmental tendencies. The closing material in particular, simultaneously suggesting distance and proximity to the part of the work that appears to be most remote from the primary material (the end of the slow movement), illustrates this combination of traits.

The intervening scherzo is substantial, and makes widespread use of *b* (cf. Ex. 9.2) and various motifs derived from it. The movement is characterised by considerable energy and forward momentum, the nervous staccato semiquaver figures of the opening (Ex. 9.8) resembling Walton.[15] The grim, determined tone more generally is notably different from the light-hearted, rustic tone of early scherzando music, in keeping with the wider turn away from idyllic pastoralism towards a more complex, abstract stylistic conception. Compare it, for instance, with the rustic 'giocoso' styles of the first of the *Three Dances* (HH 48ii) or the Second Piano Concerto finale (or indeed the initial 'Hard and Bright' Allegro) (HH 152), a change in mood also felt in the 'giocoso' finale of the Concerto for Strings (HH 215).

The harmony of the Scherzo's 7/8 section is notable, with frequent C major chords, a widespread E minor orientation, and the eventual intrusion of B♭s recalling the opening chords of the movement, framing it very effectively. There is some harmonic fluctuation in the ensuing cadenza-like passage, the melismatic oboe part breaking free from the nervous energy of the Scherzo, and a sense of relaxation is achieved in a number of linked steps – first the B♭ of the opening of the movement is dropped, with the F♯ bass recalling the Locrian formations of the first movement;

1920s onwards, and E. J. Moeran's turn to chamber music in the early 1930s as he sought to improve his technical control, not least of structural parameters. The closest this group of composers came to abandoning the generic prerequisite for intricate technical working and integration of structure was in a rhapsodic tendency exemplified by Vaughan Williams's chamber music and Howells's early one-movement works.

[15] A *Musical Times* review of the Clarinet Sonata also noted the similarities with Walton (Mason, 'New Music', 25).

Ex. 9.8 Sonata for Oboe and Piano, 3rd mvt, bars 1–4

similar constellations centred on other notes are then explored before the original collection returns, now suggesting G major (bar 268), leading to the resumption of the opening material and key, A minor, two bars later (the opening of the epilogue). The Scherzo thus fills an interim position in the arch-shaped harmonic progress of the work: the first movement articulates a subtle process of destabilisation and increase of tension, linking seamlessly with the remote regions of the slow movement, which also reuses and develops motivic material (notably *a*); the Scherzo then recycles several other elements of the first movement (notably *b*) and begins to fill in the considerable harmonic distance covered by the previous material, preparing for the epilogue.

This final section opens in A minor and recreates the initial deflection from the tonic. The introduction of sharps that this involves is however absorbed by the ensuing establishment of the tonic major, neutralising the harmonic meandering and destabilising manipulation of mode observed previously. The final dissolution of key into the integrating whole tone collection then draws the disparate tendencies of the entire work into closer relation, revealing an additional, underlying sense of structural coherence. The simultaneous fluidity and purposefulness of form that Howells had aimed for in several earlier chamber works (for instance in the *Rhapsodic Quintet* (HH 107) and violin sonatas) reaches its pinnacle in the Oboe Sonata, with style and logic being mutually defining.

In contemplating this style we can distinguish all of the 'gifts of the gods' identified by Howells in Vaughan Williams's *Pastoral Symphony* – a certain reticence, the inflections of folk-song, modality, as well as parallel fifths and common chords in abundance. The first three points are closely related, most obviously 'modality' and 'folk-song', although the idea of 'reticence' is brought to bear strongly on these features. An avoidance of stark contrasts and dramatic gestures is crucial, an ebbing and flowing style of both harmony and melody being favoured. Howells's admiration for both Vaughan Williams's and Gurney's melodic styles, and his comparison of their typical 'gentle' melodic outlines to 'the Malvern Hills … when viewed from afar', is a useful point of reference.[16] The simplicity of Gurney's mature

---

[16] 'Vaughan Williams's tunes will not "draw faces", or produce crude pictures of craggy heights. But they will often give you a shape akin to such an outline as the Malvern

style is contrasted with the unsuccessful complexity and confusion of his earliest efforts, exemplified by 'piano preludes thick with untamed chords' and 'violin sonatas strewn with ecstatic crises'.[17] In the references to the Malverns, alongside other allusions to English culture, from Gurney's engagement with English poetry to an implied connection of the *Pastoral Symphony* to a great national heritage (through an indirect comparison with Byrd and Weelkes), there are clear implications of Englishness, along with connotations of pastoralism, that also shed some light on Howells's views on his own music. Specifically, elements of style are related to Englishness and its essential traits of restraint and reticence.

Howells's early pastoral style followed in the footsteps of composers such as Vaughan Williams, Holst and Bax, with whom it shared a prominent French influence. Like his English precursors, Howells and contemporaries such as Moeran and Warlock soon moved away from their earlier naive and idyllic styles, towards a grimmer tone and exploration of more complex expressive areas. In Howells's music in particular this trend seems to have encouraged a type of abstract pastoralism in line with his comments about the Malverns and the measured and integrative approach to influences such as folk-song and Tudor music. His music tends to be more absolute, in a sense more technical, than that of the prominent earlier English pastoralists, and the development of a greater ambivalence of mood in his later music can be related to an increasingly complex structural conception, reflected in his use of mode. Thus a desire for structural coherence and integration interacts with a desire for formal ingenuity, in an attempt to create relationships appropriate to the specific expressive concerns of each work. The manipulation of elements such as mode and texture widens the range of options open to Howells in the constitution of formal-structural units.

Although aspects of these techniques are quite radical in their own way, the exploratory aspects of Howells's music are nevertheless clearly in line with what Arnold Whittall identifies as the 'sane and socially responsible' modernity envisaged by Vaughan Williams,[18] a view closely bound up with the English attitude to nature (and tradition) as a spiritual tonic and force for moral good, exemplified, for instance, by Gurney's mystical and evocative article 'The Springs of Music'. The emphasis on nature as a wholesome artistic inspiration establishes for this type of art a heightened function as positive moral expression and stimulant, relating to the issues of national identity already alluded to, and contributing to a construct of healthy, moral Englishness strongly at odds with much (perceived) over-intellectualised, morally and aesthetically suspect continental modernism.[19] Thus musical nationalism was related to a celebration of the English countryside as an embodiment of

> Hills present when viewed from afar' (Howells, 'Vaughan Williams's "Pastoral" Symphony', 127); 'Gurney's melodic speech is a "kindly" human utterance – as gentle as the outline of the Malverns' (Howells, 'The Musician', 15).

[17] Howells, 'The Musician', 13.
[18] Whittall, 'British Music in the Modern World', 14.
[19] For a discussion of implications of health and morality in musical discourse in Britain, see Scott, 'The Sexual Politics of Victorian Musical Aesthetics'; and Heckert, 'Schoenberg, Roger Fry and the Emergence of a Critical Language'. For a more general discussion, see Collini, *Public Moralists*.

moral superiority, a discourse to which Howells's contributions cited above clearly contribute (building on the writings of both Vaughan Williams and Gurney).

The prominence of pastoralist art throughout this period, investing nature and rurality with 'a talismanic significance as everything that contemporary, urban England was not but yet might be',[20] further relates to a nostalgic view of nature encouraged by war and imperial contraction. Jed Esty notes that in 'shrinking back to its original island centre, England would no longer be a world-historical nation, but it might recapture the humanist, aesthetic, and pastoralist values that had been eroded or degraded by imperialist capitalism'.[21] It is interesting to note that Howells and contemporaries such as Vaughan Williams, Bax, Bliss and Moeran quickly moved away from the experimental elements and obvious cosmopolitan influences (notably French and Russian) of the 1910s and 1920s. The naive, almost exoticist use of folk material is also largely discarded, leading to a more abstract, inward-looking approach. Edwin Evans's comments in a 1920 article on Howells are a particularly subtle, early example of how this process operated – he notes that nationalism is a limiting interim position between a 'false internationalism' orientated towards Germany and a 'true internationalism in which all idioms alike will be admitted full citizenship'.[22] Imperialism is aligned with false internationalism, while the local influence of the Gloucestershire countryside ('a better school than any academy') on Howells is aligned with true internationalism.[23]

The result is a personal, self-contained language with a strong English identity and clear roots in dominant aesthetic trends of the 1910s and 1920s. The Oboe Sonata explores some of the furthest limits of this style, developing an intricacy of structure that draws on the full breadth of Howells's technical apparatus and stylistic palette, and is in fact facilitated by the generic constraints. His withdrawal of the work suggests that he was unsure whether the result was viable, and the simplification of certain elements in the Clarinet Sonata represents a retreat into safer territory. Most noticeably, there is a tendency towards a greater transparency of structural relationships, allied to simplification of local complexities. The opening, for instance, is more straightforward in texture and presentation of principal material (Ex. 9.9). A recurring ambiguity of key and mode is introduced by the D pedal, however, suggesting a Dorian mode, although the subsequent appearance of G♯s also suggests a possible A minor orientation; the reappearance of this material at the end of the movement, over an A pedal, is an extremely simple form of stabilisation, contrasting strongly with the continuous unfolding, across several movements, of the Oboe Sonata.

Howells uses a clear sonata form, with the second subject preceding the first in the recapitulation. The subtleties of texture, motivic working and harmony/mode of the earlier work are noticeably toned down. Instead of the complex interrelations of key and mode, for example, he often restricts himself to the Dorian/Aeolian ambiguity just mentioned. This is revisited in a sort of false recapitulation, in a

---

[20] Mandler, 'Against "Englishness"', 170.
[21] Esty, *A Shrinking Island*, 39.
[22] Evans, 'Herbert Howells', 87.
[23] *Ibid.*, 88.

Ex. 9.9 Sonata for Clarinet and Piano, 1st mvt, bars 1–4

Dorian G♯ minor, at [8], and something similar can be observed at [2], where a reappearance of the opening theme occurs during a transition from a Dorian C♯ minor to G♯ minor/A♭ major, precisely the key centre used at [8]. Further ambiguity is created by the alternation between major and minor modes (as observed at the two points just mentioned, and, most prominently, the final gesture of the work), as well as the simultaneous use of major and minor thirds, and the use of false relations. Structural divisions are clear, suggesting an episodic formal conception with obvious rotational aspects; thus the later appearances of the first subject – that is, the 'false recapitulation' and final paragraphs in A minor – balance the initial harmonic deflection in the exposition, while also moving further to stabilise the first subject itself. The second subject prepares for this final resolution, while the intervening reappearance of the development's syncopated chords (themselves derived from the 3 + 3 + 2 pattern of the first subject) helps to release the tension accrued during the development. There are obvious parallels with the Oboe Sonata in the concluding integration of initially disparate strands to achieve a final stabilisation, but the outlines of the process are simpler, with obvious divisions between self-contained, relatively static blocks of material.

The structural tension created through these devices is more immediately obvious than comparable processes in the Oboe Sonata, also leading to simpler local relationships and long-range structural outlines. The similarities between the two sonatas suggest that Howells was still mulling over aspects of the earlier work, however. Besides the similarities of construction, the Scherzos in particular have many parallels; the rhythmic central part of the first movement also resembles the corresponding section of the Oboe Sonata, and the accumulation of harmonic tension in the first movement, leading to a resumption of primary material in G♯ minor, is another direct parallel.

Despite similarities in the basic form of the second movement, the closure at the end of the first movement makes for a very different structural dynamic. The second movement does not now need to bear the full responsibility of resolution (or dispersal) of tension, and as a result both the Scherzo and the reappearance of first-movement material fulfil different roles than their counterparts in the Oboe Sonata. The Scherzo is more independent, and the opening is more emphatically anchored in an obvious key centre – F♯, suggesting a Phrygian mode that occasionally points towards B minor. This shifts towards C♯ and less stable harmony,

Ex. 9.10 Sonata for Clarinet and Piano, 2nd mvt, bars 194–5

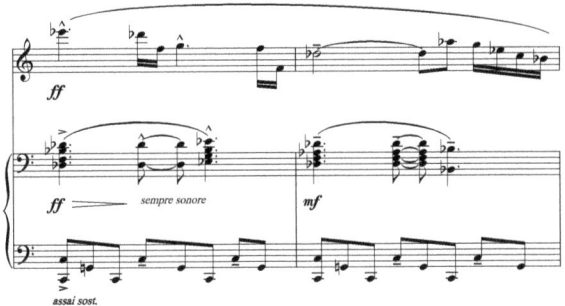

Ex. 9.11 Sonata for Clarinet and Piano, 2nd mvt, bars 272–3

including a rhythmic section recalling the syncopated chords of the Oboe Sonata's 7/8 segment. The progression from primary scherzo material in F♯ to more remote areas, leading to a syncopated section, is then repeated (after 7), the second rotation building in intensity and merging into a climactic, dissonant outburst (Ex. 9.10), whose harmony is suggestive of Phrygian and Locrian formations on C, with suggestions of bitonal combinations (D♭ and G♭ over the C pedal).

The use of the Phrygian mode obviously relates to the initial F♯ material, and further destabilisation after four bars, as dynamic intensity subsides, suggests a suspension of tension. There are parallels here with the cadenza section in the Oboe Sonata, a similarity highlighted by the sudden stabilisation provided by first-movement material in the home key, in this case the second subject in A major. Rather than simply staying in this key, Howells elects to move back to scherzo material in A minor, via a brief, self-contained reference to the first subject of the first movement. This resumes the D pedal that opens the work, but tends towards the minor and makes much of the alternation of C♯ and C♮, suggesting a destabilisation of mode that ultimately shifts the focus onto the tonic note in the final gesture (Ex. 9.11).

There are thus some arch-like formal elements, particularly the progressive harmonic motion and the reappearance of first-movement material to bring about stabilisation, but their effect is gentler than that of the large, suspended spans of the Oboe Sonata and their eventual absorption and dispersal. In both works, Howells experiments with frameworks that provide the type of structural solidity felt to be required in this genre; in the Oboe Sonata this leads to a rather mystical conclusion, while the Clarinet Sonata, with its simplified outlines, can be more lighthearted. The relationship of Howells's explorations of form and structure to his stylistic/aesthetic preferences varies in other substantial works from this period and subsequently, according to his expressive intentions, and is often informed by generic tradition. It is interesting to note that this consideration becomes more pronounced in the later music, establishing a curious parallel with his contemporaries Walton and Bliss, whose early experimental tendencies similarly appear to be reined in through the adoption of traditional genres from the later 1920s onwards.

In parallel with this development, there is an increasing depth to elements of Howells's style and language, and their expressive potential. We can observe a much more complex interrelation of elements in the later music, resulting in more tightly knit structures, while also encouraging greater vividness of expression and variety of mood. This is heavily influenced by the advanced manipulation of mode and harmony, and the imaginative treatment of texture and thematic/motivic material. In the Clarinet Sonata, Howells applies the concision of presentation and structural outline of his shorter works to a larger, more complex framework. In the Oboe Sonata he does the opposite, testing the potential of numerous technical elements; perhaps he felt, in hindsight, and spurred on by Goossens's comments, that the result was too obscure, too forbidding. Both works, however, present an imaginative engagement with the technical requirements of the duo sonata genre, within whose constraints Howells's strategies of integration of disparate technical elements and procedures achieve a remarkable coherence of style and structure.

PART IV

Howells the Modern

CHAPTER 10

'Tunes all the way'? Romantic Modernism and the Piano Concertos of Herbert Howells

Jonathan Clinch

THE release in May 2000 of not one but two piano concertos by Herbert Howells was hailed as 'an astonishing revelation'.[1] Both technically advanced and well crafted, Howells's piano concertos make a significant contribution to British music at the start of the twentieth century and, although discarded by the composer, demand a central position in any reassessment of Howells. For the scholar of British music, these are major artistic statements that function as significant commentaries on their period; and as an increasing number of publications emerge critiquing the ways in which British composers adapted and reacted to Continental Modernism, Howells, in particular, demands attention.

The piano concertos date from 1913 and 1924. The first (HH 31), written during Howells's initial year of study at the Royal College of Music (RCM), could arguably be regarded as the last Romantic British piano concerto, focusing heavily on models of Elgar, Stanford and Parry. The second (HH 152), premiered in 1925, could equally be considered the first British Modernist piano concerto. The piano concertos (and specifically Howells's journey from the first to the second) give us a vivid picture of Howells the modernising[2] composer, working through a period Constant Lambert labelled 'The Revolutionary Situation'.[3] Their reception, likewise, demonstrates much about the critical press and general state of music in Britain at the time.

Aesthetically, to view Howells as a Modernist, especially through the lens of his piano concertos, is difficult to justify, particularly when 'modern music' now represents far more avant-garde musics. Ultimately, Modernism is a chronologically moving target, making it a dangerously vague term to use at such an early stage of reappraisal. However, it is the subtle mixing of Romantic and Modernist elements that makes Howells particularly interesting to scholars of British culture – positioning him as a leading 'Romantic Modern'.[4] Alexandra Harris uses the term to critique the specifically English way in which artists and writers of the 1930s

---

[1] Herbert Howells, Piano Concerto no. 1, Piano Concerto no. 2 and *Penguinski*, Howard Shelley (piano), BBC Symphony Orchestra, Richard Hickox (conductor), audio CD (Chandos, 2000), CHAN 9874. Reviewed in the *Gramophone* (March 2001), 58.

[2] Michael Levenson writes 'it will prove better to be minimalist in our definition of that conveniently flaccid term *Modernism* and maximalist in our accounts of the diverse *modernizing* works and movements' (Levenson, *The Cambridge Companion to Modernism*, 3).

[3] Lambert, *Music Ho!*, 11–15.

[4] Harris, *Romantic Moderns*.

and 1940s 'showed that "the modern" need not be at war with the past',[5] a reconciling of Modernist and Romantic elements, whose tempered Modernism could be argued to have had a greater impact than the great Modernist 'statements', which often suffered from a lack of understanding in Britain. Like the subject matter it describes, the term offers a more subtle account of British modernism in relation to its more extreme foreign neighbour, Continental Modernism. This chapter is therefore about the way in which Howells pursued this new artistic agenda. There is a significant advance in technical sophistication and artistic maturation between the concertos, and it continued through the 1930s in works such as the Concerto for String Orchestra (HH 215). Neither piano concerto, therefore, could be used to define Howells's music for more than a short period, but they are both part of an overall progression that needs to be historically contextualised. In the context of Howells's career we need to understand their significance and what they tell us about his later works. Within that specific period we need to understand how they reflect the foremost influences, how each of the works functions, and what they tell us today.

It is clear that Howells was extremely aware of the latest trends within contemporary composition. Not only did he attend numerous concerts, but he met many of the leading modernists of the day in person, including Stravinsky, Bartók and Ravel. He also admired Debussy, Berg and Prokofiev. Like Parry, he went out of his way to hear and study the latest music, even though he admitted it was often not to his taste. He was also very much involved in a wider discourse, asking the specific question 'What is modern music?' in a radio lecture series entitled 'Music and the Ordinary Listener: The Modern Problem' in 1937.

The first lecture began:[6]

What is 'modern music'?
That's a question for whose answer many a jesting Pilate will not wait. <u>What</u>, indeed is it? Is it the gospel of a brutal chord, like my half-crown expletive?
Is it found in the melancholy fugal beginning of the Hindemith Quartet some of you heard last Sunday night?
Is it Richard Strauss in 'Rosenkavalier', where he turns the harmonic series into an entrancing kaleidoscopic confusion of upper-partials?
Are we to find 'modernity' in the cut-throat opposition of two dove-like common chords used in a diabolical admixture by Stravinsky to express Petrushka's impotent rage?
Is the answer to be found in Gustav Holst's 'Planets'? – in 'Neptune'? Or is it in the hurtling clash of 'Mars', in the same work?
Does modernity wear a sour visage? Maybe it's a roguish brilliance called 'Facade' – or last night's thundering at aural doors, called 'Belshazzar's Feast'. Is it a display of power? Ask Mr Bela Bartok – and his answer may be this: (1st 'Bagatelle' – on piano).

---

[5] *Ibid.*, jacket back.
[6] 12 February 1937. Script contained in the Herbert Howells Archive, Box B.

And where does 'modernity' live? Is its G.H.Q. set up where Schonberg, von Webern and the lamented Alban Berg have lived and worked so much – in the city of Johann Strauss and his enchanting waltzes? Is it Paris – the city of musical sixes-and-sevens and of strutting Art Manifestos? Does it issue from Germany with a passport bearing the signature of Paul Hindemith? It is not for us to deny it a home in Tokyo, or Fiji, or Matabeleland. Some will say Harlem is its abode, and Tin Pan Alley its paradise – others, that it lives most comfortably in our own most tolerant capital city – where it surges in apparently uncontrollable tides about the strands of Langham Place. Who shall say?

It's a complex business. And there are extraneous difficulties. There even occurs, sometimes, the terrifying thought that, after all, modern music is merely an '-ism'.

Whether an '-ism' or not, Howells's two piano concertos certainly differ significantly in conception and style, and chart significant changes in his compositional direction.

Piano Concerto No. 1 in C Minor (HH 31)

On 10 July 1914 Herbert Howells's First Piano Concerto received its premiere at the Queen's Hall, London. Howells, at the age of twenty-one, and despite coming from one of the poorest of imaginable family circumstances, had produced a piano concerto of such merit that it was recommended by Charles Stanford to be included as the major work in the Twenty-Third RCM Patron's Fund Concert.

Howells had very little orchestral experience. Whether his lessons with Herbert Brewer included orchestration is unknown, but the claim in the preface to the Novello edition that this was his first orchestral work is contrary to Edwin Evans's 1919 *Musical Times* article, which lists an 'Overture for Orchestra' (1910/11) that has never come to light. More importantly, Howells certainly would not have *heard* any orchestral music in a backwater like Lydney, so it is likely that his only experience of a live orchestra would have been when the Three Choirs Festival came to Gloucester in 1907 and 1910.

Although the initial impetus to write a piano concerto remains unknown, it seems likely that the suggestion would have come from Stanford. Stanford's own Piano Concerto in C minor (no. 2, Op. 126) had been finished in July 1911 but was still awaiting its first performance. Stanford's own major influence, that of Rachmaninoff's Second Piano Concerto in C minor, was certainly passed on to the young Howells. Stanford had conducted the Rachmaninoff work at the RCM in 1908, but the work 'undoubtedly made a more profound impression at Leeds in 1910', when he conducted it at the festival with the composer himself as soloist.[7] Howells dedicated his concerto to its first soloist, Arthur Benjamin. As well as being an extremely talented pianist, Benjamin was also a composition pupil of Stanford. Although younger than Howells, he had arrived at the RCM earlier, in 1911. Their friendship had developed early, and Benjamin took Howells on his first trip abroad when they visited Switzerland together in the summer of 1913.

---

[7] Dibble, *Charles Villiers Stanford*, 425.

Howells's command of concerto form seems remarkable at such an early stage, but he did have some experience of articulating such a large structure. As part of his submissions for an open scholarship he had included a Violin Sonata in B minor (HH 24). In both style and form Edward Elgar's music leaps from every page,[8] from the stately opening in octaves to the second subject of the final movement (marked 'Nobilmente – sul G', a typical Elgarian 'big tune' with marching bass[9] – replicating the opening of Elgar's Symphony no. 1). It is most likely that Howells used Elgar's recently composed Violin Concerto as a model for his sonata. In addition to the features already noted, the choice of B minor and a three-movement structure are unusual. Howells had recently met Elgar at the 1910 Three Choirs Festival and may even have been at the private run-through of the Violin Concerto given by Elgar and Kreisler. Following the success of the first performance in London, the second performance at the 1911 Three Choirs Festival (in Worcester) would have made that particular piece the talk of the area at the very time that Howells had abandoned lessons with Herbert Brewer to write his portfolio for the scholarship. Howells later said that English composers 'suddenly woke up around 1900', and it was Elgar who showed that we 'could be a nation of orchestral composers'.[10]

Alongside the influence of Elgar, that of Parry should also be noted. The introduction, during which all of the subjects appear, could quite easily be mistaken for Parry as it mirrors a typical formula used at the start of his big choral works. As the opening mirrors Parry, the quasi-folk-dance of the final movement is a significant nod to Stanford's *Irish Symphony*, with its notable *hopjig* Scherzo. The harmonic language throughout could be seen as an extension of Parry's own use of diatonic dissonance; the frequent appoggiaturas, use of pedal points and dissonant bass moves are all traits of Parry's symphonic style. The most significant foreign influences are those of Rachmaninoff and Debussy. So much of Howells's pianism stems from the example of Rachmaninoff, and Howells even played Rachmaninoff's Prelude in C♯ minor for his Royal Academy of Music audition.

The programme booklet for the first performance contains an eight-page analytical note on the concerto, presumably by Howells himself, highlighting the function of the introduction: 'This Concerto consists of three movements, of which the last two are linked. The first is prefaced by what amounts to an introduction … But the relationship of this introduction is as much to the latter movements as to the first, and contains derivatives of most of the themes on which the work is built.'[11] Despite Howells's prodigious talent the first performance was not a huge success. Arthur Bliss, a contemporary student of Stanford, later commented 'I can play the first phrases of your early Piano Concerto in C minor which I heard at the College, badly conducted by Stanford I believe. Certain things remain.'[12] Hubert Parry's diary makes two references to the concerto:

---

[8] Clark, *Elgar and the Three Cathedral Organists*, 33.
[9] RCM, MS 4655, 29, third system.
[10] Interview with Herbert Howells, May 1977, British Sound Archive, B2951.
[11] Programme of the Twenty-Third RCM Patron's Fund Concert, 4.
[12] Palmer, *A Centenary Celebration*, 373.

> March 27th 1914: Henschel [conductor of the Scottish Orchestra] to examine compositions & orchestra etc. Some very good compositions. Benjamin's Clarinet & String 5tet interesting. Howells' Concerto strenuous but too long. Benjamin played it very well.
>
> July 10th 1914: To Queen's Hall for Patron's Fund rehearsal. Howells' concerto presenting great difficulties.

It seems that Howells agreed, referring to 'its murder by critics' in a later speech.[13] The reviewer of the *Musical Times* opined: 'Mr Howells greatly taxed his powers of imagination in attempting a Pianoforte concerto; in aiming at breadth and dignity he only arrived at a certain stiffness of manner that did not engage the hearer's interest. There is no doubt of Mr Howells's great ability, and no reason why he should put it to such ascetic use.'[14] However, it did make a positive impact on several people, including the critic Eaglefield Hull, who referred to it as 'a magnificent work, well worth ranking by those of Rachmaninov which we hear so frequently',[15] and fellow student Ivor Gurney, who wrote to Howells from the trenches: 'I often think of your Concerto and its strength and beauty. It is a work which must one day force itself on the attention of a world whose mind, alas, must for sometime be fixed on other things.'[16]

In later life Howells abandoned the concerto completely, giving the manuscript to his close friend, Sydney Shimmin. When Christopher Palmer came to write about it in his initial study of Howells's music he dismissed it as 'a student work'[17] – no doubt reflecting Howells's own rejection of the work. The manuscript was donated to the RCM library in Shimmin's bequest, but by that time the final page of the manuscript had come loose and was missing. In order to prepare the concerto for publication in 1999, John Rutter wrote a new final page to complete the work. He also found that there were:

> numerous errors and inconsistencies in the manuscript ... The piece, though impressive and accomplished, was an apprentice work, his first essay in orchestral writing, and not surprisingly he wasn't always very accurate in his notation, though there were few places where his intention was not clear even though there might be missing accidentals, inconsistent phrasing between instruments, illogical dynamics, transposing instruments mis-transposed etc.
>
> ... The problem with the piece is not the orchestral writing but the finger-breaking piano writing. Nevertheless it does deserve being played, as a work – a fascinating might-have-been. There are echoes of Rachmaninov, Brahms and Debussy (*La Mer*, which he clearly knew, had been published only five years earlier) but you can hear Howells speaking with his own voice.[18]

---

[13] Speech to the RAM Club in 1955, Herbert Howells Archive, Box D.
[14] Review of Howells, First Piano Concerto, *Musical Times* (1 August 1914), 540.
[15] Spicer, *Herbert Howells*, 37.
[16] Letter from Ivor Gurney to Howells, 19 August 1916; see Palmer, *A Centenary Celebration*, 42.
[17] Palmer, *Herbert Howells: A Study*, 30.
[18] John Rutter, interview with author, 16 August 2010.

Howells adopted these influences in a very direct way. Stanford's own book on musical composition (written in 1911) takes the student through the writing of a sonata movement by mirroring one by Beethoven, bar by bar.[19] It is therefore not surprising that Howells would replicate the form of Rachmaninoff's Second Piano Concerto so closely in his own concerto. A later talk by Howells addresses the practice of imitation directly:

> I speak as an individual, ordinary Englishman. That may very well mean my views will not be shared by any of my fellow-countrymen! In our musical tastes and preferences we are *a race of individualists*. Our composers do not seek common ground. They do not group themselves in *schools*. We have no equivalent of the French preoccupation with the numeral called 'six'. We do not pull together. Our estimates of musical values do not tally.
> ... Today English music is *restless* but *vital*. It is technically assured to the point of brilliance ... The history of English music is a fantastic story of Death and Resurrection – a thing of *periodic* rather than *sustained* triumph.
> ... we have never been shy of borrowing. But we have borrowed *creatively*. We have done that in *all* the arts, not least in *music*. Like the Germans, we have been *improvers* rather than *inventors*.[20]

Given how strongly Howells rejected the concept of nationalism in music here, the initial preoccupation of Katharine Eggar's 1922 article on Howells, 'An English Composer', may come as a surprise, and emphasises the preoccupations of a highly conservative press: 'Mr Howells is a composer who is not afraid to own to his nationality. It is for him a matter of deep and happy satisfaction – a matter to be daily grateful for – that he is English, that he belongs to England and that England's great and long musical heritage belongs to him.'[21] There is an obvious tension between a perceived 'foreign' Modernism and the (newly) established British music, and Howells clearly encouraged this – 'I am a "modern" in this, but a Britisher too!'[22] In the years following the First Piano Concerto Howells courted considerable success with awards from the Carnegie Trust and Cobbett Phantasy Competition; performances at the Three Choirs and the Proms; and his first employment, briefly at Salisbury Cathedral, and then Westminster Cathedral and the RCM. Through his success, Howells also becomes a major influence on others: for example, William Walton in an interview of 1968 related having consciously modelled his Piano Quartet (1918–21) on Howells's in order to achieve success.[23] Howells had become an established composer.

Piano Concerto No. 2 in C Major (HH 152)

Howells's return to the piano concerto genre was a significant statement. To date, his major successes had been in two fields – chamber music and short orchestral

---

[19] Stanford, *Musical Composition*, 79.
[20] Herbert Howells, untitled talk given in July 1956, Herbert Howells Archive, Box D.
[21] Eggar, 'An English Composer'.
[22] Spicer, *Herbert Howells*, 57.
[23] Lloyd, *William Walton*, 24.

pieces – and there was quite a deliberate difference in style between them. In his chamber music, Howells addressed important composition problems (primarily of form) in a serious way. His orchestral music on the other hand was far lighter in character (examples include 'Puck's Minuet' (HH 83i), *Procession* (HH 125) and 'Merry-Eye' (HH 83ii)) with a concentration on Stravinskian colour and wit. By writing a piano concerto at this stage, Howells brought together these two sides of his compositional personality, attempting to write a piece of absolute music that would impress both the critical and compositional establishments, and the general public in search of 'tunes'. Our two major questions are, therefore, how did he reconcile these two elements (which have a direct parallel in the dualistic Romantic Modernism concept) – and was he successful?

In terms of reception history, the answer is a firm no. As will be explained below, there was a major incident that overshadowed the music itself. From the very beginning, however, Howells was giving the public mixed messages about the function of his concerto. On the one hand the Second Piano Concerto was the biggest of Howells's 'experiments with sonata form';[24] on the other, Howells created significant anticipation of a far more popular and conservative work by referring to it as 'a diatonic affair – deliberate tunes all the way'. An article in *The Music Teacher* introduced the work in some detail:

> The work which Mr Howells has just finished is a concerto in C for piano and orchestra. This was composed for Harold Samuel, who will give the first performance of it on his return from South Africa. The composer calls it 'a diatonic affair – deliberate tunes all the way – even episodes taking on the semblance of new themes (but themes which are closely derived or developed from the main subjects). As with the first violin sonata's form, so with this, there is no break between movements. But the two works have nothing else in common. The concerto, for the most part, is extremely definite in expression; jolly in feeling; and attempts to get to the point as rapidly as may be. There are no cadenzas; and the piano takes, as it were, a place among the orchestral instruments from time to time. The work is more concerned with counterpoint (of a modern sort) than with harmonic "colour", and it will take less than 20 minutes in performance ... there's little time for symphonic lengths, these days.'[25]

Howells's dismissive tone in this passage seems remarkable, given how modern the piece was. Through his output to date Howells would have come across as a highly ambitious and precocious talent; this passage seems to show Howells moving away from that, possibly in search of mass appeal. Perhaps it is not surprising that critics went to the premiere in a hostile frame of mind – they certainly did not get what they were expecting. The critical reception to his orchestral music had been very positive up this point; 'Puck's Minuet', 'Merry-Eye' and *Procession* had all been given celebrated Proms performances thanks to the interest of the conductor Sir Hamilton Harty.[26] A *Times* review of 1922 recounts how a 'new

---

[24] An essay of the same title by Howells has now been lost.
[25] Eggar, 'An English Composer', 129.
[26] British Sound Archive, B2951.

Work by Mr Howells ... went brilliantly, and was so well received that it had to be repeated.'[27] As a result of this success with small orchestral pieces there was considerable interest in the longer concerto. The concerto, however, received far more press coverage for an incident that occurred just after the final bars:

> [A]fter Mr Howells had taken his call, a tall, fair man rose from his seat in the top circle, walked to the balustrade and said in a clear, intelligent voice that could be heard all over the hall: 'Thank goodness that's over!' There was a moment's hush to mark the shock of surprise, and then came bursts of laughter from audience and orchestra, frowns and hisses and applause. Dr Malcolm Sargent, who was conducting, looked up at the top circle with an angry, shocked expression. A counter-demonstration sprang up, and the applause – much louder than on the first occasion – drew Mr Howells from the artistes' room, ignorant of what had happened, back again on to the platform. After he had made his bow and retired once more the applause died down, whereupon the fair-haired stranger once again walked to the parapet and in the same clear tones said: 'That's the last of him!' At which a voice behind me called out: 'He's drunk!' and looking round, I saw it came from a young lady, leaning forward with an expression of intense pain. That concluded the incident which enlivened me and the rest of the audience a good deal, and sent us home in a much happier condition than we should otherwise have been.[28]

The tone of such coverage seems remarkable today, but the writer was by no means alone in his opinion, and as a result Howells withdrew the piece altogether, despite the fact that Curwen was in the final stages before printing. Howells later claimed that he 'wasn't surprised that that man got up – there were cliques in those days. He got up for purely political reasons. He was furious I'd been asked and commissioned to do this work.'[29] The outbursts were made by a critic called Robert Lorenz, a well known friend of Philip Heseltine (Peter Warlock). Howells stated that the clique were annoyed that he had been commissioned over the composer E. J. Moeran. However, Howells's dislike for Warlock was well known,[30] and the minutes of the Royal Philharmonic Society's meetings show no evidence of any such commission:

> 14 February 1924 – A letter was read from Mr Howells saying that he had a pianoforte concerto which he had written for Mr Harold Samuel well advanced. The Hon. Sec was asked to tell Mr Howells that the committee would be pleased to hear him play it over.
>
> 4 September 1924 – A letter was read from Herbert Howells – his pianoforte concerto would probably be finished and ready for committee's consideration at the end of September.

[27] *The Times* (30 August 1922).
[28] Turner, 'Barbarism at The Queen's Hall'.
[29] Interview with Herbert Howells, May 1977, British Sound Archive, B2951.
[30] For example, in a report for the BBC Howells described a recital of Warlock's songs as a 'warning against mis-handling of the English poets'. Herbert Howells, BBC Report, Herbert Howells Archive, 48.

18 September 1924 – notes that they had heard from Mr Howells that his p.f. concerto was approaching completion.

25 September 1924 – programme was finalised.[31]

Howells had quite a few problems with the piece, and the organisation of the first performance did not go smoothly.[32] On 4 October 1924 *The Times* announced that 'a new pianoforte concerto by Herbert Howells will be played by Mr Harold Samuel' in its forthcoming series of seven concerts, conducted by Sir Hamilton Harty. However, Harty wrote to the Royal Philharmonic Society in December 1924 asking to be released from the engagement.[33] This was followed by a letter in January from Harold Samuel:

> A letter was read from Mr Samuel asking for a postponement of the production of the Howells pf. concerto to next season as he was unable to find time to prepare it – Resolved to write to Mr Samuel pointing out that he would place the committee in the fiercest difficulty if he did not play the concerto on April 27th and asking him to do so if necessary with the music.[34]

Samuel subsequently agreed to play as arranged.[35] Thomas Armstrong, one of Howells's earliest pupils at the RCM, spoke of the interest in Howells at the time: 'everything was looked at with interest – the highest hopes were entertained of him'. He attended the performance and noted, after the outburst, other groups stood up in support of Howells – led by Vaughan Williams. Ultimately it was Samuel's lacklustre performance that upset Howells most. The highly conservative press turned against Howells, having previously lauded him as a traditionalist, and Howells was doubly unlucky in that *The Times* covered it twice:

> 28th April 1925
>
> There was a breathlessness about the whole which never seemed to get relief, even in the comparatively quiet slow movement. One wanted to forget 'What I say is', and listen in a calmer mood to the threads of musical thought which lie behind the clangour of the piano and the strenuous insistence of the orchestra, but one was not allowed to do so. No doubt this was partly because everyone was too anxious to make the work go, and a more complete study of the *ensemble* might remove some of the discomforts of the listener. If so, the remedy is to repeat it on another occasion.

> 19th May 1925
>
> ENGLISH MUSIC – Compositions and Performances
> AMERICAN CRITIC'S IMPRESSIONS.
> By Richard Aldrich, Musical Editor of the 'New York Times'.
> The concert of the Royal Philharmonic Society, arduous listening though it was – and apparently arduous performing, insufficiently rehearsed on the

---

[31] British Library, Royal Philharmonic Archives, MS 292, 144.
[32] Spicer, speaking on 'Out of the Deep', British Sound Archive, H749.
[33] British Library, Royal Philharmonic Archives, MS 292, 204.
[34] *Ibid.*
[35] *Ibid.*, 211.

part of skilful players under an obviously talented young conductor (Mr Malcolm Sargent) – was a deeply interesting showing of what the British composers nowadays are doing ...

The new production of Mr Herbert Howells's Pianoforte Concerto gave the American listener pause, as it did, apparently, some others in the audience besides the audibly vocal protestant in the gallery. Its vigour of conception, its prodigal use of all the resources of pianoforte and orchestra, as well as the composer's unconcern over clashing dissonance, were, of course, borne in upon the listening ear. But is it not too little considered in all manner of details and structure; too much an improvisation, sometimes a reckless improvisation? Excellent things are said about Mr Howells; but the question could not be escaped whether here was not an undoubted talent improvidently spending itself, too little mindful of Horatian maxims, too little regarding sane and wholesome examples of reticence and reflection.

Clearly Howells's attempt to bring formal clarity and an overall rigour to the concerto with a condensed sonata structure and overt formal gestures (such as the Classical false recapitulation at the end of the slow movement) was perceived as precisely the opposite – 'reckless' free form. In many ways Howells could not win: in some circles he had already been branded a conservative as early as 1920, but to the press he was too modern, although the accusation that he was 'too little considered in all manner of details and structure' is certainly false.[36] The amalgam of this inconsistency of musical criticism, the inability of people to listen to 'symphonic lengths' and the trauma of that particular humiliation was too much for the desperately sensitive composer.

From the opening marking – 'Hard and Bright' – we can see that Howells's compositional aesthetic had come a long way from the first concerto. The principal influences on the second concerto are Parisian – Debussy, Ravel and Stravinsky. Howells had been exposed to their rich sonorities from his early days at the RCM (where the Ravel String Quartet received one of its first English performances) and at the London performances of the Ballets Russes.[37] Ravel's music in particular, with its soft modal dissonances and use of Classical forms, appealed to Howells, who quite rightly equated the wonderful sonorities he heard in Vaughan Williams's *Fantasia on a Theme by Thomas Tallis* with the composer's 1908 period of study with Ravel. Other composers had been drawn to the French impressionists too, and John Ireland, in particular, had enormous success with his Debussyesque Second Violin Sonata (1917). It seems extraordinary to think that when Arthur Bliss left for the trenches in the First World War he took only 'the 48 and Debussy's Préludes'.[38] In his autobiography Bliss mentions the period leading up to this:

---

[36] 'Some said at the time he was too clever ... and musically too elaborate ... it was said that if he had a piece of manuscript in front of him, he couldn't bear to leave any bit uncovered' (Sir Thomas Armstrong, British Sound Archive, B2951).
[37] See Thomas, 'Modernism, Diaghilev and the Ballets Russes'.
[38] Letter from Arthur Bliss to Howells, 30 May 1918 (Palmer, *A Centenary Celebration*, 27).

Howells, Goossens and Benjamin became close friends of mine, and it added greatly to the zest of evenings at the Diaghilev ballets and operas to have them alongside me in the gallery at Drury Lane or His Majesty's Theatre. These evenings were shot through with unexpected excitements, as the curtain went up on a Bakst design or the opening notes of a Stravinsky score were heard.[39]

Another shared experience was a concert at Queen's Hall in 1923, when Bliss's own *Colour Symphony* was performed alongside Prokofiev's First Piano Concerto in D♭, with the composer as soloist. Considering the Prokofiev alongside the concertos of Howells and Bliss,[40] we can see that they have many traits in common: sudden sharp dissonances caused by the juxtaposition of unrelated simple triads; unprepared melodic dissonances; light and energetic pianism; highly sectional structure articulated by interruptions rather than resolutions; and most importantly three-movements-in-one cyclic form, which recapitulates the start of the concerto at the end. They also rely on the development of very small amounts of thematic material, concentrating on the shapes of small motifs. Bliss wrote of his:

> As an Oriental Print is often developed from one small and seemingly inconspicuous pattern, so the form of this work is knit closely together by the development of a two-bar theme that makes its appearance in the second bar. The pianos are not used in the classical concerto, where they fill the role of star performer to a background or chorus, but are of [sic] an equal integral part of the whole composition, and can be regarded as two great arabesque-making machines.[41]

Howells, likewise, put enormous strain on two ideas – the opening piano theme, with its characteristic parallel triads (owing a lot to Debussy's pianism), and a second more rhapsodic idea based on a minor third.[42] These principles of motivic organicism in Howells (and Bliss) undoubtedly stemmed from Stanford's teaching and are demonstrated by the frequent prioritising of 'economy of material' and variation technique in *Musical Composition*.[43]

> What Stanford can do with a few notes!
> And then think of the score of *L'Après Midi* ... Quite apart from the sound of it ...
> The form of a work ought to interest its modern composer *chiefly as an accomplished fact*: at any rate in pure music. (I'm not of course pleading for dispensing with a knowledge of musical form. One presumes that a composer

---

[39] Bliss, *As I Remember*, 28.
[40] Arthur Bliss, Concerto for Two Pianos (1924).
[41] Arthur Bliss, programme note for Boston Symphony Orchestra (19 December 1924), reproduced in Roscow, *Bliss on Music*, 48.
[42] Rudolph Reti analyses two similar patterns in Debussy's 'La cathédrale engloutie' in *The Thematic Process in Music*, 194, and it is not unthinkable that Howells had the structural consistency created by these thematic contours in mind for his concerto.
[43] Stanford, *Musical Composition*, 49.

knows his business.) What always matters to a modern is to express a complex mood. Now for that, sonata form is not always suitable; or sonata form as hitherto accepted may not be suitable ...

In my first violin sonata, and again in the new piano concerto, I found myself using a form of 'First Movement' to cover the whole work. I said just now that what matters to one is to express a complex mood. Perhaps it is a triplex mood: then see how the truth of the old form adapts itself to that. I found that what would have been the exposition made my first movement, what would have been the development made the slow movement, what would have been the recapitulation (modified) made the last movement; and then I felt need of a long retrospective coda, summing up not merely the movement which it ended, but the whole work.[44]

The retrospective coda was to be a device that Howells would use throughout his career: the finest examples being found in the Third Violin Sonata (HH 136 – 1923), the Oboe Sonata (HH 239 – 1942) and the Organ Partita (HH 334 – 'Epilogue' – 1971). In a sense, in using a modified recapitulation, there was a need for a coda to resolve the tonal and motivic processes, but it is more than a device for righting what could be seen as a structural failure. The bridge passage at the end of the second concerto's slow movement, when the piano tries several times to initiate a return to the opening material but fails (and so the final movement begins with a modified version of the first subject), is perhaps the most effective structural device of the concerto. Combining this with the stasis of the held string chord, Howells creates a moment when we are very aware of his temporal game. It is a passage of extreme nostalgia, highlighting that although the piano solo wants to recapitulate (in the classical mode), the world has moved on from such things. Bearing in mind Howells's critique – 'no time for symphonic lengths these days' – the concerto's form seems to reflect his modernist commentary in a very direct way.

Howells's form is particularly special. Given his description of it, one might view it as an instance of double function form. However, the cyclic element is more usefully dealt with as an instance of two-dimensional sonata form[45] with independent rhetorical and tonal functionality arising from a series of interrupting sections of varying length. The overall sonata structure is defined by two ideas in two different areas, but is perhaps most strongly articulated by the false recapitulation at the end of the slow movement. After several abortive attempts to return to the opening music of the concerto, the piano leads into a highly modified return to the tonic, a move that resolves the overall sonata structure tonally but not rhetorically (i.e. we expect the opening piano motif to return with the initial affirmation of the orchestra). Howells then makes us wait to the very end of the final movement for a full thematic and tonal resolution. While only two bars in length, the orchestral introduction presents a very strong cadential resolution into the tonic. The piano's responses take on a Classical syntax, leading to a dominant cadence (rehearsal mark 1). However, at bar 23 there is highly unexpected chromatic move to a B♭

---

[44] Eggar, 'Herbert Howells'.
[45] Vande Moortele, *Two-Dimensional Sonata Form*.

major seventh chord. This sort of tonal shift is highly effective after the stability of the piano's opening in C major. By the time the piano returns to C major (rehearsal mark 4) the opening material has already changed significantly. Howells's form relies on this continuous variation and, as Howells himself said (when analysing Vaughan Williams's *A Sea Symphony*), 'more than half of the harmonic and tonal values of this work reside in the relationship of common chords'.[46]

Following the Second Piano Concerto's premiere, Howells did have some critical success with the first performance of *Paradise Rondel* (HH 159; a reworking of the *Pastoral Rhapsody* – HH 134),[47] but his music began to be overshadowed by other composers as he devoted more time to teaching, adjudicating and family life. This came to a head in 1928 with the first performance of *In Green Ways* (HH 172), which was completely eclipsed by the premiere of William Walton's Viola Concerto (with Paul Hindemith as soloist). Howells did return to orchestral composition with the Cello Concerto (HH 205–7) and the Concerto for String Orchestra, but never with the same experimental vigour. A radio interview reveals more:

[INTERVIEWER]: Have you ever wanted to write a symphony?

HOWELLS: Never – I've never wanted to – I've never wanted to write an opera … and that is not an intellectual standpoint. I don't think that I could do it in the way that I would justify calling it a symphony … I have composed out of sheer love of trying to make nice sounds … if there is just sufficient intellectual quality in the way that I've done it that's merely because I've slogged at an understanding of music.[48]

Of the two sides that Howells tried to reconcile in his second concerto, it seems that the aesthetically focused 'light' music won, but there was certainly more to it than that. Howells did want to write a symphony; there are sketches for the opening of a 'Symphony in D' (HH 97) in the RCM, possibly linked to a request from Harty in 1919: 'From an orchestral point of view – what is badly needed is a work of medium length – with a central interest – not a suite – but a poem of 12–15 minutes – Failing this a symphony of 30 minutes – are you in sympathy with these ideas?'[49] His denial of ever wanting to write an opera is also untrue, as an article in 1922 mentions his plans to write an opera on the 'troubled relationships between Richard the First and the famous, determined, noble Bishop Hugh of Lincoln',[50] a plot that Howells brought up again in a lesson with Joan Littlejohn.[51] Both these instances highlight the psychological complexities in defining Howells the composer, with a clear ten-

---

[46] Notes for a broadcast on Vaughan Williams's *A Sea Symphony*, Herbert Howells Archive.

[47] The two works share several identical sections and a number of others that differ only in points of detail; where they differ more substantially the underlying structure is, nonetheless, the same. It seems likely that the *Pastoral Rhapsody* was withdrawn by the composer because of its being superseded by the later work.

[48] Interview with Herbert Howells, May 1977, British Sound Archive, B2951.

[49] Letter from Sir Hamilton Harty, 10 March 1919, Herbert Howells Archive.

[50] Eggar, 'An English Composer'.

[51] Unpublished interview with the author, 6 April 2012.

sion between his own assessment of his compositional career in later life, and the composer he had hoped, during his early years, he would become.

For historical convenience it is tempting to view the second concerto as a breaking point, separating the early Howells (focused on orchestral and chamber works) from the church composer, about whom rather more is known. However, it is more representative to view the concerto as one of several experiments that led Howells to his later aesthetic. The trio formed by the concerto, the Organ Sonata no. 2 (HH 189 – 1932) and *Lambert's Clavichord* (HH 165 – 1927) can be seen as defining the later Howells. Far from abandoning the principles of the concerto's experimental form, we see Howells use it again in the organicism and motivic organisation of the Organ Sonata (and later in the Oboe and Clarinet Sonatas), alongside many of his most characteristic rhythmic gestures. Equally, *Lambert's Clavichord*, in which Howells presents the most perfect synthesis of Elizabethan and Ravelian styles, represents the moment when he found his default aesthetic mode. The Second Piano Concerto, far from being a breaking point, was actually a major stepping stone on the path to compositional maturity as Howells came to terms with what it meant to be a Romantic Modern – reconciling Modernism with his traditional spirit.

To come back to my initial investigation looking at the lasting significance of the concerto, it tells us a great deal about the cultural demands on a British composer in this period. Howells's music presents significant commentaries on the changing nature of popular culture – of high and low art. The overall preoccupation is with form, although arguably the second concerto could almost be regarded as a parody of the sonata form – the bedrock of absolute music's privileged status. The critical reception seems to suggest that Howells's overall message (whatever you regard it as) was missed. That said, his own descriptor – 'tunes all the way' – seems to point to an inherent self-consciousness that, along with experiments to reconceptualise the sonata for a new age, appears not only Modernist, but representative of this new era. Their historical significance is therefore arguably even greater than their musical significance.

Howells once wrote that it was 'the highest compliment' to be thought of as 'traditional';[52] but it is important to recognise that that does not make him a conservative composer. As Sir David Willcocks summed up perfectly: 'he's not conservative – he wrote new things using conventional means'.[53] This conservatism can now be seen as a polar opposite to the Modernism with which Howells experimented, particularly during the 1916–25 period, as he sought to find a middle ground in a new 'Romantic Modernism'. Nevertheless, his great experiment backfired as he lacked the emotional strength to ignore his critics. Towards the end of his life, Howells was interview by the BBC: 'If you were to say to me, "Have you been happy to be a composer?" – I don't think any man in musical history has been happier. "Have you been disappointed?" – so often that I wouldn't like to tell you.'[54] It is hard not

---

[52] Herbert Howells, BBC Report, 50 (referring to his former pupil, Gordon Jacob).
[53] *Herbert Howells: Echoes of a Lifetime* (17 October 1983), British Sound Archive, T5237BW C1.
[54] Interview with Herbert Howells, May 1977, British Sound Archive, B2951.

to imagine that he was thinking back to 1925, and the failure of his Second Piano Concerto; but whatever the composer's own views of either concerto, it is becoming more and more clear that Howells's own views on his music need to be taken with a considerable pinch of salt. In the context of his overall career, the concertos represent major achievements, but it is perhaps in an even wider context, as scholarly reassessments of British composers such as Howells continue to emerge, that the full impact of these concertos and their 'astonishing revelation' is beginning to be realised. Regardless of whether or not opinions of Howells change, we come to understand the musical life of the period in a new way, and the ongoing debate on British Modernism provides a perfect context for a revaluation.

CHAPTER 11

'I am a "modern" in this, but a Britisher too': Howells and the Phantasy

David Maw

The Phantasy Challenge

BRITISH chamber music during the first half of the twentieth century was convulsed with a 'phantasy mania'.[1] The competition for 'phantasies' inaugurated by W. W. Cobbett in 1905 was enthusiastically received and became the first of a series that continued under differing aegises through the next four decades.[2] The genre that it spawned was also taken up outside this context, both through Cobbett's own commissioning and through the independent interest of composers beyond his sphere. In a short period of time, the genre had established itself; yet it did not long survive Cobbett's death in 1937 and had all but entirely vanished in the postwar period.

Cobbett's idea with the competitions was to encourage the writing of short chamber works of modest technical demands. The first competition specified a string quartet in one movement not exceeding twelve minutes in length: 'The old English Fantasy may be suggested as a typical form which presents possibilities of modern development.'[3] Cobbett intended the phantasy label to refer to the Tudor-Jacobean consort-and-keyboard genre, the fantasy; the initial 'ph' was his own faux-archaising touch. He later confessed that at the time of advertising his first competition, his own knowledge of the 'old English Fantasy' was 'very restricted';[4] and it is highly unlikely that those taking part in the early competitions were any better informed. The fantasy repertoire was not yet published, and knowledge of the works in early sources was limited to a very small number of experts. So the challenge that Cobbett presented to composers was to all intents and purposes the creation of a new genre, with the phantasy word being an open concept that would be filled through usage. For the first competition, he added the suggestion that the phantasy 'may consist of different sections varying in *tempi* and rhythms'.[5]

There was nothing new about single-movement forms incorporating the contrasts of a multi-movement work; it was a challenge that had attracted many composers through the nineteenth century. The novelty of the phantasy was its condensed length. Liszt's Piano Sonata in B minor lasts thirty minutes – as long, in other words, as a work in four independent movements. What Cobbett demanded

---

[1] Caldwell, *The Oxford History of English Music*, Vol. II, 392.
[2] A historical overview of the genre is given in Maw, 'Phantasy Mania'.
[3] From a notice in *Musical Times*, 46 (1905), 455.
[4] Cobbett, 'The Beginnings', 50.
[5] From a notice in *Musical Times* 46 (1905), 791.

was that the same feat be accomplished in not much more than a third of this length, a considerable challenge and one that Stanford recognised as 'not the broad and easy way out of difficulties that it appears to be at first sight'.[6]

It is testimony to the power of Cobbett's influence that writings about the phantasy should have appeared quickly upon the genre's inception. There was a brief article in 1910 by Fuller Maitland for the Appendix of the second edition of Grove's Dictionary, a sizable paragraph in Stanford's treatise *Musical Composition* (1911) and a substantial overview after the genre's first decade by Ernest Walker in *The Music Student* (1915).[7] Fuller Maitland recognised the phantasy as an expanded single-movement sonata form interpolating a slow movement and possible Scherzo; whilst Walker, reviewing a greater body of compositions and in more depth, despaired of any commonly typifying features save the presence of contrasts of rhythm and tempo within a single movement. Stanford's comments are the most pertinent for consideration of Howells, whose professor he became the year after *Musical Composition* appeared. His account of the fantasy, as he spelled it, is curiously positioned at the end of a chapter on 'Extraneous Influences in Instrumental Music', predominantly concerned with the accommodation of extra-musical ideas in instrumental compositions. The 'experiment' of the 'revival of the old "Fancies" or "Fantasies" of early times' counted for Stanford in a similar way. Perhaps he considered it an extraneous influence because it represented an attempt to contravene the natural evolution of forms, whose value he had already expounded in the sixth chapter of the treatise. At the same time, he quite reasonably dismissed the novelty of the idea on the grounds that single-movement forms had already been tackled by Schumann and Mendelssohn.

Stanford would have had good knowledge of the early phantasies, as several of his former pupils had been amongst the prize winners in the first competitions. He recognised three approaches to writing the genre, and was presumably drawing on acquaintance with his pupils' compositions in doing so. It could be conceived as a single movement, as a series of connected short movements or as something 'amorphous'. What he meant by this third is unclear, as he offered no further comment on it. The centrality of received forms to his account in the earlier chapter suggests that the 'single movement' possibility would be an extended composition in an established form (normally sonata form); so something 'amorphous' would then be a composition proceeding without reference to such convention.

Howells was a teenager when the first phantasies were written. He was thus of the first generation that could take up the challenge of the phantasy not as pioneers but as refiners. Foundations of the genre had already been laid by, amongst others, Hurlstone, Bridge, Friskin and Ireland, and codified in the writings mentioned above. Shortly after completing his studies in 1916, Howells set about composing a work for Cobbett's fifth competition, which demanded phantasies for string quartet or piano trio 'based on folk songs'. His *Fantasy String Quartet* (HH 71) won

---

[6] Stanford, *Musical Composition*, 163.
[7] Fuller Maitland, 'Fancy'; Stanford, *Musical Composition*, 162–4; Walker, 'The Modern British Phantasy'.

second prize in 1917, and in the same year he composed a *Phantasy Violin Sonata*, now known as the Sonata no 1. in E major for Violin and Piano, Op. 18 (HH 78).[8] As will become apparent, a third work, the *Rhapsodic Quintet*, for clarinet and string quartet, Op. 31 (HH 107) of 1919 also merits consideration as a phantasy, despite the absence of the word phantasy from its title.[9]

The phantasy was an important genre in the compositions that were establishing Howells as a major new voice in British music during the late 1910s. Howells himself recognised this. Commenting in 1919 on his *Fantasy Quartet* he wrote: 'I am a "modern" in this, but a Britisher too! One of my best works, I think.'[10] His appreciation of the success of the work is tied up with its balancing the twin objectives of formulating a compositional aesthetic in tune with modern musical developments whilst also articulating his national identity. Study of his use of the phantasy in the early compositions reveals the technical concerns and aesthetic priorities that motivated him at this crucial time in his development.

'New experiments in form'

By 1919, form was very much in Howells's mind: 'I have long ponderous thoughts on problems of Musical Form ... We want new experiments in form, and a sympathetic consideration of them when they are made.'[11] These remarks, made during the process of writing the *Rhapsodic Quintet*, show not just a concern with form, but a deliberate intention to explore its possibilities in new ways. Form was again a subject of concern in an interview that Katharine Eggar conducted with Howells three years later. The differences between a published interview and the confidences of a private diary occasion discussion below; but there is no reason to think that in discussing an abstract technical matter like form Howells would not have said more or less simply what he thought. The interview reflects also on the phantasy works, so its remarks are relevant for consideration here: 'The form of a work ought to interest its modern composer *chiefly as an accomplished fact*: at any rate in pure music ... sonata form is not always suitable; or the sonata form as hitherto accepted may not be suitable.'[12] He marks here a duty on the composer's part to follow through his ideas without concern for preconceived schemes. So whilst the stress on formal experimentation is still present, the means of arrival at this experimentation seem to be different. Form-thinking implies a process of pre-compositional planning on form, whereas form as 'an accomplished fact' suggests the shape that the music has

---

[8] HH 71 was published as *Fantasy String Quartet* but bears the Cobbettian spelling ('Phantasy') on the autograph; Andrews, 'A Documentary and Bibliographical Study', Vol. I, 122.

[9] This chapter builds on the survey of Howells's use of the phantasy given in Hodgson, 'The Music of Herbert Howells', 161–5. Hodgson's account is particularly important for establishing the connection between the single-movement phantasy and Howells's concept of mood, a point elaborated below in some detail; *ibid*., 165–76.

[10] Palmer, *A Centenary Celebration*, 72.

[11] Howells, diary entry of 1 March 1919, quoted in *ibid*., 77.

[12] Eggar, 'Herbert Howells', 214.

assumed in the process of having been composed, something that is appreciated once composition has been completed. This shift in perspective will be noted again below in connection with the *Rhapsodic Quintet*.

Formal experimentation was at the heart of the phantasy; and it is possible that it was the phantasy competition of 1916/17 that pushed Howells in the direction of the formal experimentation that his diary was to acknowledge so enthusiastically by the time of the *Rhapsodic Quintet*. The Piano Quartet (HH 66) of 1916 provides a gauge against which to measure the works that followed soon after it. Certainly it seems at first glance more straightforward from a formal perspective. It comprises a conventional sequence of three movements: sonata Allegro, ternary slow movement and Rondo finale. Closer scrutiny reveals that the individual forms of these movements are not always easily reconciled with the traditional models. The first movement, for example, clearly has aspects of sonata-form organisation: there are two clearly characterised themes (at the opening and at figure 6) and tonal contrast between them (A minor/C minor); development of these elements follows, and then there is a clear point of recapitulation (figure 10, bar 9), with the first theme returning in its original key. Here, though, the resemblance ends: the second theme returns in the tonic major (figure 13), but is still in the process of development; indeed, its return launches the movement on another extensive development, treating that like a further element in the rotational process. So there is no sense of resolution or arrival. The treatment of the second theme responds to a large-scale sonata procedure across the whole piece, being developed in the middle section of the second movement and returning as a contrasting theme in the finale, where its final appearance (figure 51, bar 6) is in the tonic, supplying the recapitulation that it did not have in the first movement. In this respect, the Piano Quartet seems to be looking forward to the unification of multi-movement form that the subsequent phantasy chamber works would explore. There are, then, already aspects of formal experimentation in this, Howells's first fully accomplished work; but they are subtle, and fall within the well-established framework of the genre.

Cobbett's fifth competition demanded phantasies 'based on folk-songs of any of the four nations [of the United Kingdom]'.[13] Howells opted to write for string quartet but did not base his work on a known folk-song; instead he wrote his own tunes. In a brazen display of his independence from Stanford, Howells adopted the approach to the phantasy that Stanford characterised as 'amorphous'. The phantasy challenge galvanised the spirit of formal experimentation in him, and he completely discarded precedents to create something of his own. There are five sections united by the deployment and transformation of a single stock of material. In Howells's words, the work 'is governed by the motto theme heard in the first bars'.[14] The style, and to some extent material, of the opening recurs in the middle and at the end, giving the whole an outline broadly similar to that of a rondo; but the style, tonal and thematic construction are so unlike the rondo in every other respect that a listener is unlikely to be struck by any such connection. To all intents and purposes, it is an essay in original form (Table 11.1).

---

[13] 'Occasional Notes', *Musical Times*, 57 (1916), 366–67 (367).
[14] Palmer, *A Centenary Celebration*, 405.

Table 11.1 Form of *Fantasy String Quartet* (HH 71)

	Bar	Fig.	Tempo	Material	Time	Key
1. Motto theme	1		Moderato, assai espressivo (crotchet = 72)	Three varied presentations of motto theme	4/4	Fm
	34	2	Più mosso (crotchet = 100)	Transition drawing on elements of motto theme		Fm → Bm
2. First episode	55	4	Ancora più mosso (minim = 80)	Two statements of 16-bar folk-song-like transformation of motto theme	2/2	Bm
3. Motto theme	103	8	Meno mosso (crotchet = 60)	Free return of motto theme	4/4	Gm → Fm
	123	9	Molto tranquillo e mistico	Reminiscence of folk-song-like transformation		Dm
	140	10	a tempo, e poco a poco accel.	Transition	(irregular → 3/4)	
4. Second episode	155	11	Allegro, assai vivace (crotchet = 138)	Dance-type transformation of motto theme	3/4	Dm → C
	206	16, bar 2	(crotchet = 138)	Further transformation of motto theme acting as trio to surrounding dance material		Em
	227	18	Più animato (crotchet = 138)	Free return of dance material	3/4 → 4/4	F/Cm → C
5. Motto theme and coda	268	20, bar 18	Meno mosso e più tranquillo	Dissolution of motto theme	3/4	Fm → Am
	287–8	20, bar 37	Più lento	Fragmentary reminiscences of earlier phrases	4/4	Am → C

The quartet was to be the most formally original of Howells's phantasy essays. His next chamber work, the First Violin Sonata, was also a phantasy work, as is clear despite the loss of the word 'phantasy' from its title. Ostensibly, it is an example of what Stanford dubbed the 'tabloid preparation', a multi-movement sonata in miniature. Yet although it is conceived in distinct separate movements, those movements are assimilated into a single formal span, thereby reconciling the seemingly contradictory single and poly-movement types of phantasy in an impressive display of compositional virtuosity.

Howells outlined the form of the sonata in some detail:[15] the three parts of a sonata-form movement (exposition, development, recapitulation) are superimposed on the three movements of a sonata composition (fast, slow, fast), though with the recapitulation becoming a transformation of the exposition rather than a simple repetition.[16] A further complexity is a gradual accumulation of ideas as the sonata progresses, new material being added in each of the second and third movements. Thus, the recapitulatory third movement does not fully close the processes of the sonata, and the scheme requires a short fourth movement, reminiscing each of the main thematic ideas, as a coda.

The form (Table 11.2) takes the double-function idea of earlier single-movement works a step further, as here the three sections of sonata form map exactly onto the three movements of a sonata: the opening Allegretto acts as an exposition, the slow movement as a development; and the Allegro molto serves as a modified recapitulation. So whereas in Liszt's Piano Sonata in B minor the slow movement section acts as an interruption to the form and the recapitulation is effected with a substantial amount of literal repetition, in Howells's form the slow movement effects development, maintaining the momentum of the whole, and the recapitulation is achieved (in part, at least) through the ongoing process of transformation. It should be noted, though, that the slow movement really comprises two parts: the slow

---

[15] *Ibid.*, 448–9; see also Chapter 10 of the present volume.
[16] The work can be viewed as a cogent, if complex, example of what William Newman dubbed double-function form (Newman, *The Sonata since Beethoven*, 134, 373–8). This concept has recently been challenged by Steven Vande Moortele on account of a lack of compositions in which sections of the form precisely coincide with movements of the cycle (Vande Moortele, *Two-Dimensional Sonata Form*, 20–4). Howells's Violin Sonata is, though, precisely such a composition; and on the basis of the composer's formal description, it might be seen to have manifested Newman's idea deliberately had it not predated that by fifty years. Complexities in the design arise from dual function within the sonata form (for example, the development continues also the expositional function); but these do not undermine the basic plan. More generally, some of the force of Vande Moortele's criticism of Newman's concept may be attenuated by a more sympathetic appraisal in this context of Hepokoski and Darcy's deformational account of sonata form, which recognises interpolations into or over a development. The insertion of a slow movement, for example, merely manifests the phenomenon on a larger scale. From a historical perspective it is precisely such deformational insertions into traditional sonata form that can be seen to have opened up the possibility of the formally integrated and through-composed sonata cycle in the first place. Hepokoski and Darcy, *Elements of Sonata Theory*, 212–15, 220–1.

Table 11.2 Form of Sonata no. 1 for Violin and Piano (HH 78)

	Bar	Tempo	Material	Time	Key
I. Exposition	1	Allegretto, sempre un poco rubato (dotted crotchet = c. 84)	Presentation and elaboration of first theme (A)	9/8	E (iv–i)
	27	Poco più mosso, agitato (crotchet = dotted crotchet)	Development of motifs from A building to climactic gesture (α) at 76–7	3/4 → 9/8	Roving
	80	Tempo primo	Return to mood of opening	9/8	E (vi–IV) → E♭
II. Development	1 (103)	Meno mosso (quasi lento)	Presentation and elaboration of second theme (B) by violin over development of A in piano	Vln 3/4 Pno 9/8	Roving (E♭ → C etc.)
	41		Closing statements of B, dissolving at cadences	3/4	B → roving
[Transition]	65	Doppio movimento	New theme (C) introduced in piano against continuation of B in violin; builds to climactic return of α at 77–8	3/2	E (ii)
	79	Più mosso, e ritmico	Preparation of material (transformation of A) and style of coming allegro	6/4 + 2/4	
III. Recapitulation	1 (194)	Allegro molto (dotted minim = c. 116)	Transformation of A	6/4 + 2/4	E (vi)
	23	Più deciso	Introduction and elaboration of new material (D) in dialogue with transformed A	4/2 + 3/2	(iv … v)

Table 11.2 continued

	Bar	Tempo	Material	Time	Key
	66	Poco meno mosso, più espressivo (minim = 104)	C	3/2	(I)
	78		B worked to a climax	3/2 → 9/4	Roving (E♭ → D♭ etc.)
	100	Un poco più lento	α extended to six bars: climax of whole sonata	9/4	E (I–IV)
IV. Coda	1 (304)	Assai tranquillo (dotted crotchet = 69)	A	9/8	(vi–IV)
	13	Ancora meno mosso (crotchet = dotted crotchet)	D and C	6/4 + 2/4	
	29–45	Più lento	B transforming into A with echo of α at 36–39	3/4 → 9/8	(vi–V–I)

movement proper and a substantial transition, during which material of the slow movement overlaps with ideas that are to become the substance of the third movement. A further ingenious piece of architecture binds the whole form together: each of the movements reaches its climax on the same gesture (α in Table 11.2), a derivative of the opening theme. From a purely technical point of view, the Violin Sonata is the most daring of the phantasies; indeed, it remains one of Howells's most ambitious and accomplished compositional essays.

Two years later followed the third of the phantasies, the *Rhapsodic Quintet*. Howells offered seemingly contradictory accounts of the birth of its form. In 1922 he told Katharine Eggar that the quintet 'composed itself without any conscious interference on my part: at least I can recall no interference; only when I had finished it did I sit down to study it ... At any rate, there was no attempt to throw my thoughts into any stereotyped form'.[17] His diary of 1919 gives a rather different picture. On Friday 7 February: 'All my thoughts were on the Clarinet Quintet, towards a new second half', suggesting that the work had been finished and was now being revised. The following day: 'Today ... my thoughts would run on the final things in the Clarinet Quintet; and after some useless attempts, I at last sat down to it – at 9 p.m. – and saw right to the end', suggesting that the revisions were now finished. Completion was only temporary, however, as on Friday 28 February: 'Even now I'm not satisfied with the Clarinet Quintet I have done for [Oscar] Street. Perhaps, now that I have begun the method of revising everything, I shall become an abject slave to it'; and the following day there were 'hours spent in an easy chair, fire-gazing, form-thinking. Most of it focused on the Clarinet Quintet'.[18]

The contrasts between these accounts may simply result from the different sorts of representation of compositional process appropriate in the private (if, in this instance, rather self-conscious) context of a diary on the one hand and an interview for publication in a widely circulated journal on the other. It is possible that Howells thought it better in this latter context for a work of rhapsodic kind to have been composed spontaneously, and so mythologised the compositional process in order to encourage an appropriate reception. If so, the apparent contradiction is a matter of differing registers between the genres of writing. It is also possible, though, that the difference in these accounts is less considerable than it first seems. Perhaps the work was written more or less spontaneously in its first version, as he later recounted. It was at this point (in early February) that Howells reviewed it and set about some revisions, which were more laboured to accomplish. Certainly, there was 'form-thinking' involved during the revision, so the insouciance that he adopted in 1922 was misleading as a representation of the finished work. In any case, formal planning was an important part of the work's compositional process at some level, as the careful structuring of its final form attests; and although he did not exactly 'throw [his] thoughts into any stereotyped form', the finished work follows a carefully structured plan that owes much more to traditional sonata form than its two phantasy precursors, even if not to 'sonata form as hitherto accepted' (Table 11.3).

---

[17] Eggar, 'An English Composer', 130.
[18] Palmer, *A Centenary Celebration*, 75–7.

Table 11.3 Form of *Rhapsodic Quintet* (HH 107)

	Bar	Fig.	Tempo	Material	Time	Key
Exposition (1st rotation)	1		Lento, ma appassionato	First theme (A), two balanced paragraphs leading to climax and transitional continuation	2/4	Unsettled (Em →)
	70	4	a tempo, tranquillo	Second theme (B), two sequential statements		E♭ → E
Development (2nd rotation)	98	5	agitato, ed accel.	Development of A	(2/4)	C♯m
	124	7	Più mosso, inquieto	Introduction of new theme (C) over continued development of A	Changes of metre	Roving
	164	11	Doppio movimento ritmico, e non troppo allegro	Contrapuntal development of B and C over ostinato	Polymetric: 3/2 over 4/2 (minim = crotchet)	Chain of minor thirds (D–F–A♭)
Recapitulation (3rd rotation – reversed)	212	21	più elato	Climactic restatement of B	4/2	E♭/Cm → E
	229	22	più quieto	Transition using fragments of A and B and giving last appearance of C		E → E♭
	242	23	Mezzo movimento	B	4/4 (crotchet = minim)	G
	252	24	Meno mosso	A (fragment), material completely reworked	2/4	Cm → A♭
Coda (4th rotation – themes combined and fragmented)	303	26	Lento, assai tranquillo	Combination of A and B	(2/4)	Chromatic
	311–20	27	Più adagio	A and B (fragmented)		C

NB bar numbers follow the cello line during the polymetric section (169–98).

In the light of the overt formal experimentation in the two previous works and of the 'form-thinking' that Howells had put into the work, it is at first glance surprising that the quintet should be so conservative from a formal perspective: it comprises a single sonata-form movement of expanded scale. Its broad conformity to the sonata-form outline should not conceal some importantly original and arguably experimental aspects within it. The addition during the development of a new *scherzando* theme in counterpoint with the treatment of the two themes of the exposition unifies the character of this section, giving it the semblance of a separate movement interpolated into the whole. This contrast of character and style within the single-movement design is what justifies regarding the piece as a phantasy. The free handling of the recapitulation is another novelty: it begins with a climactic statement of the second theme, which is the culmination of the developmental process that has just been pursued; then it subsides to a calmed reminiscence of the first subject, now reduced to its opening fragment, before the two themes are combined in the coda. There is, then, justification for arguing that the greater challenge remaining to Howells after having succeeded in the task of writing two evidently experimental forms was that of finding originality within the framework of the established form, and thus the *Rhapsodic Quintet* is very much in the line of the works preceding it.

Howells's three phantasy chamber works exhibit, each one, a different solution to the challenge posed by the phantasy genre. Moreover, together they illustrate the validity of Stanford's fantasy taxonomy by supplying one each of the types identified by it. Whether consciously or not, Howells's phantasies at once acknowledge Stanford's influence and go beyond it as they employ a language that Howells acknowledged had by this time ceased to please his former teacher.[19] Under the influence of the phantasy, Howells was experimenting daringly with form; but this experimentation was not an abstract pursuit for its own ends: it was at the service of a modern sort of musical expression.

'To express a complex mood'

In accounting for his approach to form to Katharine Eggar, Howells commented: 'What always matters to a modern is to express a complex mood.'[20] The expression of mood is not normally allied to a consideration of form. It is usually thought to arise from choices of harmony, texture, rhythmic movement and melodic outline that are independent of the dispositions of these materials that create form.[21] Even in a sonata-form composition where the contrasts between different themes may represent changes of mood, the form arises from processes that are independent of these contrasts. Howells, though, points to a more central role of form in the expressing of mood, and in particular a 'complex mood'. It seems that the ways in which the

---

[19] Howells's diary for February 1919 recounts Stanford's negative reaction to the Second Violin Sonata; Palmer, *A Centenary Celebration*, 375.
[20] Eggar, 'Herbert Howells', 214.
[21] Leonard Ratner, for example, recognises the topical variety that may be apparent within a sonata form without according it a formal role; Ratner, *Classic Music*, 1–30.

music is sustained and developed directly govern the mood. Howells developed this idea in his commentary on the formal 'experiment' of the Violin Sonata:

> I conceive the value of such a form to be in this: that while it ensures a logical growth *as a whole*; and while it preserves in itself the contrast of line and of colour which is provided by the sequence of three separate movements as commonly adopted in the Sonata or Symphony; it at the same time draws all three moods under a closer, unified spell. It becomes more a triple mood (if so it may be called) than a succession of three more intensely contrasted and separated moods.[22]

The complex, triple mood is achieved here through the formal integration of the moods that are articulated separately in the movements comprising the whole. This integration is a product of the compositional processes working throughout. Two processes are especially revealing in this connection: tonal design and thematic development.

At the centre of the Violin Sonata's expression of a triple mood is the handling of the first theme. It is the unifying element of the whole work, running through each of the three movements; and it is the only theme to be subjected to thorough development. The construction of a theme suitable to serve this purpose – having varied elements for development but also a strong identity that will be maintained under transformation – is a challenge in itself. Howells settled upon a melodic arabesque in a wide arch shape comprising several distinct motivic elements (row 'a' of Ex. 11.1a, which identifies three paradigms, α, β and γ). Although the theme is more complicated in its combination of elements than the other themes of the piece, its broad arch shape and wide span give it also a strong identity that differentiates it from them.

Even within the initial expository section, during which the melody is presented and restated, the motivic elements begin to be detached from it and undergo separate development (see rows 'b' to 'i' of Ex. 11.1a). The second section of the movement takes this process further, being the most intensive development of the whole work, concomitant with the normal role of a first movement in multi-movement sonata design. It moves far from the initial phrase, exploring its constituent elements before then recombining them at the climax. The transformation reached at this point becomes the starting point for the second movement (Ex. 11.1b); and it is the treatment of it over the changeable harmonic patterning that justifies Howells's description of this as a development section.

The use of the first theme in a transformed state (Ex. 11.1c) in the third movement means that this does not have the simple effect of recapitulation that Howells's description of the form ascribes to it. Indeed, both tonal and thematic returns are side-stepped at the beginning of the movement. Tonal resolution arrives with the return of secondary material that begins the climactic part of the movement (and of the whole work), but the true thematic return awaits the coda, where the mood is reflective rather than triumphant. The framing function of the first theme is further realised in the mutation of the second theme into the first right at the end of the piece, where it picks up the cadence of the first movement that had been

---

[22] Palmer, *A Centenary Celebration*, 448.

Ex. 11.1a Sonata no. 1 in E major for Violin and Piano, 1st theme and motivic development in its exposition

Ex. 11.1b Sonata no. 1 in E major for Violin and Piano, climactic and developmental transformation of 1st theme

Ex. 11.1c Sonata no. 1 in E major for Violin and Piano, first theme transformed in 3rd mvt

interrupted by enharmonic mutation then but now finally achieves closure (Ex. 11.2a and 11.2b).

The first theme thus assumes the role of the subject (one might say persona) of the whole work; and it becomes the focus of the changing moods that the music passes through. Yet, Howells's expression 'triple mood' implies simultaneity within this subject of the different moods in the piece. Recognition of the unity of the theme through its different instantiations brings with it an appreciation of the unity of the three moods as a single, complex mood. This idea was to be echoed later by Howells in writing about Vaughan Williams's *Pastoral Symphony*: 'He builds up a

Ex. 11.2a Sonata no. 1 in E major for Violin and Piano, enharmonic mutation in transition between 1st and 2nd mvts

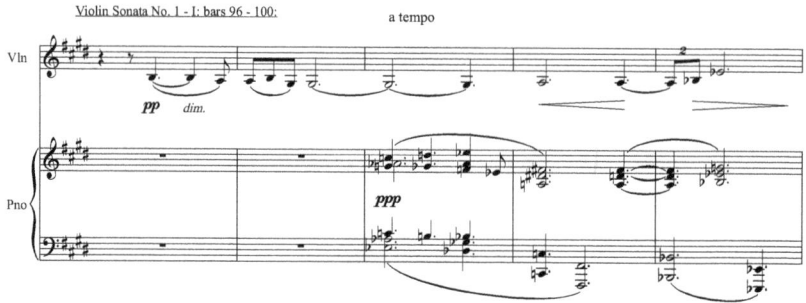

Ex. 11.2b Sonata no. 1 in E major for Violin and Piano, enharmonic mutation avoided to achieve final closure

great mood, insistent to an unusual degree, but having in itself far more variety than a merely slight acquaintance with it would suggest ... Even its detractors (and they may be many) will admit its compelling sense of unity ... If you like, it is a frame of mind.'[23] The metaphor of the music as 'a frame of mind', or the psychology of a persona, is apposite to the Violin Sonata and, in fact, to both the other phantasies. It is consistent with the view of the music as articulating moods, but beyond this, it provides revealing terms within which to interpret the compositional processes.

The formal conception of the Violin Sonata as the fusion of distinct movements creates a tension between the needs of these to be shaped as to some extent complete in themselves, and the ongoing momentum in the sonata-form plan. Howells meets this by a subtle interplay between closure and continuity in the thematic

---

[23] Howells, 'Vaughan Williams's "Pastoral" Symphony', 123.

and tonal discourses. In the thematic form (Table 11.4), each movement pursues a ternary plan, though between the second and third movements this is complicated by overlap in the transition. The outline of the third movement's thematic plan is further complicated by the use of the first theme in transformation and the sketchy initial presentation of the subsidiary material (C), whose recurrence marks the beginning of the recapitulation. Formal closure could not be too strong or self-contained in a section intended to function as closure to the whole; and it would be similarly contradictory to embark on the wholescale exposition of new material.

The thematic form works also on the larger scale. The two main themes are placed one in each of the first two movements, so that exposition and development functions overlap within the first rotation. The second rotation constitutes the recapitulation and presents A in a transformed state, separating it from B by the interpolation of new material. The third rotation is the coda, in which both themes are reduced to single statements, and are again separated by the additional material, also in reduced form. The normal three rotations of a sonata form are thus shifted in relation to the formal functions with which they usually coincide, and their proportions are correspondingly altered, so that in place of three presentations of roughly balanced length, they pursue a progressive diminution in their periodicity.

Similarly, the formal approach requires important tonal modifications to the normal scheme of sonata composition. The desire to give a rounded shape to the first movement exposition removes the tonal tension derived from the opposition of two tonal centres typical of the sonata exposition. Only one key is presented; the central section develops tonal contrast by moving away from and back to this initial key, but it does not establish an opposing secondary key. Howells replaces the dynamic opposition of keys by the development of ambiguity within the tonic key area itself. There is, for example, frequent confusion of the tonic and its relative minor, so that cadential direction is at times unsure, as where C♯ overlays the cadence on E at the end of the first section of the first movement (Ex. 11.3a). Harmonic ostinati are also used to create ambiguity, their repetitions at once anchoring the tonality whilst their circularity undermines any sense of progression. The third section of the first movement begins with a three-chord ostinato comprising descending fourths against arpeggiating fifths (Ex. 11.3b). Each of the chords is a seventh chord, and the second of them is the tonic chord, but there is no progression to this chord: the three seem equally weighted. So whilst the tonic is certainly present in the opening and closing parts of the first movement, it is shrouded with ambiguity, which gives it a complexity that makes up for the lack of a competing key centre.

The conflation of tonic and relative is a feature that is played out later on in the piece, where the relative comes to stand for the tonic at the beginnings of both the recapitulation and the coda. In each case, this is to delay the real tonal resolution whilst reinforcing a formal point of arrival tonally. At the beginning of the recapitulation, the conventional harmonic gesture of arrival is subverted. The dominant is reached but interrupted by a semitonal descent to a B♭ major chord. The recapitulation then commences an augmented second higher in C♯ minor. The true moment of tonal return is situated towards the latter end of the movement with the return of material C, and this is preceded by a substantial dominant preparation in the conventional way. Its placement is calculated to reinforce the subsidiary idea C

Table 11.4 Overlay of formal levels in the Sonata no. 1 for Violin and Piano

	Bar	Section type	Material	Movement form	Thematic rotations
Mvt I	1	Exposition	A	a ⇩ternary	⇩1st rotation
	27	Development		a´	
	80	Recapitulation		a	
Mvt II	103	Statement	B	a ⇩ternary	
	119	Continuation		a´	
	143	Restatement		a	
	167	Transition/	B/C		
	179	⇩Exposition	A´	a ⇩ternary	⇩2nd rotation (D/C interpolated)
Mvt III	194				
	213	Episode	D	b	
	259	Recapitulation	C	a	
	271		B		
	293		A		
Mvt IV	304	Recapitulation		⇩Reminiscence coda	⇩3rd rotation (D/C interpolated)
	316		D/C		
	332		B → A		

Ex. 11.3a Sonata no.1 in E major for Violin and Piano, confusion of tonic and its relative undermining cadential direction

Ex. 11.3b Sonata no.1 in E major for Violin and Piano, ostinato repetition undermining harmonic direction

that had been introduced seemingly in passing during the transition between the second and third movements. The return of B soon after is marked by a further destabilising of the tonality, the reason being that here, as with the first theme, the true point of resolution will occur in the coda, when B finally does arrive in the tonic.

The return of the second theme in the third movement is marked by a sudden move from E to E♭ major that picks up a recurrent tonal shift in the piece. The first hint of it is in the progression in the first movement into the middle section. The cadential g♯ is enharmonically reconfigured as a♭ in a progression that seems to lead towards E♭ minor, though this is quickly side-stepped. At the end of the movement, the same thing happens, this time successfully cadencing in E♭ major (Ex. 11.2a); and although the music moves quickly on again to C major, it returns to E♭ major at the climactic elaboration of the theme. E♭ major is once more hinted at in the transition's progression back to the tonic via two half-diminished sevenths a diminished third apart, the first the minor supertonic of E♭, the second the leading-note seventh of E. E♭ major does not form in these occurrences a secondary key in the usual sonata-form dichotomy. Rather, it haunts the tonic, derailing the tonal progress at important moments. There even seems to be a remembrance of this right at the end of the work, in the tentative way in which the final chord arrives after an ambiguous octave G♯ at the crucial point in the first movement's cadence that had previously been enharmonically mutated (see again Exx. 11.2a and 11.2b). The bare octave offers no indication whether the G♯ has once again mutated to A♭. The ending acquires a psychological charge of doubt, so that when the E major chord arrives, it could even be the flat supertonic of E♭ major. Rather than being clear or final, the chord is faint and whispered. Here is complexity of mood conveyed right to the end.

As in the sonata, the *Fantasy Quartet* unifies the diverse moods of its various episodes into a single 'complex mood' through the development and transformation of a single theme. It is every bit as unified thematically as the Brahmsian model of chamber music that Stanford taught, but its method of arriving at this end is quite different, in virtue of the folk-type materials it employs. In his interview with Katharine Eggar, Howells was quite clear about the benefits and traps of composing with folk-song materials:

> The most that [folk-song] influence should be permitted to do is (1) to put one into its own genial mood, (2) to impart its own 'inflections', as it were, (3) to find itself logically developed in a manner that is always inherent in it (at its best), in a way that it has rarely been able to enjoy because of its almost continuous servitude to dance-schemes and metrical verse ... When you dwell for a moment on the possibilities of any really fine folk tune, you may be struck with the thought that the eternal A. B. A. of it (despite a limited sort of adequacy) is the real curse (if there be one) of folk music.[24]

For this reason, Howells ducked the prescription of Cobbett's competition to compose on a known folk-song and instead used materials of his own devising. His own folk-song achieves its most formal statement in the first episode, where it assumes an AA′BB′ form (Ex. 11.4b), a more open-ended shape than the ABA he criticises. Even here, the formality of its presentation derives more from the regular four-bar phrasing, as on each repetition the phrases of the melody start to recompose themselves.

The key to Howells's approach lies in the idea that folk-song should 'find itself logically developed in a manner that is always inherent in it (at its best)'. So the techniques of motivic variation and manipulation within sections draw on procedures similar to those found in folk-song. The first section comprises three varying statements of a melodic phrase followed by a transition (Ex 11.4a). The first, the motto theme itself, is an arch that rises sharply a minor tenth from the tonic before falling

[24] Eggar, 'Herbert Howells', 214.

Ex. 11.4 (a) *Fantasy String Quartet*, Op. 25, presentation and unfolding of motto theme. (b) *Fantasy String Quartet*, Op. 25, transformation of motto theme in 1st episode

Ex. 11.4c *Fantasy String Quartet*, Op. 25, transformation of motto theme in 2nd episode

back down to it more gradually, with a caesural punctuation on the dominant at the midpoint. Taken on its own, it reveals a free, quasi-improvisational shape, characterised by certain distinctive and recurrent intervals – the opening fifth, and the apposition of a tone and minor third – but presenting no repeated motivic elements. The second phrase is a paraphrase of it, the opening fifth acquiring a lower auxiliary that will prove characteristic later on, the rise of a tenth now being exceeded to the twelfth, and the caesura being composed through with emphasis on the subdominant in place of the dominant. Other changes involve re-rhythmicisations of elements in the original melody. The cello's third phrase repeats the violin's first, but its cadence is avoided and drives on into a closing statement from the violin that epitomises the motto theme. This epitome phrase is the launching point for the transition, which draws also on elements from earlier phrases, now assuming a motivic role. Whereas the phrases of the opening expositional section constitute a series of paraphrases of the initial statement, the melodic line of the transition is generated by a continuous progression through variants of three paradigms.

The informality in the nature of the development and tendency for the melody as a whole to remain in view as it changes seem to be symptomatic of a desire to evoke vernacular musical speech. Such techniques ensure continuity in the progression of the music. The transformation techniques that are used to derive the materials of the episodes are not wholly different, but they are designed to achieve contrast (Exx. 11.4b and c). The folk-song of the first episode is foreshadowed by the epitome phrase of the opening paragraph. It is the simplification of the rhythm, and in particular the use of repeated notes, allied with the imposition of a regular four-bar phrase structure, that effect the change of character. In the second episode, Howells begins the folk-dance with a clear paraphrase of the opening of the motto theme, now in triple time. The new figures generated by this procedure quickly become themselves the basis for the subsequent melodic development, and the motto theme as a distinct entity is lost from view.

The reliance on melodic development of materials tends to encourage a slow rate of harmonic change and textures that focus on one instrument at a time, with relatively little counterpoint. Even in the faster sections, rapid chord movement arises often from a mere oscillation between chords. This procedure suits the episodic construction, with static harmony accentuating the contrasts between the sections – contrasts that have been designed to be pronounced. So the F minor seventh chord of the opening is maintained with only the briefest interruption of auxiliary harmonies for the first twenty-three bars; and the music remains closely tied to it for the next twenty-three bars. The movement from F minor to B minor is then achieved by a succession of two half-diminished sevenths a major third apart (Ex. 11.5). The progression is deliberately abrupt, and the starkness of the contrast between the F minor opening and the B minor of the folk-song stands out as sharply as possible.

Simplicity at the surface level of the harmony is compensated by the complexity of the tonal design. The C major chord with which the piece ends is not at all predictable from the opening. In fact, there is no hint of C as a tonic until some way into the second episode (bar 172, figure 13). This is the first perfect cadence in the piece and helps to characterise the dance style that is exploited here. The trio section moves away from C, but the resumption of the dance style leads to the

Ex. 11.5 *Fantasy String Quartet*, Op. 25, abrupt key change through progression of half-diminished seventh chords

re-establishment of C through a ten-bar dominant preparation (249–58), which is the most unambiguous tonal gesture of the whole piece. A direct resolution is avoided by progression to the subdominant, but expectation of resolution to C is maintained as the bass continues down to the supertonic, the first violin rising energetically against it. The music breaks off just before the resolution is attained and there is a return to the material of the opening (Ex. 11.6a). The work's opening chord (an F minor chord with minor seventh) returns, now revoiced so that it provides the resolution in the melody and bass. This is the first moment in the work at which any connection between the opening chord and C major has been revealed.

This revelation suggests that the tonality of the whole piece will emerge as an expanded plagal cadence, but the subsequent harmony does everything to avoid so neat and simple a resolution to the wayward tonal design (Ex. 11.6b). The melody of the beginning returns over the F minor seventh chord but is quickly dissolved into a flourish and trill, and the simple diatonicism of the opening is now unsettled by augmented chords. A succession of two augmented chords a tone apart takes on the semblance of an altered ♭II–V progression with the arrival of an A minor chord; and this establishes the harmonic theme of the closing page: two approaches to closure in C, each interrupted by chords of A. Despite the use of unusual chord types, the underlying harmonic progression can be related to a straightforward vi–ii–V–(I) cadential descent of fifths; but the voicing of these chords is designed to conceal the root progression. With the failure of the second attempt, the texture dissolves, leaving the second violin's melody line to descend on its own to C. The final harmonic progression arrives at the long-delayed C major chord without affording it any sense of resolution. A descent of two second-inversion seventh chords leads to a chord that sounds as if it might be a supertonic chord in C, but this again is interrupted by A minor, and the final progression from this to C is one of resignation, not attainment. Just at the point when a conventional tonal work should find its sharpest access of harmonic direction and focus, Howells's loses its way. The final chord sequence sounds less like a directed progression than an apposition of attractive but only loosely related harmonies.

Ex. 11.6a *Fantasy String Quartet*, Op. 25, textural and harmonic rupture initiating closing section

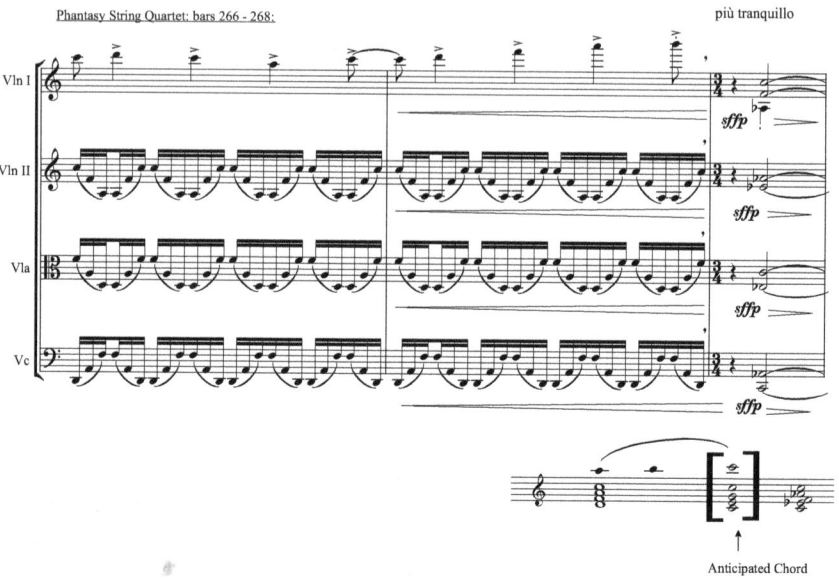

As in the Violin Sonata, the motto theme is treated as the subject or persona of the work, its resilient identity unifying the contrasting moods of the episodes into a complex whole. The tonality does not pursue the closure of the sonata: indeed, the final cadence is a paradox, both fulfilling the anticipated C major cadence of the second episode and denying it through subversion of the harmonic logic that would invest it with tonal meaning. The tonality, then, is less unified than that of the sonata, suggesting a narrative dimension to the mood complex enacted by the theme. The unequivocally folk-like themes in the episodes are projected within a frame that is doubtful and interrogative. The genial atmosphere of folk-song seems like a distant dream to the modern consciousness that experiences it.

Whilst the sonata and the quartet are both constructed around the evolution of a single dominating thematic idea, the quintet represents the confrontation of two distinct and contrasting themes, in true sonata fashion; and these are joined by a third element in the middle section. Howells nonetheless conceived the work as embodying an underlying unity of mood, noting a 'mystic feeling about the whole thing'.[25] In his conversation with Katharine Eggar, he said of the quintet: 'I got interested in the form it took, and tried my best to decide which of two things in it most governed the ultimate form it took: the melodic ideas, or the moods'.[26] It is not necessary to make the decision that Howells was attempting here. It is, though, possible to glean from the terms of Howells's discussion an insight into the formal processes of the piece. The precedent of the quartet and sonata suggests that mood and melody are symbiotic elements in the expression of complex mood. Thus in

---

[25] Palmer, *A Centenary Celebration*, 72.
[26] Eggar, 'An English Composer', 130.

Ex. 11.6b *Fantasy String Quartet*, Op. 25, harmony of closing section

the quintet, the interplay between the melodic ideas and the moods is central to the dynamic of the piece and consequently to the shape that it assumes. Part of the resolution that the recapitulation achieves is to force the two main themes to exchange their moods, so that it is less a restatement in the simple sense than a terminal transformation. The initially tranquil B theme adopts the passionate character of the A theme, which in its turn is calmed. It is clear from the remarks discussed above that Howells thought these features more important than any overall resemblance to sonata form, though the sonata-form framework is analytically useful and generically appropriate.

The contrast between the two themes is one of melodic direction and rhythmic movement (Ex. 11.7): the first is an upwards arch shape in an animated rhythm of diverse elements; the second outlines an overall descent, in a smoother and slower rhythmic movement. There is a unity to them, in that both explore a pentatonic pitch collection; moreover, the core parts of the two themes invert one another. This underlying unity is at the heart, on the one hand, of the exchange of mood that the two themes execute during the piece and, on the other, of the question whether it is in fact the sequence of moods rather than the melodic ideas that conveys the form. The exchange of roles effected by the two themes in the recapitulation relates to the gradual exhaustion of the first theme through its development. Its florid tail is eliminated and all that remains is the turn about the initial note (Ex. 11.8). The recapitulation of this theme is less a restatement of it than a recreation of it under its new thematic guise. The return of the two themes in the coda, counterpointed against one another, is ghostly. It is not a resolution: the descending chromatic harmonies indicate as much; it is the return of an unresolved problem, and it contributes to the undermining of the piece's ending discussed below.

Ex. 11.7 *Rhapsodic Quintet*, Op. 31, unity and contrast in the principal themes

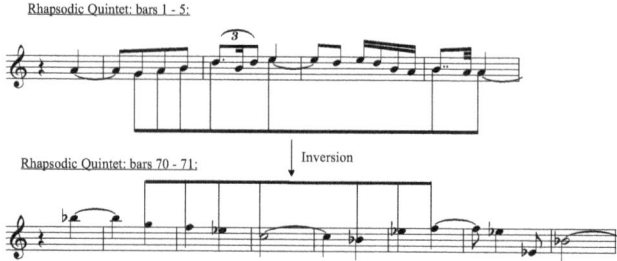

The deployment of a relatively conventional tripartite sonata-form outline is the framework for a very unusual tonal design. Despite the marked difference in formal approach between the quintet and the quartet, there is some important similarity in their tonality: each ends on a C major chord that is not predictable at its opening but emerges as a tonal goal at a late stage in the piece's evolution. Indeed, the approach to the closing C major of the quintet is even more veiled than that in the quartet, where there is, at least, a relatively straightforward section in C major. In the quintet, C major appears as a goal only right at the end of the development, where the texture and approach are similar to those at the end of the second episode of the quartet (Ex. 11.9; compare Ex. 11.6a): the progression breaks off with the anticipation of a C major chord. As in the quartet, that C major chord does not arrive. Although there is a C in the bass of the harmony, above it is an E♭ major seventh chord. The sense of arrival is thus not entirely frustrated, but the harmony is ambiguous, giving simultaneously the E♭ major of theme B and the C that was anticipated.

The conventional arrival at such a point would be the return of the opening theme in the tonic, and the implication of the build-up at the end of the development is that this will be triumphant. In fact, the key of the opening theme was not securely established at the outset, and there was no hint of C major in any case. The return of the second theme in its original key at this point subverts the form both tonally and thematically. The motivation for such an occurrence can be located in the unusual tonal configuration of the exposition.

Of the three phantasies, the quintet begins with the weakest assertion of its initial tonality. The presentation of the first theme avoids a strong declaration of its tonal centre. Rather, the tonic is revealed gradually as a framework for an elaborate architecture (Ex. 11.10a). There are two large-scale phrases, each comprising two statements of the theme, the first in the strings, the second on the clarinet culminating in a climactic descent by the strings. The first statement is in E minor Phrygian, but focuses on the modal 'dominant' (a B half-diminished seventh chord; Ex. 11.10b). The expected cadence on E is replaced by G minor, which is the basis for the second statement. Thereafter, there is a tonal progress back to E by descending fourths, tucking the third statement (a whisper-like echo of the beginning down a minor third) within the D major dominant of G and giving the fourth phrase a tone up from the second on A minor. When this fourth statement cadences on E

Ex. 11.8 *Rhapsodic Quintet*, Op. 31, progressive transformation of 1st theme

Ex. 11.9 *Rhapsodic Quintet*, Op. 31, textural and harmonic rupture at end of development

minor, the tonic that was initially withheld is finally given; but the climactic conclusion of this section is deflected once more to G minor and to a cadence onto its dominant, a D chord. Two further statements of the theme in D and E effect a transition to D♯ major, in which key the second theme arrives (see bar 70 in Ex. 11.10a). Understandably, Howells notates the D♯ major as E♭ major; and whilst the harmonic logic clearly indicates D♯ major as its outcome, an ambiguity between D♯ and E♭ is part of the tonal argument of the piece. In the present context, D♯ acts as a leading note for a second, slightly extended statement of the theme in E major;

Ex. 11.10a *Rhapsodic Quintet*, Op. 31, harmonic and tonal architecture of exposition

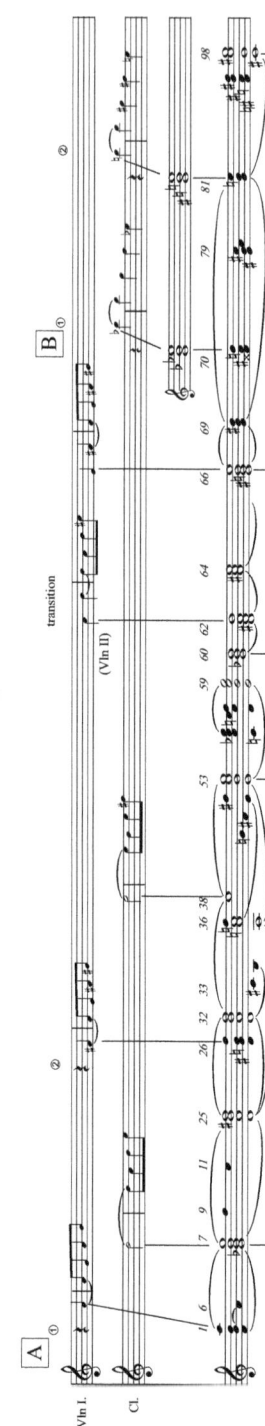

Ex. 11.10b *Rhapsodic Quintet*, Op. 31, harmonic structure of 1st theme

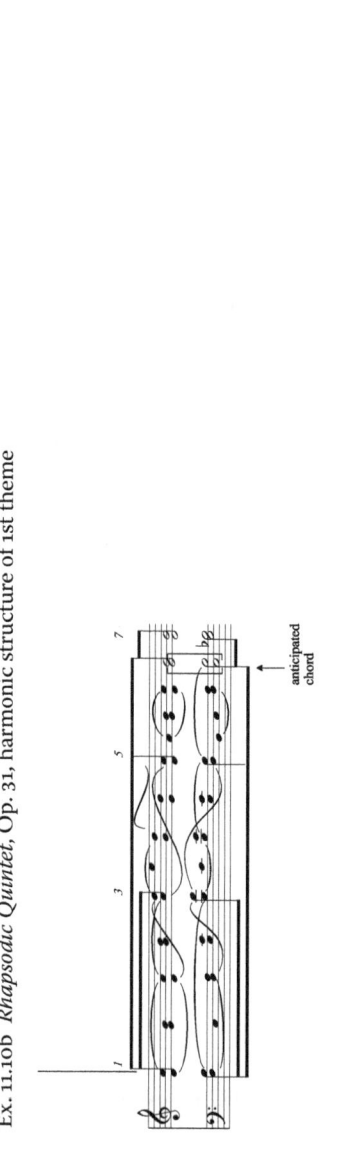

Ex. 11.10c *Rhapsodic Quintet*, Op. 31, harmonic progressions by minor third in latter part of development

so identification of it with E♭ major is purely notational. Yet the harmonic move between the keys of D♯ and E is weak, involving a tritone root progression (A♯–E) and false relation (E♯–E).

Overall, the exposition is a prolongation of E, with interruptions in G minor and D♯ major (Ex. 11.10a). It is far from the conventional establishment of a tonic and secondary key, not least because the primary key is so fragile in its presentation. Rather, the exposition announces a set of tonal elements and relationships that are the basis for what follows, without offering any hint of the possible outcome of their interaction. The exposition cadences not in E but on its relative, C♯ minor, and the first stage of the development sets this in relationship with the G minor that twice interrupted the tonal direction previously. Together with E, these form a sequence of minor thirds that prefigures the sequence of chords a semitone higher in the second half of the development (Ex. 11.10c).

The E♭ major/C minor that begins the recapitulation does not remain for long; after four bars the harmony starts to move flatwards, and then after a further three bars sharpwards, cadencing on E̲ at bar 22. The harmonic logic of this progression plays on an ability to take E̲♭ as D̲♯, and the same is true of the following transition, which falls back to E̲♭ before arriving on a G chord (Ex. 11.11). This section of the recapitulation picks up the D♯ major from the exposition and plays with its enharmonic ambiguity. The result of this process is that D̲♯ is changed into E̲♭, and it is this key that inflects the C of the following restatement of the first theme. The lie is given to this as a resolution of the tonal argument, however, by the descending chromatic sequence that begins the coda (Ex. 11.12), which serves, like that of the *Fantasy Quartet*, to undermine what seemed to have been achieved previously in order to return to the original condition of the materials. The closing cadences do nothing to remedy this, as the C major that is attained seems imposed on what preceded it rather than the inevitable or logical outcome of it. The 6–5 sigh over the C major chord is a final gesture of ambiguity: hinting at the opening of the first theme, it offers cyclic closure, but in giving just the first two notes of that theme, it suggests also its continuation and thus no real closure at all. This openness is the more subversive for the reassuring, low-tessitura voicing of the chord and its lengthy sounding (two and a half bars with a pause). It has the semblance of late Romantic closure but neither the context nor the force.

The Violin Sonata contains its substantial lexicon of harmonic invention within the traditional frame of an end-stopped tonality. It finishes with the E major of its beginning; and if the finality of that gesture is undermined by attenuation of the texture and the lingering ghost of E♭ major, it remains a conventional rounded tonal statement nonetheless. The great achievement of the quintet is in balancing the harmonic tools that Howells had recently fashioned within a command of large-scale form that nonetheless maintains the exploratory open aesthetic of the *Fantasy String Quartet*. Like the string quartet, it ends on a C major chord that does not relate to the key of the beginning; but where in the quartet C major emerges as a goal only late on, befitting its episodic construction, in the quintet C is less a goal or point of resolution than it is an attempt to mediate the subtle tonal play between E̲ and D̲♯/E̲♭ that has been sustained since the beginning. Such tonal play – shrouded by ambiguity and left only provisionally resolved at the end – is at the heart of the

Ex. 11.11 *Rhapsodic Quintet*, Op. 31, enharmonic duality in transition of recapitulation

Ex. 11.12 *Rhapsodic Quintet*, Op. 31, harmonic process of closing section

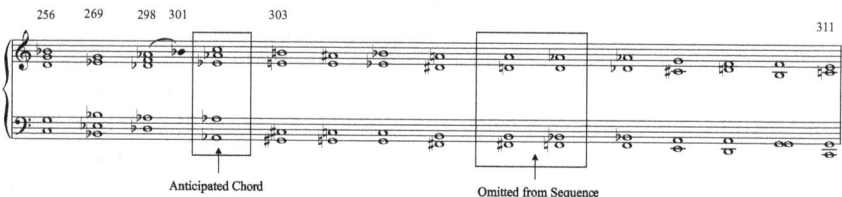

'complex mood' that Howells sought to express in his music at this time. Unlike the sonata and the quartet, the quintet plays two contrasted but related themes off one another, complementary but irreducible foils of a single identity, just as D♯ and E♭ are complementary parts of a single pitch identity. The hidden connection between them is a cipher for the unity that they manifest in their exchange of mood, and also in their combination. They represent not contrasted agents in a drama but opposing facets of a single 'frame of mind'. In this case, then, they are part of the complexity of the mood that the piece enacts.

The Phantastical Phantasy

Howells's engagement with the idea of the phantasy was not limited to works in the Cobbett mould. He used the phantasy label for several works of a very different kind: there was a now-lost *Phantasy Ground Bass* for organ (HH 52 – 1915), a *Phantasy* for piano (HH 74 – 1917), a *Phantasy Minuet* for pianola (HH 105 – 1919) and the choral-orchestral phantasy *Sine nomine* (HH 126 – 1923). The word 'phantasy' exists, of course, in ordinary language, with a meaning of spectral apparition or hallucination. A number of composers writing in the 1910s and 1920s called pieces phantasies having in mind only such associations. Howells's own former teacher, Herbert Brewer, composed a *Midsummer Phantasy* for piano (1927), which comprised four miniatures: 'Mutual Attraction', 'Pandean Pipes', 'Pixies' and 'The Love Philtre'. The term 'phantasy' is justified here only for its loosely programmatic association with the magical and other-worldly, and this seems to be the sense intended by Howells in his other phantasy compositions.

Representative is the *Phantasy* for piano, which was written in March 1917 between the *Fantasy String Quartet* and the Violin Sonata. The piece is complete and in fair copy; and although the manuscript indicates an intention to write three such pieces, only the one is copied in and no others are known. The piece is strongly influenced by Debussy and Ravel, to the extent that Howells's own usually strong style is at times hard to discern – a possible reason for its exclusion from the list of works that he drew up for Edwin Evans in 1919.[27] The opening seems to have been modelled on the piano writing of Ravel's *Jeux d'eau*; and Howells borrows towards the end Ravel's subdominant augmented-sixth chord of the third bar, which he uses as a subtonic auxiliary chord (the spelling is revealing of the derivation, as Howells writes B♯ when in fact the note functions as an auxiliary C♮ to the Bs of the adjacent tonic chords; Ex. 11.13). There are also reminiscences of Debussy's piano writing (Ex. 11.14). Howells seems to have been taken with the retransitional phrase in the *Première arabesque*, where the dominant-ninth chord of the dominant circumvents its expected resolution and leads instead to the first inversion of the subdominant, the third and ninth of the chord progressing outwards by a semitone rather than following the normal inwards resolution. In adopting this progression, Howells intensifies it, leading to an arrival on the root position of the subdominant and exaggerating the repetitions, drawing them out over nine bars. Similarly, the orchestral-seeming texture of the climactic section that follows (figuration at the top, a low sustained bass and prominent tenor), and a pair of adjacent augmented triads from a few bars further on, also seem to have derived from Debussy – perhaps *Le jardin sous la pluie* in this instance.

The music follows a bipartite scheme (Table 11.5), the second part being a varied rotation of the material introduced in the first, which is capped by a short coda. Much of the writing consists of short fragments that follow one another in a sort of mosaic formation. There is a hint of the sonata principle in the transposed restatement of secondary material, but it is very brief and does not generate any sense of resolution of the tonic key, as a strong climactic section in the subdominant follows. There is nothing here that is reminiscent of the phantasy principle at work in the chamber compositions; and the assemblage of fragmentary materials into a free form seems to be less governed by a sense of formal propriety than by a pictorial intention. *Jeux d'eau* carries the motto 'Dieu fluvial riant de l'eau qui le chatouille …' ('The river god giggling as the water tickles him …'), which is a plainly phantastical image. Howells's phantasy suggests similar imagery, even though its title falls short of anything specific.

Two years after the piano *Phantasy*, Howells was amongst a group of European composers responding to a request from the critic Edwin Evans to write or arrange something for the Aeolian Company's pianola.[28] A number of composers offered arrangements, but five supplied newly composed works: Stravinsky, Malipiero, Casella, Goossens and Howells. Howells's *Phantasy Minuet* was the

---

[27] Palmer, *A Centenary Celebration*, 69–70.
[28] Andrews, 'A Documentary and Bibliographical Study', Vol. I, 175–6. Andrews relates the difficulties that the medium posed to Howells: 'there is that dreadful sense of mechanism which almost petrifies my musical mind'.

Ex.11.13 *Phantasy*, Op. 29, no.1, indebtedness to Ravel, *Jeux d'eau*

longest of the five, running at nearly nine minutes' playing time. It has an unusual construction, falling in two sections: the first a ternary-form modal minuet and trio, the second presenting two free variations of the minuet theme in slower time. Writing for a mechanical instrument, Howells took the opportunity to employ some unusual textures. The opening minuet observes a moderate triple time, as a minuet should, but the upbeats of the theme are florid groups harmonised in chords of fourths and fifths, and in the middle of the texture run decuplet-over-sextuplet figurations in Dorian harmony. The muted character of the music, its tendency to florid textures and decoration, and the unusual

Ex. 11.14 *Phantasy*, Op. 29, no.1, indebtedness to Debussy

[* A '5' in the MS suggests that Howells thought at one stage of a 3+3+5 grouping for the L.H. figuration]

Debussy, *Première Arabesque*, bars 14 - 17:

Ex. 11.14 *continued*

deceleration of movement in the second half are suggestive of a phantastical inspiration. It is possible that Howells had the supernatural appearance of the playerless pianola in mind and intended the whole as a ghostly reminiscence of past times.[29]

Howells's final work to carry the 'phantasy' label, this time as a subtitle, was the choral-orchestral work, *Sine nomine*. Katharine Eggar wrote: 'The work is written in an entirely original form, hence its title, and the composer (for the sake of weaker brethren) allows it to be called a phantasy.'[30] Here the subtitle *Phantasy* carries both formal and figurative associations. The piece is a single movement of

---

[29] Strictly speaking, the pianola is not playerless, as it is controlled by a human agent who influences performance variables such as tempo, phrasing and dynamic; however, the keys depress automatically, thereby giving a spectral appearance to the performance.

[30] Eggar, 'An English Composer', 130.

Table 11.5 Form of *Phantasy* for piano, Op. 29, no. 1 (HH 74)

	Bar	Material	Comment	Key
I. Exposition	1	A	Triplet demisemiquaver figuration in right hand over quaver dyads arpeggiating F#m7 chord in left (ii7). Harmony develops latterly, but F#m7 remains point of reference.	E (ii)
	29	B	Figuration and harmony intensifies and melodic line emerges from right-hand figuration. 9/8 bars of arpeggiated harmonic flourish punctuate phrases.	
	43	C	E7 dominant prolongation (alternating with Gm) – compare *Fantasy String Quartet*, figure 10.	A (v)
	52	D	Resolution of dominant to low A undermined by B♭m harmony above, marked by return of A texture, thickened and widely spaced across keyboard, harmony developed.	I
	58	B′	Continuation of developed texture and melody leading to sequential descending cadence seeming to head for E♭ major but interrupted at end.	
	87	C′	Variant of E7 prolongation.	A (v)
II. Recapitulation	96	A′	Transformation of opening (return to initial tonality); some rhythmicisation of left-hand quavers and new figuration in right hand. Second phrase takes different tonal turn.	E (ii)
	120	E	New continuation of A figuration, E♭m–D7.	
	131	B′′	Further continuation of B including some specific transposition of B′.	
	150	F	Climactic section on A, B figuration continued in right hand, new melody in tenor.	
	159	D′	Harmonically modified, now over E (dominant).	A (v)
	165	C′′	Harmonically varied, E7 no longer alternating with Gm.	
III. Coda	171	B′′′	Rising over rhythmicised E pedal.	E
	183	A′′	Return of right-hand figuration over new sustained harmony; figuration gradually liquidated.	
	195–207	G	Descending single line in bass leading to final chord of E, *ppp* sustained over seven bars.	

about fifteen minutes' length with an arch shape characteristic of phantasy-type compositions, initial and closing slow sections framing a central, faster, dance-like section. The closing section is a free reprise of material from the first. In relation to this piece, Eggar described the plainsong style inspiring it as 'the folk-song of the Church', thereby making a connection with the place of its first performance, Gloucester Cathedral.[31] The phantasy in this case is a hallucination of the cathedral's past, evoking ghosts of bygone worship; but the phantastical expression is reconciled with the phantasy-type formal design of the Cobbett-inspired chamber works.

This group of pieces invites reflection on the *Fantasy String Quartet* from their alternative expressive perspective; and the piece lends itself readily to this. Howells commented on it: 'No break; tho' there are two distinct moods, the first much more subjective than the second.'[32] What he characterised as changes in mood might be more clearly thought of as changes in voice. As he says, the first is more subjective, or interior and self-reflective, with a recitative-like style. The second, by implication, is more objective, appearing first as a fully fledged folk-song and later as a folk-dance: the individual in society. There is, though, no indication of a change of subject between these voices. On the contrary, there are almost no cadences in the piece – the only exceptions are within the exterior-voice sections, at certain phrase boundaries – and certainly not at the limits of sections. The interior voice is roused to lead into the exterior voice, with transitions that accelerate into the new movement and prepare the coming tonality. The smooth progressions from the interior voice into the exterior one indicate contrasting articulations of the same consciousness. The exterior voice, though, is dependent on the other. At the end of the first episode, it dissolves back into the interior voice – whilst the second episode is abruptly broken off, as if suddenly roused from a dream. The exterior voices are hallucinations, dreams of action on the part of the introverted consciousness of the piece. One might speculate that they are dreams of love (the first episode) and marriage (the second) that are thwarted or unfulfilled. The rupture of the second episode prompts the interior mind to an extravagant dissolution of its motto theme. The tension between vocal melody and instrumental figuration that the preceding episode had developed are now galvanised in a mini-cadenza, prompting the work's most striking harmonic progressions. Thereafter, both melodic and harmonic syntax all but collapse; and the closing cadence, if it seems to provide the resolution sought by the previous episode, does so under a veil of doubt or despair about successful action in the exterior world.

In Howells's oeuvre, the aesthetic, phantastical side of the phantasy concept should not be dissociated from the formal side that Cobbett instigated. Although Howells developed the aesthetic side in pieces that do not have a strong generic connection with the phantasy, all three of his formal phantasies have veiled, mysterious endings and play with high levels of ambiguity in their tonal construction, suggestive of phantastical inspiration within their complex moods. The switches between interior and exterior voices in the quartet play particularly to this aspect, suggesting a crypto-programme of reverie and visions. The phantasy for Howells

---

[31] *Ibid.*
[32] Palmer, *A Centenary Celebration*, 72.

was not simply a formal game but an important component in an aesthetic of the magical and mystical, one that can be related to what Christopher Palmer has identified as the 'Celtic' aspect of his artistic makeup.[33]

'A "modern"...but a Britisher too'

Howells's reflection on why the *Fantasy String Quartet* particularly pleased him is revealing both for the terms in which he saw his own compositional aspirations at the time, and for its implication of a possible divide between these two ends. It echoes his remarks on the cantata *Sir Patrick Spens* (HH 77): 'it is an example (I hope) of a fit compromise and union between the spirit of Folk Music and modern organized musical expression'.[34] Here the necessity of compromise in reconciling the two ends is explicit. As Howells saw it, the intention to be a modern would not necessarily be married to that of manifesting a British national consciousness. It is consistent with this view that the most overt representations of folk idiom in the quartet are in the episodes (presented, as it were, in inverted commas), whereas the idiom of the framing sections tends towards uncertainty, fragmentation and discontinuity.

Englishness was certainly a quality that Howells prized in his own work. Katharine Eggar reported:

> Mr Howells ... is certain that an Englishman expressing himself in composition must, if he is natural, have a turn of speech as unmistakably native in that medium as in his speaking or writing of his mother-tongue. And in the case of his own works, he most considers that those which are his most characteristic – the most unmistakable 'H.H.ish', shall we say? – are also 'the most Englishy'.[35]

Yet the outcome of such thinking was not a style saturated with folk-song. Neither the sonata nor the quintet makes use of such materials. For Howells, a 'native' turn of speech could be conceived more abstractly. Later, he claimed that 'sticking to the point' was an English trait in his work, and Eggar added to this 'remoteness'.[36] Such qualities may reasonably enough be attached to the phantasies, with their compact form, focused thematic development and tendency to muted dynamics, particularly in their closing pages. More striking, though, is the detachment of such terms from the specifics of the musical language. They seem like an attempt to deflect the discourse of national style away from musical specifics towards qualities of a more abstract and moral kind.

Although happy to express himself as an Englishman, Howells did not favour overt nationalism in music. In an article for the *Athenaeum* in November 1916, around the time he was working on the *Fantasy String Quartet*, he wrote 'After long years of musical mumblings and incoherence, plain speech is a salutary asset;

---

[33] *Ibid.*, 129–42.
[34] *Ibid.*, 438.
[35] Eggar, 'An English Composer', 129.
[36] Eggar, 'Herbert Howells', 214. For an exploration of the quality of 'remoteness' in Howells's music, see Hodgson, 'The Music of Herbert Howells', 171–6.

and if we do not lose ourselves in the fashion for Nationalism in Art, we shall not be unduly perturbed that this speech is not always confined to one language, and that our own.'[37] Even as he was writing a work ostentatiously grounded in the style of folk-music he was more at pains to stress the validity of straying from a national language in the interests of 'plain speech'. The language of the *Fantasy Quartet*'s second episode comes close to that of Stravinsky's *Petrushka*. The piano *Phantasy*, which was written only a few months later, showed very directly his engagement with French style, an influence that thoroughly permeated his own idiom, its harmonic and textural aspects in particular. Stylistic characteristics were a superficial matter; it was the attitude of the music that differentiated modern English music from French: 'Too much and too careful consideration … goes to make "precious" music, which is all very natural in a modern Frenchman, but is no part of an English musician's make-up.'[38]

There is a concern for a potential internationalism behind these remarks that underpins also Howells's emerging discontent with the phantasy concept. Cobbett had always been clear that the genre should be a national one: 'a type of composition which fits the British composer like a glove'.[39] For Howells, in the 7 January entry of his 1919 diary, it was problematic: 'My 1917 "Phantasy Sonata" jumped back into my life this morning, pleading "guilty" of being unfit. I set about redressing wrongs in it. … I began this morning by changing the Sonata's name. By deed poll I have dropped "Phantasy" from it: the word has begun to frighten onlookers at British Music!'[40] Howells seems not to have been alone in this retreat from the word phantasy. Ireland named his Second Piano Trio (1917) merely *Trio in One Movement*, though it was as much a phantasy as its precursor of 1906. Ernest Austin's *Trio in One Movement* was originally called *Phantasy*.[41] Frank Bridge continued to explore the single-movement architecture he had forged in his early phantasies but without the label, his *Rhapsody Trio* of 1928 being the next example. It is not hard to see why the phantasy label could have been viewed as problematic. Single-movement forms were not new with Cobbett, so use of the phantasy label to refer to them may have suggested that English composers were unaware of the Continental works that already followed this trend; and the works using the title did not allude to or develop the style or form of the Tudor-Jacobean genre bearing the name, which may thus have seemed like false advertising. At worst a presumptuous national claim to musical common property, at best simply misleading, the phantasy might well have given composers cause to fight shy of it.

Howells's concern for being a modern and a 'Britisher' tilts towards the former: it is being modern that matters to him more. Being a Britisher is not so much a matter of adopting a certain style, or even a certain language, but a matter of a musical attitude: concision, remoteness, plain speaking and avoidance of preciousness. Of the phantasy works, it is the *Rhapsodic Quintet* that seems to come most often closest to these ideals, particularly with its frequent recourse to the diatonic

---

[37] Howells, 'Younger British Composers', 560.
[38] Eggar, 'Herbert Howells', 214.
[39] Cobbett, '*Obiter dicta*', 34.
[40] Palmer, *A Centenary Celebration*, 74.
[41] Cobbett, 'Chamber Music Notes', (1918).

dissonance that Howells inherited from Parry. The opening, saturated with seventh chords; the simple static harmonisation of the second theme; and then the bristling counterpoints at the beginning of the recapitulation are moments where the writing most clearly embodies these qualities. It is here that the tension between being a Britisher and being a modern becomes most clearly visible, for there is no obvious place for 'a complex mood' amongst these terms, and at these points in the work the musical expression seems almost disarmingly direct.

For Howells the phantasy was a vehicle for formal experimentation. His purpose with this was not to establish the identity of the genre; on the contrary, he wanted to move beyond it. His phantasies paved the way for single-movement orchestral works such as *Pastoral Rhapsody*, Op. 38 (HH 134) of 1923; *Paradise Rondel* (HH 159) of 1925; and the Piano Concerto no. 2, Op. 39 (HH 152), also of 1925, whose formal plan owed a great deal to the Violin Sonata. However, the phantasy, to the extent that it was established when Howells took it up, provided a context and motivation for developments in modern musical expression. In particular, it was the inclusion of contrasting moods within a single, united form that attracted Howells. Formal experimentation was not an end in itself for him but a means to express the complex mood that he associated with modern music. Complex mood appears as a facet of a frame of mind in these works. The development and transformation of thematic subjects through the course of them represents changing states within a single consciousness; but the phantasy carried also an association of the phantastical: the consciousness could be assailed by visions and hallucinations, suggesting its disintegration under the influence of mysterious exterior forces. Howells's phantasies were portraits of modern man in his psychological complexity and emotional confusion tinged with a mystic hue.

CHAPTER 12

Austerity, Difficulty and Retrospection: The Late Style of Herbert Howells

Phillip A. Cooke

HERBERT Howells's setting of the *Stabat mater* (HH 309) of 1965 is rightly held up as his masterpiece, the culmination of all that he had been striving for in his compositional career, a work that not only defined his mature musical language but also represented a composer at the height of his artistic powers, comfortable with his highly wrought and idiosyncratic idiom. It was a piece that would cast a shadow on all Howells's work both during and after its composition, and its place is as important in the composer's oeuvre as the early chamber music successes or the triumph of *Hymnus paradisi* (HH 220). However, if we view the *Stabat mater* as being the zenith of Howells's career, how do we then view the works that followed? For Howells continued to compose regularly for another thirteen years and composed in excess of forty works. It is easy to view these final works as being a somewhat irrelevant addition to his legacy, lacking the burning intensity of the *Stabat mater*, dealing mainly with smaller-scale genres and invariably being written for cathedrals, Oxbridge colleges and various luminaries. The difficulty, austerity and modernity of these final works has led to few performances, which only emphasises the perceived irrelevance of these pieces and the composer's slow, autumnal coda.

However, this is not necessarily the case, and I aim to show in this chapter that there are many fine later works, with much imaginative, beautiful and finely constructed music that provides more than the 'soft pedalled'[1] coda that many presume these works are. Although in his final years Howells would rarely reach the high levels of musical complexity and emotional anguish that characterise the *Stabat mater*, I aim to show that there is a constant process of refinement, modification and aesthetic fine-tuning that makes many of these works worthy additions to his body of work, and in some cases eclipses some of their more celebrated earlier cousins.

But what exactly characterises 'late style'? What are the fundamental hallmarks of music of this broad term and how do they differ from music written earlier in a composer's career? In his comprehensive article 'Disability and "Late Style" in Music', Joseph Straus states:

> Music in a late style is presumed to have certain internal qualities (such as fragmentation, intimacy, nostalgia, or concision) and to be associated with certain external factors (such as the age of the composer, his or her proximity to and foreknowledge of death, a sense of authorial belatedness with respect to significant predecessors, or a feeling of having lived too late within a historical period).[2]

---

[1] Spicer, *Herbert Howells*, 172.
[2] Straus, 'Disability and "Late Style" in Music', 3.

He elucidates further on this idea by suggesting six key terms associated with late style: 'introspective', 'austere', 'difficult', 'compressed', 'fragmentary' and 'retrospective'.[3] The late works of Herbert Howells certainly have elements of all these six terms, and throughout this chapter I will show how Howells's work of this final period adheres to Straus's description of the style, though with particular emphasis on three key terms that are the most prominent and pertinent to the composer's aesthetic: austerity, difficulty and retrospection.

We cannot underestimate the importance of the *Stabat mater* when viewing Howells's oeuvre, life and compositional aesthetic; the work is too thoroughly intertwined with all of them. It was always going to be a work that defined Howells, mainly because of the choice of text, with its vivid description of suffering and mortality heightened in coming from a grieving mother's point of view. The poem is so close to his own life and his own experiences that it would be impossible for him to have been objective in his setting; lines such as 'Vidit suum dulcem natum, / Moriendo desolatum, / Dum emisit spiritum' ('She beheld her tender Child, / Saw Him hang in desolation, / Till his spirit forth He sent')[4] strongly mirror the helplessness of Howells watching his son quickly succumb to advanced polio.

There is a strange masochistic quality to the poem that no doubt appealed to Howells, ever the purveyor of both agony and ecstasy in his sacred works, with both the expressive range of the text and powerful descriptive language being a boon for such a composer. Lines such as 'contristatam et dolentem / pertransivit gladius' ('His bitter anguish bearing, / now at length the sword has passed') and 'Sancta Mater, istud agas, / crucifixi fige plagas / cordi meo valide' ('Holy Mother! Pierce me through, / in my heart each wound renew / of my Saviour crucified') are full of dramatic, expressive potential, crying out for setting in an equally powerful manner. And Howells certainly responded in kind with a work that captures the anguish and grief of the text, but also ratchets up the emotion to an almost unbearable level with each new section seeking to increase the level of emotional torment and unease. As the *Guardian* critic Hugo Cole noted after the first performance, 'The *Stabat Mater* seems to be one of those works in which the subject has chosen the composer rather than the composer choosing the subject';[5] Howells could not have chosen a more suitable text for a work to crown his compositional achievements and to highlight his own idiosyncratic aesthetic.

To create this disturbing aural landscape Howells would continue to evolve his musical language, honing many of the contrapuntal and harmonic techniques and mannerisms that he had used throughout his career. What is most striking about the work is the level of polyphonic complexity that is present throughout; from the stark, two-part bitonality of the opening to the declamatory outbursts of sections such as 'Quis est homo' ('Is there one'), Howells shows a mastery of contrapuntal writing. This is no great surprise, as works from the early *Missa sine nomine*

---

[3] *Ibid.*, 12. Straus uses these terms as 'metaphorical clusters of late-style characteristics' in which associated terms taken from a survey of authors writing on the subject are applied.

[4] Translation of the *Stabat mater* from Caswall, *Lyra catholica*, 46.

[5] Spicer, *Herbert Howells*, 171.

(HH 28) right through to the celebrated services of the 1940s and 1950s all rely on Howells's polyphonic dexterity to propel them forward. He was a master of imitative, contrapuntal writing: each subsequent vocal entry adding the necessary degree of tension, creating motion through the continual search for resolution. A fine example of this is the *Gloucester Service* (HH 249 – 1947), which is characterised by Howells's constant use of imitative counterpoint: from the soft, dovetailing lines in 'For behold from henceforth' with the divided sopranos entering a minim beat apart to create a nuanced heterophony, to the strident imitative entries at the beginning of the 'Gloria' with each subsequent entry increasing the dramatic rendering of the 'Glory be to the Father', Howells's polyphonic proficiency is present. However, the sheer polyphonic density of the *Stabat mater* creates a certain sense of wonderment; the ever-questing, weaving chromatic lines never seem to find the repose that they do in earlier works, rather moving to another dissonance, another moment of anguish and unease. It was to be the most contrapuntally progressive work that Howells would ever compose, and one can only imagine the reaction of some of the members of the Bach Choir (who gave the premiere) when they were presented with this fiendishly difficult and angular score.

He augments this polyphony with an extended harmonic vocabulary, again expanding upon many of the facets already present in the previous works. The *Stabat mater* takes many of the key harmonic ingredients of Howells's mature style but subjects each one to emotional and psychological intensification: the soft appoggiaturas of earlier works become tortured dissonances almost totally dislocated from their chord of resolution, the tritone is elevated from a piquant colour to an integral force, and the false relation that so colours works such as *Like as the Hart Desireth the Waterbrooks* (HH 230iii) and the *Collegium regale* (HH 246) is now lost in a tormented sea of minor seconds. The harmonies are made more striking by the style of delivery that Howells engages; the *Stabat mater* is characterised by sudden declamatory outbursts, almost as if the level of emotional intensity becomes too great to hold in, these then swelling to 'shattering climaxes which can only be described as orgasmic'.[6] This rhetorical style can be found in all of Howells's works for chorus and orchestra from the opening, *Sea Symphony*-inspired choral outburst in *Sir Patrick Spens* (HH 77: 'The King sits in Dunfermline town drinking the blood-red wine'), through to the impassioned opening entry in the Kyrie of the *Missa sabrinensis* (HH 275), but not to the same level of painful distress as encountered in the *Stabat mater*.

The *Stabat mater* holds a unique position in Howells's oeuvre, as it is not only the culmination of his 'mature' compositional career but also sows the seeds of the beginning of his late style. Though it may not be fragmentary or compressed (as a work in a holistic sense), nor retrospective (though it does find the composer grappling with moments of personal grief), it is certainly introspective, austere and difficult. It is the beginning of Howells's preoccupation with death as a subject matter – perhaps not the 'proximity to and foreknowledge of death' that Straus suggests, but an awareness of self-mortality and a refusal to accept it willingly. Of all of Straus's six terms, 'difficulty' seems the most apposite for the *Stabat mater*: it is a

---

[6] Palmer, *Herbert Howells: A Study*, 59.

Ex. 12.1 *A Sequence for St Michael*, bars 4–7

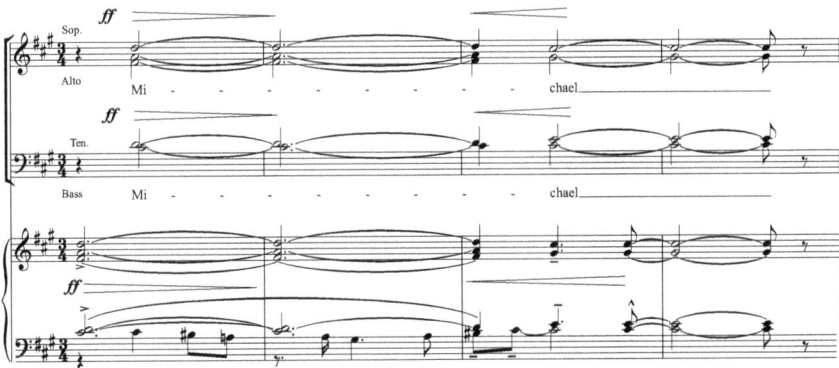

hugely complex (even complicated) work, texturally complex with dense polyphonic writing (in both the choir and orchestra) that can verge on the incomprehensible; it is a technically advanced, if not virtuosic, work pushing the boundaries of what is capable from a large choir; it is severe in its rhetoric, declamatory and monumental with an often oblique succession of musical ideas and harmonic progressions; it is manneristic and totally uncompromising; it is a difficult, late-style work.

The influence of the *Stabat mater* and its genesis can be felt on two works composed by Howells whilst the larger work was an ongoing concern: *A Sequence for St Michael* (HH 299) and *Take Him, Earth, for Cherishing* (HH 307). Both these bear the musical hallmarks of the *Stabat mater*, but also directly relate to events in Howells's life during the composition of the oratorio. *A Sequence for St Michael* was written in 1961 and is a setting of the medieval poet Alcuin, translated by Howells-favoured Helen Waddell, for choir and organ. Although ostensibly about the warrior archangel Michael, the opening *fortissimo* eruption of 'Michael' suggests the desolate cry of a disconsolate father, still grieving after twenty-five years, still searching for some catharsis in his composing life. This opening chord gives us a snapshot of Howells *circa-Stabat mater*: the declamatory outburst, the dissonant appoggiatura, the chromatic weaving line, and the total laying-bare of emotion and raw pain in these two chords (Ex. 12.1). Here, the association of this Michael with the Mary of the *Stabat mater* and her grieving by the cross for her son is extremely strong.

Howells cements the link between *A Sequence* and the *Stabat mater* throughout the work, no more so than with the extensive tenor solo in G♯ minor that follows the *Sequence*'s opening material. This moment of necessary repose is cut from the same cloth as the 'Eia, Mater' ('O thou Mother!') tenor solo section of the *Stabat mater*; it treads the same expressive path and provides the same function in each. The choice of tenor solo for both these works is interesting; in his diary of the time Howells states: '1961, *September 4*: Rain and gloom. Morning on S. M. ... Evening work on "Eia Mater" (with Mick very present)'.[7] The plangent, weaker tone of the

---

[7] As quoted in Palmer, *A Centenary Celebration*, 444.

tenor is obviously linked indelibly with the voice of a younger man, in this case that of Howells's son, Michael – it is almost as if this voice speaks personally to the composer, cutting through the rest of the choral texture to intone its message.

Take Him, Earth, for Cherishing is unusual in that it is a late work by Howells that has found a place in the repertoire and is celebrated as one of his finest compositions, certainly in the genre of shorter choral works. Christopher Palmer suggests that *Take Him, Earth* is 'noticeably bathed in the afterglow of *Hymnus paradisi*',[8] and there is much to be said for this proposal – certainly it is a warmer and more homophonic setting than *A Sequence for St Michael*. However, it is the looming spectre of the *Stabat mater* that informs the sound-world of *Take Him, Earth*; amidst the unison sections and resonant major chords (both of which will be found in later works) are moments of increasing tension, contrapuntal complexity and dramatic outbursts, all of which are associated with the *Stabat mater*. In *Take Him, Earth*, the final mood is one of acceptance and consolation, very different from the resignation and exhaustion of the final F major chord in the *Stabat mater*, following as it does the 'crippled funeral march'[9] of the final movement with its emphasis on the tritone and an ungainly 5/4 metre.

Both of these works exhibit traits associated with late style with, perhaps surprisingly for a high profile work, *Take Him, Earth* being the most apparent. Although not as austere or difficult as the *Stabat mater* it is certainly an introspective work and suggests a detached, almost personal sound-world, somewhat at odds with the very public nature of the commission. It also has an element of the fragmentary, with regular dramatic outbursts puncturing the reflective undertone. *A Sequence for St Michael*, although difficult in terms of harmonic and polyphonic complexities, actually demonstrates fewer of those stylistic traits suggested by Straus.

The vast majority of Howells's post-*Stabat mater* works were either commissioned by, or written for, leading church and cathedral choirs on both sides of the Atlantic; and because of this it is easy to suppose that Howells was simply going through the motions with these myriad settings, 'mainly to satisfy the apparent insatiable appetite of organists who wanted the kudos of their own Howells dedication'.[10] These final years resulted in a large body of service music, including eight settings of the evening service, four settings of the *Te Deum* and a Mass setting – it is understandable why people might question the composer's artistic intentions. Why Howells wrote so much church music in his final years is a moot point; it does not appear to be primarily financially motivated, as he would often compose a service before finding a willing cathedral choir to perform it, such as with the earlier *Worcester Service* (HH 263 – 1951) which was initially to be a service for York Minster, or the enduring possibility that the *Dallas Canticles* (HH 345 – 1975) were to be a setting for Durham Cathedral.[11] He also stated to the organist of Washington Cathedral, Thomas Pratt, in 1977 whilst corresponding about a new setting of the

---

[8] Palmer, *Herbert Howells: A Study*, 76.
[9] Palmer, liner notes to Howells, *Stabat mater*.
[10] Spicer, *Herbert Howells*, 172.
[11] For more information see Andrews, liner notes to *The Complete Morning and Evening Canticles of Herbert Howells*, Vol. III.

Te Deum (HH 355), that he would compose it 'without any question of a commission fee',[12] suggesting that perhaps the prestige of a performance or a performer outweighed the possibility of financial remuneration.

There are two settings of the evening service that stand out, and that are fabulous examples of Howells's late style, and how its idiosyncrasies help to breathe new life into the composer's reaction to this text: the *Chichester Service* (HH 317) and the *Dallas Canticles*. The *Chichester Service* (written in 1967) is arguably Howells's first setting of the evening canticles after the *Stabat mater*, and it is one of the most reactionary, individual and harrowing settings he would ever attempt.[13] It would initiate the final group of settings that would finish with the *Dallas Canticles* in 1975. The *Chichester Service* feels very much like an off-shoot from the *Stabat mater*, in a much more obvious and organic way than *A Sequence for St Michael* or *Take Him, Earth, for Cherishing*; it almost acts as a microcosm for the techniques and emotions employed by the larger work. Patrick Russill refers to the work as 'spiritually unsettling',[14] and it is easy to see why. The divided soprano voices enter on a major second, and this sets the mood and harmonic palette for the work; in fact the opening line of the text ('My soul doth magnify the Lord, and my spirit hath rejoiced in God my Saviour') contains some remarkable intervallic material, with major and minor seconds and diminished and augmented fourths being the predominant colours (all taking place over a tonic pedal). Howells's emancipated intervallic vocabulary stems from the apparent desire to make all that is usually glorious and redemptive about this opening line seem unsettling and sullied. Words such as 'soul', 'Lord' and 'Saviour' are major seconds; 'spirit' and 'rejoiced' diminished fourths; and 'God' a minor second – at every juncture Howells takes the harrowing route. There is very little that is either magnificent or rejoicing about this music.

These twisting chromatic lines persist throughout the work, continuing the atmosphere of restlessness, the suggestion of a fruitless search for some sense of certainty. The interval of a second at the opening entry is found at prominent places right through the work: 'For behold from henceforth' (bar 22), 'For he that is mighty' (bar 29) and 'He hath filled' (bar 71), to name a few. It binds the work together and gives the impression of unresolved anguish, seeking a final resolution to pacify the trauma of earlier. One may expect this resolution in the final 'Amen' of the Magnificat, but Howells reserves some of his most unsettling music for this final cadence. The 'Gloria' begins with soft, understated polyphony, gradually growing in volume and intensity. This intensification peaks on the phrase 'world without end', where Howells brings back the minor second in declamatory fashion over a *fortissimo* D minor ninth chord, rich in dramatic and emotional power. He then moves to the 'Amen', first with a diminished harmony before moving to B♭

---

[12] Buttrey, 'The Washington Canticles', 363
[13] The work is predated by the *Sarum Service* of 1966, but it is believed that large parts of it were written in the 1950s (around the time of the setting for Westminster Abbey), which gives it a slightly anachronistic feel. More information on this can be found in Andrews, liner notes to *The Complete Morning and Evening Canticles of Herbert Howells*, Vol. I.
[14] Russill, 'The Evening Canticles of Herbert Howells, 1945–1975' (n.p.).

Ex. 12.2 Magnificat, *Chichester Service*, bars 150–5

dominant seventh, which then propels the music to cadence in the voices on a bare fifth of A and E. This unusual and striking sonority (rarely heard in this fashion in mature Howells) is enhanced by the final cadence in the organ, a simultaneous false relation with a C♮ in the upper voice against an A major chord below (Ex. 12.2).

The use of false relations is not a new technique for Howells (they can be found in his work from the *Collegium regale* right through to the *Dallas Canticles*); however, they have rarely been used in such a dramatic and disturbing fashion as here. The major second that began the work is denied its final resolution, both with the 'empty' sonority of the fifth in the voices and with the false relation of the final cadence. Here Howells makes the point that there is no final peace and rest in this 'world without end' – rather a raging against an untimely and inevitable end.

It is easy to feel the looming spectre of the *Stabat mater* hanging over the *Chichester Service*; they are too closely linked. The Mary of the *Chichester Service* is very similar to the figure of the larger work; gone is the wide-eyed young woman filled with awe and wonderment (as in the reticent recitation of the opening of the *Collegium regale* or the same, joyous section of the *Gloucester Service*, with its strident rising fifth and melismatic setting of 'magnify'); she is replaced by the grieving mother, weeping at the feet of her crucified son. It makes the *Chichester Service* one of Howells's most original settings: his post-*Stabat mater* aesthetic and musical language shining a whole new light on the canticles, making the listener (or the worshipper) reconsider his or her relationship with the text. It is 'spiritually unsettling'; everything is more extreme than in earlier settings: the opening is more questioning, the mighty are put down from their seat with a greater force and the 'Amen' is neither conclusive nor consoling. This continues in the Nunc dimittis, with the voice of Simeon now a resigned and exhausted plea rather than the voice of spiritual fulfilment that is found in the earlier settings.

The *Chichester Service* is a very difficult piece to comprehend, full of complex contrapuntal material and totally unconcerned with 'pleasing' an audience or congregation. It is an austere work in a way that the *Stabat mater* and the satellite works are not; it moves quickly from moments of the impersonal to elemental outbursts of drama and distress. The introspective and fragmentary qualities of *Take Him, Earth* may be less obvious in this work, but it is undeniably an uncompromising one – more of a *cri de coeur* from the composer than a work of congregational devotion.

Eight years separate the *Chichester Service* and the *Dallas Canticles*, but they are very different in mould, design and tone; and they highlight Howells's changing view on mortality, both of his loved ones and of his own. If the *Stabat mater* and the *Chichester Service* represent Howells refusing to accept mortality and railing against it, then the *Dallas Canticles* show a composer gradually contemplating his own end and approaching it in a more serene fashion. Nowhere is this more clear than in the Nunc dimittis, in which the opening line – 'Lord, now lettest thou thy servant depart in peace' – begins to take on extra significance to the composer, especially one who had devoted the best years of his composing life to church music. The exhausted tenor of the *Chichester Service* is now replaced by a warm baritone: secure, accepting and somewhat poignant. What makes this section yet more poignant is that Howells chooses to accompany the solo with the male voices (alongside the organ), accentuating the plaintive tone of the baritone, enhancing the subtle masculinity of this section. There is something nostalgic about the work: not that Howells is trying to ape his previous style or successes, but perhaps he is trying to recapture something of the tone and rhetoric that define those celebrated settings of the 1940s and 1950s.[15]

The rest of the *Dallas Canticles* is cast in a similar mold to the opening of the Nunc dimittis: it retains the extended harmonic language of post-*Stabat mater* and much of the polyphonic and declamatory writing of the *Chichester Service*; however, everything in this late work seems to be done in a more tranquil and refined way. The move to a new key for the section 'He remembering his mercy', which felt forced and transitory when done in a similar way in the *Chichester Service*, here feels like a natural moment of stillness and repose. Howells indulges himself with a solo soprano intoning the opening line of the Magnificat over the unison remainder of the choir – a subtle 'remembering of his mercy', but also a dream-like reminiscence of past glories?[16] Patrick Russill suggests that the *Dallas Canticles* 'is

---

[15] The inclusion of the same cadence that heralds the arrival of the 'Gloria' in the Nunc dimittis of the *Collegium regale* just before the 'Gloria' in the Magnificat of the *Dallas Canticles* (a D major chord with added F♮) perhaps hints at this nostalgia. As already highlighted, the false relation has a striking role in the *Chichester Service*, but is used there in a stark, severe manner; in the aforementioned cadence in the *Collegium regale* and the *Dallas Canticles* its use is much softer, as a tonal colouring rather than a dramatic utterance. The differences in the use of this interval help emphasise the difference in tone between the two settings.

[16] In his liner notes to the Signum Classics release (SIGCD 190) and the Priory Records disc (PRCD 782), Paul Andrews states that this repetition of the opening words is 'an innovation ... found nowhere else in Howells's many settings'. This is not actually the case, as Howells had used this formal idea earlier than the *Dallas Canticles*, in the *Hereford Service* of 1969, to similar effect.

probably the finest set ... of late Howells. Proportion, texture and tonality seem to be handled with judiciousness and renewed affection.'[17] Certainly there is a strong *raison d'être* behind this setting, perhaps lacking the beady-eyed conviction of the *Chichester Service* but certainly with more purpose and more relish than the intervening works. Whether this renewed compositional affection stemmed from a new challenge and a new audience in the United States one cannot conclusively say; however, the success of this setting and its serene, autumnal tone seem to suggest a composer at one with his mortality and happy with his own musical idiom.

The *Dallas Canticles* shows a very different side to Howells's late style from that of the *Chichester Service*; it is not a work that is hugely difficult or austere (in terms of Howells's late style), nor particularly introspective or fragmentary; what makes this work adhere to Straus's six key terms are the retrospective qualities that it exhibits. It is a serene, nostalgic work, not necessarily archaic, but one that looks back to the works of Howells's mature style and aims to capture something unquantifiable of that period.

One of the defining characteristics of Howells's late style is the increasingly important and soloistic role of the organ in the choral works. Throughout his mature composing career the organ had played a pivotal role in his output and had more than just an accompanimental role in the canticles and other choral works. In the post-*Stabat mater* works the organ writing becomes more advanced and more florid, and often provides a very different and distinct musical discourse from that taking place in the choir. All of the late canticle settings benefit from this advanced writing, often augmenting the declamatory eruptions and shattering climaxes that characterise these later works. The *York Service* (HH 340 – 1973) makes full use of the emancipated organ, with Howells revelling in the famous 'tuba mirabilis' stop of the Minster organ to great, exuberant effect (particularly to herald the arrival of the 'Gloria' in both the canticles). The increased floridity of the organ writing is perhaps at odds with Straus's notion of austerity in late style; one might expect a more pared-down, spare form of organ writing to become the norm. However, what it does exhibit is the idea of difficulty in late style, adding more voices to the ramified contrapuntal complexities already present in the vocal writing, increasing the intransigent, technically advanced musical language. Indeed, we can view the role of the organ as a microcosm of Howells's late style at large. There is an increasing tension between austerity and difficulty; from the *Stabat mater* onwards we find an often restrained, elemental tone harnessing music of a formidable and increasingly complicated manner. This incongruity in style perhaps adds more weight to the difficult part of Straus's definitions, with contradiction featuring amongst his sub-definitions of difficulty.

One of Howells's most substantial works for the organ dates from this period: the Partita (HH 334) from 1972. Written for the newly elected Prime Minister Edward Heath (to whom Howells had earlier promised a work if he should become Prime Minister), the work is a five-movement piece and features many of the fingerprints of Howells's late style. There is a general feeling of unease and agitation throughout (even in the more reflective second movement, 'Interlude'), lacking a moment

[17] Russill, 'The Evening Canticles of Herbert Howells, 1945–1975'.

Ex. 12.3 'Interlude', Partita for Organ, bars 1–2

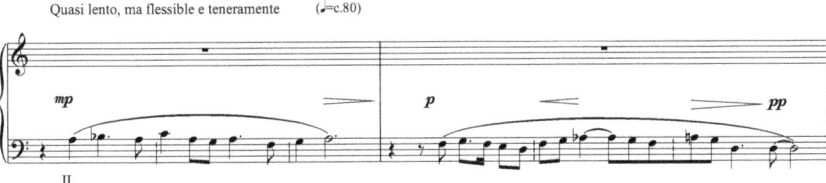

of pure triumphalism such as the 'Paean' of the earlier *Six Pieces for Organ* (HH 226 –1939–45) or the celebratory feel of the Rhapsody no.4 (HH 289 – 1958).

The 'Interlude' is perhaps the most interesting movement and taps into another trend in Howells's more meditative, slower later works: that of a burgeoning influence of Gregorian chant. Plainchant had always been present in Howells's compositional genetic makeup right from his early experiences at Westminster Cathedral in the early 1910s, but the austere modality of chant begins to find a more solid home in these late works. The opening line of the 'Interlude' has a strong flavour of plainchant; it is mainly conjunct with a rhythmic freedom and harmonic simplicity not often found prior to these works (Ex. 12.3). The way the line is then embellished and varied but rests at the heart of the composition is somewhat similar to Benjamin Britten's 'church parables', though in the Partita it remains one of several principles guiding the work rather than the fundamental concept, as in the younger composer's works. Howells would use a similar technique in various other later works, the Magnificat from the *Winchester Service* (HH 319) and *Take Him, Earth, for Cherishing* both benefiting from long quasi-Gregorian sections.

The Partita is a less obvious late-style work than some of the choral works that surround its composition. Being in five movements it quickly moves through passages of difficult, austere and fragmentary material, though the overriding concern is that of introspection and retrospection. The 'Interlude' is characteristic of Howells's late style: it is introverted and detached, suggesting the 'private' world of *Take Him, Earth* and earlier works such as *The House of the Mind* (HH 274 – 1954). The reference to Gregorian chant (though not explicit) suggests a sense of timelessness and a communing with the past, not just of a previous musical epoch, but of a previous time in the composer's life (here the world of Westminster Cathedral and his first public performances) – a moment of wistful nostalgia. It also reiterates the austerity aspect of late style; the impersonal, expressionless quality of chant, stripped down and restrained, is transferred to the 'Interlude', increasing the already present sense of detachment.

Another key element of Howells's late style that is highlighted by the Partita is the growing sense of metrical irregularity that creeps into his later works. Many of Howells's most celebrated mid-period works (*Hymnus paradisi, Like as the Hart* etc.) utilise changes of metre and time signature to great effect, often in a subtle way to emphasise particular melodic patterns or word setting. In a work such as the Magnificat from the *Gloucester Service* Howells switches often between two, three and four minim beats (four times in the opening ten bars); he reserves his two bars of irregular time (7/4 – both a change of beat and metre) for the line '[he hath] scattered the proud in the imagination of their hearts'. This metrical change is generated by the speech patterns of the line and helps to give the setting a natural, human feel in keeping with Howells's ethos of stressing the poetic qualities of the text.

By the time we reach the *Stabat mater* and the later works, the sense of metrical irregularity and ambiguity has increased greatly to the point where it has moved from being an important part of the composer's technique (such as the above example from the *Gloucester Service*) to become an indelible part of his style. Howells regularly shifts between crotchet and quaver beats and between regular and irregular groupings: there are long sections in 5/8 and 7/8, with the asymmetrical rhythms caused by the addition or subtraction of a quaver to a regular crotchet beat becoming manneristic. In a work such as the late anthem *The Fear of the Lord* (HH 349 – written in 1976 for the chapel choir of Clare College, Cambridge) these metrical irregularities are played out in full with constant changes of metre and accent. Many of the changes of metre are utilised in a similar fashion to the earlier works, following the natural inflection of the speech pattern; but often Howells plays with these patterns, changing phrase lengths to create different effects, changing the emphases of different lines. In the opening of *The Fear of the Lord*, the first line, 'The fear of the Lord is honour', is set in three subtly different ways, each changing the emphasis and accentuation of the text. Although the intervallic shape of the line remains intact, the change of accentuation and lengthening of certain notes helps to enhance the urgent, unsettling nature of this opening phrase. Constant change of metre and beat in the late works is such a strong aspect of Howells's late style that it becomes a mannerism, and transcends its initial impulse for metrical freedom and change of emphasis. It is entirely bound up with Straus's description of late style: particularly, the notion of difficulty as another musical fundamental is modified and experimented with to create subtly disturbing effects.

Although the majority of Howells's late works are sacred pieces, there are a handful of very fine secular choral works that the composer wrote in his final years – notably the two unaccompanied settings of George Herbert (1593–1633) composed in 1975–6. These two works, *Antiphon* (HH 347) and *Sweetest of Sweets* (HH 348), were written following the suggestion of Sir David Willcocks that Howells might write some unaccompanied music for the Bach Choir. They illustrate that, even with his final works, Howells was striving to refine and expand his expressive musical language. The two pieces continue in a similar polyphonic vein to the *Stabat mater*, particularly *Sweetest of Sweets*, whose supple, sensuous contrapuntal lines are most indebted to the earlier work. Harmonically the two settings are as progressive as Howells would ever get: the long chromatic lines spin and spin, rarely giving the sense of a strong tonic, thus enhancing the searching, questing quality that we associate with the late works. The multiple appoggiaturas and prominent false relations of the *Chichester Service* are found in abundance, as well as the constant clashes of minor and major consonances, all building the mood of uneasy but sensuous chromaticism that mirrors Herbert's intense poems.

One of the key features of these late Herbert settings is the constant reminder of Howells's own mortality and how these two works exhibit the same tone and mood

Ex. 12.4 *Sweetest of Sweets*, bars 47–50

as the *Dallas Canticles*. There is an even greater feeling of finality to the works, especially in the choice of texts – the opening of *Antiphon* ('Let all the world in every corner sing, "My God and King!"') feels like an exultant coda to any composer's life and work, and the haunting final line of *Sweetest of Sweets* ('But if I travel in your companie / You know the way to heaven's door') is as poignant a goodbye as Richard Strauss's 'Im Abendrot' from the *Four Last Songs*. Howells emphasises certain emotional moments in these texts by relaxing his chromatic language for short sections, reeling in the contrapuntal lines for relative stasis and repose. This is most evident in *Sweetest of Sweets*, where a four-bar section on the text 'Comfort, I'll die' is harmonised in F♯ major (complete with tonic pedal) in a solid 3/4 metre (Ex. 12.4).

Howells returns to this tonality for the final bars of the piece, with tenor and soprano solos intoning the final 'You know the way' over hushed F♯ major chords in the rest of the choir. Howells draws particular prominence to these lines, the relatively homophonic and diatonic harmony (which is in such contrast to the surrounding material) signposting them as having special importance. He achieves a similar effect in *Antiphon* on the line 'But, above all, the heart must bear the longest part', where the music slows and quietens to a G major triad, heralding another short section of relative repose and emotional intimacy.

Both *Antiphon* and *Sweetest of Sweets* are difficult works by Straus's definitions: they continue the rhythmic and metrical advancements of the post-*Stabat mater* works, they are declamatory and technically advanced, and they show little if any concern to please performer or audience member. They are austere works; and for all Howells's seemingly valedictory choice of texts, they are remarkably impersonal and restrained. They continue the contradiction between difficulty and austerity that is present throughout the late style. The two settings certainly show Howells's 'proximity to and foreknowledge of death'. As well as being difficult and austere we may view the works as being compressed: they are microcosms of the contrapuntal

Ex. 12.5 *The Fear of the Lord*, bars 88–91

and harmonic devices Howells had employed throughout his final years, though now found in a concentrated and distilled form (each setting is under five minutes long). Although the poems deal specifically with the more retrospective qualities of late style, Howells's music is anything but this, with the chromatic, polyphonic lines seeming to be more progressive and more challenging than in any other work previously. They are virtuosic works, manneristic and obdurate, and the music sometimes seems at odds with the text; but they are settings of great sensitivity and expressivity, and fine examples of Howells's late style.

We have seen in the *Chichester Service* and the *Dallas Canticles* how Howells's changing view on mortality had caused him to see certain sections of the evening service in a different light from that of his earlier years. This sensitivity to the choosing and setting of texts and their meaning is expanded by the two Herbert settings, and suggests that in his final years Howells was refining this sensitivity. The choosing of texts that stressed the awareness of mortality becomes a growing concern, and many of the late choral works feature prominent references to death and what lies beyond. The motet *Thee Will I Love* (HH 332 – a setting of Robert Bridges written for Peterborough Cathedral in 1970) has the final lines 'This prayer I make for Jesus' sake, / That thou take me in thy possession', and Howells makes the most of this final line with resonant added-note homophony. The motet *Come, My Soul* (HH 336 – a setting of John Newton for his friend Richard Latham, organist of St Paul's, Knightsbridge from 1972) has the final line 'Lead me to my journey's end', and in a similar fashion to *Sweetest of Sweets* Howells has a much more questioning and reflective end to an optimistic text, emphasising the journey into the unknown that he himself was soon approaching. The anthem *The Fear of the Lord* (1976) is no different, with a final line of 'it shall go well with him at the last, and he shall find favour in the day of his death' (Ex. 12.5). Again Howells reserves some of his most expressive music for these lines (especially the cadences on the word 'last'), and the final cadence to G major is as striking as it is poignant and heart-felt.

We can almost describe Howells's late style as being preoccupied with death. From the grieving mother of the *Stabat mater* to the opening of 'heaven's door' in *Sweetest of Sweets* the spectre of death is never far from the composer's mind. This is no surprise for any person reaching their final years, but is particularly pertinent when we consider that Howells was a meticulous diary keeper, constantly aware of the anniversaries of long-dead friends, family members and luminaries – none more so than the anniversary of his beloved son, Michael. The influence of Michael's death was paramount in Howells's work; and rather than receding in the composer's later years, it grew stronger and deeper. Like many elderly people Howells retreated to his past for comfort, as loneliness became more and more unavoidable; the more time Howells spent in the past, the greater the influence of Michael grew. If there were ever doubts about the influence of Michael on the late works, we only need to look at the diary entries for the compositional period of the *Stabat mater*, such as that of 4 September 1961 quoted above (p. 225), and of 6 September: 'Mick's day …'.[18]

This preoccupation with death can lead casual observers to presume that the works of Howells's late period are serious, weighty and, at worst, morose and gloomy: that they lack the vigour of the *Rhapsodic Quintet*, the power of *Like as the Hart* or the melodic simplicity of *A Spotless Rose* (HH 109). Even Howells scholars refer to the lack of light in these works, Christopher Palmer mentioning a 'tendency to veiled half-lights'[19] in the *Stabat mater* and other works. Certainly the aspect of light in the post-*Stabat mater* works has changed dramatically from the *Gloucester Service*, for which Palmer suggested that 'It *sounds* like what Gloucester's east window *looks* like',[20] or from the light as the ever-present companion in *Hymnus paradisi*. Light is present in the late work but not shining with burning luminosity: rather an autumnal light, weak and wan, even more valued for its very being. None of Howells's later works will ever reach the luminous qualities of the *Gloucester Service*, nor 'Holy Is the True Light' from *Hymnus paradisi*, but when listening to *Sweetest of Sweets* we are struck by how, amidst the complex polyphony and unstable harmonies, light is present, right through to the final tranquil cadence.

For popular appeal, the late works are just too complex, too austere and too 'grey'; they lack the colour and magic of their earlier counterparts. The sensual, kaleidoscopic harmonies of the mid-period works have been chromatically extended to a level where they no longer just colour traditional tonal writing: the excitement of the loose-limbed contrapuntal lines is now dampened by their never-ending pursuit of consonance and certainty. There are too many similar church pieces: despite his consummate skill and professionalism, Howells's late settings of the *Te Deum, Exultate Deo* (HH 343), *Jubilate Deo* (HH 316) and a handful of the late evening canticle settings (including the *St Augustine's Service* (HH 320) and the *Magdalen College Service* (HH 330)) never seem to hit the heights of the earlier works. For many performers there seems little incentive to learn the *Dallas Canticles* when you have the *Collegium regale*, *The Fear of the Lord* when you have *Like as the*

---

[18] Palmer, *A Centenary Celebration*, 444.
[19] Palmer, *Herbert Howells: A Study*, 59.
[20] Palmer, *A Centenary Celebration*, 147.

Hart or, for that matter, the *Stabat mater* when you have *Hymnus paradisi*. The earlier church music redefined Anglican music in the mid twentieth century, introducing hitherto unencountered levels of sensuality and expressivity, challenging performers and congregation alike. It would appear that the disturbing power of the *Chichester Service* or the dramatic, quasi-oratorio of the *Te Deum (for St Mary Redcliffe, Bristol)* (HH 310) have yet to find a permanent (or even temporary) home in the repertoire.[21] Even performances of the *Stabat mater* are incredibly rare, mainly owing to the huge costs incurred in mounting such a large work, but also to the difficulty in comprehending such a complex and distressing piece. As mentioned above, *Take Him, Earth, for Cherishing* is unusual in being the only late work to have found a place in the regular repertoire; and although it is a very fine piece, one wonders (perhaps uncharitably) if it is only played regularly because of the tragic circumstances behind its commission.

Herbert Howells's late works, from the epoch-straddling *Stabat mater* to the final short choral pieces, are all undeniably statements of late style; they adhere without question to Straus's description in 'Disability and "Late Style" in Music'. How we view a composer's late style varies from composer to composer: from the admiration and veneration of the complexities of Beethoven and Bach to the wonderment and bewilderment when faced with Stravinsky's final works. As well as being late style, the salient characteristics of austerity, difficulty and retrospection mean that these late works are undeniably Modernist works: they are progressive to the core, experimental and increasingly self-conscious (thus increasing the abstraction suggested by Straus). Though the aesthetic distance traversed by Howells from his earlier works is not as marked as with other composers, these late works confirm the modern direction of travel that he established early on, and are very much at odds with the widespread understanding of him as an arch traditionalist and conservative.

There is a trend in twentieth-century British composers for their work to become more austere, more complex and less popular in their final years. One need only look at Holst, Walton and Britten to prove this point. Howells undeniably follows this same course: for *Hymnus paradisi* read *The Planets*, *Belshazzar's Feast* and the *War Requiem*; for the *Stabat mater* read the *Choral Fantasia*, *Variations on a Theme by Hindemith* and *Phaedra*. But as we are now re-evaluating Britten's late works as being a continuation of his aesthetic and technical progression and worthy additions to his oeuvre, it is probably time to reassess Howells's works post-*Stabat mater* in the same light.

The late-style descriptions of austerity, difficulty and retrospection that characterise the *Chichester Service* and the *Dallas Canticles* are precisely what make these settings stand out in Howells's oeuvre; it is what makes them strong artistic

---

[21] In his book *A Century of Cathedral Music: 1898–1998*, John Patton notes that the *Chichester Service* was performed once in 1986 and twice in 1998 (the most recent years of the survey) compared with eighty-four performances of *Collegium regale* in 1986 and seventy-one in 1998. The *Te Deum (for St Mary Redcliffe, Bristol)* was not performed. These statistics refer to eighty-four choral establishments in Britain.

statements. It is these characteristics that draw us to them, to experience a unique vision of how this text can be interpreted and reimagined. Though neither is as comforting nor as musically satisfying as the mature settings for Gloucester and St Paul's, they are not a pale imitation of these earlier works: rather a new and expressive 're-encountering' of the text channelled through the composer's emotions and experiences. The same can be said of *Antiphon* and *Sweetest of Sweets*: they do not represent a composer going through the motions or imitating past glories; rather, they are the refinement and fine-tuning of a life-time's building of aesthetic and technique. These two settings are difficult and austere, but amongst the finest works Howells would write for unaccompanied choir. Many of the late-style pieces will never replace the works on which Howells's reputation is built (the early carol-anthems, the mid-period services and *Hymnus paradisi*), but they will enhance and define our full understanding of the composer's music, and give the fuller picture of Herbert Howells as man and artist.

PART V

Howells in Mourning

CHAPTER 13

In modo elegiaco: Howells and the Sarabande

Graham Barber

THERE is a characteristic rhythm that occurs persistently throughout Howells's works. In slow, triple metre, it emanates from his apparent obsession with the sarabande[1] and appears to be associated with elegiac thoughts, both personal and religious. It almost always appears in conjunction with intense, chromatic harmony. What are the origins and characteristics of this manner and mood? Why does Howells keep returning to the sarabande as a vehicle for expression, especially when in melancholy spirits? What is the relationship between instrumental and sung sarabande? And what other, subliminal effects does this modus operandi have on his music? These are the questions I shall attempt to answer in this chapter.

While some early works contain the seeds of Howells's fixation, from 1940 he wrote a steady flow of stylised dances in sarabande form, spanning more than thirty years:

(a) 'Saraband (for the Morning of Easter)' (HH 226ii – 1940)
(b) 'Saraband (*in modo elegiaco*)' (HH 226v – 1945)
(c) 'Dart's Saraband' (HH 237iv – 1956)
(d) 'Malcolm's Vision' (Quasi alla sarabanda) (HH 237xvi – 1956)
(e) 'Eia mater' (Espressivo: alla sarabanda), from *Stabat mater* (HH 309 – 1959–61)
(f) 'Ile's Interlude' (Poco lento, quasi come Sarabanda, molto serioso), from *Three Figures* (1960 – HH 297ii)
(g) II (Quasi adagio: serioso ma teneramente), from Sonatina (HH 333 – 1971[2])
(h) Sarabande, from Partita (HH 334 – 1971)

With the exception of 'Eia mater' and 'Ile's Interlude', they are all keyboard works. Ex. 13.1 demonstrates how consistently Howells used the sarabande formula: slow, triple time, with no initial anacrusis; accented second beat; four-bar phrases; modal ambivalence; and ornamented melody. Within this basic template a diverse array of rhythmic and harmonic inflexions can be observed, built around a strict, metrical core. There is almost always an arch form over the first eight bars, the exception being (g), which starts on the highest note. Beyond this structure, phrases often break down further into smaller units: (a), (b), (d), (e) and (f) follow the pattern 2 + 2 + 4 bars, while (c), (g) and (h) have 2 + 2 + 2 + 2. As we shall see later, the basic four-bar unit, whether subdivided or not, plays a significant role in identifying the

---

[1] When referring to the generic dance I use the spelling 'sarabande' unless quoting Howells. He usually wrote 'saraband', both for titles and in his diary notes, though he seems to adopt the French form from the late 1960s.
[2] In the published score there is no mention of sarabande. However, a manuscript of this movement is inscribed 'Sarabande for Hilary' (MacNamara). See also Howells's diaries, 25 August 1968: 'copied the revised Sarabande'; RCM, MS 7831.

Ex. 13.1 Eight sarabande incipits (a) to (h)

presence of the sarabande tendency in works not overtly associated with the dance. There is frequent, tangy dissonance: the English cadence is much in evidence, for example (b) 7–8 and (c) 7–8, and unprepared clashes occur in (c) 3, (g) 6 and (h) 3. The only exceptions to this acerbic flavour are (a), where the mood is one of jubilation as appropriate for Easter Day, and (f), 'Iles's Interlude', which, apart from a harmonic frisson in the first bar, is smoothly diatonic.

Crucially, the distinctive sarabande rhythm ♩♩ appears in almost every bar, either in the melody or in the accompaniment, the suspension of movement on the second beat having the effect of time standing still.[3] Even where the formula is softened with an upbeat, as in the rhythm ♩♩♪, the effect is the same,[4] and there is a noticeable absence of the more yielding ♩♪♩ rhythm.[5] It is remarkable that Howells manages this without monotony. Indeed, he harnesses the swaying, ritual motion to evoke a sense of heaviness, even weariness. As the dances develop there is a natural tendency towards more continuous figuration, but the underlying impulse is never far beneath the surface. Before considering these key works in more detail it is appropriate to explore Howells's formative years for any stimuli that may have led him to develop this predominantly elegiac manner and form.

Howells openly acknowledged his debt to Tudor keyboard music, not least in his vivid account of taking tea with Béla Bartók in the early 1920s and playing him some examples from the English virginals repertoire.[6] *The Fitzwilliam Virginal Book*, published in 1899,[7] was probably his main source, but he would also have had access to modern editions of *Parthenia*[8] and *My Lady Nevells Booke*.[9] The closest equivalent to the sarabande in these volumes is the galliard. Originally a lively dance, it slowed considerably when absorbed into the virginals repertoire.[10] Howells might have savoured this example by Orlando Gibbons (Ex. 13.2),[11] especially its delicious false relations in almost every bar.[12] Gibbons seems to be paying homage here to John Dowland's 'Flow My Tears', one of the most famous songs of the early seventeenth century, also set in pavane form by William Byrd, Thomas

---

[3] In poetic metre, the spondee: a metrical foot consisting of two accented syllables.
[4] The antibacchius: two accented syllables followed by one unaccented.
[5] The dactyl: one accented syllable followed by two unaccented.
[6] See Palmer, *A Centenary Celebration*, 407–9 for a full transcript.
[7] In an edition by J. A. Fuller Maitland and W. Barclay Squire.
[8] The first modern edition was published in 1848 by The Musical Antiquarian Society.
[9] This manuscript of works by William Byrd in an edition by Hilda Andrews was published in 1926, with a preface by Howells's mentor, Sir Richard Terry.
[10] In *A Plaine and Easie Introduction to Practicall Musicke* (1597), Thomas Morley describes the galliard as 'a lighter and more stirring kind of dancing than the Pavan'. In *Musick's Monument* (1676), Thomas Mace describes it as 'performed in a *Slow and Large Triple-Time*; and (commonly) *Grave, and Sober*', whereas he characterises the sarabande as 'the *Shortest Triple-Times … more Joyous and Light* than Corantoes'.
[11] Rimbaud, *Parthenia*, 44.
[12] Notwithstanding this example, Howells's own galliards are of the faster type: namely 'Sir Hugh's Galliard', *Lambert's Clavichord* (HH 174; no. 10); and 'Ralph's Galliard', *Howells' Clavichord* (HH 237xiii).

Ex. 13.2 Galiardo (Orlando Gibbons, *Parthenia*), bars 1–7

Morley and Giles Farnaby.[13] It has the feeling of a slow dance with strongly accented second beats, though it has an untypical seven-bar phrase structure.

The outcome of immersion in this repertoire and of experimenting with the historical instrument for which it was written was a collection of twelve pieces called *Lambert's Clavichord* (HH 165).[14] In these recreations of antique forms compiled in 1926–7, Howells borrows features from the keyboard works of Byrd, Bull, Gibbons etc. while at the same time adding his own modern slant. For instance, the first piece, 'Lambert's Fireside', with its 'modal' key signature (Ex. 13.3), subtly evokes the harmonic ambiguity of the Tudor-Jacobean composers to whom he pays homage, but pushes at the boundaries of their constrained style. As Frank Howes remarked, 'Not one of the pieces could conceivably have been written by an Elizabethan'.[15] Prophetic of the later Howells sarabande are the solemn mood, the lack of anacrusis, the second beat phrase endings, the false relations and the four-bar strains. 'My Lord Sandwich's Dreame' (Ex. 13.4) is another dance from the same collection, which in its initial gesture and grave air clearly hints at Howells's later fascination with the sarabande. While Howells delights in the melodic mannerisms and harmonic conceits of a bygone age, he is careful to avoid the most

---

[13] Maitland and Squire, *The Fitzwilliam Virginal Book*, Vol. II, 42, 173 and 472 respectively.
[14] Named after Howells's friend Herbert Lambert, harpsichord and clavichord maker, of Bath. It is typical that Howells should have been most intrigued by the expressive clavichord, despite the likelihood that most English virginals music was conceived for a plucked instrument.
[15] Howes, *The English Musical Renaissance*, 100.

Ex. 13.3 'Lambert's Fireside', *Lambert's Clavichord*, Op. 41, bars 1–8

obvious sign of pastiche, binary form, favouring instead a ternary structure in most cases.

In drawing on the past, Howells was not only indebted to the virginalists. An equally powerful source of inspiration was Henry Purcell, of whom he said 'no English composer ever had a graver beauty in his counterpoint … nor a more "modern" voice'.[16] He may have had in mind the famous *Chacony* in G minor (Ex. 13.5), in which the sarabande rhythm is pervasive. When, in 1950, he wrote a programme note on this piece for a concert of English music at the Royal Albert Hall, he drew particular attention to the minor-ninth clash between melody and bass in the second bar, but that is just the first in a litany of dissonances arising from the irresistible logic of Purcell's part-writing, of which Ex. 13.5 gives a taste. It was this exquisitely judged linear technique that Howells came to emulate in his own works. In this passage Purcell uses affective dissonances arising by step and by leap, daring clusters of adjacent notes, and surprising false relations. The melody comprises short motifs, which connect through increasingly insistent rhythms to form a perfectly proportioned arc.

The chaconne form might be described as a sarabande on a ground bass. Purcell used all three forms extensively. When Howells tried out a ground bass of his own, his model was Purcell rather than Byrd. In the concluding passage from 'Wortham's Grounde', no. 4 from *Lambert's Clavichord* (Ex. 13.6), the melodic stresses fall repeatedly on the second beat while the lyrical line obscures the four-bar periodic

---

[16] In one of his *Music and the Ordinary Listener* talks, 12 March 1937, quoted in Palmer, *A Centenary Celebration*, 149.

Ex. 13.4 'My Lord Sandwich's Dreame', *Lambert's Clavichord*, Op. 41, bars 1–8

Ex. 13.5 Chacony in G minor (Henry Purcell), bars 102–9

structure: traits that also characterise Howells's approach to word setting, as we shall observe later.

Like the galliard before it, the sarabande slowed considerably during the first half of the eighteenth century. Handel furnished exquisite examples of his own, such as the sung sarabande 'Lascia ch'io pianga' from *Rinaldo* (HWV 7), while Bach elevated the slow dance to one of the most soulful forms of expression, in the Sarabande and Chaconne from Partita no. 2 for Violin (BWV 1004), for example. Meanwhile, the keyboard sarabande became festooned with elaborate roulades and graces. There is a glimpse of this manner in the middle section of 'Samuel's Air' (no. 8 from *Lambert's Clavichord*) that suggests the rhythmic shape and feel of the mature, stylised sarabande in tempo, mood and rhetorical gesture (Ex. 13.7).

Ex. 13.6 'Wortham's Grounde', *Lambert's Clavichord*, Op. 41, bars 31–40

Howells would doubtless have been familiar with more recent reminiscences of the Baroque dance by Continental composers such as Grieg[17] and Debussy,[18] as well as by those nearer home. The third movement of Hubert Parry's *English Suite* for strings[19] is an expressive Sarabande in E minor (Ex. 13.8) cast in strictly formal four-bar units. However, like most other romantic samples of the form it lacks the *spirit* of the seventeenth-century dance. While the generating sarabande rhythm is employed in every bar, it is constantly undermined by Parry's suave melody, which favours the long line over metrical characterisation. While Howells would have been respectful of such sophisticated music by his esteemed mentor he would not have derived much from such a model, except perhaps its sense of pathos.[20] Grieg's well-known Sarabande from the *Holberg Suite* is unashamedly sentimental in its evocation of the dance, though it does suggest a template for Howells in its adoption of ternary form. Debussy's Sarabande from *Pour le Piano*

---

[17] Edvard Grieg, 'Sarabande', *Holberg Suite* for strings (1884).

[18] Claude Debussy, 'Sarabande', suite *Pour le Piano* (1901); and 'Hommage à Rameau', *Images* (1905).

[19] Completed around 1914 and first performed posthumously at a private performance at the Royal College of Music (RCM) on 4 June 1920 in memory of the composer, who was Principal of the College till his death in 1918. It was in 1920 that Howells was appointed composition teacher at the RCM. Other pastiche Baroque suites by Parry were *Lady Radnor's Suite* (1894) and *Hands across the Centuries* (1918), both containing sarabandes.

[20] '... a quality that has moved me more than any other in music ... even since boyhood'. Hodgson, 'The Music of Herbert Howells', 8.

Ex. 13.7 'Samuel's Air', *Lambert's Clavichord*, Op. 41, bars 14–23

(Ex. 13.9) perhaps provides Howells with a more provocative paradigm in its modal ambivalence; its insistence on regular, non-elided phrase patterns (albeit in six-bar composite units); and, above all, its evocation of the mystical.

In 1921, Howells heard the first, informal play-through of Ralph Vaughan Williams's *Pastoral Symphony*,[21] a work in which the composer expresses his reactions to the First World War – in Michael Kennedy's words, 'not by anger nor upheaval but by a profounder look into the recesses of the human spirit'.[22] The

---

[21] At the RCM, conducted by Adrian Boult; Palmer, *Herbert Howells: A Study*, 12.
[22] Kennedy, *The Works of Ralph Vaughan Williams*, 155.

Ex. 13.8 'Saraband', *English Suite* (C. H. H. Parry), bars 1–14

theme that dominates the fourth movement (Ex. 13.10) is, in effect, a slow dance in sarabande rhythm, and is quoted in an analysis of the work by Howells dating from 1922 in which he defends Vaughan Williams's use of folk-song, parallel fifths, common chords and modal inflexions, though he simply refers to it as 'a slow-moving tune'.[23] There is a world-weariness about the repetitive rhythm that seems entirely apt, and there could be no clearer model for Howells's association of this gesture with elegiac thoughts and feelings. The prevailing sense of resignation is disturbed by subversive undercurrents in the middle section leading to a tormented outburst, but the quasi-sarabande theme re-emerges with an even greater sense of consolation. The regularity of the dance rhythm is all the more evident in contrast to the wordless vocal solos *senza misura* that open and close the movement.[24] If there is a fundamental difference in outlook between the two composers it is that Vaughan Williams ultimately takes an optimistic view, while Howells's tortured pessimism remains largely unrelieved.

In 1930, a new kind of synthesis between secular dance and sacred ritual was forged by Vaughan Williams in *Job, A Masque for Dancing*. Scene 1 includes the majestic 'Saraband of the Sons of God' (Ex. 13.11), an elated but restrained triple-time dance, in which he embodies the *idea* of the sarabande, without recourse to its defining rhythm. Strength, elegance, grace, formality, symmetry, movement,

---

[23] Howells, 'Vaughan Williams's "Pastoral" Symphony'.
[24] The same technique was used by Howells himself in *Sine nomine: A Phantasy* (HH 126), written for the Three Choirs Festival in 1922.

Ex. 13.9 'Sarabande', *Pour le piano* (Claude Debussy), bars 1–14

euphony – these are the qualities that evoke the dance here.[25] Also featured in *Job* were a minuet, a pavane and a galliard.[26] Vaughan Williams's falsely optimistic antiwar work *Dona nobis pacem*, dating from a few years later in 1936, features a stark distillation of the sarabande rhythm in its desolate opening (Ex. 13.12). There is an obsessive quality here, in the soloist's repeated cries of 'Dona' echoed with even more stridency by the chorus a moment later, creating the same sense of pain that Howells was to evoke in the first, agonised utterance in his *Stabat mater* (HH 309), and using the same dominant minor thirteenth chord. It is not surprising that Howells should have dedicated it to his beloved Ralph 'in affectionate memory', its extensive use of the elegiac sarabande mode perhaps an unconscious tribute.

While Howells's early keyboard works are the most fruitful source of features of the sarabande style in nascent form, a glance at his vocal works reveals further possible evidence. From his earliest songs Howells showed a sensitive and refined response to lyrics and a meticulous approach to word stress. Although he could not entirely ignore the influence of folk-song and sung dance he was very wary of it. Interviewed by Katharine Eggar in 1923 he condemned 'continuous servitude to dance-schemes and metrical verse', advocating instead 'freeing our minds from the tyranny of verse and dance'.[27] It is certainly true that he was at pains to

---

[25] Howells later parodied the theme in 'Ralph's Galliard', one of two tributes to his friend included in *Howells' Clavichord*. The other was the companion piece, 'Ralph's Pavane'.
[26] Howells wrote a detailed programme note on *Job* for a BBC Symphony Orchestra Concert on 12 October 1949. See RCM, HH Papers, Box B.
[27] Eggar, 'Herbert Howells', 214.

Ex. 13.10 *Pastoral Symphony*, 4th mvt (Ralph Vaughan Williams), letter A, bars 4–10

Ex. 13.11 'Saraband of the Sons of God', *Job, A Masque for Dancing* (Ralph Vaughan Williams), bars 1–8

avoid predictable patterns and verse structures, and showed a strong preference for through-composed schemes as well as a flexible application of musical metre. However, what appears on the surface to be freely evolving musical prose often has a covert metrical sinew that holds the music together. A case from an unlikely source is one of his best-loved songs, 'King David' (HH 102), which, if re-barred in 3/2, starts to take on the movement and semblance of a dance (Ex. 13.13). Is it too fanciful to see in this early combination between underlying slow, triple metre and sorrowful text an anticipation of the sarabande manner and its associated yearning quality? Several of the identifying features are present, even the regular phrase structure if you discount the two-bar introduction. In the following twelve-bar passage from 'The Goat Paths' (*In Green Ways* (HH 172 – 1928)), the word stress in

Ex. 13.12 'Agnus Dei', *Dona nobis pacem* (Ralph Vaughan Williams), bars 1–13

Howells's setting is almost always on the second beat (Ex. 13.14). Although seemingly remote from the idea of dance, there is a lightness and grace arising from the repeating patterns that carries the music forward in measured steps. At the same time the impression of metrical freedom is preserved because the phrases of the vocal line do not coincide with the fundamental four-bar periods.

In the two-part song 'To Music Bent' (HH 194 – 1933) Howells sets up a swaying sarabande rhythm in the piano accompaniment, and exploits the first- and second-beat stresses to accommodate the five metrical feet of the poem. In Ex. 13.15 the words of the second verse are added to demonstrate the utility of this solution, though the song is through-composed. It is intriguing to note that the first trebles do not slavishly imitate the second trebles in their opening phrase. The second trebles have a smoother, scalic version, starting on low C, while the first trebles' simpler, sarabande rhythm begins a third higher on E♭ in order to arrive on the same dominant note. This provides a prophetic glimpse of the eventual solution to the 'Cujus'/'Eia mater' impasse encountered later in discussion of the *Stabat mater* (Exx. 13.1e and 13.26).

Finally, in Ex. 13.16, 'Thou that takest away the sins of the world' from the 'Gloria' of the *English Mass* (HH 276 – 1955), the word stress again falls on the second beat. Lurking in the shadows are the customary four-bar dance units, but Howells conceals the symmetry by extending the vocal phrase into the fifth bar. The more direct rhythmic outlines in the accompaniment, however, make the quasi-sarabande reference explicit.

Such examples as these recall the melodic stress patterns noted earlier in 'Wortham's Grounde' (Ex. 13.6), and similarly disguise the underlying, symmetrical four-bar periods. However, the closest fusion of the sarabande manner with

Ex. 13.13 'King David', bars 1–10, rebarred in 3/2

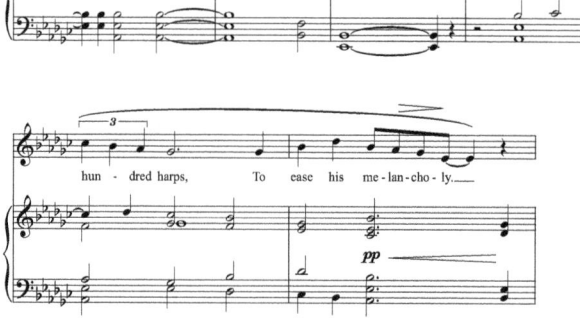

vocal writing before the *Stabat mater* is to be found in settings of the Nunc dimittis, a text that Howells set repeatedly, especially from 1945 onwards. He almost invariably chooses triple metre and the tempo is always solemn in keeping with the reflective text. The Gloucester setting (HH 249) is a particularly poignant example, completed at his mother's side in the last few days of her life. A diary note on 6 January 1946 records 'a lovely day with mother. The F sharp Magn. and Nunc finished while talking to her'.[28] It is an affecting emanation of the elegiac manner, expressing resignation tinged with sadness (Ex. 13.17). The organ having established the sarabande pulse, the sopranos' long-breathed melody propels the music forward in a wide lyrical arc, disguising the underlying periodic structure (three times four bars, counting from the soprano entry). A similar response to the text can be found in the *Worcester Service* of 1951 (HH 263), also closely connected to a death.[29]

---

[28] At the family home in Lydney, Gloucestershire. Quoted in Spicer, *Herbert Howells*, 142.

[29] Of Howells's friend and patron Lady Olga Montagu, sister of George, Earl of Sandwich, commemorated in 'My Lord Sandwich's Dreame' (Ex. 13.4).

Ex. 13.14 'The Goat Paths', *In Green Ways*, Op. 43, bars 26–37

These tendencies in Howells's word-setting practice seem to draw on the sarabande's accentuation pattern and demonstrate a connecting thread from Howells's earliest vocal works leading up to the *Stabat mater*. They also highlight the subtle balance between surface rhythm, metrical undercurrent and periodicity that plays such a decisive role in that work.

Towards the end of 1939, having been fired up by writing the second set of Psalm-Preludes, Howells embarked on what would ultimately become the *Six Pieces for Organ* (HH 226 – 1939–45). Apart from *Howells' Clavichord* this set represents the strongest concentration of work in his mature sarabande manner.

Ex. 13.15 'To Music Bent', bars 1–18

Ex. 13.16 Gloria, *An English Mass*, five bars before figure 52

The first piece to be composed, 'Fugue, Chorale and Epilogue', was completed on 16 December 1939, followed immediately by 'Master Tallis's Testament' on 23 December. Howells regarded the latter as a 'footnote' to Vaughan Williams's *Fantasia on a Theme by Thomas Tallis*, another of the older composer's works that had a profound influence on Howells.[30] It has quite rightly achieved iconic status among organists, so much so that it is all too easy to miss some of its unique qualities. Clearly it is a tribute to Vaughan Williams, to Tallis and to Tudor music in general; but look at it another way, as in Ex. 13.18, barred in simple triple rather than compound duple metre, and you sense the motion of the stately sarabande in its four-bar phrase structure, its slow tempo (quasi lento, teneramente ♪ = 60) and its accentuation. Is this yet another in the succession of elegiac pieces that Howells seems constantly to characterise by reference to the dance?

[30] 'My own organ piece "Master Tallis's Testament" (1940) is a footnote to the Vaughan Williams work, and even more a personal "throw-back" to the Tudors.' Howells in correspondence with Peter John Hodgson, November 1968, quoted in Hodgson, 'The Music of Herbert Howells', 8.

Ex. 13.17 Nunc dimittis, *Gloucester Service*, bars 1–17

Ex. 13.18 'Master Tallis's Testament', *Six Pieces for Organ*, bars 1–8, barred in 3/4 instead of 6/8

Three of the remaining pieces were composed in April 1940, during a period of convalescence. These included the 'Saraband (for the Morning of Easter)', the only sarabande in Howells's output not in elegiac mode. It joins a succession of ebullient organ pieces in C major spanning thirty-five years, most of which (though not this piece until the coda) exploit prominently some of Howells's most recognisable melodic fingerprints, the sharp fourth and flat seventh degrees of the scale: Psalm-Prelude no. 3 (second set, HH 219 – 1939), 'Saraband (for the Morning of Easter)' (1940), Rhapsody no. 4 (HH 289 – 1958), *Flourish for a Bidding* (HH 326 – 1969), 'Finale and Retrospect' (the fifth movement of the Partita (HH 334 – 1971) and *Epilogue* (HH342 – 1974). One has only to recall the resplendent C major outburst on 'Sabaoth' in the fourth movement of *Hymnus paradisi* (HH 220) to find a choral equivalent for this exultant mode of expression, and with the same modal inflexions. The choice of dance form for the day of Resurrection may seem strange, but not if one recalls Vaughan Williams's sacred dances. There may even be a conscious reference to the 'God' theme from *Job*, found in that work at letters K and Xx (Ex. 13.19). This theme, in resplendent C major with a halo of sonorous harps and low brass, describes the descending interval G to C, much elaborated over pedal notes on C, A and F, of which Howells's first bar could be seen to be a conflation (see Ex. 13.1a). Certainly, in its visualisation of celestial radiance this 'Saraband' has a strong affinity with Vaughan Williams's seminal work, at the point at which 'God pronounces sentence of banishment on Satan'. The approach to the recapitulation is Howells at his most intense, and the release of energy at Tempo I is explosive. Palmer reads it as 'the actual moment of Resurrection when the gates of Paradise

Ex. 13.19 'Scene VIII', *Job, A Masque for Dancing* (Ralph Vaughan Williams), letter Xx, bars 1–5

are flung wide and the main theme returns, having broken all bonds asunder'.[31] It stands apart from the other examples cited because of its triumphal subject matter; nevertheless, it exhibits typical sarabande characteristics of formality and grace, as well as strong evocation of stylised gesture and movement.

There was a gap of five years before the 'Saraband (*in modo elegiaco*)' was added to the set. In contrast to the dance for Easter Day it is a bleak affair. Paul Spicer suggests the sombre mood could be attributed to the depression that descended on Howells every September, caused by memories of his beloved son Michael[32] – the work is dated 16 September 1945, ten days after the tenth anniversary of Mick's death, duly noted in Howells's diary. However, he appears to have been frantically busy while the 'Saraband' was taking shape. The entry a few days later reveals that he left for Scotland on Monday 10 September, not returning until Monday 17th. Despite a crowded schedule of examining, he was 'composing saraband' in Glasgow on the 15th, completing it the next day in Edinburgh ('saraband morning'). The following day he notes: '"Saraband" copying'.[33] It may, therefore, be naive to assume that Howells was reflecting his own mood at the time, however concentrated the mode of expression.

Notated in minims rather than the usual crotchets, the piece exploits the triadic appoggiatura D♭ minor to C minor as its leading motif (Ex. 13.1b). Peter Hodgson categorically associates the work with Good Friday, although no subtitle survives in the published score. In his thesis he writes without equivocation: 'The *Saraband* was composed for the morning of Good Friday, thus complementing the second piece, also a *Saraband*.'[34] In the chronological list of works he states '1945: Saraband

---

[31] Palmer, *Herbert Howells: A Study*, 65.
[32] Spicer, *Herbert Howells*, 140.
[33] Howells, diaries, Vol. x, RCM, MS 7831.
[34] Hodgson, 'The Music of Herbert Howells', 126.

for Good Friday',[35] and again in the list of organ works: '1945: *Saraband in Modo Elegiaco* (for Good Friday)'.[36] Perhaps, as a recent pupil of Howells, and someone who was in close correspondence with him at the time (1968), he knew about the Good Friday attribution directly from the composer. Perhaps Howells's diary note 'saraband morning' of 15 September is shorthand for 'morning of Good Friday'. The fact that Howells turned once again to the sarabande form for the 'Cujus (Saraband for the Morning of Crucifixion)' (see below, p. 261) would tend to strengthen the case for the Good Friday connection. In the absence of documentary evidence it is impossible to solve the mystery, but, undeniably, there is a sharp, stabbing dissonance in almost every bar, and it is not difficult to imagine a slow, sorrowful procession as an insistent pedal ostinato takes hold from the midway point (Ex. 13.20) leading to a searing climax in bar 39 at the return of the opening theme. If the recapitulation in the Easter 'Saraband' is the moment of the Resurrection, then this recapitulation is surely the point at which Christ stumbles and falls under the weight of the cross. The substitution of C major for C minor on the second beat fails to dispel the prevailing sense of despair, which continues to the bitter end.

While the *Six Pieces for Organ* contain the main concentration of organ sarabandes, there is evidence of the dance in other organ pieces. For example, the *Intrata* no. 2 (HH 233), written in 1941 for Sir Walter Alcock's eightieth birthday, has clear references to the sarabande in its opening measures. Even more noticeable are those in the separate *Prelude: 'De profundis'* (HH 288), which appears to have been written during a time of mental anguish.[37] Whatever the motivation, Howells turned once again to Psalm 130: 'De profundis clamavi ad te, Domine'. The marking is 'Quasi lento, tristamente', and the initial pulse ♩ = 48. At first the metre fluctuates between common and triple time, but the latter is soon established as the norm, the rhythmic devices and false relations of the sarabande suffusing the musical discourse. This works up to a shattering, grief-stricken climax, the four-bar periods ruthlessly controlling the pacing of the music, while the leading melody takes rhapsodic flight, ebbing and flowing around these structural pillars with complete abandon as the struggle subsides (Ex. 13.21). This is not a sarabande, but it evinces many of its qualities, and is certainly cast *in modo elegiaco*.

Howells' *Clavichord* (HH 237) had an even longer gestation period than the *Six Pieces for Organ* and underwent many changes along the way. In all, the project spans twenty years: from the first manuscripts, dated 1941, to final publication in 1961. Howells's use of the sarabande both overt and by implication becomes especially pronounced from about 1940 – in fact it would be no exaggeration to claim it as a fingerprint of his mature style from then onwards. As well as the works already cited, there are further examples from *Howells' Clavichord* that are close to the

---

[35] *Ibid.*, 240.
[36] *Ibid.*, 284.
[37] A diary note for 12 April 1958 reads: 'Michael birthday (32nd). Composing a new work for USA'. More work on an organ piece is noted on 13–14 April and then on 19 April: 'Completed the 2nd new organ work for New York'. The two works were the *Prelude: 'De profundis'* and Rhapsody no. 4, destined for H. W. Gray, music publishers. It is not clear which work was composed first; Palmer, *A Centenary Celebration*, 120. Concurrently, his daughter Ursula was in hospital, having been suffering from tuberculosis since November of the previous year.

Ex. 13.20 'Saraband (*in modo elegiaco*)', *Six Pieces for Organ*, bars 28–46

sarabande concept in feel and appearance. These include 'Goff's Fireside' (1941), one of the first of the set to be written, originally entitled 'Walford's Rest' (Ex. 13.22).[38] Had it been called 'Goff's Sarabande', it would not have been out of place in

---

[38] Numerous pieces were reassigned between inception and publication. The original commemorative title was presumably occasioned by the death of Sir Walford

Example 13.1. Perhaps the melodic lines are smoother, the dissonances milder – but the gestures and the metrical shape are unmistakable. It appears that Howells's language was becoming infused with enriching elements from the dance, so that any slow, triple-time piece was likely to encompass features of the sarabande. When an element of emotional turmoil is added, this manner becomes especially compelling. A striking example is 'Rubbra's Soliloquy', in which heavily accented first and second beats contribute dramatically to the climax at bar 27, from which point a controlled decay in diminishing waves of intensity occurs over regular, four-bar intervals (Ex. 13.23).

Turning to the explicit use of the sarabande in *Howells' Clavichord*, the essence of the dance is laid bare in the two uncompromising archetypes quoted in Ex. 13.1. From a manuscript source it appears that 'Malcolm's Vision' may have originally been intended for Thurston Dart. A surviving scrap of just five bars in RCM, MS 4711, with the inscription 'Recapitulation of "Dart's Sarabande [*sic*]"' turns out to be almost identical to bars 39–43 of George Malcolm's piece as published.[39] This must mean that Dart's eventual 'Saraband' was a new piece written later, or alternatively, that Howells switched attributions at some point. Both are in ternary form, but he manages to disguise his recapitulations so skilfully that one is hardly aware they have taken place – compare Ex. 13.24 with Ex. 13.1d. 'Dart's Saraband' is stripped of all but essential movement, while Malcolm's, in Howells's favoured Phrygian mode, is more elaborately figured, though still with remarkable economy of material. For example, the eight-bar exposition just cited presents a study in different ways of repeating the note E, showing a level of detail and refinement that became a touchstone of Howells's style.

The incubation period for the *Stabat mater* was similarly protracted. *Hymnus paradisi* had been performed in 1950[40] after languishing for fifteen years, and this was followed by the *Missa sabrinensis* (HH 275) in 1954.[41] Then, in the same year, came the commission from the Bach Choir for another major work. Howells took a considerable while to decide on a text, and did not start composing until 1959. Palmer provides a detailed timeline of Howells's diary entries starting on 26 August 1959, revealing the slow and often painful process by which the *Stabat mater* took shape before it finally saw the light of day in 1965.[42] The section that caused most difficulty was the second movement, 'Cujus animam gementem'. It is clear from the sketches that this began life as a 'Saraband for the Morning of Crucifixion'.[43] Conversely, the 'Eia Mater' ('alla sarabanda') started out as a piece in 4/4.[44] A transcription of the putative 'Cujus' is given in Ex. 13.25. Howells's attempt to write a *sung* sarabande proved problematic. The tension seems to be that words need the freedom to subvert the metre, whereas the sarabande rhythm is tyrannical in its

---

Davies on 11 March 1941, a further elegiac reference.
[39] RCM, MS 4711, fo. 9a.
[40] First performance at Gloucester Cathedral, 7 September 1950.
[41] First performance at Worcester Cathedral, 7 September 1954.
[42] First performance at the Royal Festival Hall, London, 22 November 1965.
[43] RCM, MS 5267/15.2, fo. 1a (numbered 12). See reference to the '"Cujus" Saraband' quoted in Palmer, *A Centenary Celebration*, 443.
[44] RCM, MS 5267/15.2, 15.2c and 15.2d.

Ex. 13.21 *Prelude: 'De profundis'*, bars 93–116

insistence and does not readily allow such flexibility. Added to this, the complex strands of the four-part chorus quickly become congested. Nevertheless, Howells perseveres for nine pages of continuous music as far as a recapitulation of the opening material, before abandoning the tortuous path. It is unclear at what point Howells decides to switch the sarabande to the fourth movement. When he does so, he keeps the function of the accompaniment – to convey the rhythm of the dance – and that of the now *solo* vocal line – to project the text – almost entirely separate (Ex. 13.26).

Ex. 13.22 'Goff's Fireside', *Howells' Clavichord*, bars 1–8

Ex. 13.23 'Rubbra's Soliloquy', *Howells' Clavichord*, bars 27–38

In writing the 'Eia mater' as a sarabande, Howells appears at first to have simplified the original 'Cujus' theme in a more direct statement of sarabande characteristics. The complete ink draft shows equally weighted first- and second-beat chords in the first two bars. However, at some point the quaver

Ex. 13.24 'Malcolm's Vision', *Howells' Clavichord*, recapitulation

appoggiatura from the 'Cujus' sarabande was reinstated in pencil (Fig. 13.1).[45] At the same time the harmonic approach became more oblique. This adjustment may have been made at quite a late stage, possibly to effect a smoother transition from the preceding movement, 'Quis es homo'.

Quite early in the *Stabat mater* saga, Howells produced another sarabande, seemingly with little effort. Towards the end of 1959 he was asked to write a test piece to commemorate the centenary of the National Brass Band Contest held at the Crystal Palace, London, on 10 July 1860. This gave rise to *Three Figures: Tryptych for Brass Band*, of which the middle movement 'Iles's Interlude' is marked 'Poco lento, quasi come Sarabanda, molto serioso' (Ex. 13.27). It was scored for brass band by the noted arranger Frank Wright, and the contest took place on 15 October 1960.[46] In just thirty-nine impeccably crafted bars, Howells seems to find the kind of lyrical response to the sarabande that he failed to discover in the 'Cujus'. In contrast to the other models in Ex. 13.1, there is no discernible theme at the outset, the music emerging mysteriously from the profoundest regions of the bass instruments. The clouds lift as the soprano instruments enter, their meandering lines moving almost exclusively by step, and in Phrygian mode on C. Only occasionally does the melody partake of the sarabande rhythm, which is entrusted almost exclusively to the inner parts and basses. Shifting harmonies add to the enigmatic effect. Nominally in F minor, the precise tonal centre is obscure until a radiant B♭ major is established at bar 21. This certainty is short-lived, however, and there are several enharmonic swerves before the music evaporates, leaving a solitary note E.[47] The impression remains of one long, arching shape – it is difficult to believe that it is all built on

---

[45] RCM, MS 4640, Book IV.
[46] Andrews, 'A Documentary and Bibliographical Study', 458–9. See also Palmer, *A Centenary Celebration*, 405–6.
[47] This continues into the final movement without a break, though the alternative ending, for separate performance, settles on F major.

Ex. 13.25 'Cujus: (as a Saraband for the Morning of Crucifixion)', *Stabat mater*

Ex. 13.26 'Eia mater', *Stabat mater*, bars 9–16 (continuing Ex. 13.1e)

Fig. 13.1 'Eia mater', *Stabat Mater*, opening page of the complete ink draft, with pencil emendations

regular, subterranean, four-bar units. While all three movements in the triptych commemorate important figures in the brass band movement, the choice of a sarabande for the middle movement further establishes Howells's association of the dance with the elegy.

Writing 'Iles's Interlude' may well have been cathartic, but it did not seem to cure the *Stabat mater* doldrums. Howells continued to wrestle with the 'Cujus' on and off until August 1963. A thorough analysis of the sketches is beyond the scope of this chapter but, in summary, there were at least three further attempts at an

Ex. 13.27 'Iles's Interlude', *Three Figures*, bars 1–27

Ex. 13.28 'Cujus animam gementem', *Stabat mater*, reduction of accompaniment from six bars before figure 18

opening, with pedal points tried out on D in the bass, and F♯ in the treble, before finally settling on low B, for which the string basses have to tune down. It seems likely that the plainsong-like motto theme that appears as a connective tissue in all but the first movement was a relatively late development arising out of the 'Cujus' struggle. What should not surprise us is that the revised 'Cujus' retains vestiges of the sarabande from its former incarnation (Ex. 13.28). Moreover, every other movement falls under the spell of the dance as Howells draws the work together. For example, the third movement, 'Quis es homo', prefigures the 'Eia' sarabande at figure 30 in the score. At the end of the fifth movement, 'Sancta mater', Howells finds at last the elusive sung sarabande for the words 'Virgo, virginum praeclara' (Ex. 13.29). (See discussion of 'To Music Bent', above, p. 251). The sixth, 'Fac ut portem', can be read as an immense sarabande (Ex. 13.30, at the words 'Et plagas recolere'). Apart from a few interpolations, the whole movement is in regimented four-bar phrases, increasing in menace towards the shattering climax at 'in die judicii'. The music finally subsides, leading to a recapitulation of the 'Eia mater' sarabande to the words 'Fac me cruce'. With the exception of its ruminative introduction, the sarabande rhythm is largely absent from the last movement, 'Christe cum sit hinc exire', as it was from the first. It is as if the slow dance of death has come to an end. As the choir dissolves into a succession of 'Amen's there is just one ultimate sarabande effort at figure 77 before, exhausted, it expires.

In this work Howells achieves a concentration of style exceeding even that of his previous, extended choral works, *Hymnus paradisi*, *Missa sabrinensis* and *An English Mass*. It demonstrates a complex relationship between the elegy and the dance, in which the sarabande, never far from the surface, plays a pivotal role. There were two further sarabandes after the *Stabat mater*, the first written in 1968 as a gift for Hilary MacNamara, a piano student at the RCM (Fig. 13.2). With the later addition of incisive outer movements this became the formidable Sonatina (HH 333), completed in December 1971, though in the published edition, the

Ex. 13.29 'Virgo, virginum praeclara', *Stabat mater*, from one bar before figure 50

Ex. 13.30 'Fac ut portem', *Stabat mater*, reduction of accompaniment only from seven bars before figure 55

title 'Saraband' for the middle movement was dropped for some reason. It shows Howells in total command of the form, and relishing expansion into the wider palette of the piano after the self-imposed restriction of the clavichord. There is not the slightest deviation from the four-bar phrase unit, and there is little attempt to subvert the sarabande rhythm through melodic elision. The form is once again

Fig. 13.2 Autograph manuscript of 'Saraband', Sonatina for Piano

ternary, and once again Howells disguises the recapitulation, adding spice and colour. The prevailing mood is melancholy, rather than tragic. The ensuing movement is marked 'Agile, destro, sempre veloce' but has a moment of reflection in the middle at 'Tranquillo, assai con tristezza', where a suggestion of sarabande rhythm materialises briefly.

While Howells was working on the Sonatina he was also wrestling with an extended organ work that he had promised to Edward Heath in the event that the latter should ever become Prime Minister.[48] It is this quest that eventually led to the

[48] Which he did, on 19 June 1970.

composition of the other post-*Stabat mater* Sarabande, which became the fourth of five movements comprising the Partita for Organ. Diary entries are once again revealing.[49] It seems Howells could not decide on an overall form. On Thursday 30 May 1971 he refers to an 'organ suite'. On 2 September he claims to have finished the 'Sonata in Division'. However, he must have thought better of it because on 9 September he reports 'some copying of the strange Sonata for Organ – which may become a Partita'. The entry of 16 September records work on a 'Scherzo'. The Sarabande is not mentioned, so it is impossible to know at what stage it was written. Inscribed 'for the 12th day of any October', the piece is an elegiac tribute to Ralph Vaughan Williams in his centenary year, the repeated sighs in memory of Howells's friend almost palpable. Two pages of an incomplete draft survive (Fig. 13.3).[50] The opening theme is lacking bars 3–4 and 7–8 (compare Ex. 13.1h). Perhaps Howells added these two-bar phrases to establish the sarabande rhythm more emphatically. Alternatively, it may be an earlier varied form of the recapitulation. Whatever the case, the abbreviated format was adopted for the final version of the recapitulation. The second page includes what appears to be a self-quotation of the 'Cujus'/ 'Eia Mater' theme (see bar 25 in the published score). There is also a hint of this theme in the Sonatina Sarabande, in the alto voice of the first bar (Ex. 13.1g), and there are further melodic correspondences with 'My Lord Sandwich's Dreame' (Ex. 13.4) and 'Goff's Fireside' (Ex. 13.22).[51] It is even possible to read the theme as an inversion of the head motif in 'Saraband (*in modo elegiaco*)' (Ex. 13.1b). Given Howells's predisposition toward the sarabande it is not surprising that such reminiscences should emerge.

For Howells, the sarabande represented much more than a quaint artefact from musical antiquity. Solemn yet tender, it was a perfect vehicle for expressing elegiac thoughts and feelings, both personal and religious. By using a stylised dance, a sense of distance is preserved from painful associations. An essential element is the undeviating four-bar phrase structure, which lends an inexorable quality to the music. The defining sarabande rhythm takes on a life of its own, subsequently permeating Howells's mature style, and becoming embedded in the fabric of many works that have no apparent connection with the dance. The origins of this process can be traced to his study of forms and sounds of the past, absorbed both directly and through the prism of composers such as Vaughan Williams. Particularly conspicuous in the keyboard works, the sarabande manner is assimilated into works in other genres, of which the *Stabat mater* furnishes the ultimate consolidation of the style. Here, as well as providing an objective counterbalance to the lurid text, it functions as a strengthening agent, a tool in the composer's gestural apparatus and an unobtrusive unifying force. There is a common assumption that, for Howells, the bar line is more or less arbitrary, or as Palmer expressed it, 'everything fluid,

---

[49] Palmer, *A Centenary Celebration*, 475.
[50] RCM, MS 5270.11.
[51] Other possible echoes are of the Sarabande from Grieg's *Holberg Suite*, and Sigfrid Karg-Elert's tribute to that piece, the funerary chorale prelude 'Freu dich sehr, o meine Seele', Op. 65, no. 5.

Fig. 13.3 First page of an early draft of 'Sarabande', Partita for Organ

timeless, mystic, wonderful'.[52] That may hold true at a superficial level, but we have seen that even when the surface is apparently rhapsodic there is often a metrical undercurrent that controls the flow of the music and gives it a sense of inevitability; and this often stems from the rhythmic discipline of the dance. In his commentary

[52] Palmer, *Herbert Howells: A Study*, 149.

on Holst's *Hymn of Jesus* Howells drew attention to the association in that work between dancing and the mystery of the cross, which he said identified 'the spirit of the dance with the nature of religious experience'.[53] This undoubtedly struck a chord with Howells who, like Vaughan Williams, in his sensual realisation of the Magnificat (1932), saw no contradiction in expressing sacred thoughts through secular means. It goes some way to explaining Howells's mystic communion with the sarabande *in modo elegiaco*.

---

[53] Palmer, *A Centenary Celebration*, 318.

CHAPTER 14

On Hermeneutics in Howells: Some Thoughts on Interpreting His Cello Concerto

Jonathan Clinch

HERBERT Howells was notorious for revisiting works, revising and restructuring – from chamber works like the Third String Quartet, *In Gloucestershire* (HH 62, which exists in at least three versions: see Chapter 8) to the substantial reworking of the Requiem (HH 188) to form *Hymnus paradisi* (HH 220), it seems that Howells was rarely satisfied. However, one work stands apart in personal significance – his Cello Concerto (HH 205–7). Starting it in 1933, Howells worked on it throughout his life, even revisiting it close to his death. It was clearly an important work for him, and on more than one occasion he referred to its slow movement as his finest work. This article serves as an introduction: to contextualise it by outlining its history; to discuss elements of structure and style; and to consider our hermeneutical approach to Howells, here and in the rest of his output.

There are several compelling reasons why a hermeneutical approach to Howells should be considered, and is, arguably, overdue. This particular branch of analysis, within which the emphasis is shifted from issues of structure and technique, towards issues of meaning and context, which are 'empathetic rather than empirically verifiable',[1] is perhaps the key to demonstrating why Howells the composer deserves a more widespread consideration. Through the success of Christopher Palmer's *A Centenary Celebration* and Paul Spicer's biography, a clearer picture of Howells the man is starting to emerge, but the next step, of linking our understanding of Howells the man and his music, is much harder. However, it is Howells's music in the first place that drives people to read such biographies, so the link is clearly a desirable one. I am therefore advocating an approach to examining the relationship between man and music that leads to a better understanding of both. This approach does not constitute the revealing of any kind of hidden narrative, but rather considers a shared field of experience that both listener and composer might have.

This article considers one single work, his Cello Concerto, in which I argue the soloist represents the composer in a very striking and direct manner. This kind of representation has broad implications for the ways in which we listen to Howells and the dynamics at play within his works. The principal goal is therefore to have new ways of listening to Howells, rather than subscribing to any particular viewpoint. Following interviews with many of Howells's former pupils, a common image of Howells the restless poet emerged – a teacher concerned that each pupil develop a language and voice of their own, of 'distinctive subjectivity'.[2] Naturally, this leads us to consider Howells's own voice. It is clear to anyone who knows even a little of

---

[1] Bent, 'Hermeneutics'.
[2] Edwin Roxburgh, interview with the author, 12 September 2012.

Howells's output that he has a very distinctive language, which is both personal and consistent. Our challenge is to explore what that language means. In his texted works this musical language acts as a powerful commentary that is often extremely subtle and informative. In his absolute music, this kind of reflection is much harder, but ultimately the test of such analysis is in the hearing, and if we can consider new ways of listening to Howells's music that are convincing to any listener, we have made progress.

Edward Cone took on this challenge in his 1974 book *The Composer's Voice*, beginning with the basic question: 'If music is a language, then who is speaking?'. At several points he wrote specifically on the concerto genre; it is:

> the obvious instrumental form in which recognition of the protagonist and sympathy for his point of view are prerequisite to a synoptic understanding of the composition ... One who achieves full identification with the complete persona of any complex work must not only participate in the fortunes of each component persona, character, and leading agent, but also experience, vividly and intimately, the course of events produced by that relationship.[3]

It is therefore with the attitude that we have much to gain, and nothing to lose, from this approach, that we come to the Cello Concerto.

There is no evidence to tell us exactly when Howells started to write the Cello Concerto, but his 1935 diary suggests it was at some point during 1933: 'December 30 [1935]: Played through the Cello Concerto – and realised I'd almost forgotten its tunes! I have worked at it in distinctive and baffling intermittencies for nigh on 3 years.'[4] Another major work that Howells was writing at this time was the Organ Sonata. Both works show that his compositional craft was at its peak, demonstrating a profound logic in the use of small motivic cells to form all of the material for a large work, and an overall confidence and consistency of musical language. At a time when England was hailing Sibelius above all living composers, Howells's music displays very little of Sibelius's style but much of his logical process. Stylistically, Howells's absorption of traits from the Renaissance counterpoint of Tallis and Byrd was coming to the fore. Works such as *Lambert's Clavichord* (HH 165) demonstrate Howells's complete mastery of this style. In other works (such as the Cello Concerto) the influence is more subtle and can be detected in the counterpoint, with its rich independence of line both rhythmically and harmonically. Howells made the use of modal counterpoint his own, and while stylistic comparisons are often made to Vaughan Williams, Howells's music is quite different. In general his use of modality is entirely horizontal, whereas Vaughan Williams's concentrates on harmonic (vertical) colouring. Howells's overall textures are also much lighter, possibly as a result of his concentration on vocal counterpoint, such that the luminance of Byrd's style comes through in many works. Howells's textures in the Cello Concerto are quite thin, and correspondingly his orchestration is very light, concentrating on a string orchestra to carry the weight of material, coloured by the other orchestral sections as necessary.

---

[3] Cone, *The Composer's Voice*, 123, 25.
[4] Palmer, *A Centenary Celebration*, 94.

Howells marks the short score of the second movement 'sketched in the autumn of 1935', which suggests that he had finished his short score of the first movement before the death of his nine-year-old son Michael in September of that year. This moment was a watershed in his output, and despite the success of numerous pieces before this point, in many ways the 'post-Michael Howells' is of more interest to us. It certainly brought about a renewed interest in church music, which came to dominate his creative activities; and while not all of his works are 'about Michael', Howells's intense form of spirituality could be seen as stemming directly from this event. Although Howells struggled to believe in a Christian God, there can be little doubt that he did have an intense spiritual relationship with Michael, which continued throughout his life and often manifested itself in his most natural form of communication, his music.

The trauma of the death is well documented,[5] and it was at his daughter Ursula's suggestion that he began to compose again – as an act of catharsis. Howells referred to the works composed at that time as very private 'medical documents', which freed his 'frozen state of mind'.[6] The most celebrated of these was the large-scale work for soloists, chorus and orchestra, *Hymnus paradisi*, widely acknowledged as his masterpiece. The dates on the manuscript of the Cello Concerto show that he sketched the slow movement throughout 'the autumn of 1935', finishing it in 'the summer of 1936'.[7]

Having mentioned the concerto, Howells's 1935 diary continues:

> December 31 ... terrific rain (2pm) then a walk over Painswick Beacon ... And midnight thoughts for and on Michael.
>
> January 1 1936: People and Places. First, beloved Michael, to whom, at Twigworth, D, U and I went.[8]

Howells continued to work on the concerto, and in 1937 he used the first movement (alongside the song cycle *In Green Ways* (HH 172)) in his portfolio for the Oxford D.Mus. degree. For this purpose he orchestrated the short score, renaming the movement *Fantasia for Solo Cello and Orchestra* (HH 205). The short-score manuscript shows that the first movement had grown to such a size by then (around seventeen minutes) that Howells had given it the title *Concerto in One Movement*. However, he continued to sketch out the further two movements and may even have been considering reducing the *Fantasia* first movement.

The *Fantasia* is characterised by its enormous range of orchestral and harmonic colours – there is an extensive exploring of modal harmony, a richness and smoothness of harmonic shifts – with a heavy use of non-functional, extended sevenths; shared-note and enharmonic shifts; and parallel motion, a post-Ravelian chromatic style within a Sibelian form. This was Howells at his most dissonant, while at the same time maintaining a diatonic architectural framework – a framework projected clearly from the harmonic discourse of the opening pages. Howells's process is a

---

[5] Spicer, *Herbert Howells*, 96; Chapter 15.
[6] Interview with Herbert Howells, May 1977, British Sound Archive, B2951.
[7] Cover of Royal College of Music (RCM), MS 8845b i.
[8] Palmer, *A Centenary Celebration*, 96.

continuous one: no overt gestures but, rather, a subtle building over an extended period. In a way the protracted forms of organ rhapsodies come closest in precedent to the *Fantasia*.

Howells continued to work on the concerto throughout his life, and references can be found in letters and his diaries. He told Joan Trimble, a pupil at the time, that he was at work on a cello concerto 'for Mick'.

> Friday August 11th 1939
> I've been working for Mick all morning till just now ... it helps to keep Danzig out of my mind ... only all the time I grow anxious lest what I write will not be good enough for the beloved lad. I'm going to try to get the work really finished before the new term's joy or the old world's destruction ... I can't bear hearing the international news.[9]

The concerto reappears in a letter to Arthur Bliss (17 June 1942) that refers to a 'work for cello and orchestra which I keep pulling to pieces and remodelling'.[10] In the process Howells seems to have gone back to work on the completed first movement, as he required help from H. K. Andrews to get his D.Mus. score back from the Bodleian Library in Oxford: 'I had a job to get leave to have them out of Bodleys ... Such a lot of red tape you never saw.'[11] And so it continued in the 1950s and 1960s. By the late 1970s Nicholas Webber referred to the slow movement as: 'the best music he has ever written ... There was a kind of lobby movement to get Howells to complete it in time for this year's Proms.'[12]

Joan Littlejohn (a librarian at the RCM and close pupil) recalls further composing and revising in the latter years of Howells's life as she, like H. K. Andrews, had to contact the Bodleian and obtain a photocopy (posted 29 March 1979); Howells then donated the photocopy to the RCM library, only to ask for it back again in October 1980.[13] This work was possibly spurred on by the number of people encouraging Howells to finish the work, including his godson, the cellist Julian Lloyd Webber, and Lloyd Webber's teacher, Pierre Fournier.[14] Several sketches suggest that Howells was also considering reworking the concerto as a double concerto for cello and viola;[15] however, when Novello enquired about the possibility of publishing a cello piece, Howells refused to acknowledge that the score even existed.

Around the same time, the original *Fantasia* manuscript was found in the Bodleian by the cellist Gillian Matthews, who then set about organising its first performance, given in January 1982. In the weeks following Howells's death in February 1983, Palmer and Littlejohn were both invited by Ursula to go through the manuscripts that were still at his house in Barnes. This was probably the first time that anyone

---

[9] Transcribed in notes from Joan Trimble to Christopher Palmer, RCM, Herbert Howells Archive.
[10] Andrews, 'A Documentary and Bibliographical Study', 310.
[11] H. K. Andrews, letter to Howells, dated 24 March 1947, quoted in *ibid*.
[12] Webber, 'Herbert Howells at 85', 26.
[13] Joan Littlejohn, interview with the author, 27 July 2011.
[14] Julian Lloyd Webber, interview with the author, 4 April 2011.
[15] See RCM, MS 8845d, 'Concerto for Viola, Violoncello and Orchestra'.

had seen the second movement and sketches for the third. Subsequently, Palmer orchestrated the second movement (already complete in short score) for the same forces as the *Fantasia*, and it was first performed at a concert to celebrate Howells's centenary, held in Westminster Abbey on 17 November 1992 – Palmer gave the movement the title *Threnody* (HH 206). In the concert's programme note, Palmer dismissed the last movement as 'no more than a collection of random sketches and jottings. The MS of the Cello Concerto is now in the RCM.'[16]

When the folio was returned to the RCM in 2011, it revealed that Howells had left twenty-four pages of sketches for the final movement. It also revealed that the final movement was significantly different from the preceding ones – far more angular, rhythmic and less rhapsodic, with a more clearly defined tonal structure. Its rhetorical style (see Exs. 14.1 and 14.2) was in line with several other works from the same period, including the final movements of the Concerto for Strings (HH 215) and the last Psalm-Prelude (second set, no. 3 (HH 291iii) – Ex. 14.3).

Within Howells's output, the concerto shows an interesting lack of Howellsian traits; for example, there is no use of stylised dance. Its form throughout shows that linear counterpoint was central to his music. As so often in the church music, the Cello Concerto is constructed of long lines, although none longer than the opening cello exposition (forty-two bars), which is almost continuous – a form of soliloquy from the soloist. In its chromaticism and rhapsodic phrase structure (it is really an accompanied recitative), the first movement looks back to the third organ rhapsody. The opening itself, with the three orchestral chords, evokes the similar minor sevenths at the start of Vaughan Williams's *The Lark Ascending*.

The length and rhythmic fluidity of the cello's opening phrase cause any specific thematic identity to be lost. We are presented with a collection of small melodic outlines and rhythmic gestures that appear frequently with constant, subtle reworking – a continuous process. There are melodic cadential moments but they immediately lead into very brief bridge sections and the process starts again, almost immediately. Howells often positions climaxes at the start of new sections – moments of harmonic concordance that reveal that, although the overall work comes across as highly rhapsodic and harmonically turbulent, the overall harmonic structure is a simple oscillation between modes of E; E♭; and its relative, C minor. Howells, like Stanford, taught that form was to be dictated by the musical material (not vice versa); thus we see a strictness of organisation, within music that appears to be free and lacking in form, that is ingenious and a natural succession to the kind of formal innovations of Stanford (who mixed elements of sonata and variation form in many works) and Parry (for example the *Ode on the Nativity* begins with two separate themes that subsequently coalesce as their identities merge).

This combination of neo-Baroque rhetoric; modal counterpoint; and extended, functional harmony makes Howells's style unique, though it is also worth mentioning the success that Kenneth Leighton had in his orchestral works, albeit

---

[16] Palmer, *A Centenary Celebration*, 455.

Ex. 14.1 Opening of 'Sketches for a Finale', Cello Concerto, RCM, MS 8845c

Ex. 14.2 An earlier sketch of the opening of the finale, Cello Concerto, RCM, MS 8845c

Ex. 14.3 Psalm-Prelude, set 2, no. 3, bars 1–3

with rather sharper edges and sonorities. On one occasion Howells, discussing the difficulties of dissonance and his admiration for Leighton, played the opening phrase of Bach's first trio sonata for organ to a student and said 'why can't we go back to that!'[17] – the rhetoric of this movement is not dissimilar in intent.

The examples quoted show an almost indiscriminate use of various kinds of articulation markings, and it could be argued that Howells's short scores suggest that he was first and foremost a string composer. Certainly his orchestration was centred on the use of a string orchestra, with highly pointillistic use of the brass, wind and percussion – which was never structural. Their approach to linear counterpoint is particularly important in a concerto context, which often hinges on the relationship and hierarchy of parts (or lack thereof). The relationship between

---

[17] Peter Wright, interview with the author, 19 July 2011.

soloist and orchestra in particular is clearly one of colour and contrast in Howells's mind, rather than serving any specific Classical function; and while there is some rhetoric in the dialogue between the two, its importance is to the overall line, rather than being instrument-specific.

Howells's use of dissonance is a topic in itself. His use of cross-relations, suspensions, dissonant anticipations and other unessential dissonance in his lines seems to stem from his love of Renaissance counterpoint; and, while he clearly extends the harmonic vocabulary (often by not resolving decorative dissonance), its basis is in the music of Byrd.[18] At the opening of the final movement (Ex. 14.1) three distinctive dissonances are emphasised: a highly dissonant leap down to E (bar 2), the E♭ colouring of the consequent and the dissonant leap to the high B♮. Howells's melodic dissonance emphasises dissonances on E (tonic), B (dominant) and E♭ (enharmonic leading note), while, at the same time, the repetition of the pitch of D within the rhetorical patterns, along with the functional dominant thirteenth at the end of the example, suggest the key of G major rather than E minor. Such subtle contradictions as this bitonal ambiguity between tonic and relative are extremely common in Howells and suggest a very careful consideration of dissonance. This is often over-simplified, especially in reference to a specific augmented dissonance (dominant seventh with augmented eleventh) as the 'Howells chord'. Certainly his use of the acoustic scale (sharp fourth, flat seventh) was frequent, but his handling of it in a vertical and horizontal manner is much more subtle, having greater structural implications. In this movement it is the implied harmony of melodic dissonance that takes centre stage and, with a frequent simultaneity of major and minor thirds, the resulting polymodal chromaticism has far greater impact than 'that chord' alone.

In the second movement, Howells develops his use of dissonance within the movement to reinforce its form. The opening is characterised by soft diatonic clusters of string chords upon a repeated E♭ pedal, over which the haunting melody of the cello floats. The adagio placido section that follows appears much calmer at first, with its light texture and lack of bass, but the introduction of trills building in sequence (heard in the first movement too) heightens the sense of tension. High strings enter with repeated accented appoggiaturas (high F to E – almost like screams), and the passage leads into an orchestral tutti presentation of the opening material. But this time it has been transformed: it is not a glorious climax in a Beethovenian sense, but rather the centre of a nightmare. Palmer's orchestration is overwhelming, but all clearly implied by the short score. Again, a calm

---

[18] Although Howells was most often associated with Thomas Tallis (particularly through the homage *Master Tallis's Testament* (HH 226iii)), his own music takes far more from William Byrd's procedures and style. Found throughout his works (but most fully realised in *Lambert's Clavichord* (HH 165)), Byrd's most expressive traits are incorporated by Howells in his stylised cadential procedures, vertical interval technique, use of unessential dissonances, constant reworking of small motivic cells and writing of keyboard music that could quite easily be idiomatic string music.

(*estinto*) coda with an E♭ pedal dissipates the tension, but the overall impression is of emotional exhaustion rather than relief.

The ostinato bass in the slow movement acts, as throughout Psalm-Prelude, first set, no. 3, like a heartbeat. That Psalm-Prelude takes the text 'Yea, though I walk through the valley of the shadow of death, I will fear no evil' (Psalm 23:4). Composed in 1918 after the death of several close friends in the First World War, the music replicates the footsteps of that walk. Again, it is interesting that Howells alludes to an existing piece with such inherent optimism. In alluding to the final Psalm-Prelude (second set, no. 3) in the Cello Concerto finale, Howells may have been considering the message of that Psalm (33:3) – 'Sing unto him a new song' – in his process of grief at the stage of wanting to be able to move on. The Cello Concerto finale certainly has a violence rarely heard in Howells (the openings quoted above (Exx. 14.2 and 14.3) start with similar unexpected clashes) but it is also worth noting that this was not the first time Howells alluded to music from the Psalm-Preludes. The *Elegy* for viola, string quartet and string orchestra (HH 70) in memory of Francis Purcell Warren takes its climax directly from the first Psalm-Prelude (Psalm 34:6: 'Lo, the poor crieth, and the Lord heareth him').

Considering the central role poetry played in Howells's life, it is perhaps not surprising that he would be drawn to the Psalms when considering the emotional content of a work; they would have been the first forms of poetry he experienced, first at Lydney Parish Church and then at Gloucester Cathedral. One direct example exists in some unidentified sketches for a string suite where Howells quotes from Wordsworth's autobiographical poem *The Prelude*: '... there is a dark / Inscrutable workmanship that reconciles / Discordant elements, makes them cling together / In one society'. The original line begins 'Dust as we are, the immortal spirit grows / Like harmony in music'.[19] The quote reinforces the need to approach Howells's absolute music with poetic and literary models in mind.

In his book *Concerto Conversations*, Joseph Kerman, in a similar way to Cone, looks at the many dramatic roles that are played out in the concerto genre. Kerman's creative readings of concertos work in a very direct way when applied to Howells. If we view a concerto as a conversation from 'the composer's voice' (as Kerman and Cone advocate) we can consider what Howells was trying to say in his cathartic concerto. Howells gives the soloist an extremely dominant role from the very beginning. The soloist's line is repetitive and rhythmically (as well as harmonically) fluid – the overall effect is to focus all attention on the soloist. For listeners who know the reasons for composition, this focus on the individual, who is clearly in a state of emotional distress, acts as a powerful proxy, both as a personification of the composer through music, and of the actual individual in front of them. In the first movement the economy of material and its initial presentation come across as obsessive, and this acts in sharp contrast to the other two movements. The first movement is naturally tense, but at the same time the constant shifts of phrase and metre mean that the music never quite settles or resolves. The second movement's directness, the strictness of the ostinato pedal and overt emotion of the cello's opening melody are therefore extremely unexpected. Again, there is no

---

[19] William Wordsworth, *The Prelude* (1805), I.340–4.

sense of resolution in this movement, but the contrast with the first movement and the constant yearning appoggiaturas make the movement extremely disturbing, particularly when the context is fully appreciated. The final movement is far more direct and energetic. Again, whether the context is acknowledged or not, the music is extremely nervous and makes frequent use of sudden and hard dissonances that just stop, rather than resolving. The overall effect is a more extreme version of the relationship between the second and third movements of the Concerto for String Orchestra, in which we are presented with a troubled, almost Bergian second movement (dedicated to the memory of Michael Howells and Elgar), which grinds along, before bursting into a nervous *perpetuum mobile* finale.

The late Dr John Birch was close to Howells and worked with him at the RCM. When I asked him to describe Howells, he replied: 'H. H. was, in one word, restless. Music and man were tense, always moving forward.'[20] This gives us an image of Howells that seems to match the personified soloist of the concerto; and in the context of similar works (such as the *Elegy* and the Concerto for Strings) it seems that this is an emotional facet that took on more than a specific significance. It is also important to know that Michael had shown a lot of interest in music already (it was the common ground of the pair),[21] and that the choice of instrument too had meaning. We gain an insight here from one of his RCM lecture plans of 1951:

> The Cello ....
> Its nature as an extension of the male voice,
> an Extension of compass, flexibility and variety of touch
> The extension of compass gives the cellist an almost moral uplift in these days ...
> He is melodically a man or woman of (generally) precise terms. But Bach, in these suites never allows him to be an out-an-out [sic] melodic agent: never grants him a monopoly in the sphere of melody. He makes the cellist address in a mixture of exact melodic terms and implied (half stated) harmonic terms. After many bars of almost exclusive-melodic procedure, he suddenly enforces the harmonic consideration. That enforced harmonic nature of things touches nearly every cadence.[22]

His comments on the cello as an extension of the male voice have direct relevance here, reaffirming Kerman's personification and, in turn, perhaps explaining why Howells did not push the work for performance or publication. This is further supported by comments of his daughter ('Michael's death affected everything for the rest of his life'[23]) and other close friends such as Harold Darke ('he was a broken man, never the same again'[24]). His choice of an instrument that often

---

[20] John Birch, interview with the author, 6 August 2011.
[21] Joan Littlejohn, interview with the author, 2 August 2011: 'Michael was musical. H. H. often spoke of Sunday music sessions at home when he played the Sparrow tune to Mick; this tune and its story of a little sparrow that gave its legs to help build a bridge always reduced Mick to tears, but he would then ask H. H. to "Please play it again!".'
[22] Herbert Howells Archive.
[23] British Sound Archive, B2941.
[24] Quoted by Michael Darke (his son) in an interview with the author, 28 November 2011.

communicates in implied terms mirrors Howells's own inclination to write music full of ambiguity and subtleties of meaning that demand that the listener form their own interpretation.

External thoughts are therefore essential to the interpretational process. For example, by considering contemporary theories of grief, and specifically of parental bereavement, we come to look at Howells in a very different way. In fact it could be argued that it is Howells's experience – his relationship with Michael and with death itself – that is a unique and powerful feature of his music. In *The Spiritual Lives of Bereaved Parents*, Dennis Klass has argued that far from getting over the loss of a child, parents develop a new type of relationship or 'continuing bonds'.[25] By considering the way in which Howells's new relationship was formed through music, we can look at the Cello Concerto as an example of this transformation in attitude. In a sense, Michael's death acted as a release from the critical anxiety that came to a head through the Second Piano Concerto. By losing Michael, Howells's own sense of mortality and meaning changed, and such trivial matters as critical success started to loosen their grip on his creative mind.

Bereavement generally does not trigger sudden changes, and in Howells's post-Michael music we see all of the traits of his earlier music; but it does change the way in which we interpret the music he wrote as he began this new relationship, one of profound spirituality, intensity and significance. Howells defined himself using the past like no other; and in a way Howells the Modernist gave way to Howells the visionary – with a particular obsession with the accrued meaning of places and people. It may therefore be that we need to rethink how we interpret statements like: 'there is not a day that I don't have a thought of Michael'[26] in a more positive light. Michael's death was a defining, but not limiting, factor. As Howells himself said, composition had the 'power to offer release over any other medium',[27] and that offers a fascinating and crucial element to our interpretational process.

Howells's music is full of subtle and carefully thought-out gestures; and in seeking to interpret these it may be true that the influence of Michael has sometimes been exaggerated;[28] but it is the 'gritty wistfulness and intense spirituality' that is without 'sentimentality or nostalgia'[29] that draws people to his music.

The harmonic, rhythmic and melodic processes articulating the overall architecture of his music can suggest many contradictory ideas – ideas that are often hinted at rather than expressed directly – and many of his choral works exploit this, the text itself adding a further layer of interpretational material.[30]

---

[25] Klass, *The Spiritual Lives of Bereaved Parents*, Chapter 2: 'The Spiritual Aspects of Parents' Grief'; and Chapter 3: 'Community and the Transformation of the Parent-Child Bond'.
[26] Howells quoted by Andrew Green on 'Out of the Deep', British Sound Archive, H749.
[27] British Sound Archive, M1350R TR1.
[28] Hilary MacNamara expresses the view in British Sound Archive, B2951.
[29] Paul Spicer, British Sound Archive, B2951.
[30] For a discussion of the interaction between text and music in Howells's setting of Robert Bridges, see Clinch, 'Beauty Springeth Out of Naught'.

In the Cello Concerto we not only share with Howells in a prolonged period of grief but also in all of the various other (sometimes contradictory) emotions too. Yes, Howells's personal sound-world is highly pleasing on an aesthetic level, but his music and its study offer so much more. Sir Keith Falkner remarked that Howells was 'very inhibited talking about Michael. So sensitive and reserved – He didn't give himself away.'[31] His music offers a very different commentary on the human condition, and that is perhaps the true sign of his artistic genius.

[31] British Sound Archive, H749.

CHAPTER 15

Musical Cenotaph: Howells's *Hymnus paradisi* and Sites of Mourning

Byron Adams

To the memory of Mark William Highleyman

'What humanity can endure and suffer is beyond belief'.
Sir Edwin Lutyens, letter of 12 July 1917

A N horrible story: one that causes sickening knots of dread to tighten in the pit of any loving parent's stomach. The events unfold simply, inexorably, as if the chill hand of the Erlkönig guided the tragedy. A family is on holiday in Gloucestershire when the youngest child, a bright, resolute, and charming little boy, falls ill. A local doctor is summoned, makes an accurate diagnosis and urges the family to return to London as quickly as possible. On the ride to the train station and on the train hurtling through the darkening countryside, the gasping child, held by his powerless father, struggles to breathe, turning blue and black from lack of oxygen, a sure sign of bulbar poliomyelitis. On arrival in London, an ambulance rushes the little boy to a nursing home; as the doctors debate about what to do – an iron lung, perhaps? – the child proves their irrelevance by dying. The boy, named Michael, left behind a father immured in a grief that time did not assuage; a mother whose feelings were doubtless keen but went virtually unnoticed; and an older sister whose secondary place in her father's affections would be felt again and ever again in the decades to come.

The parents mourned separately: the emotional distance already apparent between them at the time of Michael's death gradually widened, although there was no question of divorce. The father's need for distraction led him to intensify his hunger for sexual gratification.[1] The waves of erotic bliss always receded too quickly, however, leaving in their wake only the dark, cold waters of depression, grief and regret. The shy mother, Dorothy, remained in the background, a marked contrast to the public mourning of her husband, who was a distinguished composer and professor at the Royal College of Music (RCM). In a touching attempt to console her father, the daughter, Ursula, gently suggested that he should channel his emotions into music. In the end, however, he turned neither to his wife nor his daughter, but to a series of lovers and to the construction of a musical score designed to memorialise his dead child.

Several curious features marked Michael's funeral. It was presided over by Canon Alfred Cheesman, rector of St Matthew's, Twigworth, and Michael's godfather, a rather louche cleric whose role in the life of the young Ivor Gurney was equivocal at best.[2] A striking aspect of the service was the music, as the grieving father

---

[1] Ridout, 'Herbert Howells Remembered', 12–13.
[2] For a brief discussion of Canon Cheesman's curious and, indeed, inappropriate behavior towards Gurney, see Adams, 'Review of Pamela Blevins' *Ivor Gurney and Marion Scott*', 673–4.

instructed the organist to improvise on nursery rhymes, something that would have affronted the sensibilities of any healthy nine-year-old boy: Michael would surely have disapproved. The macabre, almost Mahlerian, pall cast by this request – the poor organist! – continued well past the funeral itself. When the distressed father noticed that his son had been buried in a part of the damp churchyard prone to flooding, Michael's body was reinterred on higher ground. His grave stands in front of that of the composer and war poet Ivor Gurney. Gurney had been a close companion of Michael's father during their shared youth in Gloucestershire. Driven to insanity by mental demons exacerbated by the agony of active service at the front, Gurney died in an asylum in London just two years after Michael's passing. On the cross that marks Michael's grave is etched a verse poignantly wrenched from its context in St Luke's Gospel, and transmuted into a lament: 'Where your treasure is, there will your heart be also.'[3]

The composer, of course, was Herbert Howells; the score is, of course, his *Hymnus paradisi* (HH 220). Howells conducted the premiere of *Hymnus paradisi* in Gloucester Cathedral at the Three Choirs Festival on 7 September 1950, fifteen years and one day after Michael's death. During this period, Howells wrote other music, it is true. But *Hymnus paradisi* was his recurring preoccupation between 1935 and 1950. Much of the music that he composed after this great work continued to mourn the loss of his son. Listening to the twisting anguish of the opening section the *Sequence for St Michael* (HH 299), composed in 1961 when Howells was sixty-nine years old, with its chromatic screams of 'Michael, Michael' is to experience directly a father's raw, unceasing grief. During the years of brooding that preceded that Gloucester premiere of *Hymnus paradisi*, and over the years of brooding that followed, the composer created a touching 'origin story' for the score that subordinated – or simply omitted – many facts as he developed an uplifting master narrative.

Howells did not seek consciously to mislead anybody with his story of the creation of *Hymnus paradisi* – far from it. The creation of narrative, personal and musical, is a basic instinct of all human beings regardless of culture. The compulsion to make sense retroactively of tragedy is irresistible, and in the creation of personal history some details necessarily take priority over others – or are left by the wayside. As she revealed to her father's biographers, Christopher Palmer and Paul Spicer, Ursula Howells developed her own narrative of the events surrounding her brother's death: she was a twelve-year-old girl at the time, and doubtless a good part of her later testimony was shaped by family lore. As for Michael's mother, she must have developed her own version of the story as well, but, unlike her daughter or husband, she never divulged it.

But the narrative – the plot outlined in the opening paragraph of this essay – is itself elusive and contested. Surely the most valuable lesson learned from Jacques Derrida, Roland Barthes and other of the French critical theorists of the 1980s is that narratives and, indeed, the words that make up those narratives, are essentially subjective and open to divergent interpretations, as Kurosawa portrayed in his film *Rashomon* (1950). For instance, Ursula Howells recalled to Paul Spicer:

---

[3] Luke 12: 34.

it was lucky in one way that there was only one iron lung in London, and it was on the other side of London. It would have been possible to get it to him, but the doctors felt that it might be kinder to let him die given that he would anyway be totally paralysed for the rest of what would have been a much shortened life. So they had this awful decision to make, but fortunately he died while they were deliberating.[4]

In his preface to the full score of *Hymnus paradisi*, Spicer muddies the waters by asserting that 'there was no hope: in the process of his parents having to make the difficult decision as to whether or not to put the boy in an iron lung, Michael died on the evening of the 6th from the most virulent form of polio'. In this variant, it is not the doctors but rather the *parents* who had to make the 'difficult decision'.[5] What neither biographer nor daughter mentions is that watching a child die from bulbar poliomyelitis had to be a ghastly experience almost beyond endurance even for doctors. Given the constant references to consultations with doctors in Howells's diary in the days and hours leading up to his son's passing, and given the Howells' profound distress, it is unlikely that Howells and his wife took this decision upon themselves; indeed, it is almost inconceivable that a pair of anxious, middle-class parents in the Britain of 1935 would have had the temerity to second-guess a physician.

Their daughter's contention that 'there was only one iron lung' in London at the time of Michael's death is, however, amply supported by evidence. Iron lungs were not yet common in 1935 and were considered a somewhat experimental treatment. Why the doctors treating Michael hesitated can never been known, of course. Even if there was only one iron lung on the other side of London, it would have been easy enough to transport Michael to the machine, if not the machine to Michael. Reading of the delay is disheartening, as a large body of medical evidence suggests that had Michael been placed immediately in an iron lung he might well have lived, albeit handicapped.

To posterity, the only tales that matter are the ones that survive, whether told by artists, memoirists or historians. A grieving mother receives little attention from the wide world unless she is a distinguished author, such as Joan Didion, who chronicled the deaths of her husband and her daughter in two searing books, *The Year of Magical Thinking* (2005) and *Blue Lights* (2011). During the cold aftermath of her son's death, Dorothy Howells's silence meant that her experience would be met with general indifference except for those rare twinges of compassion felt by the more empathetic readers of programme notes for *Hymnus paradisi*: 'What must his mother have felt?'. It is unrecorded whether or not Dorothy Howells had a personal circle of friends to console her.

Sometimes disasters become more bearable when they are translated into art. The mere idea that a series of events occurs without moral logic – a little boy contracts a deadly virus, is rushed home and dies as physicians discuss his fate – dismays

---

[4] Ursula Pélissier (née Howells) quoted in Spicer, *Herbert Howells*, 97. For simplicity's sake, she will be referred to throughout this essay as 'Ursula Howells'.

[5] Paul Spicer, 'Introduction' to Herbert Howells, *Hymnus paradisi*, full score (London, 2007), ix.

most human beings: the sheer randomness is almost unendurable. But if a story is created from happenstance, and if that story continues past an otherwise senseless death to the creation of a masterpiece, then a comforting measure of healing is given a vehicle and outlet.

In his classic study of western attitudes toward dying and death, Philippe Ariès notes that the deaths of knights were always foreshadowed in legends. In the footsteps of Malory and other chroniclers of old, Howells retrospectively detected portents in the days just before Michael fell ill.[6] Part of the function of Howells's narrative was to make sense of the rapid onset of his son's illness and death and, perhaps, to lessen any lingering sense of his own responsibility: parents justly feel guilty when an already sick child is pushed past endurance. Of a fraught journey that occurred on 1 September, Howells remembered, 'a forbidding evening ... all the way, bats flew about our heads, and this worried D[orothy] deeply for some strange reason. Somehow I hated the eerie nature of the walk from the Bus to the Farm.' After quoting this passage, biographer Christopher Palmer asks, 'Was Howells, with hindsight, reading signs and omens into things perfectly innocent in themselves?'.[7] Palmer allows his reader to supply the most obvious of answers: 'yes'.

Another retrospective portent was the 'luridly spectacular' sunset over Gloucestershire that, as Paul Spicer writes, 'Howells always said that he never forgot'.[8] Would Howells have remembered that sunset so vividly had Michael survived? Sunsets, after all, are not just natural phenomena, but can be potent symbols for the end of life. In one of her most poignant poems, 'Because I Could Not Stop for Death', Emily Dickinson evokes the power of this symbol, which dates back to the Egyptians: 'We passed the School, where Children strove / At Recess – in the Ring –/ We passed the Fields of Gazing Grain – /We passed the Setting Sun.' Such scene painting is found in Dickens's *The Old Curiosity Shop*, a book that pervaded British culture from its publication in 1841 until the turn of the twentieth century, when its sentimentality caused it to fall out of favour. Like the rest of the literate British population, Howells must have been familiar with the scene in which the doomed Little Nell climbs the tower of a chapel and gazes on the setting sun: 'Oh, the glory of the sudden burst of light ... It was like passing from death to life; it was drawing nearer Heaven' (Chapter 53).[9] In his volume *Angels and Absences: Child Death in the Nineteenth Century*, Laurence Lerner comments upon this passage, 'But [Dickens'] image of drawing nearer heaven might more easily suggest passing from life to death. Life – the life of rustic England that she sees from the top of the tower – is impregnated with death.'[10] It is unsurprising, therefore, that a deeply literate man like Howells grasped instinctively the retrospective importance of that lurid sunset and incorporated it into his scenario of the augury of disaster.

All artists weave the detritus of life into a tapestry that assuages what Wallace Stevens famously called 'the blessed rage for order'. Indeed, this essay is no different

---

[6] Ariès, *The Hour of Our Death*, 5–7.
[7] Palmer, *A Centenary Celebration*, 92.
[8] Spicer, *Herbert Howells*, 97.
[9] While Dickens does not specify a sunset here, Nell returns to her lodging in the gathering darkness of twilight.
[10] Lerner, *Angels and Absences*, 95.

from any other of these constructed narratives. While advancing expansions, alternatives and explications predicated upon the words and music created by Howells, this investigation seeks to bring some order to the untidy history of Michael Howells's senseless death, as well as to speculate on his father's compulsive mourning. Despite his strivings, Howells never found a way to encompass his loss verbally: his words were necessarily fragmented, misleading, contradictory and, at times, inchoate. By contrast, he eloquently fashioned a musical narrative – not just *Hymnus paradisi* but also the other works in which he memorialised his son – that simultaneously expressed and transcended his pain. As much as its creation may have been given impetus by the death of a nine-year-old boy in 1935, *Hymnus paradisi* is not just 'about' Michael Howells – it is about the nature of grief, that most human of sufferings.

Of Magical Thinking

'Herbert was an extremely emotional person. I don't know what he was like religiously before Michael's death', recalled Ursula, 'but afterwards, every weekend we went to Gloucester [from London to Twigworth]'. Then comes the telling memory: 'We used to live in church. But that was an emotional thing as Michael was buried there.'[11] That a bereaved father – religious or not – should pray obsessively after the death of a child is not all that unusual; Ursula Howells's repeated and not altogether approving use of 'emotional' strikes a jarring note, however, born perhaps of a lingering resentment at having her childhood blighted by an atmosphere of perpetual mourning for a sibling, not to mention those weekly elegiac sorties to Gloucestershire.

What she does not speculate upon, however, is what exactly her father was praying for during those long weekends spent in St Matthew's, Twigworth. Prayers for the repose of Michael's soul could have been offered anywhere, in any London church close to home. But Howells felt the need to be near the actual physical remains of his son. Only when Howells began to find prayer in the church somehow ineffective did the creation of *Hymnus paradisi* proceed in earnest and with surprising rapidity. The act of composing this work became part of an elaborate inner ritual of supplication that returned at intervals over the course of its composer's life.

One plausible answer to the question 'What was Howells praying for?' can be put simply: he may have been praying for Michael to return from the realm of the dead into that of the living. After the first phase of numb shock, the second stage of reacting to a sudden death is often denial. In his classic study, *Loss: Sadness and Depression*, psychologist John Bowlby writes that this phase is one of a 'yearning and searching for the lost figure lasting some months and sometimes for years'.[12] Mourning his father, who had perished in the sinking of the Lusitania, Geoffrey Gorer recalled, 'As rational hope diminished, I constructed elaborate fantasies that my father was surviving on some desert island in the Atlantic … it was only by such magical thinking that my father could be kept from extinction.'[13]

---

[11] Spicer, *Herbert Howells*, 98.
[12] Bowlby, *Loss: Sadness and Depression*, 85.
[13] Gorer, *Death, Grief, and Mourning in Contemporary Britain*, 3. Note that Gorer's use of the term 'magical thinking' precedes that of Joan Didion by almost half a century.

Gorer's desire was impossible, yes, but the suddenly bereaved, who feel abandoned in an irrational world, lose their bearings as grief consumes their lives. The sudden and violent nature of Gorer's loss exacerbated his grief. When the victim is a child or young person who dies with unaccountable swiftness, the emotional reaction is magnified further. The death of a child is commonly considered by psychologists as one of the most – if not *the* most – traumatic possible event for an adult to experience.[14] Bowlby notes, 'For many parents, it is clear, some degree of disbelief persists for many months after a child's death.'[15] For some parents, the passing of a child results in a form of mourning that can persist for decades, or, indeed, in the case of some, continue indefinitely.[16] Describing the death of a child in her novel *The God of Small Things*, Arundhati Roy observes, 'It is curious how sometimes the memory of death lives on for so much longer than the memory of the life that it purloined.'[17]

In *The Year of Magical Thinking*, Joan Didion explores her own irrationality, including her desire not to be parted from the physical artefacts left behind by her dead husband, such as clothes and shoes, in case he might return and need them. Didion delineates how certain routines take on a profound significance as rituals that, if performed regularly and properly, might bring back the dead. In her poignant successor to *The Year of Magical Thinking*, *Blue Nights*, Didion creates a subtle chronicle – initially diffuse but growing ever more cruelly clear and final – of the illness and passing of her only daughter, Quintana. Didion writes of a 'period during which I believed that I could keep people fully present, keep them with me, by preserving their mementos, their "things", their totems.'[18] In *The Year of Magical Thinking*, Didion returns over and over to the immediate circumstances of her husband's fatal coronary thrombosis; she does the same in *Blue Nights* when relating the gradual dissolution of her daughter's health and decline into oblivion.

The reactions of both Didion and Howells represent a species of unresolved grief that constantly circles back upon itself. The American psychologist Theresa A. Rando has indentified this syndrome as 'complicated mourning'. In her volume *Treatment of Complicated Mourning*, Rando observes, 'In all forms of complicated mourning, the mourner attempts to do two things: (a) deny, repress, or avoid aspects of the loss, its pain, and the full realization of its implications for the mourner and (b) hold on to and avoid relinquishing the lost loved one.'[19] Among the clinical indicators of complicated mourning, Rando finds an 'excessive and persistent overidealization of the deceased' and 'compulsive, or ritualistic behavior sufficient to impinge on the mourner's freedom and well-being', as well as 'obsessive thoughts and preoccupation with the deceased and elements of the loss.'[20] Commenting on the hypotheses of psychologist Samuel R. Lehrman, Rando reports, 'an untimely death is a

---

[14] Nelson and Frantz, 'Family Interactions of Suicide Survivors and Survivors of Non-Suicidal Death,' 131–46.
[15] Bowlby, *Loss: Sadness and Depression*, 119.
[16] See Rubin, 'The Death of a Child Is Forever', 285–99.
[17] Roy, *The God of Small Things*, 17.
[18] Didion, *Blue Nights*, 44.
[19] Rando, *Treatment of Complicated Mourning*, 149.
[20] Ibid., 152.

death involving a relatively young person and implying disadvantageous timing in terms of an actual sudden death or diagnosis of incurability'. As she observes, 'The absence of forewarning compromises the ability to understand and explain the death because the loss seems so disconnected with anything that preceded it ... One's entire world, world view, and assumptions are violated instantly.' [21]

These indicators of complicated mourning flared up repeatedly in the decades of Howells's grief for his son. Just one indicator was the way he constructed an idealised version of Michael. In comparing her brother's determined endurance to her own 'floods of tears' during their father's punishing piano lessons, Ursula Howells succinctly conjures up the living boy: 'Michael was much tougher.'[22] All photographs of Michael Howells bear out this innate toughness: his fearless gaze into the camera suggests these are pictorial records of a masculine boy who loved games and hardly aspired to be the acme of Victorian notions of perfection.

Paradoxically, in the process of trying to hold on to the memory of his son, Howells tended to idealise away any real and personal characteristics so that 'Michael' became a metaphor for the grief itself, which had to be occasioned by the departure of an angelic presence. Indeed, the name itself became fungible in this regard: this tendency is evident as early as Howells's Concerto for Strings (HH 215 – 1938), the searing slow movement of which is dedicated to both Michael and the memory of Elgar, who had died in 1934.

While conflation here of the old and the young is disconcerting in its incongruity, it is but a precursor of the myriad ways in which Michael's death would be conflated with the deaths of others who were dear to Howells. His behaviour indicates that the experience of grief has a compulsion all its own, regardless of, and perhaps separate from, the lost object. Even when not as explicit as the dual dedication of the concerto, the spectre of Michael haunts other works composed *in memoriam*. Spicer aptly observes that in his *Stabat mater* (HH 309 – 1965), a work ostensibly dedicated to Vaughan Williams's memory, Howells set the hymn attributed to Jacopone Da Todi, which, whatever else it may be, is the lament of a parent over the violent agony and death of a beloved child.[23] Another instance of this practice is the motet on the death of President Kennedy, *Take Him, Earth, for Cherishing* (HH 307 –1964). As Christopher Palmer noted, the shocking assassination of a vital young statesman sent Howells back to Helen Waddell's English translation of the same poem by Aurelius Clemens Prudentius (348–c. 405) that he had quoted in the original Latin in the dedication to Michael affixed to *Hymnus paradisi*: 'Nunc suscipe, terra, fovendum, / gremioque hunc concipe molli.'[24]

Spicer is certainly correct when he asserts, 'What many people find difficult with post-Michael Howells is the unrelenting nature of the grief in the music ... There is music to come, even of this period, which manages to free itself from the deepest of this obsession with grief, but almost everything is touched by the hem of the

---

[21] *Ibid.*, 174–5.
[22] Spicer, *Herbert Howells*, 87.
[23] Palmer, *A Centenary Celebration*, 442. The *Stabat mater* was premiered in 1965, when its composer was seventy-three and Michael had been dead for thirty years.
[24] *Ibid.*, 122–3.

shroud which is ever present.'[25] True enough, but exceptions to the rule do exist and should be acknowledged. In fact, one of the first pieces that Howells completed after his son's death was the elaborately voluptuous song 'The Lady Caroline' (HH 111ii), which was sketched out on 2 January 1936.[26] There were periods in Howells's creative life when his mourning receded and he could compose a lovely, untroubled score such as his Clarinet Sonata (HH 251 – 1946), as well as several of the more extrovert pieces, including the witty 'Walton's Toye', found in the two books written over twenty years and published in 1961 as *Howells's Clavichord* (HH 237).[27]

At the same time, it is true that most of the music written by Howells after 1935 consists of choral works that are sacred or elegiac or both. Howells returned insistently to religious texts as part of his recurring ritual of mourning and remembrance. *Hymnus paradisi* and the many other choral works that commemorate Michael either explicitly or implicitly rely for both their expressive qualities and their formal designs upon the texts chosen by their composer. Indeed, a prominent component of the 'creation' narrative of *Hymnus paradisi* is the gradual process by which its text was assembled. Given his repeated use of sacred poetry and prose, Howells's religious convictions positively demand interrogation.

For many who know Howells only as a composer of liturgical music for the Anglican Communion, frank investigation into his personal convictions can prove unsettling. Ursula Howells reports her elderly father's late confession of unbelief: 'I know he said to me, about a year before he died when we were sitting one day in the dining room: "I don't believe there's anything."' Displaying a marked lack of empathetic imagination, she continues, 'I was very surprised that he said it as definitely as that. That was the only surprise I had. Not that he didn't believe. It was the fact that he said it, and come [sic] out with it.'[28] But in the face of God's implacable silence, why should an octogenarian who had spent decades of his life performing rituals in the hope of regaining his lost child have continued to believe in what must have finally seemed a coldly indifferent – indeed, ungrateful – deity? Why should he not say so? All of that ravishing music – *Hymnus paradisi*, those motets, anthems, *Te Deum*s, *Jubilate*s, Magnificats, Nunc dimittises, the epic *Missa sabrinensis* (HH 275 –1954), the *Stabat mater* – offered up in vain.[29]

Spicer uses Ursula Howells's testimony to remark censoriously upon the 'flimsiness of [Howells's] religious convictions'.[30] Spicer opines that 'the inordinate amount of time Howells spent in church' during the period after Michael's death, 'especially at Twigworth, says more about his emotional state, and his unwillingness to let go of the physical trappings of his son, than of any religious revelation or conversion'.[31] It is well known among psychologists that many of the bereaved,

---

[25] Spicer, *Herbert Howells*, 109–10.
[26] Palmer, *A Centenary Celebration*, 500.
[27] This collection also contains one of Howells's most affectingly simple memorial pieces, 'Finzi's Rest'.
[28] Quoted in Spicer, *Herbert Howells*, 98.
[29] The Kyrie of the *Missa sabrinensis* ('Mass of the Severn') was originally intended for *Hymnus paradisi*; see Palmer, *A Centenary Celebration*, 105.
[30] Ibid., 110.
[31] Spicer, *Herbert Howells*, 110.

such as Joan Didion, have had the very same reactions to the sudden deaths of loved ones. In particular, a number of parents who have been robbed of their children by death – as if by a thief in the night – are easy prey to the pathologies of 'complicated grief'.

Neither daughter nor biographer seems to have entertained the possibility that Howells was never a Christian believer in the first place: faith cannot be considered flimsy if it never existed to start with. There are relatively few religious works from the youthful period during and just after the composer's matriculation at the RCM. Like Vaughan Williams and others, Howells might best be labelled an 'aesthetic Anglican'. As Howells's student Alan Ridout remembered, 'A complete unbeliever theologically, he nevertheless had a strong feeling both for religious architecture and literature.'[32] He loved the Jacobean majesty of the Authorised Version of the Bible, and the Tudor eloquence of Cranmer's Book of Common Prayer; he adored the poetry of George Herbert; he responded deeply to the mysterious, indeed almost occult, beauty of cathedrals, whose decoration often contains echoes in stone of pre-Christian Britain; and he valued highly the grave beauty and reassuring constancy of ancient ritual. After all, he was trained as an articled pupil of Herbert Brewer in Gloucester Cathedral, one of loveliest sacred spaces in Great Britain. Although his book on Howells is wild, dishevelled, at times inaccurate and sometimes maddening, Christopher Palmer comes closest to the essence of the composer's religious connoisseurship by evoking the pre-Christian paganism of the Celts to characterise Howells's sensuous love of beauty – a love that embraced the beauties of warm, sensuous bodies as well as the beauty of holiness.[33]

Only when faced with his anguish at Michael's death did Howells fall to his knees at Twigworth. What he prayed for during those anguished hours was something quite outside the tenets of Christian doctrine, an incantation that has its origin in the deepest and most primitive regions of the human psyche. Howells did not petition a beneficent God for his son to join the company of angels in heaven surrounded by the nimbus of Christ's everlasting glory; he wanted his child returned as if by magic, corporeally, to his arms. Howells cannot be censured for being merely human.

A Musical Cenotaph

While Michael's death was clearly the defining event in his father's life, it was not his first painful, unresolved bereavement by any means, nor was it Howells's first brush with death. The years of the First World War were deeply traumatic: during this time, after all, doctors gave Howells a death sentence when they diagnosed him in 1915 as suffering from Graves' disease, then invariably fatal. Indeed, his doctor gave Howells six months to live, but suggested an experimental treatment using radium. In desperation, Howells went to St Thomas's Hospital in London for injections of radium directly into his neck at a time when the uses of the substance and its potential dangers were barely understood. Astonishingly, this primitive use of radium – Howells was reputedly the first person in Great Britain to have been so

---

[32] Ridout, *A Composer's Life*, 54.
[33] See, for example, Palmer, *A Centenary Celebration*, 129–30, 197–8, 200.

treated – was successful, and the composer lived to be ninety. The process of recuperation was both protracted and unimaginably painful, however; one can only imagine the adverse reactions to the injections that Howells endured during these years. It should also be remembered that this treatment was absolutely a shot in the dark, for there was no guarantee whatsoever that it would work. Active service in the war was out of the question, as Howells suffered from uncertain health through the 1920s.[34] One can only speculate if a faith in medical miracles was born from this reprieve, a faith that later turned to guilt that he was saved but not his son.

During this time, wracked with illness, Howells had to endure the loss of a beloved friend, the young violist and composer Francis Purcell Warren (1895–1916), whom Howells called 'Bunny' (it is not clear if Howells bestowed this moniker on Warren, or if it predated Warren's arrival at the RCM). Howells portrayed Warren in the graceful fourth movement of his early orchestra suite entitled *The Bs* (HH 42). According to Thomas Dunhill, Warren, who had risen to the rank of Second Lieutenant in the Second Lancashire Regiment, 'was reported "missing" on July 3, 1916 at Thiepval, in the Battle of the Somme'.[35] Like tens of thousands of British troops who perished at the Somme, including George Butterworth, Warren's body was never found, probably sucked under the mud, blood and other detritus of the battlefield. Alan Ridout, one of Howells's students at the RCM, recalled:

> There is no doubt in my mind that Howells loved Francis Purcell Warren. He had a snapshot of him on his mantelpiece, standing together with Leon Goossens ... But once he dwelt on him and stood before the picture gradually becoming inarticulate with grief. After a long silence, he said, 'He was *everything* to me' and sobbed, then swiftly pulled himself together.[36]

In a reminiscence published three years before his own autobiography, Ridout stated even more directly, '[Howells] was as overt as he could be about his early love for Francis Purcell Warren, "Bunny" of his orchestral suite, "The Bs".'[37]

While Howells associated Michael's death with other beloved figures who departed after his son, it is clear that it resonated intensely with his earlier loss

---

[34] Spicer, *Herbert Howells*, 43–5.
[35] Dunhill, 'Francis Purcell Warren', 358–9. Although Warren is usually identified as a violist, Dunhill reports that he won the Open Scholarship for Violin at the RCM. In a wartime address to the students of the RCM quoted by Dunhill, Sir Hubert Parry, the director of that institution, refers to Warren as a violinist.
[36] Ridout, *A Composer's Life*, 55.
[37] Ridout, 'Herbert Howells Remembered', 13. Paul Spicer recoils at the very notion of a homoerotic component to Howells's love for Warren: 'Ridout is at pains to point out that this was no homosexual love' (Spicer, *Herbert Howells*, 63). This statement is certainly true of the chapter about Howells found in Ridout's memoir, published in 1995. However, in his article for the *RCM Magazine* published four years earlier, Ridout is at pains to point out quite the opposite and speculates upon Howells's bisexuality. One wonders what happened to cause Ridout's narrative to change in the intervening years. While an exploration of Howells's complicated erotic life is beyond the scope of this essay, see also Palmer, *A Centenary Celebration*, 39–40, 212.

of 'Bunny' Warren. Ridout insightfully recognised Howells's tendency towards making such emotional connections: 'To say that he was "half in love with easeful death" would be an understatement; and with it went a nostalgia for childhood, and a vast area of regret for lands of lost content.' Ridout's allusion to A. E. Housman's achingly nostalgic poem 'The Land of Lost Content' also illumines the sense of loss that permeated Howells's life after the death of Warren.[38] Ridout noted that if Howells 'was depressed, and he was often tormented by depression, he said so'.[39] The death of Warren and, most devastatingly, that of Michael exacerbated this persistent sense of loss, perhaps born during his own harrowing and near-fatal bout with Graves' disease.

In this context, it is chilling to read Ridout's memory of a lecture that Howells gave in 1952 on music and mourning shortly after the death of George VI:

> He said, too, that he had arranged for the organist to play nursery rhymes at Michael's funeral, and asked 'Why not?' The lecture culminated in something like a testament; so far as I know, and simply by chance, only I fully understood it. He said that he was going to play a recording of a work – what it was, and who it was by, was of no consequence – which summed up all that could be stated in music about death. His exact words were: 'If there is a better expression of mourning music, I have yet to hear it.'[40]

Ridout indentified the work that Howells played on that occasion: 'It was in memory of 'Bunny' [Warren] that he wrote the Elegy for Viola, String Quartet and String Orchestra in 1917 [HH 70] – the piece he so cryptically spoke about in his lecture on the music of mourning.'[41] The close juxtaposition of Michael's funeral with the threnody for Warren can hardly have been accidental.

That Howells conflated Warren's ghastly fate with that of Michael is entirely understandable when viewed within the context of the First World War and its effect upon the British population. After all, Warren was barely an adult when he was killed at the Somme. As the slaughter depleted the ranks of adult troops, especially in the army, soldiers at the front became both younger and older; thus Vaughan Williams, who initially served in the Royal Army Medical Corps, was allowed as a middle-aged cadet to train as an artillery officer. In the verse of the war poets, such as Wilfred Owen and Siegfried Sassoon, the young infantrymen are often referred to as 'lads' – a term that eloquently suggests their tender years. Owen and Sassoon expropriated this term from Housman's volume *A Shropshire Lad*; as Paul Fussell has observed, 'Perhaps Housman's greatest contribution to the war was the word *lad*, to which his poems had given the meaning "a beautiful brave

---

[38] Housman's poetry became enormously popular during the First World War and was often invoked as a model for the wartime elegy. See Fussell, *The Great War and Modern Memory*, 281–2. The young Howells once met Housman, who complained so vociferously about his verse being set to music that the composer took the drastic step of destroying all of his songs to texts by the choleric poet; Spicer, *Herbert Howells*, 59.

[39] Ridout, 'Herbert Howells Remembered', 11–12.

[40] Ibid., 12.

[41] Ibid., 13.

doomed boy".[42] For Howells, both Warren and Michael bore the marks of a 'beautiful brave doomed boy'.

The connection between Warren and Michael was not just emotional for Howells: it became musical as well. The first author to unravel the complex chronology of the creation of *Hymnus paradisi*, Christopher Palmer, identified the score's principal antecedent as the a cappella Requiem (HH 188) for double choir, cast in the key of D major, that Howells completed in 1932 but that was not published or performed in the composer's lifetime.[43] In a letter to Diana Oldridge dated 13 October 1932, Howells wrote, 'Dinna! I've added a complete new short work to my holiday list – a brief sort of "Requiem" (on the Walford Davies model, but more extended). I finished it yesterday and am copying it out. It's done specially for King's College, Cambridge – otherwise I might not have dreamed of it.'[44] Why did Howells suppress this work? He might well have hesitated to send it on to Boris Ord at Cambridge because of its difficulty: few if any choirs of the 1930s could have coped with such a complex, highly chromatic and dissonant score. In any case, there is no evidence that Ord ever enquired about his undelivered Requiem or even knew of its existence.

A further reason may have been its resemblance, acknowledged by Howells himself, to the *Short Requiem in D major, in Memory of Those Fallen in the War*, composed in 1915 by one of Howells's former teachers at the RCM, Sir Walford Davies. Not only are both scores cast in the same key, but, as Palmer accurately observes, 'the similarities between nos. 1, 3, 4, 5 and 6 in the two works are striking, particularly (in terms also of layout and phrase-structure) in "I heard a voice from heaven".'[45] The differences between the two are marked, however. Davies's work is uncomplicated, essentially diatonic (with the very occasional use of borrowed or altered chords for local effect) and curiously placid. By contrast, Howells's Requiem is complex, modal and octatonic, and is often tormented.[46]

People who are not shocked in the least by the piecemeal manner in which Johann Sebastian Bach assembled his Mass in B minor are nevertheless disconcerted to learn that Howells based his *Hymnus paradisi* on a musical source that predates Michael's demise: it is as if Howells was somehow less than respectful to his son's memory by doing so. The composer may have anticipated such future opprobrium when he suppressed his Requiem over the course of his lifetime, as he may not have wanted to complicate his carefully crafted narrative of the genesis and completion of *Hymnus paradisi*. It is just possible, in addition, that he may

---

[42] Fussell, *The Great War and Modern Memory*, 282.
[43] Palmer, *A Centenary Celebration*, 93–127.
[44] *Ibid.*, 98.
[45] *Ibid.*, 61.
[46] Through his close study of Stravinsky, Ravel and Vaughan Williams, Howells was very much aware of the potential of the octatonic scales. As the composer Anthony Scott recalled, 'If I told him that I had enjoyed a work, say Vaughan Williams's Fourth Symphony, he would analyse it for me very clearly and simply, indicating how most of the themes used an individual scale which VW was thinking in while writing that work.' Vaughan Williams's Fourth Symphony (1934) is drenched in octatonic pitch materials. Palmer, *A Centenary Celebration*, 235.

Ex. 15.1a *Elegy*, Op. 15, bars 1–4

Ex. 15.1b Psalm 23, Requiem, bars 1–2

have refused to share his Requiem with the world in 1932 because of its connection, made through the use of the Davies score as a model, with the losses of the First World War, specifically the death of 'Bunny' Warren.

Indeed, Warren's wraith haunts both the 1917 *Elegy* for viola, string quartet and string orchestra, and the 1932 Requiem. The *Elegy* was a turning point in Howells's style: Vaughan Williams's *Fantasia on a theme by Thomas Tallis*, which Howells first heard at its premiere in Gloucester Cathedral in 1910, suggested to him an array of inspiring techniques, including the use of unaccompanied lines; modal inflections that deepen gradually into intense octatonic passages; and prolonged climaxes, at once ecstatic and saturated with dissonance, that are built up from the gradual accretion of polyphonic density. Howells uses these techniques as well as strikingly similar thematic ideas in both the Requiem and the *Elegy* – indeed, parts of the Requiem sound as if they are choral variants of passages drawn from the instrumental work (Ex. 15.1).

In a birthday tribute to Howells published in 1967, Hugh Ottaway placed this commingling of pleasure and pain in a broader context: 'For Howells, as for Elgar and Delius, the ecstatic and the elegiac – the visionary glory and the sense of loss – are closely bound up together.'[47] As he neared the conclusion of this short but insightful essay, Ottaway marginalised the influence of Elgar in order to link the music of Howells and Delius. It is certainly true that Delius influenced Howells in general and that the younger composer was clearly impressed by *Sea Drift* (1904) in particular, with its luscious harmonies surrounding the boy narrator with a nimbus of melancholy as he learns of death from a bereaved sea bird. However, it must be remembered that the second work at that 1910 premiere of Vaughan Williams's *Fantasia on a theme by Thomas Tallis* at the Three Choirs Festival in Gloucester Cathedral was Elgar's oratorio *The Dream of Gerontius*, conducted by Elgar himself.[48] Indeed, this performance of *Gerontius* was the first allowed in Gloucester Cathedral, as clerical objections to the Roman Catholicism

---

[47] Ottaway, 'Herbert Howells and the English Revival', 899.
[48] Spicer, *Herbert Howells*, 22.

Ex. 15.2a 'Prelude', *The Dream of Gerontius* (Edward Elgar), bars 1–4

Violas (con sord.), 2 Clarinets in A, 2 Bassoons

Ex. 15.2b 'Preludio', *Hymnus paradisi*, bars 1–4

Violas, 2 Clarinets in A, 1 Bassoon

of Newman's poem had put the oratorio under interdict until that year.[49] There are several striking similarities between *Gerontius* and *Hymnus paradisi*: both works open with single lines that are orchestrated for violas, clarinet and bassoon in unison (Ex. 15.2).[50]

It is hard to imagine that Howells did not consciously allude to Elgar's oratorio in this opening gambit, given that the rest of the prelude to *Hymnus paradisi*, which was the last part of the score to be completed and scored, is modelled on the prelude to *Gerontius*. While the recurring themes in *Hymnus paradisi* – most drawn from the earlier Requiem – cannot be labelled as clearly as the leitmotifs that pervade *Gerontius*, they are nevertheless transformed in a manner remarkably reminiscent of Elgar's practice.

Howells had good reason to be grateful to Elgar, who was on the whole suspicious of young composers trained at the RCM by his nemesis, Sir Charles Villiers Stanford. In a generous gesture, Elgar commissioned Arthur Bliss, Eugene Goossens and Howells for new works to be presented at the 1922 Gloucester Three Choirs Festival.[51] Howells fulfilled this commission by composing one of his most original works, *Sine nomine: A Phantasy*, Op. 37 (HH 126), for soprano and tenor soloists, chorus and large orchestra – much the same forces that he would employ for *Hymnus paradisi*. Unfortunately, neither critics nor audiences appreciated *Sine nomine*, which, among other innovations, did away with the use of a text altogether; it waited seventy years to receive a second performance.[52] Although Palmer treats this work as a precursor to *Hymnus paradisi*, it deserves

---

[49] McGuire, 'The English Music Festival, 1910', 260–1.

[50] The subtle difference between the two is that Elgar uses both clarinets and both bassoons, whereas Howells uses only a single bassoon – the difference in timbre at such low volume is virtually imperceptible, however. In addition, Elgar's violas are muted; Howells's are not.

[51] Palmer, *Howells: A Centenary Celebration*, 28.

[52] Palmer writes, '*Sine Nomine* is a complex and difficult piece which poses many problems of balance and integration. Elgar, seeing the young composer-conductor harassed at rehearsal, offered to give up some of the time allocated to his own

attention by itself as an extraordinary piece of innovation. *Sine nomine* is the first work for chorus and orchestra by Howells in which harmonic resources derived from Debussy, Ravel and, in particular, Vaughan Williams's recent *A Pastoral Symphony* (the Third Symphony, premiered on 26 January 1922) are wedded to a polyphonic technique predicated upon the weaving of multiple discrete layers into a luminous web of sound.[53] The subdued but lapidary orchestration, the choice of soloists, the disposition of choral forces, the luminous contrapuntal textures, the stylistic allusions to plainchant, the evocation of ringing and tolling bells – indeed the entire sound-world – of *Sine nomine* prefigure to an uncanny degree the musical elements that will pervade *Hymnus paradisi*, but the use of these stylistic features in the later score to express grief-stricken remembrance and occult hope retrospectively illumines the essentially elegiac nature of the earlier work.

Although Spicer has compared *Sine nomine* to a cathedral, it might also justly be compared to one of the many war memorials designed by the great Modernist architect Sir Edwin Lutyens (1864–1944) that were being erected in Britain and France during the 1920s. While the Latin phrase *sine nomine* literally means 'without name', Howells would have known this tag from at least two sources: from Tudor keyboard music and as the title of one of Vaughan Williams's most popular hymn tunes, first published in the *English Hymnal* of 1906.[54] It is inconceivable that Howells would not have known this tune and the third and sixth stanzas of its text:

> O may thy soldiers, faithful, true, and bold,
> Fight as the Saints who nobly fought of old,
> And win, with them, the victor's crown of gold ...
>
> The golden evening brightens in the west;
> Soon, soon to faithful warriors cometh rest:
> Sweet is the calm of Paradise the blest.

Sine nomine is an inimitable achievement, in that Howells worked mightily to eschew as many obvious external references as possible. No wonder that its first audience was puzzled, forced to wait patiently through a quarter-hour of enigmatic and complex sonority before they could hear their beloved *Elijah*. Nothing even remotely like *Sine nomine* had ever been heard before in a British music festival. Its very title seems to undercut its standing as a title. The wordless melismas of the soprano and tenor soloists can be construed as ecstatic or elegiac or both. The choral entries are so integrated into the orchestra that the choral sonority becomes even more impersonal than the women's voices in the final movement, 'Sirènes', from Debussy's *Nocturnes* (1897–9). Howells surely took the *Nocturnes*

Gerontius rehearsal in the hope of alleviating matters. Needless to say, Howells was unforgettingly grateful.' *Ibid.*, 28–9.
[53] *Ibid.*, 154.
[54] Howells originally called his early *Mass in the Dorian Mode* (1912) the *Missa sine nomine*. See Palmer, *A Centenary Celebration*, 69. In addition, the first of his *Six Pieces for Organ* is entitled 'Preludio "sine nomine"'.

as a model in this instance, but, unlike the composer of *Sine nomine*, Debussy gave his work a suggestive title so that listeners are prepared to make connections with an episode from familiar mythology. Even the disembodied women's voices at the end of 'Neptune' in Holst's *The Planets* (1914–16) are implicitly associated with the idea of interstellar space. By contrast, the sonority of *Sine nomine* approaches the 'white radiance of Eternity' of which Shelley wrote in his elegy for Keats, *Adonais*.

Like Elgar's *Spirit of England* or Vaughan Williams's *A Pastoral Symphony*, *Sine nomine* reflects a cultural shift that occurred in British life during the First World War, embodied most conspicuously in Lutyens's war memorials. Faced with casualties of unprecedented magnitude, as well as the diversity of religious beliefs held by the colonial troops who fought and died for Britain during the war, mourning rituals changed drastically over the course of just a few years. The elaborate customs used to mourn the departed – especially dead children – during the Victorian and Edwardian eras, with elaborate codes of dress and etiquette, had to be jettisoned, lest national morale be compromised under the weight of crushing sorrow. Mourning thousands and, on some horrific days, such as during the Battle of the Somme, tens of thousands of casualties individually was, as if by a national consensus, recognised to be impossible both during and immediately after the war. The task of remembrance was made even more challenging by the all-too-common circumstance that there were no remains to bury. Like Frances Purcell Warren, the bodies of ten of thousands of soldiers were lost; they departed without a trace, their graves forever unmarked, *sine nomine*.

In the face of such calamity, musical responses to death changed dramatically. A crucial difference between Elgar's *The Dream of Gerontius* and his *Spirit of England* can be located in a distinction between the personal and the communal. In the earlier work, the listener is drawn into the fate of a single individual who undergoes death and whose soul is transported to supernal realms; in the later one, Romantic individuality is abandoned so that listeners can participate in a communal rite. In *Sine nomine*, Howells subsumes the individual into the abstract far more completely than Elgar ever could have imagined; one wonders what the aging composer thought of the score that he had commissioned. Indeed, Howells was so thorough in his removal of signifiers that listeners and critics at the premiere were mystified rather than moved. From the experience of composing the *Sine nomine*, Howells learned that it was necessary to give his listeners sufficient signposts so that they could find their own way into a work, as he does with notable success in *Hymnus paradisi*.

Hymnus paradisi stands in the direct line of the *Elegy*, *Sine nomine* and the Requiem, in that it combines elegiac anguish, impersonality, sublimated mourning and generalised religious sentiment into a single, masterful musical edifice. An extraordinary aspect of this work is that, like *Sine nomine*, it is drenched in its creator's personal idiom, yet personal allusions have been suppressed: nowhere is there anything like the viola solo that gestures towards Warren's gifts as a string player, and the impulse that requested the nursery rhymes for Michael's funeral is conspicuously absent. Indeed, a listener coming to *Hymnus paradisi* for the first time without prior knowledge could never guess that two very specific spirits hovered over the creation of this score: a young soldier who perished in battle and a child

Fig. 15.1 The Cenotaph in Whitehall, London. Armistice Day, 1920

who died of poliomyelitis. In and of itself, *Hymnus paradisi* is at once expressive and impersonal, as its composer selflessly declines to indulge in his personal grief so that listeners may find a vehicle for their own experiences of loss and thereby gain a measure of consolation. In other words, *Hymnus paradisi* functions as a cenotaph.

Derived from the Greek word *kenotaphion*, a cenotaph is an 'empty tomb'. The most famous modern example is the Cenotaph that stands in Whitehall in London, designed as a war memorial by Lutyens, who famously replied to Lloyd George's request for a non-denominational catafalque, or empty casket stand, by declaring that what was needed was not a catafalque – the word is French, after all – but a cenotaph, the very tomb itself.[55] At first merely a temporary edifice constructed of wood and plaster erected for a joint Allied Peace Procession that occurred on 19 July 1919, the initial monument was later replaced by the government, persuaded by public sentiment, with a permanent one carved from Portland stone. Occupying the same site as the provisional monument, the stone Cenotaph was unveiled by George V on Remembrance Day, 11 November 1920.[56]

Despite objections from a few Anglican clergymen who protested that the Cenotaph was not traditionally Christian owing to its lack of a cross, it immediately became a locus for postwar mourning in London.[57] In her biography of Lutyens, Jane Ridley writes, 'it caught the public mood and made an immediate impact ... Men doffed their hats as they rode past on London buses. It was the people's shrine.'[58] Viewers were moved by the apparent simplicity of the Cenotaph, its 'absence of all ornament', as one correspondent wrote to *The Times*.[59] But the uncomplicated surface of the Cenotaph belied the complexity of Lutyens's design. Lutyens described his concept in detail: 'all its horizontal surfaces and planes are spherical, parts of parallel spheres 1801 ft 8 in. in diameter; and all its vertical lines converge upwards to a point some 1801 ft 8 in. above the centre of these spheres.'[60]

The Cenotaph's power derives from its essential Modernism: indeed, Lutyens used his formidable skill as geometrician to great effect in all of the commemorative monuments that he designed. As historian Jay Winter observes, 'A striking minimalism is evident in two of the most important British war memorials, the Cenotaph in Whitehall and the Memorial to the Missing at Thiepval on the Somme ... so different from wartime patriotic commemorative forms and from postwar exercises in civic or religious art.' Of the Cenotaph, Winter writes that 'by announcing its presence as the tomb of no one, this one became the tomb of all who had died in the war.' He sums up the lasting significance of this memorial when he writes, 'Lutyens's Cenotaph leapt over the mundane into myth, and by doing so provided a focus for collective mourning of a kind unknown before or since in Britain.'[61]

There is more to the Cenotaph than geometry, however. Through his wife Emily, a devoted Theosophist, Lutyens had come into contact with one of the most massive collective examples of 'magical thinking' in modern history, as interest in

---

[55] Skelton and Gliddon, *Lutyens and the Great War*, 40.
[56] Ibid., 47.
[57] Winter, *Sites of Memory, Sites of Mourning*, 104.
[58] Ridley, *Edwin Lutyens*, 288–9.
[59] Skelton and Gliddon, *Lutyens and the Great War*, 43.
[60] Quoted in Winter, *Sites of Memory, Sites of Mourning*, 104.
[61] Ibid., 102, 104.

spiritualism expanded with dizzying rapidity during and after the First World War. Although Lutyens himself was an inveterate sceptic with a certain nostalgia for Christianity, he and his wife moved in circles that included such noted spiritualists as Annie Besant, the Theosophist; Arthur Balfour, the politician; and Sir Oliver Lodge, a distinguished physicist who was the Chancellor of Birmingham University.

After Lodge's son was killed in the war, his interest in spiritualism increased dramatically. He wrote a book, *Raymond* (1916), that contains an extended section concerning his child's posthumous adventures in the afterlife that is at once unbearably poignant and curiously corporeal.[62] Like Howells praying for Michael at Twigworth, Lodge sought to conjure back his son, if only fleetingly, in order to have some sign of his continued existence and, through reincarnation, his eventual return. As Winter compassionately notes, 'Once we read his letters it becomes easier to imagine what Lodge and millions of others dreamed of: the continued development and growth of those whose lives were brutally cut short.'[63]

A veteran of the First World War, Ralph Vaughan Williams, echoed this sentiment in a characteristically equivocal manner. Casting about for something appropriate to send to Howells after Michael's death, Vaughan Williams wrote, 'I don't think it is really any comfort – indeed "comfort" would be just an impertinence – but I cannot help believing that a life once begun can never really stop – though it has stopped for us and that there may, after all, be a real joining up some day.'[64] That Vaughan Williams, whose mature attitude towards religion has been memorably and accurately characterised as a 'cheerful agnosticism', employed in 1935 the very phrases that pervaded British society at the time of the First World War shows the persistence of such ideas, whether he truly entertained the possibility of a realm beyond or not.[65]

After the war Howells resorted to a vaguely spiritualist vocabulary like that used by Vaughan Williams, phrases permeated by the tenuous hope that the dead continued in a life beyond the realm of ontology.[66] He may have been comforted by such ideas during the period of his own brush with death and after the disappearance of 'Bunny' Warren. What is likely, however, is that the embers of such inchoate speculations flamed into magical thinking after the death of his son, leading Howells inexorably towards the creation of *Hymnus paradisi*.

---

[62] *Ibid.*, 61–2.
[63] *Ibid.*, 62.
[64] R. Vaughan Williams, *Letters*, 240.
[65] U. Vaughan Williams, *R.V.W.: A Biography of Ralph Vaughan Williams*, 29.
[66] The interest in spiritualism and the occult that developed during the First World War and after informs a curious story told by Ursula Howells concerning Gustav Holst's unpropitious astrological chart made for her younger brother. Of course, this tale is yet another search for an augury to help make sense of the disaster to come. Palmer, *A Centenary Celebration*, 275–6.

Just as Lutyens's Cenotaph and Memorial to the Missing of the Somme at Thiepval are examples of Modernist architecture, so a particularly British form of musical modernity informs Howells's *Hymnus paradisi, Sine nomine* and the other works written in memory of Warren and Michael. One of the puzzling aspects of the critical reception of Howells's music has been an almost wilful refusal to view him as a Modernist composer, just as Lutyens's reputation has suffered because of the lack of obviously radical elements in his style. Yet both men assimilated the aesthetic and cultural shift towards important aspects of modernity that came to prominence during the First World War.

In this regard, several analogies can fruitfully be drawn between Lutyens's work as an architect and Howells's music written *in memoriam*. Indeed, Howells was interested in architecture from an early age, having been introduced to the appreciation of great sacred buildings by his father; as Spicer writes, 'This early exposure to great architecture, and the place of music within it, awoke in Herbert what was much later to become his principal creative force.'[67] Both composer and architect maintained astonishing technical control over their material, but both made sure that their elaborate calculations remained well below the deceptively smooth surface of their creations. Listeners to *Hymnus paradisi* are no more aware of Howells's dazzling skill as a contrapuntist than viewers can calculate how Lutyens was able to make the top of the Cenotaph seemingly disappear into the empyrean as they move closer to the base of the shrine, unaware of the way he employed the ancient Greek architectural technique of *entasis*.[68]

In formal matters, Howells evinces a sense of right proportion that can be compared to that of Lutyens. Indeed, Howells was fascinated with the question of form in music from a very early stage of his career (see Chapter 11). *Hymnus paradisi* itself is an experiment in form, constructed as it is in broad arcs of sound that rest on a subtly disguised symmetry. While a detailed analysis of *Hymnus paradisi* is beyond the scope of this chapter, the rising and falling key areas, often related by interlocking major thirds, move the music forward in a series of extended tonal arches that stretch from the opening unaccompanied lament in B minor to the compromised solace of the final triad of E♭ major. Howells's formal innovations have their architectural analogue in the astonishing design of interconnected arches that is a chief feature of Lutyens's Memorial to the Missing of the Somme at Thiepval, which was unveiled in 1932. A striking feature of Lutyens's design is the over 72,000 names inscribed on that memorial's pillars – including that of Francis Purcell Warren.[69]

Lutyens and Howells share an even more essential trait in that they both emphasised the communal over the personal. Just as Luytens aimed to subsume the names of individuals under the overall effect of the Memorial to the Missing of the Somme at Thiepval, and to make communal mourning paramount at

---

[67] Spicer, *Herbert Howells*, 15.
[68] *Entasis* is a process by which seemingly horizontal lines are subtly modified into a whole by almost imperceptible curves.
[69] Skelton and Gliddon, *Lutyens and the Great War*, 139.

Fig. 15.2 Memorial to the Missing of the Somme, Thiepval, Picardie, France

the Cenotaph, so Howells did not dwell upon his own sorrow in the *Hymnus paradisi*, but rather transmuted personal grief into a musical gathering place of memory and mourning. Howells banished anything remotely like the personal cry of 'Libera me, Domine' from the traditional Requiem Mass and instead chose the most widely understood and elemental parts of the Latin liturgy, intermingling these with the two most popular Psalms, the 23rd and the 121st, and a short extract from the Sarum Diurnal translated into English. The name of the Christian Saviour is conspicuous by its complete absence. Like the Cenotaph, *Hymnus paradisi* is relevant to persons of all faiths, or, indeed, to those who hold no faith whatsoever; as Winter writes of the Cenotaph, *Hymnus paradisi* was intended to be 'a form on which anyone could inscribe his or her thoughts, reveries, sadnesses'.[70]

The Valley of the Shadow

As this narrative draws towards its necessarily inconclusive close, Lutyens's Cenotaph in London must be left behind, and, tracing the westward route of the Cheltenham Flier that took Howells to Twigworth, attention must return to the verdant countryside of Gloucestershire. Only with reference to Gloucestershire can a crucial question be asked: if *Hymnus paradisi* is, as its title proclaims, a 'hymn of paradise', where, then, is this particular paradise located? Is it a supernal, distant realm far from earth where Michael would remain forever distant? Or is this paradise something closer to home, not the Elysian Fields but the bruised Arcadia of Gloucestershire?

In a searching essay on the ways in which 'war composers' such as Vaughan Williams and Bliss subverted the 'pastoral' style after the First World War, Eric Saylor muses on a peculiar aspect of the British pastoral tradition: 'Additionally, and contrary to most other traditions, representations of death were integral parts of English pastoral art. Images of skulls, tombstones, or the phrase *Et in Arcadia ego* ('Even in Arcadia there am I [Death]') had been present in pastoral art since the early seventeenth century'.[71] Basing his work upon that of literary critic Terry Gifford and others, Saylor makes a useful distinction between the 'soft pastoral', redolent of nostalgia and a vague pantheism, and the 'hard pastoral', in which the Arcadian landscape of the British countryside is permeated with reminders of dissolution.

While certain of Howells's earlier works fall under the category of the 'soft pastoral', the 'hard pastoral' is given a new kind of treatment in *Hymnus paradisi*. The work is divided into two kinds of settings. Extracts from the Latin liturgy of the Requiem Mass based on conjunct and modal chant-like themes stand in contrast to settings of English texts that are inflected with gestures familiar from British folk-song. Only the capstone fourth movement, the Sanctus, combines English and Latin texts. The moment that Howells introduces music redolent of plainchant or

---

[70] Winter, *Sites of Memory, Sites of Mourning*, 104.
[71] Saylor, '"It's Not Lambkins Frisking at All"', 42.

folk-song, however, swift changes follow: there is slippage away from the established tonal centre, contrapuntal complexity increases, dissonance intensifies, and freely chromatic and octatonic elements intrude insistently upon the diatonic and modal music. The inexorable intensification of chromaticism and ever denser polyphony creates a sense of smothering aural claustrophobia that threatens to overwhelm the listener in a manner that anticipates such later scores as Ligeti's Requiem (1965). Simply put, Howells employs the pastoral tropes of *The Bs* or his *Pastoral Rhapsody* (HH 134 – 1923) only to undermine them. Even the final movement, 'Holy Is the True Light', a setting of a fragment from the Salisbury Diurnal translated into English, shares this musical slippage from light into darkness. The music rises to exultation only to conclude in shadow, as the return of the lamenting theme that opens *Hymnus paradisi* smutches the radiance of the concluding cadence of E♭ major: the final chord sounds less like a harbinger of dawn than an exhalation of the spirit.[72]

In his comparison of Howells to Delius, Hugh Ottaway recognised the valedictory significance of this final movement: 'Howells's vision is "evermore", Delius's "nevermore", but the music speaks of a similar yearning. There is no mistaking a sunset, whichever way you happen to be facing ...'.[73] Of course, the slim semantic difference between 'evermore' and 'nevermore' is immaterial for a parent obsessively yearning for the return of a dead child. Like the sunset viewed from the chapel tower by Little Nell in Dickens's *The Old Curiosity Shop*, the light of the sunset depicted in 'Holy Is the True Light' is the 'sudden burst of light' that, as Lerner observes, reveals a view downward. The 'life of rustic England' it illuminates is permeated by decay and death.

Part of the symbolic potency of any sunset derives from the pattern enacted daily: the light from the setting sun rises to a pitch of glory only to dissolve slowly into darkness. Little Nell's 'sudden burst of light' is no different from the 'lurid sunset' that was burned into Howells's memory on the nightmarish ride to the train station as he held Michael's writhing, gasping body, and the same sunset that he portrays in the final movement of his musical cenotaph. After his son's death, Howells did not need to be reminded by a passage from Dickens that the Gloucestershire countryside was home to death, for his son contracted the deadly virus in its bucolic surroundings and his coffin was lowered into that rural earth. Howells grasped that the paradise of Gloucestershire could be fatal, that the beauty of a sunset could turn lurid and the bloom on the cheeks of a healthy child could pale forever in the twinkling of an eye. The musical metaphors Howells employs with such cunning in *Hymnus paradisi* tell this narrative with an eloquence and honesty unmatched by words. Yet the score is not merely a personal cry but a poignant reminder of the terrifying fragility of life: no-one understands fully that they are in paradise until

---

[72] Within this context, it might be noted that Howells's *Elegy* for viola, string quartet and string orchestra also ends on a triad of E♭ major, which is the key of Elgar's autumnal Second Symphony (1912) as well as the 'Nimrod' variation from his *Enigma Variations*, Op. 36 (1899).

[73] Ottaway, 'Herbert Howells and the English Revival', 899.

it is abruptly snatched away. Howells used the objectivity and abstraction offered by postwar Modernist aesthetics in order to console that community of fellow-mourners whose own vanished Edens rested eternally in the silent earth, a silence that remains unbroken despite incantations and offerings: 'Where your treasure is, there will your heart be also.'

APPENDIX

Catalogue of the Works of Herbert Howells

Paul Andrews

THIS catalogue is based on the one that forms part of my doctoral dissertation.[1] Its aim is to set down as complete a record of Howells's work as a composer as present information allows, always taking into account the possibility of new discoveries or new information about known works coming to light in the future. To that end, in addition to listing every complete published, performed and recorded work, it also includes entries for works for which there is some primary or secondary documentary evidence, but that are no longer extant, or are known or assumed to be missing. As in the earlier catalogue, Howells's works are arranged in chronological order so far as it is possible to be certain of the date of completion. But Howells was an artist who was far from consistent in his recording of these details on his manuscripts or elsewhere, and, for example, in cases where there was a gap sometimes of some years between composition and publication or performance, the date of a number of works has to be a best guess, based on all the available information. This relative uncertainty is reflected in some of the entries. In addition, as some works, including a few major compositions, were revised or added to over a considerable period of time or existed in more than one version (HH 61 and HH 111 are cases in point) the decision has been taken to assign the earliest date at which a viable version is known to have existed. The catalogue concludes with a short list of undated works for which not even a speculative date can be risked, and the titles of a number of songs appearing in early self-compiled lists that have not survived.

The entry for each work sets out its title and constituent parts, the medium of performance, whether it is published or unpublished and, in the latter case, if the manuscript is missing. The constituent parts of a work comprising separate numbers are given in roman numerals within the main entry and multiple versions are indicated by lower-case letters.

A small number of mainly early pieces has come to light in the years since I compiled the original version of the catalogue. As this is its first appearance in published form, the numbering of Howells's compositions has been completely revised to take account of these new discoveries, and therefore entirely supersedes the numbering scheme of the earlier catalogue. Howells made a number of attempts to assign opus numbers to his own works as a student and in the early part of his career, but he was never consistent in this practice, frequently changing his mind, and eventually abandoned it completely in the 1920s. Where works were published with opus numbers, however, they are noted in the catalogue, but clearly some other unique siglum is desirable if Howells's compositions are to be

---

[1] Andrews, 'A Documentary and Bibliographical Study'.

precisely identified by their numbers. Howells was frequently in the habit of using his own initials as a shorthand signature and he was invariably referred to as 'HH' by his friends and pupils, so it seemed appropriate and intuitive to use 'HH' as the identifying siglum for this catalogue. Thus the complete works of this remarkable musician are encompassed by HH 1 through to HH 381.

Year	HH no.	Title	Instruments	Texts (if applicable)	Publisher
1907–9	1	*To the Owl*: two part-songs (i) 'When Cats Run Home' (ii) 'The Tu-whits Are Lulled'	Treble voices, pno	A. Tennyson	Novello (1911)
1908	2	*Four Romantic Pieces* (i) 'Norwegian Tune' (missing) (ii) 'The Arab's Song' (MS) (iii) [unidentified] (missing) (iv) 'Peasant's March' (missing)	Pno		Unpublished
1908	3	'By the Sea' (MS – incomplete)	Pno		Unpublished
1908	4	'A Visit from the Sea' (MS)	Voice, pno	R. L. Stevenson	Unpublished
1908	5	'Windy Nights' (MS)	Voice, pno	R. L. Stevenson	Unpublished
1908	6	'To a Wild Flower' (MS)	Pno		Unpublished
1908	7	'Charm Me Asleep' (MS)	Voice, pno	R. Herrick	Unpublished
1908	8	'Humoreske' in E minor (MS)	Pno		Unpublished
1908	9	'Romance' (MS)	Pno		Unpublished
1909	10	'Melody' (MS)	Pno		Unpublished
1909	11	'Marching Song' (MS)	Pno		Unpublished
1909	12	'My Shadow' (MS)	Voice, pno	R. L. Stephenson	Unpublished
1909	13	'From a Northern Land' (MS)	Pno		Unpublished
1909	14	'Gnomes' (MS)	Pno		Unpublished
1909	15	'Saga' (missing)	Pno		Unpublished
1910s	16	Prelude in E major (missing)	Pno		Unpublished

Year	HH no.	Title	Instruments	Texts (if applicable)	Publisher
1910s	17	Gavotte in F major (missing)	Pno		Unpublished
1910–11	18	*Betty's Ballads* (missing)	Voice, pno		Unpublished
1910–11	19	Overture (missing)	Orchestra		Unpublished
1911	20	*Hymn for Coronation: 'God of Our England'* (MS)	Voices, pno	H. B. Parker	Unpublished
1911	21	'Longing'	Voice, pno	F. Macleod	Unpublished
1911	22	Prelude in E♭ (missing)	Org.		Unpublished
1911	23	Postlude in C (missing)	Org.		Unpublished
1911	24	Sonata in B minor (MS)	Vln, pno		Unpublished
1911	25	Sonata in C minor, Op. 1	Org.		Novello (1992)
1911	26	*Five Songs* (MS) (i) 'The Twilight People' (ii) 'The Devotee' (iii) 'The Waves of Breffny' (iv) 'The Sorrow of Love' (v) 'The Call'	Low voice, pno	(i) S. O'Sullivan (ii) E. Gore-Booth (iii) S. O'Sullivan (iv) T. Keohler (v) G. Roberts	Unpublished
1911	27	*Summer Idyls* (sic) (MS) (i) 'Meadow-Rest' (ii) 'Summer-Song' (iii) 'June-Haze' (iv) 'Down the Hills' (v) 'Quiet Woods' (vi) 'Near Midnight' (vii) 'In the Morning'	Pno		Unpublished

Year	No.	Title	Forces	Text	Publication
1912	28	*Missa sine nomine* (*Mass in the Dorian Mode*), Op. 2	SATB	Latin Mass	Church Music Society (1990)
1912–17	29	[*Three Double Chants*] (i) in A major (ii) in C# minor (iii) in B♭ minor	Voices		*The New St Paul's Cathedral Psalter* (1997)
1913	30	*Four Choral Preludes* (missing)	Org.		Unpublished
1913	31	*Concerto in C minor*, Op. 4	Pno, orchestra		Novello (2001)
1913	32	*Comedy Suite*, Op. 8 (missing)	Cl., pno		Unpublished
1913	33	*Two Doxologies for the Compline Hymn 'Te lucis ante terminum'* (missing)	SATB		Unpublished
1913	34	*O salutaris hostia*	SATB	St T. Aquinas	Novello (1987)
1913	35	*Even Such Is Time*	SATB	W. Raleigh (attr.)	Novello (2008) (ii) Novello (2011)
1913	36	*Two Pieces* (i) Menuetto (missing) (ii) 'Cradle Song'	Org.		Unpublished
1913	37	*Psalm-Prelude* (missing)	Org.		Unpublished
1913	38	*Songs for Low Voice*, Op. 7 (i) 'The Valley of Silence' (ii) 'When the Dew Is Falling' (iii) 'By the Grey Stone' (iv) 'St Bride's Song' (v) 'When There Is Peace'	Low voice, pno	F. Macleod	Thames (1999)
1913	39	'The Evening Darkens Over' (missing)	Voice, pno	R. Bridges	Unpublished

Year	HH no.	Title	Instruments	Texts (if applicable)	Publisher
1913	40	*Two Songs from 'A Shropshire Lad'* (missing) (i) 'The Street Sounds to the Soldiers' Tread' (ii) [unidentified]	Voice, pno	A. E. Housman	Unpublished
1913	41	*Variations for Eleven Solo Instruments*, Op. 3 (missing)	Unknown		Unpublished
1914	42	Suite for Orchestra, *The Bs*, Op. 13 (MS) (i) 'Overture (to Bublum)' (ii) 'Scherzo (to Blissy)' (iii) 'Lament (to Bartholomew)' (iv) 'Mazurka alias Minuet (Bunny)' (v) 'March (Benjee)'	Orchestra		Unpublished
1914	43	Fugue for Five Voices and Strings, *The Lord Shall Be My Help*	SSATB, strings	Unknown	Unpublished
1914	44	Nunc dimittis	SATB (double choir)	Latin text	Novello (1989)
1914	45	*Five Part-Songs*, Op. 5 (i) 'Love's Secret' (missing) (ii) 'Is the Mood Tired?' (missing) (iii) 'Weep You No More' (iv) 'The Winds Whistle Cold' (v) 'A Dirge'	TTBB	(i) W. Blake (ii) C. Rossetti (iii) J. Dowland (iv) D. Terry (v) W. Shakespeare	S & B (1914) [iii–v only]
1914	46	'The Primrose' (MS)	Voice, pno	T. Carew	Unpublished
1914	47	'The Tinker's Song'	Voices, pno	Unknown	Oxford University Press (1923)

Year	Op.	Title	Forces	Text/Author	Publisher
1914	48	*Three Dances*, Op. 7	Vln, orchestra		Novello (1990)
1914	49	Madrigal for Five Voices, 'In Youth Is Pleasure'	SSATB	R. Wever	Novello (1916)
1914	50	*Lady Audrey's Suite*	String quartet		Novello (1917)
1914	51	Minuet in A minor (MS)	Pno		Unpublished
1914	52	*Phantasy Ground Bass* (missing)	Org.		Unpublished
1914	53	Prelude no. 1	Hp		S&B (2000)
1914	54	*Two Songs* (missing) (i) 'O Mistress Mine' (ii) 'His Poisoned Shafts'	Voice, pno	(i) W. Shakespeare (ii) R. Bridges	Unpublished
1915–16	55	*Four Songs*, Op. 22 (i) 'There Was a Maiden' (ii) 'A Madrigal' (iii) 'The Widow Bird' (iv) 'Girl's Song'	Voice, pno	(i) W. L. Courtney (ii) A. Dobson (iii) P. B. Shelley (iv) W. W. Gibson	WR (1919)
1915–16	56	*Three Psalm-Preludes*, Op. 32 (Set 1) (i) Psalm 34:6 (ii) Psalm 37:11 (iii) Psalm 23:4	Org.		Novello (1921)
1915/1918	57	*Three Rhapsodies*, Op. 17 (i) No. 1 in D♭ major (1915) (ii) No. 2 in E♭ major (1918) (iii) No. 3 in C♯ minor (1918)	Org.		Augener (1919)

Year	HH no.	Title	Instruments	Texts (if applicable)	Publisher
1915–17	58	*Five Part-Songs*, Op. 11 (i) 'The Shepherd' (ii) 'The Pilgrim' (iii) 'A Croon' (iv) 'A Sad Story' (v) 'Come All Ye Pretty Fair Maids'	Female voices, pno	(i) W. Blake (ii) W. Blake (iii) Anon. (iv) Anon. (v) Anon.	Curwen (1919)
1915–17	59	*Three Rondeaux*, Op. 12 (i) 'Roses' (ii) 'A Rondel of Rest' (iii) 'Her Scuttle Hat'	Voice, pno	(i) C. C. Tarelli (ii) A. Symons (iii) F. D. Sherman	S&B (1918)
1915	60	*Five Songs*, Op. 10 (missing) (i) 'Wanderer's Night Song' (ii) 'Merry Margaret' (iii) 'Close Mine Eyelids' (iv) 'Under the Greenwood Tree' (v) 'On the Merry First of May'	High voice, orchestra	(i) J. W. Goethe (trans. Howells) (ii) J. Skelton (iii) T. Storm (iv) W. Shakespeare (v) H. B. Parker	Unpublished
1916–18	61	*Snapshots*, Op. 30 (i) 'The Street Dancer' (ii) 'The Polar Bear' (iii) 'Wee Willie Winkee'	Pno		Swan (1921)
1916–30s	62	String Quartet no. 3, *In Gloucestershire*, Op. 34 (a) First version (1916; missing) (b) Second version (1920; rev. 1957) (c) Third version (MS) (d) Fourth version (1930s)	String Quartet		(d) Novello (1992)

Year	No.	Title	Forces	Text	Publication
1916	63	The Breathless Ballad of 'Peter Pan' Quartets	Voice, pno	Anon.	Unpublished
1916	64	Four Anthems to the Blessed Virgin Mary, Op. 9 (i) 'Alma redemptoris mater' (missing) (ii) 'Ave Regina' (missing) (iii) 'Regina coeli' (iv) 'Salve Regina'	SATB		Novello (1988) [iii–iv only]
1916	65	Two Short Pieces (missing)	Org.		Unpublished
1916	66	Quartet in A minor, Op. 21	Pno, string trio		S.. & B (1918; rev. 1937)
1916	67	The Skylark	Treble voices, pno	J. Hogg	Unpublished
1917	68	By the Waters of Babylon: A Rhapsody	Bar, vln, vcl, org.	Psalm 137	Novello (1992)
1917	69	Dansons (MS)	Vln, pno		Unpublished
1917	70	Elegy, Op. 15	Vla, string quartet, string orchestra		B&H (1938)
1917	71	Fantasy String Quartet, Op. 25	String quartet		Curwen (1925)
1917	72	'Here She Lies a Pretty Bud' (MS)	Voice, pno	R. Herrick	Unpublished
1917	73	'An Old Man's Lullaby'	Voice, pno	T. Dekker	Edwin Arnold (1948)
1917	74	Phantasy, Op. 29, no. 1 (MS)	Pno		Unpublished
1917	75	Three Pieces, Op. 28 (i) 'Pastorale' (ii) 'Chosen tune' (iii) 'Luchinushka'	Vln, pno		S&B (1923)

Year	HH no.	Title	Instruments	Texts (if applicable)	Publisher
1917	76	Suite for Piano, *Sarum Sketches*, Op. 6 (i) 'The Ooce March' (ii) 'The Drudge Talks to Himself' (iii) 'The Drudge Forgotten' (iv) 'Ooce Reads "Arabian Nights"' (v) 'Ooce at Leisure' (vi) 'Charades'	Pno		Augener (1921)
1917	77	*Sir Patrick Spens*: traditional ballad, Op. 23	Bar., SATB, Orchestra	Trad.	S&B (1928)
1917	78	Sonata no. 1 in E major, Op. 18	Vln, pno		WR (1924)
1917	79	Sonata no. 2 in E♭ major, Op. 26 (MS)	Vln, pno		Unpublished
1917	80	Suite for String Orchestra, Op. 16 (MS)	String orchestra		Unpublished
1917	81	'Upon a Summer's Day' (MS)	Voice, pno	M. Baring	Unpublished
1917	82	'Up on Their Brooms the Witches Ride' (MS) – incomplete	Voice, pno	W. de la Mare	Unpublished
1917/1920	83	*Two Pieces for Small Orchestra*, Op. 20 (i) 'Puck's Minuet' (1917) (ii) 'Merry-Eye' (1920)	Orchestra		G&T (1918/1920)
1918	84	'Before Me, Careless Lying': A Madrigal	SSATB	A. Dobson	S&B (1919)
1918	85	'Cradle Song', Op. 9, no. 1 (MS)	Vln, pno		Unpublished
1918	86	[*Two Fragments for Piano*] (MS) – incomplete (i) 'Semplice' (ii) (In Cafe 'Lyons' at Paddington, June 3rd)	Pno		Unpublished

Year	No.	Title	Forces	Text	Publisher
1918	87	'Haec dies'	SSATB		Church Music Society (1992)
1918	88	'Harlequin Dreaming' (MS)	Pno		Unpublished
1918	89	'Here Is the Little Door': carol-anthem	SATB	F. Chesterton	S&B (1918)
1918	90	'Love the Lily' (MS) – incomplete	Voice, pno	J. W. Haines	Unpublished
1918	91	Evening Service in G major	SATB, org.	Book of Common Prayer	S&B (1920)
1918	92	'Mally O!'	Voice, pno	Anon.	S&B (1918)
1918	93	'Old Skinflint'	Voice, pno	W. W. Gibson	Curwen (1920)
1918	94	'The Restful Branches'	Voice, pno	W. A. Byrne	S&B. (1920)
1918	95	*Three Two-Part Songs*, Op. 24 (i) 'Under the Greenwood Tree' (ii) 'A North Country Song' (iii) 'A True Story'	Female voices	(i) W. Shakespeare (ii) Anon. (iii) T. Campion	Edward Arnold (1918)
1918	96	[*Three Songs*] (MS) – incomplete (i) 'The [Illegible] Has Fled with a Scream' (ii) 'Flight' (iii) 'When Day Darkens'	Voice, pno	(i) [unidentified] (ii) W A Byrne (iii) [unidentified]	Unpublished
1918	97	Symphony in D major (MS) – incomplete	Orchestra		Unpublished
1918–19	98	*Four French Chansons* (arr. Howells), Op. 29 (i) 'Sainte Catharine' (ii) 'Le Marquis de Maine' (iii) 'Le petit couturier' (iv) 'Angèle au couvent'	Voice, pno	Trad.	J. & W. Chester (1920)

Year	HH no.	Title	Instruments	Texts (if applicable)	Publisher
1918–19	99	*Three Pieces*, Op. 14 (i) 'Rhapsody' (1919) (ii) 'Jackanapes' (1919) (iii) 'Procession' (1918)	Pno		AHC (1920)
1918–21	100	*Whin*: song set (i) 'Old Skinflint' (ii) 'Merry-Eye' (iii) 'Fallowfield Fell' (iv) 'Stow-on-the-Wold' (v) 'Blaweary' (vi) 'The Mugger's Song'	Voice, pno	W. W. Gibson	Unpublished as a set: (i) and (vi) published separately (See HH 93 and HH 103)
1919	101	'The Duel'	Voices, pno	E. Field	Edwin Ashdown (1922)
1919	102	'King David' (see HH 111)	Voice, pno	W. de la Mare	WR (1923)
1919	103	'The Mugger's Song'	Voice, pno	W. W. Gibson	B&H (1924)
1919	104	*Peacock Pie*, set 1, Op. 33 (i) 'Tired Tim' (ii) 'Alas, Alack!' (iii) 'Mrs MacQueen (or the Lollie-Shop)' (iv) 'The Dunce' (v) 'Full Moon' (vi) 'Miss T.'	Voice, pno	W. de la Mare	E. & B. Goodwin (1923)

Year	No.	Title	Forces	Text	Publisher
1919	105	*Phantasy Minuet*, Op. 27	Pianola		Aeolian Company (as a piano roll – 1919)
1919	106	*Poem*, Op. 32 (missing)	Vln, pno		Unpublished
1919	107	*Rhapsodic Quintet*, Op. 31	Cl., string quartet		S&B (1921)
1919	108	*Five Songs* (i) 'Among the Tombs' (missing) (ii) 'Long Ago to Thee' (missing) (iii) 'Gavotte' (iv) 'Though I Wander' (missing) (v) 'By the Hearth-Stone' (MS)	Low voice, pno	H. Newbolt	(iii) Oxford University Press (1927) (v) Unpublished
1919	109	'A Spotless Rose': carol-anthem	SATB		S&B (1919)
1919	110	'Thé Dansant' (missing), from *A Dance Suite for Toy Orchestra*	Toy orchestra		Unpublished
1919–73	111	*A Garland for de la Mare* (i) 'Wanderers' (ii) 'The Lady Caroline' (iii) 'Before Dawn' (two versions) (iv) 'The Old Stone House' (v) 'The Three Cherry Trees' (vi) 'The Old Soldier'	Voice, pno	W. de la Mare	Thames (1995)

Year	HH no.	Title	Instruments	Texts (if applicable)	Publisher
		(vii) 'The Song of the Secret'			
		(viii) 'Some One'			
		(ix) 'A Queer Story'			
		(x) 'Andy Battle'			
		(xi) 'The Old House'			
		(xii) 'King David' (see HH 102)			
1920s	112	'The Poet's Song': two-part song (MS)	Voices, pno	A. Tennyson	Unpublished
1920s	113	'Sweet Content' (MS)	Voice, pno	R. Greene	Unpublished
1920	114	*Blessed Are the Dead*: a motet	SATB	Book of Common Prayer	Novello (1995)
1920	115	'The Chosen Tune' (arr. HH 75ii)	Pno		Thames (1997)
1920	116	'Goddess of Night'	Voice, pno	F. W. Harvey	B. & H. (1921)
1920	117	'Gogy-O'-Gay': two-part song	Treble voices, pno	Trad.	AHC (1920)
1920	118	'A Golden Lullaby': two-part song	Treble voices, pno	T. Dekker	Edward Arnold (1920)
1920	119	'John Helps' – missing	Voice, pno	F. W. Harvey	Unpublished
1920	120	'The Little Boy Lost'	Voice, pno	W. Blake	Oxford University Press (1920)
1920	121	'O Garlands, Hanging by the Door' (MS)	Voice, pno	A. Strettell	Unpublished
1920	122	'O My Deir Heart'	Voice, pno	J. James	WR (1923)
1920	123	Suite for Piano, *Once upon a Time*	Pno		S&B (1920)

1920	124	*Sing Lullaby*: carol-anthem	SATB	F. W. Harvey	S&B (1920)
1922	125	*Procession*, Op. 36 (arr. HH 99iii)	Orchestra		AHC (1924)
1922	126	*Sine nomine: A Phantasy*, Op. 37	Sop., Ten., SATB, Orchestra		G&T (1922); Novello (1992)
1922	127	'The Wonderful Derby Ram'	Voices, pno	Anon.	Edward Arnold (1926)
1922–8	128	'Gadabout'	Pno		Oxford University Press (1929)
1923	129	'All in This Pleasant Evening'	Voices, pno	Anon.	H. F. W. Deane (1923)
1923	130	'Creep afore Ye Gang'	SATB	J. Ballantine	B. & H. (1924)
1923	131	'Lord, who Createdst Man'	Voices, pno	G. Herbert	Oxford University Press (1924)
1923	132	'My Master Hath a Garden'	Treble voices, pno	Anon.	Oxford University Press (1923)
1923	133	'Old Meg'	Voice, pno	W. W. Gibson	Oxford University Press (1928)
1923	134	*Pastoral Rhapsody*, Op. 38 (MS)	Orchestra		Unpublished
1923	135	'The Shadows': part-song	SATB	S. O'Sullivan	B. & H. (1924)
1923	136	Sonata no. 3, Op. 38	Vln, pno		Oxford University Press (1925)

Year	HH no.	Title	Instruments	Texts (if applicable)	Publisher
1923	137	'Spanish Lullaby'	Voices, pno	Anon.	H. F. W. Deane (1923)
1924	138	'Bells': two part song	SS, pno	Anon.	Augener (1924)
1924	139	'First in the Garden': two-part song	Voices, pno	Anon.	Oxford University Press (1924)
1924	140	'Holly Song'	Voices, pno	Anon.	Oxford University Press (1924)
1924	141	'Irish Wren Song': two-part song	SS, pno	Anon.	B. & H. (1924)
1924	142	'A Mersey Tune'	Pno		*Liverpool Post and Mercury* (1925)
1924	143	'Mother Mother'	Voices, pno	Anon.	Augener (1924)
1924	144	'Robin Hood's Song': two-part song	Treble voices, pno	A. Munday	Cramer (1924)
1924	145	Morning Service	Voices, org.	Book of Common Prayer	Oxford University Press (1925)
1924	146	Communion Service	Voices, org.	Book of Common Prayer	Oxford University Press (1925)
1924	147	Evening Service	Voices, org.	Book of Common Prayer	Oxford University Press (1925)
1924	148	*Te Deum*	Voices, org.	Book of Common Prayer	Oxford University Press (1925)
1924	149	'Sing Ivy': two-part song	Voices, pno	Anon.	Oxford University Press (1924)

1924	150	'Singe Lully By, Lully': two-part song	Voices, pno	Anon.	Augener (1924)
1924	151	'Swedish May Song': two-part song	Voices, pno	Anon.	Oxford University Press (1924)
1925	152	Concerto no. 2, Op. 39	Pno, orchestra		Novello (2001)
1925	153	'A Country Tune'	Vln, pno		ABRSM (1925)
1925	154	'A Croon'	Vln, pno		ABRSM (1925)
1925	155	'The Days Are Clear'	Voices, pno	C. Rossetti	A. & C. Black (1925)
1925	156	'Eight O'Clock the Postman's Knock'	Voices, pno	C. Rossetti	A. & C. Black (1925)
1925	157	'Mother Shake the Cherry Tree'	Voices, pno	C. Rossetti	A. & C. Black (1925)
1925	158	'My Eyes for Beauty Pine'	SATB, org.	R. Bridges	Oxford University Press (1928)
1925	159	*Paradise Rondel* (MS)	Orchestra		Unpublished
1925	160	'St Briavels': hymn tune ('My God, I Thank Thee who Hast Made the Earth So Bright')	Voices, org.	A. A. Proctor	*Songs of Praise* (Oxford University Press, 1925)
1925	161	'When First Thine Eies Unveil'	Ten., SATB, org.	H. Vaughan	Oxford University Press (1927)
1926	162	*Two Pieces* (i) 'Slow Dance' (ii) 'Cobler's Hornpipe'	Pno		Oxford University Press (1927)
1926	163	*The Trial of Jesus*: incidental music to the play by John Masefield (MS)	SATB, strings, pno	John Masefield	Unpublished
1927	164	'Come Sing and Dance'	Voice, pno	Anon.	Oxford University Press (1927)

Year	HH no.	Title	Instruments	Texts (if applicable)	Publisher
1927	165	*Lambert's Clavichord*, Op. 41 (i) 'Lambert's Fireside' (ii) 'Fellowes' Delight' (iii) 'Hughes' Ballet' (iv) 'Wortham's Ground' (v) 'Sargent's Fantastic Sprite' (vi) 'Foss's Dump' (vii) 'My Lord Sandwich's Dreame' (viii) 'Samuel's Air' (ix) 'De la Mare's Pavane' (x) 'Sir Hugh's Galliard' (xi) 'HH His Fancy' (xii) 'Sir Richard's Toye'	Clav.		Oxford University Press (1928)
1927	166	Lento, assai espressivo (MS)	Vln, pno		Unpublished
1927	167	'The Saylor's Song': Two-Part Song	Voices, pno	Anon.	Edward Arnold (1928)
1927	168	'Slow Air'	Vln, pno		ABRSM (1927)
1927	169	'Tune Thy Music'	Voices, pno	T. Campion	Edward Arnold (1928)
1928	170	*Country Pageant*: four short pieces for piano (i) 'Merry Andrew's Procession' (ii) 'Kings and Queens' (iii) 'There Was a Most Beautiful Lady' (iv) 'The Mummers' Dance'	Pno		Oxford University Press (1928)

Year	No.	Title	Forces	Text	Publisher
1928	171	'Good Counsel'	Voices, pno	G. Chaucer	WR (1929)
1928	172	*In Green Ways*, Op. 43 (all but (ii) are from HH 67) (i) 'Under the Greenwood Tree' (ii) 'The Goat Paths' (iii) 'Merry Margaret' (iv) 'Wanderer's Night Song' (v) 'On the Merry First of May'	High voice, orchestra (or pno)	(i) W. Shakespeare (ii) J. Stephens (iii) J. Skelton (iv) J. W. Goethe, trans. Howells (v) H. B. Parker	Oxford University Press (1928)
1928	173	*A Little Book of Dances* (i) Minuet (ii) Gavotte (iii) Pavane (iv) Galliard (v) Rigadoon (vi) Jig	Pno		Oxford University Press (1928)
1929	174	*Lambert's Clavichord*: three transcriptions (See HH 165vii, ix, x) (i) 'My Lord Sandwich's Dreame' (ii) 'De la Mare's Pavane' (iii) 'Sir Hugh's Galliard'	Vcl., pno		Oxford University Press (1929)
1929	175	*Mother's Here*: incidental music for the play by Claude Aveling (missing)			Unpublished

Year	HH no.	Title	Instruments	Texts (if applicable)	Publisher
1929	176	Two Afrikaans Songs (i) 'Eensaamheid' [My Little Fire and I Are Waiting'] (ii) 'Vryheidsgees' ['Hither to Me, I Shall Lead You']	Voice, pno	F. E. Celliers	Department of Music, University of Pretoria (1999)
1930	177	'Father of Men': a hymn for Charterhouse (MS)	Voices, pno	H. C. Shuttleworth	Unpublished
1930	178	'Michael': hymn tune ('All My Hope on God Is Founded')	Voices, pno	R. Bridges	The Clarendon Hymn Book (Oxford University Press, 1936)
1930	179	'A Sailor Tune'	Pno		J. B. Cramer (1930)
1931	180	'Delicates So Dainty'	Voices, pno	Anon.	Edward Arnold (1932)
1931	181	[Three Folk-Songs] (arr. Howells) (i) 'I Will Give My Love an Apple' (ii) 'The Brisk Young Widow' (iii) 'Cendrillon' (French text) (MS)	Voice, pno	Anon.	(i) and (ii) Thames (1996) (iii) unpublished
1931	182	'Severn': hymn tune ('My God I Thank Thee who Hast Made the Earth so Bright') (see HH 160)	Voices, pno	A. A. Proctor	Songs of Praise (Oxford University Press, 1931)
1931	183	'Sweet Content'	Voices, pno	R. Greene	Edward Arnold (1932)

1931	184	'Tanz's Music': a contribution to *A Grand Private Full Dress Concert Rehearsal Performance*, RCM (1931) (missing)			Unpublished
1931–51	185	'A Maid Peerless' (rev. 1951)	SSAA, small orchestra	Anon.	Edward Arnold (1951)
1932	186	*Hymnus circa exsequias defuncti* (MS – incomplete)	SATB, org.	Aurelius Prudentius Clemens	Unpublished
1932	187	'O Mensch bewein dein Sünde gross' (J. S. Bach, arr. Howells)	Pno		Oxford University Press (1932)
1932	188	Requiem	SATB	Book of Common Prayer, Latin Requiem Mass	Novello (1981)
1932	189	Sonata no. 2	Org.		Novello (1934)
1933	190	'Bunches of Grapes'	Voices, pno	W. de la Mare	Edward Arnold (1933)
1933	191	'Flood'	Voice, pno	J. Joyce	Oxford University Press (1933)
1933	192	*A Kent Yeoman's Wooing Song*: a cantata	Sop., bar, SATB, orchestra	T. Vautor, T. Ravenscroft	Novello (1953)
1933	193	*Penguinski*: ballet music for orchestra	Orchestra		Novello (2000)
1933	194	'To Music Bent': two-part song	Treble voices, pno	T. Campion	Edward Arnold (1933)

Year	HH no.	Title	Instruments	Texts (if applicable)	Publisher
1934	195	'Lost Love'	Voice, pno	Chinese poem, trans. C. Bax	WR (1934)
1934	196	*Paegentry*: a suite for brass band (i) 'King's Herald' (ii) 'Cortege' (iii) 'Jousts'	Brass band		R. Smith (1934)
1934	197	'Triumph Tune'	Pno		Curwen (1938)
1935	198	Evening Service	TTBB, org.	Book of Common Prayer	Oxford University Press (1939) (version for ATB by J Buttrey (Oxford University Press, 1981))
1935	199	'Minuet for Ursula' (MS)	Pno		Unpublished
1935	200	*Sea Urchins*: a song-set for children's voices (i) 'Overture' (ii) 'Happy Street' (iii) 'Many Rainbows' (iv) 'The Sea-Side Landlady' (v) 'Granny Sits beside the Sea' (vi) 'The Barrel-Organ' (vii) 'A Seaside Lullaby' (viii) 'The Lair on the Cliff'	Voices, pno	G. Balcomb	S&B (1935)

1935		(ix) 'Lindy's Ballet Shoes'			
1935		(x) 'The Musical Train'			
1936		(xi) 'The Open Air'			
1937	201	'A Song of Welcome'	Voices, pno	F. W. Harvey	S&B (1935)
1935	202	Toccata (MS)	Pno		Unpublished
1936	203	'Lethe' (MS)	Ten. (or sop.), pno	H. Doolittle	Unpublished
1937	204	'David': hymn tune ('Hills of the North, Rejoice') (MS)	Voices, pno	C. E. Oakley	Unpublished
1937	205	Fantasia	Vcl, orchestra		Novello (1988)
1937	206	Threnody (orch. C. Palmer)	Vcl, orchestra		Novello (1992)
1937	207	[Finale] (MS – incomplete)	Vcl, orchestra		Unpublished
1937	208	Hunsdon House (MS)	Pno, string quartet		Unpublished
1937	209	Hymn tune ('Immortal, Invisible, God Only Wise') (MS – incomplete)	Voices, org.	W. C. Smith	Unpublished
1937	210	Hymn tune ('Jesu, Lover of My Soul') (MS – incomplete)	Voices, org.	C. Wesley	Unpublished
1937	211	King's Herald (arr. HH 196i]	Orchestra		Novello (2000)
1937	212	'The Old Mole': folk-tune arr. Howells (MS)	Pno, strings		Unpublished
1937	213	Specimen Sight-Reading Pieces	Pno		ABRSM (1937)
1937	214	'Twigworth': hymn tune ('God Is Love, Let Heav'n Adore Him)	Voices, org.	T. Rees	Hymns for Church and School (Novello, 1962)

Year	HH no.	Title	Instruments	Texts (if applicable)	Publisher
1938	215	Concerto for String Orchestra	String orchestra		B. & H. (1939)
1938	216	'Piping Down the Valleys Wild': two-part song	Voices, pno	W. Blake	B. & H. (1939)
1938	217	'Promenade for Boys'	Pno		Curwen (1938)
1938	218	'Promenade for Girls'	Pno		Curwen (1938)
1938–9	219	*Three Psalm-Preludes* (Set 2) (i) Psalm 130:1 (ii) Psalm 139:11 (iii) Psalm 33:3	Org.		Novello (1940)
1938–50	220	*Hymnus paradisi*	Sop., Ten., SATB, orchestra	Latin Requiem Mass, Psalms, Book of Common Prayer, Salisbury Diurnal	Novello (1950)
1939	221	'The History of an Afternoon – By and Large and in the Round at 49 up Amersham Hill': round for three voices	Three voices	Anon.	Novello (1991)
1939	222	Minuet (MS)	Pno		Unpublished
1939	223	'A New Year Carol': two-part song	Voices, pno	Anon.	B. & H. (1939)
1939	224	Polka	Pno, pno		Novello (1952)
1939	225	'Shadow March': two-part song	Treble voices, pno	R. L. Stevenson	H. F. W. Deane (1939)

1939–45	226	*Six Pieces for Organ* (i) 'Preludio "sine nomine"' (1940) (ii) 'Saraband (for the Morning of Easter)' (1940) (iii) 'Master Tallis's Testament' (1940) (iv) 'Fugue, Chorale and Epilogue' (1939) (v) 'Saraband (*in modo elegiaco*)' (1945) (vi) 'Paean' (1940)	Org.		Novello (1953)
1940	227	*Folk Tune Set* (MS) (i) 'Triumph Tune' (see HH 197) (ii) 'St Louis of France's Tune' (iii) 'The Old Mole' (see HH 212)	Small orchestra		Unpublished
1940	228	'Puck's Minuet' (arr. HH 83) (MS)	Pno, pno		Unpublished
1940	229	Suite for String Orchestra (missing)	String orchestra		Unpublished
1941	230	*Four Anthems* (i) 'O Pray for the Peace of Jerusalem' (ii) 'We Have Heard with Our Ears' (iii) 'Like as the Hart Desireth the Waterbrooks' (iv) 'Let God Arise'	SATB, org.	Psalms	Oxford University Press (1943)
1941	231	'Great Is the Lord' (MS)	SATB, Org.	Psalms	Unpublished
1941	232	'Ponder My Words, O Lord' (missing)	SATB, Org.	Psalms	Unpublished
1941	233	*Intrata* (no. 2)	Org.		Novello (1987)

Year	HH no.	Title	Instruments	Texts (if applicable)	Publisher
1941	234	Evening Service	Men's voices, Org.	Book of Common Prayer	Church Music Society (1995)
1941	235	'Triumph Tune' (see HH 197) (MS)	Pno, pno		Unpublished
1941–5	236	'Remember O Thou Man' (MS)	SATB	T. Ravenscroft	Unpublished
1941–61	237	Howells' Clavichord [Book 1] (i) 'Goff's Fireside' (for Thomas Goff) (ii) 'Patrick's Siciliano' (for Patrick Hadley) (iii) 'Jacob's Brawl' (for Gordon Jacob) (iv) 'Dart's Saraband' (for Thurston Dart) (v) 'Arnold's Antic' (for Malcolm Arnold) (vi) 'Andrews' Air' (for H. K. Andrews) (vii) 'Boult's Brangill' (for Sir Adrian Boult) (viii) 'Rubbra's Soliloquy' (for Edmund Rubbra) (ix) 'Newman's Flight' (for Max Newman, F.R.S.) (x) 'Dyson's Delight' (for Sir George Dyson) [Book 2] (xi) 'E. B.'s Fanfarando' (for Sir Ernest Bullock) (xii) 'Ralph's Pavane' (for Ralph Vaughan Williams)	Clav.		Novello (1961) (in two books)

Year	No.	Title	Forces	Text	Publication
		(xiii) 'Ralph's Galliard' (for Vaughan Williams)			
		(xiv) 'Finzi's Rest' (for Gerald Finzi)			
		(xv) 'Berkeley's Hunt' (for Lennox Berkeley)			
		(xvi) 'Malcolm's Vision' (for George Malcolm)			
		(xvii) 'Bliss's Ballet' (for Sir Arthur Bliss)			
		(xviii) 'Julian's Dream' (for Julian Bream)			
		(xix) 'Jacques's Mask' (for Reginald Jacques)			
		(xx) 'Walton's Toye' (for Sir William Walton)			
1942	238	'O Mortal Man Remember Well' (Sussex mummers' carol, arr. Howells)	Voices, strings, org.	Trad.	Novello (1994)
1942	239	Sonata	Ob., pno		Novello (1987)
1942	240	First Suite	String orchestra		Novello (hire only)
1942	241	Second Suite (missing)	String orchestra		Unpublished
1942–5	242	Concerto for Organ and Strings (MS – incomplete)	Org., strings		Unpublished
1943	243	'Fanfare for Schools' (MS)	Brass, timp., strings		Unpublished
1944	244	'God is Gone up with a Merry Noise'	SATB, org. (or strings)	Psalms	Novello (1958)
1944	245	*Te Deum* and *Jubilate* (*Collegium regale*)	SATB, org.	Book of Common Prayer	Novello (1950)
1945	246	Evening Service (*Collegium regale*)	SATB, org.	Book of Common Prayer	Novello (1947)

Year	HH no.	Title	Instruments	Texts (if applicable)	Publisher
1945	247	Minuet ('Grace for a Fresh Egg')	Bsn., pno		Novello (1984)
1945	248	*Six Short Pieces* (MS – incomplete) (i) Tranquillo, ma con moto (ii) [MS missing] (iii) Quasi lento (iv) Allegro impetuoso (see HH 363iv) (v) [MS missing] (vi) Untitled (see HH 342)	Org.		(i), (iv) Novello (1987)
1946	249	*Gloucester Service*	SATB, org.	Book of Common Prayer	Novello (1947)
1946	250	'A Near-Minuet'	Cl., pno		Novello (1992)
1946	251	Sonata	Cl., pno		B. & H. (1954)
1946	252	*Te Deum* and *Benedictus* for Christ Church Cathedral, Canterbury.	SATB, org.	Book of Common Prayer	Novello (1951)
1947–9	253	*New College Service*	SATB, org.	Book of Common Prayer	Novello (1953)
1948	254	'The Key of the Kingdom': two-part song	SS, pno	W. de la Mare	Edward Arnold (1948)
1948	255	*Music for a Prince* (MS) (reworking of HH 42iv, ii) (i) 'Corydon's Dance' (ii) 'Scherzo in Arden'	Orchestra		Unpublished
1948	256	*Where Wast Thou?*: Motet for Canterbury	Bar, SATB, org.	Job, Genesis, Psalms	Novello (1983)

Year	No.	Title	Instrumentation	Text/Source	Publication
1949	257	'King of Glory'	SATB, org.	G. Herbert	Novello (1949)
1949	258	Two pieces (MS) (i) 'My Lady Harewood's Pavane' (ii) 'My Lord Harewood's Galliard'	Clav.		Unpublished
1950s	259	Allegro inquieto (MS – incomplete)	Vln, pno		Unpublished
1950s	260	[Service in G] (i) *Te Deum*, Benedictus and *Jubilate* in G. (ii) [Communion service in G] (MS – incomplete)	SATB, org.	Book of Common Prayer	(i) Novello (2002) (ii) Unpublished
1950	261	'Long, Long Ago': carol-anthem	SATB	J. Buxton	Novello (1951)
1950	262	'Walking in the Snow': part-song	SATB	J. Buxton	Novello (1951)
1951	263	*Worcester Service*	SATB, org.	Book of Common Prayer	Novello (1953)
1951	264	*St Paul's Service*	SATB, org.	Book of Common Prayer	Novello (1954)
1951	265	Suite for Pipes (missing)	Recorders		Unpublished
1952	266	Alla menuetto (MS)	Pno		Unpublished
1952	267	'Behold O God Our Defender'	SATB, org. (or orchestra)	Psalms	Novello (1953)
1952	268	'Siciliano for a High Ceremony'	Org.		Novello (1957)
1952	269	*Te Deum* and Benedictus for St George's Chapel, Windsor	SATB, org.	Book of Common Prayer	Novello (1952)

Year	HH no.	Title	Instruments	Texts (if applicable)	Publisher
1952	270	'A Tune Written for Kerenski in the 1917 Russian Revolution' (MS – incomplete)	Pno		Unpublished
1953	271	*Cantata for the Waking of Lazarus* (missing)		V. Watkins	Unpublished
1953	272	'Inheritance' (from *A Garland for the Queen*)	SSAATTBB	W. de la Mare	Novello (1953)
1954	273	'Four Horses'	Voices, pno	Anon.	Edward Arnold (1954)
1954	274	'The House of the Mind'	SATB, org. (or strings)	J. Beaumont	Novello (1954)
1954	275	*Missa sabrinensis*	SATB soli, SATB, orchestra	Latin Mass	Novello (1954)
1955	276	*An English Mass*	SATB, orchestra	Book of Common Prayer	Novello (1956)
1955	277	*Evening Service in B minor*	SATB, org.	Book of Common Prayer	Novello (1956)
1956	278	'Finzi: His Rest' (MS) (different piece from HH 237xiv)	Clav.		Unpublished
1956	279	*The Office of Holy Communion* (*Collegium regale*)	SATB, org.	Book of Common Prayer	Novello (1957)
1957	280	'I Mun Be Married a Sunday' (MS)	Voices, pno	N. Udall	Unpublished
1957	281	*Westminster Service*	SATB, org.	Book of Common Prayer	Novello (1957)

1957	282	St John's College Service	SATB, org.	Book of Common Prayer	Novello (1958)
1957	283	'New Brooms' (MS)	Voices, pno	R. Wilson	Unpublished
1957	284	'Pink Almond': two-part song	Voices, pno	K. Tynan	Edward Arnold (1958)
1957	285	'The Scribe'	SATB	W. de la Mare	Oxford University Press (1994)
1958	286	'A Christmas Carol'	Voices, pno	G. Wither	Edward Arnold (1958)
1958	287	Missa aedis Christi	SATB	Book of Common Prayer	Novello (1961)
1958	288	Prelude: 'De profundis'	Org.		Novello (1983)
1958	289	Rhapsody no. 4, 'bene psallite in vociferatione'	Org.		Novello (1983)
1958	290	'Siciliana for Saint's Dom' (MS)	Pno		Unpublished
1959	291	'Aubade for a Wedding' ('Levavi oculos meos')	S voices, org.	Psalms	Novello (2000)
1959	292	Two Pieces (i) 'Dalby's Fancy' (ii) 'Dalby's Toccata'	Org. (manuals only)		Novello (1982)
1959	293	'Musica sine nomine'	Pno		Thames (1997)
1959	294	[two unidentified songs for Richard Lewis] (missing)	Voice, pno		Unpublished
1950s	295	Two Pieces (MS)	Fl., Vln.		Unpublished

Year	HH no.	Title	Instruments	Texts (if applicable)	Publisher
1950	296	*A Hymn for St Cecilia*	SATB, org.	U. Vaughan Williams	Novello (1961)
1950	297	*Three Figures: A Triptych for Brass Band* (i) 'Cope's Challenge' (ii) 'Iles's Interlude' (iii) 'Rimmer's Race'	Brass band		Weinberger (1960)
1961	298	'Coventry Antiphon'	SATB, org.	Isaiah, Haggai	Unpublished
1961	299	*A Sequence for St Michael*	SATB, org.	Alcuin, trans. H Waddell	Novello (1961)
1962	300	Hymn tune ('Love Divine, All Loves Excelling')	Voices, org.	C. Wesley	Church Music Society (1999)
1962	301	'Newnham': hymn tune ('Lord Christ, When First Thou Cam'st to Men')	Voices, org.	W. Russell Bowie	*Hymns for Church and School* (Novello,1962)
1962	302	'Salisbury': hymn tune ('Holy Spirit, Ever Dwelling')	Voices, org.	T. Rees	*Hymns for Church and School* (Novello, 1962)
1962	303	'Sancta civitas': hymn tune ('O Holy City Seen of John')	Voices, org.	W. Russell Bowie	*Hymns for Church and School* (Novello, 1962)
1963	304	[French *chanson* : 'Du temps perdu] (missing)	Pno		Unpublished
1964	305	Pavane and Galliard (MS)	Pno		Unpublished
1964	306	'The Summer Is Coming'	SATB	B. Guinness	Novello (1965)

Year	No.	Title	Forces	Text	Publisher
1964	307	*Take Him, Earth, for Cherishing*	SATB	Aurelius Prudentius Clemens, trans. H Waddell	H. W. Gray (1964)
1965	308	'God Be in My Head'	SATB	Pynson's *Horae* (1514)	Novello (2011)
1965	309	*Stabat mater*	Ten., SATB, orchestra	J. Da Todi	Novello (1964)
1965	310	*Te Deum* (for St Mary Redcliffe, Bristol)	SATB, org.	Book of Common Prayer	Novello (1965)
1966	311	'Erwin': hymn tune ('Lord by Whose Breath All Souls and Seeds Are Living')	Voices, org.	A. Young	Cambridge University Press (1967)
1966	312	*Sarum Service*	SATB, org.	Book of Common Prayer	Novello (1968)
1966	313	*Te Deum laudamus* (for Searle Wright)	SATB, org.	Book of Common Prayer	Novello (1992)
1967	314	'Benedictus es, Domine' ('Song of the Three')	SATB, org.	'Song of the Three' (Daniel: Apocrypha)	Novello (1968)
1967	315	'Et nunc et semper' (quasi menuetto) (MS)	Pno		Unpublished
1967	316	*Jubilate Deo* for the Chapel Royal (St Peter ad Vincula). HM Tower of London	SATB, org.	Book of Common Prayer	Novello (1967)
1967	317	*Chichester Service*	SATB, org.	Book of Common Prayer	Novello (1968)
1967	318	Preces and Responses	SATB	Book of Common Prayer	Novello (1970)

Year	HH no.	Title	Instruments	Texts (if applicable)	Publisher
1967	319	*Winchester Service*	SATB, org.	Book of Common Prayer	Novello (1968)
1967–8	320	*St Augustine's Service*	SATB, org.	Book of Common Prayer	Novello (1983)
1967–73	321	*Petrus Suite* (MS)	Pno		Unpublished
1968	322	*The Coventry Mass*	SATB, org.	Book of Common Prayer	Novello (1969)
1968	323	'In manus tuas': hymn tune ('This World, My God, Is Held within Your Hand')	Voices, org.	H. Swanston	Faber (1968)
1968	324	'Norfolk': hymn tune ('With Wonder, Lord, We See Your Works')	Voices, org.	B. Foley	Faber (1968)
1968	325	'One Thing Have I Desired'	SATB	Psalms	Novello (1968)
1969	326	'Flourish for a Bidding'	Org.		Novello (1987)
1969	327	*Hereford Service*	SATB, org.	Book of Common Prayer	Novello (1972)
1970	328	'H-plus-H Gavotte' (MS)	Pno		Unpublished
1970	329	'Kensington': hymn tune ('To the Name of Our Salvation')	Voices, org.	J. M. Neale	Novello (1970)
1970	330	*Magdalen College Service*	SATB, org.	Book of Common Prayer	Novello (1972)
1970	331	'"Michael": A Fanfare Setting' (arr. C Palmer) (see HH 178)	Voices, org. Orchestra	R. Bridges	Novello (1992)

1970	332	'Thee Will I Love'	SATB, org.	R. Bridges	Novello (1970)
1971	333	Sonatina	Pno		ABRSM (1976)
1971–2	334	Partita	Org.		Novello (1972)
1972	335	[Three Double Chants] (MS) (i) in C♯ minor (ii) in A minor (iii) in A major	Voices		Unpublished
1972	336	'Come, My Soul'	SATB	J. Newton	Oxford University Press (1978)
1972	337	A Grace for William Walton [A Grace for 10 Downing Street]	SATB	R. Armstrong	Novello (1992)
1972	338	'Now Abideth Faith, Hope and Charity'	SATB, org.	1 Corinthians	Novello (1989)
1972	339	'Runge: Minuet' (missing)	Pno		Unpublished
1973	340	York Service	SATB, org.	Book of Common Prayer	Novello (1980)
1974	341	[Four Double Chants] (MS) (i) in F♯ minor (ii) in G minor (iii) in G minor (iv) in E♭ major	Voices		Unpublished
1974	342	'Epilogue' (see HH 363vi)	Org.		Banks Music (1982)
1974	343	Exultate Deo	SATB, org.	Psalms	Oxford University Press (1977)

Year	HH no.	Title	Instruments	Texts (if applicable)	Publisher
1974	344	*Te Deum* for the Cathedrals of Bradford, Wakefield and Sheffield	SATB, org.	Book of Common Prayer	Church Music Society (2000)
1975	345	*Dallas Canticles*	SATB, org.	Book of Common Prayer	Calvary Press (1975)
1975	346	[Sonata for Flute and Piano] (MS – incomplete)	Fl., pno		Unpublished
1975–6	347	*Antiphon*	SATB	G. Herbert	Oxford University Press (1978)
1975–6	348	*Sweetest of Sweets*	SATB	G. Herbert	Oxford University Press (1978)
1976	349	*The Fear of the Lord*	SATB, org.	Ecclesiasticus	Oxford University Press (1977)
1977	350	'Fanfare to Lead into the National Anthem' (MS)	Brass, perc., org.		Unpublished
1977	351	'Hills of the North'	Girls' voices, org.	C. E. Oakley	Bristol Cathedral Publications (2000)
1977	352	'I Love All Beauteous Things'	SATB, org.	R. Bridges	Novello (1984)
1977	353	'St Louis Comes to Clifton'	Org.		Novello (1987)
1977	354	*Te Deum* (*Collegium regale*) (MS) (see HH 245)	SATB, orchestra	Book of Common Prayer	Unpublished
1977	355	*Te Deum laudamus* for Washington Cathedral (ed. J. Buttrey)	SATB, org.	Book of Common Prayer	Novello (1991)

Year	No.	Title	Forces	Text	Publisher
1977	356	'Tryste Noel'	SATB, org.	L. I. Gurney	Oxford University Press (1978)
1978	357	'I Would Be True'	SATB, org.	H. A. Walter	Addington Press (1978)
1970s	358	Rhapsody no. 5 (missing)	Org.		Unpublished
1970s	359	'Scherzo for Michael Smythe' (missing)	Org.		Unpublished
Undated	360	Allegro scherzando	Org.		Novello (1987)
Undated	361	[Untitled organ piece in B Dorian Published as 'Aria'	Org.		Novello (1987)
Undated	362	Chorale	Org.		Novello (1987)
Undated	363	[For inclusion in the *Five Short Pieces for Organ*] Quasi lento: teneramente. Incomplete organ piece; published in a completion by Robin Wells	Org.		Novello (1987)
Undated	364	[Two hymns] (MS – incomplete) (i) 'The King of Love My Shepherd Is' (ii) 'Fight the Good Fight'	Voices, org.	(i) H. W. Baker (ii) J. S. B. Monsell	Unpublished
Undated	365	Hymn tune ('Jesu, the Very Thought Is Sweet') (MS)	Voices, org.	J. M. Neale	Unpublished
Undated	366	Hymn tune ('Jesu, Guide Our Way') (MS)	Voices, org.	A. T. Russell	Unpublished
Undated	367	Hymn tune ('Blessed City, Heavenly Salem') (MS)	Voices, org.	J. M. Neale	Unpublished
Non-surviving	368	'The Blossom'			

Year	HH no.	Title	Instruments	Texts (if applicable)	Publisher
Non-surviving	369	'Devon to Me!'		J. Galsworthy	
Non-surviving	370	'Faces in the Night'			
Non-surviving	371	'Ghoul Care'		R. Hodgson	
Non-surviving	372	'The Huxton'			
Non-surviving	373	'Infant Joy'		W. Blake	
Non-surviving	374	'Jack Pedlar'			
Non-surviving	375	'O Maiden Maiden!' (in German)			
Non-surviving	376	'Red Roses'			
Non-surviving	377	'Song of the Apple'			
Non-surviving	378	''Tis Not in Seeking'			
Non-surviving	379	'The Village'			
Non-surviving	380	'A Wedding Song'			
Non-surviving	381	'The White Wave'			

ABRSM Associated Board of the Royal Schools of Music
AHC Ascherberg
B&H Boosey & Hawkes
G&T Goodwin & Tabb
MS Manuscript
S&B Stainer & Bell
WR Winthrop Rogers, Hopwood & Crew

Bibliography

Adams, Byron, 'Review of Pamela Blevins' *Ivor Gurney and Marion Scott: Song of Pain and Beauty*', *Music and Letters*, 92 (2011), 673–4

Andrews, Paul, 'Herbert Howells: A Documentary and Bibliographical Study', Ph.D. thesis, 2 vols. (University of Wales, Aberystwyth, 1999)

—'Howells, Herbert (Norman)', in Stanley Sadie and John Tyrell, eds, *The New Grove Dictionary of Music and Musicians*, 2nd edn (London, 2001), Vol. XI, 771

—Liner notes to Herbert Howells, choral music, Rodolfus Choir, Ralph Allwood (conductor), audio CD (Signum Classics, 2009), SIGCD 190

—Liner notes to Herbert Howells, *The Complete Morning and Evening Canticles of Herbert Howells*, Vol. I, audio CD (Priory Records, 2000), PRCD 745

—Liner notes to Herbert Howells, *The Complete Morning and Evening Canticles of Herbert Howells*, Vol. III, audio CD (Priory Records, 2000), PRCD 782

Ariès, Philippe, *The Hour of Our Death*, trans. Helen Weaver (Oxford and New York, 1991)

Banfield, Stephen, *Sensibility and English Song* (Cambridge, 1985)

Bax, Arnold, *Farewell My Youth* (London, 1943)

Benjamin, Arthur, 'A Student in Kensington', *Music and Letters*, 31 (1950), 196–207

Bent, Ian D., 'Hermeneutics', in Stanley Sadie and John Tyrell, eds, *The New Grove Dictionary of Music and Musicians*, 2nd edn (London, 2001), Vol. XI, 418–26

Bett, R.W., ed., *Tribute to Walter de la Mare on His 75th Birthday* (London: Faber and Faber, 1948)

Bickley, Nora, ed., *Letters to and from Joseph Joachim* (London, 1914), 428

Bliss, Arthur, *As I Remember* (London, 1970)

Bowlby, John, *Loss: Sadness and Depression* (New York, 1980)

Brown, A. Peter, *The Symphonic Repertoire, Vol. 3b* (Indiana, 2002)

Butterworth, Neil, *The American Symphony* (Aldershot, 1998)

Buttrey, John, 'The Washington Canticles: Herbert Howells's Last Service', *Musical Times* (1991), 363–5

Buxton, John, *Such Liberty* (London, 1944)

Caldwell, John, *The Oxford History of English Music*, 2 vols. (Oxford, 1991, 1999)

Caswall, Edward, trans., *Lyra catholica: Containing All the Breviary and Missal Hymns with Others from Various Sources* (London, 1849)

Clark, Relf, *Elgar and the Three Cathedral Organists* (Oxford, 2002)

Clinch, Jonathan, 'Beauty Springeth Out of Naught: Interpreting the Church Music of Herbert Howells', *British Postgraduate Musicology*, 11 (2011), available online at www.bpmonline.org.uk/bpm11/

Cobbett, W.W., 'The Beginnings of British Chamber Music', *The Music Student*, 7 (1915): *Chamber Music Supplement*, 13, 49–51

—'Chamber Music Notes', *The Music Student*, 11 (1918), 98

—'Chamber Music Notes', *The Music Student*, 12 (1920), 530

—'Obiter dicta', *The Music Student*, 8 (1916): *Chamber Music Supplement*, 18, 34

Collini, Stefan, *Public Moralists: Political Thought and Intellectual Life in Britain, 1850–1930* (Oxford, 1991)

Cone, Edward, *The Composer's Voice* (Berkeley, 1974)

Crocker, Richard L., 'Melisma', in Stanley Sadie and John Tyrrell, eds, *The New Grove Dictionary of Music and Musicians*, 2nd edn (London, 2001), Vol. XVI, 344–6

Davies, Douglas J., *Death, Ritual and Belief* (London, 1997)

Davies, Douglas J. and Park, Chang-Won, eds, *Emotion, Identity & Death: Mortality across Disciplines* (Farnham, 2012)

Dibble, Jeremy, *Charles Villiers Stanford: Man and Musician* (Oxford, 2002)

Didion, Joan, *Blue Nights* (New York, 2011)

Dunhill, Thomas, 'Charles Villiers Stanford: Some Aspects of His Life and Works', *Proceedings of the Royal Musical Association*, 53 (1927–8), 42–65

Dunhill, Thomas, 'Francis Purcell Warren 1895–1916', *Music and Letters*, 7 (1926), 358–9

Dyson, George, 'Charles Villiers Stanford by Some of His Pupils', *Music and Letters*, 5 (1924), 196–8

—*The New Music* (London, 1924)

Eggar, Katharine, 'An English Composer: Herbert Howells', *The Music Teacher*, 15 (1922), 129–31

—'Herbert Howells on Modern Composition', *The Music Teacher*, 15 (1923), 214–15

Esty, Jed, *A Shrinking Island: Modernism and National Culture in England* (Princeton, 2004)

Evans, Edwin, 'Herbert Howells (Modern British Composers, No. 8)', *Musical Times*, 61 (1920), 87–91, 156–9

Fellowes, Edmund, *English Cathedral Music* (London, 1969)

Finzi, Gerald, 'Herbert Howells', *Musical Times*, 95 (1954), 180–3

Foreman, Lewis, ed., *From Parry to Britten: British Music in Letters* (London, 1987)

Foss, Hubert J., 'Herbert Howells: A Brief Survey of His Music', *Musical Times*, 71 (1930), 113–16

Fuller Maitland, J.A., 'Fancy, Fantasia, or Phantasy', in J.A. Fuller Maitland, ed., *Grove's Dictionary of Music and Musicians* (London, 1906–10), Vol. V, 638

—'Stanford, Sir Charles Villiers', in H.C. Colles, ed., *Grove's Dictionary of Music and Musicians*, 3rd edn (London, 1928), 118–22

Fussell, Paul, *The Great War and Modern Memory* (Oxford, 1975)

Gorer, Geoffrey, *Death, Grief, and Mourning in Contemporary Britain* (London, 1965)

Guest, George, *The Treasury of English Church Music*, Vol. IV: *1760–1900* (London, 1965)

Gurney, Ivor, 'The Springs of Music', *Musical Quarterly*, 8 (1922), 319–22

Hadow, Henry, *Church Music* (London, 1926)

Hardwick, Peter, *British Organ Music of the Twentieth Century* (Lanham, MD, 2003)

Harris, Alexandra, *Romantic Moderns* (New York, 2010)

Heckert, Deborah, 'Schoenberg, Roger Fry and the Emergence of a Critical Language for the Reception of Musical Modernism in Britain, 1912–1914', in Matthew Riley, ed., *British Music and Modernism, 1895–1960* (Farnham, 2010)

Hepokoski, James and Warren Darcy, *Elements of Sonata Theory: Norms, Types, and Deformations in the Late-Eighteenth-Century Sonata* (New York, 2006)

Hodgson, Peter, 'The Music of Herbert Howells', Ph.D. thesis (University of Colorado, 1970)

Howells, Herbert, 'Arthur Benjamin', in *Cobbett's Cyclopaedic Survey of Chamber Music* (Oxford, 1929), Vol. I, 117

—'Charles Villiers Stanford (1852–1924): An Address at His Centenary', *Proceedings of the Royal Musical Association*, 79 (1953–4), 19–31

—'Hubert Parry', *Music and Letters*, 50 (1969), 228

—'Ivor Gurney', *Music and Letters*, 19 (1938), 14

—'The Musician', *Music and Letters*, 19 (1938), 12–17

—'The Pastoral Symphony of Vaughan Williams', *Music and Letters*, 3 (1922), 122–32

—Review of Ralph Vaughan Williams, Concerto for Oboe and Strings, *RCM Magazine*, 43 (1947), 89–90

—'Words for Musical Settings', *Athenaeum* (December 1916), 614–15

—'Younger British Composers', *Athenaeum*, 4611 (1916), 560–2

Howes, Frank, *The English Musical Renaissance* (London, 1966)

Hughes, Meirion and Robert Stradling, *The English Musical Renaissance 1840–1940: Contructing a National Music*, 2nd edn (Manchester and New York, 2001)

Huss, Fabian, 'Technical Focus and "Stylistic Cleansing" in E.J. Moeran's Sonata for Two Violins and String Trio', Gareth Cox and Julian Horton, eds, *Irish Musical Analysis*, Irish Musical Studies 11 (Dublin, 2013)

Hutchings, Arthur, *Church Music in the Nineteenth Century* (London, 1967)

Kennedy, Michael, *The Works of Ralph Vaughan Williams* (London, 1964)

Kerman, Joseph, *Concerto Conversations* (Cambridge, MA, 1999)

Klass, Dennis, *The Spiritual Lives of Bereaved Parents* (Philadelphia, 1999)

Klass, Dennis, Phyllis R. Silverman and Steven L. Nickman, eds, *Continuing Bonds* (Washington, DC, 1996)

Lambert, Constant, *Music Ho!* (London, 1937)

Layton, Robert, *Sibelius and His World* (New York, 1970)

Lerner, Laurence, *Angels and Absences: Child Death in the Nineteenth Century* (Nashville and London, 1997)

Levenson, Michael, ed., *The Cambridge Companion to Modernism* (Cambridge, 1999)

Lloyd, Stephen, *William Walton: Muse of Fire* (Woodbridge, 2001)

Lorenz, Robert, 'An Amateur on Critics', *Musical Times* (March 1923), 178

Mandler, Peter, 'Against "Englishness": English Culture and the Limits to Rural Nostalgia, 1850–1940', *Transactions of the Royal Historical Society*, 6/7 (1997), 155–75

Mason, Colin, 'New Music', *Musical Times*, 97 (1956), 24–6

Maw, David '"Phantasy mania": Quest for a National Style', in Emma Hornby and David Maw, eds, *Essays on the History of English Music in Honour of John Caldwell: Sources, Style, Performance, Historiography* (Woodbridge, 2010), 97–121

McGuire, Charles Edward, 'The English Music Festival, 1910', in Byron Adams and Robin Wells, eds, *Vaughan Williams Essays* (Aldershot, 2003), 260–1

Nelson, B.J. and T.T. Frantz, 'Family Interactions of Suicide Survivors and Survivors of Non-Suicidal Death', *Omega*, 33 (1996), 131–46

'The New Stanford Symphony', *The Observer* (25 February 1912), 7

Newman, William, *The Sonata since Beethoven*, 3rd edn (New York and London, 1983)

Noss, Luther, 'Review: *Six Pieces for Organ* by Herbert Howells', *Notes*, 12 (1954), 152–3

Novello, Henry L., *Death as Transformation: A Contemporary Theology of Death* (Farnham, 2011)

Ottaway, Hugh, 'Herbert Howells and the English Revival', *Musical Times*, 108 (1967), 897–9

Palgrave, F.T., *The Golden Treasury* (London, 1861)

Palmer, Christopher, *Herbert Howells: A Study* (Sevenoaks, 1978)

—*Herbert Howells (1892–1983): A Centenary Celebration*, 2nd edn (London, 1996 [1992])

—*Impressionism in Music* (London, 1973)

—Liner notes to Herbert Howells, *Missa sabrinensis* and *Stabat mater*, London Symphony Chorus, London Symphoy Orchestra, Gennady Rozhdestvensky (conductor), audio CD (Chandos, 1994), CHAN 241–27

Patton, John, *A Century of Cathedral Music: 1898–1998* (Winchester, 2000)

Pike, Lionel, 'Flights of Fancy: Codes and Keys in Howells', *Tempo*, 62 (2008), 11–18

—'Tallis – Vaughan Williams – Howells: Reflections on Mode Three', *Tempo*, 149 (1984), 2–13

Plunket Greene, Harry, *Charles Villiers Stanford* (London, 1935)

Rando, Therese A., *Treatment of Complicated Mourning* (Champaign, IL, 1993)

Ratner, Leonard, *Classic Music: Expression, Form, and Style* (New York and London, 1980)

Reti, Rudolph, *The Thematic Process in Music* (London, 1961)

Ridley, Jane, *Edwin Lutyens: His Life, His Wife, His Work* (London, 2003)

Ridout, Alan, *A Composer's Life* (London, 1995)

—'Herbert Howells Remembered', *RCM Magazine*, 89 (1992), 12–13

Riley, Matthew, ed., *British Music and Modernism, 1895–1960* (Farnham, 2010)

Rodmell, Paul, *Charles Villiers Stanford* (Aldershot, 2002)

Roscow, Gregory, ed., *Bliss on Music* (Oxford and New York, 1991)

Routley, Erik, *Twentieth Century Church Music* (London, 1971)

Roy, Arundhati, *The God of Small Things* (New York, 1998)

Rubin, Simon Shimshon, 'The Death of a Child Is Forever: The Life Course Impact of Child Loss', in M.S. Stroebe, W. Stroebe and R.O. Hansson, eds, *Handbook of Bereavement: Theory, Research, and Intervention* (Cambridge, 1993), 285–99

Russill, Patrick, 'The Evening Canticles of Herbert Howells, 1945–1975: A Personal Survey', *The Organist*, 3 (1992), n.p.

Saylor, Eric, '"It's Not Lambkins Frisking at All": English Pastoral Music and the Great War', *Music Quarterly*, 91 (2008), 39–59

Scott, Derek B., 'The Sexual Politics of Victorian Musical Aesthetics', *Journal of the Royal Musical Association*, 119 (1994), 91–114

Scott, Marion, 'Herbert Howells', in *Cobbett's Cyclopaedic Survey of Chamber Music* (Oxford, 1929), Vol. I, 573–5

—'Herbert Howells: His "In Gloucestershire"', *Christian Science Monitor* (25 December 1920), 12

Shaw, George Bernard, 'Going Fantee', *World* (10 May 1893)

Skelton, Tim and Gerald Gliddon, *Lutyens and the Great War* (London, 2008)

Spicer, Paul, *Herbert Howells* (Bridgend, 1998)

—'Herbert Howells's Partita', *Musical Times*, 115 (1974), 881–3

—Liner notes to Herbert Howells, Piano Concerto no. 1, Piano Concerto no. 2 and *Penguinski*, Howard Shelley (piano), BBC Symphony Orchestra, Richard Hickox (conductor), audio CD (Chandos, 2000), CHAN 9874

Stanford, Charles Villiers, *Musical Composition: A Short Treatise for Students* (London, 1911)

Stanford, Charles Villiers, *Pages from an Unwritten Diary* (London, 1914)

—'Principles for Young Composers', *Musician*, 17 (1912), 126

—'Sanity(?) in Composition', *Musical Herald* (March 1917), 78–9

—'Some Recent Tendencies in Composition', *Proceedings of the Musical Association*, 47 (1920–1), 39–53

Straus, Joseph, 'Disability and "Late Style" in Music', *The Journal of Musicology*, 25 (2008), 3–45

Sutton, Wadham, 'The Organ Music of Herbert Howells', *Musical Times*, 112 (1971), 177–8

Thomas, Gareth, 'Modernism, Diaghilev and the Ballets Russes in London, 1911–1929', in Matthew Riley, ed., *British Music and Modernism: 1895–1960* (Farnham, 2010), 67–92

Turner, W.J., 'Barbarism at The Queen's Hall', *The New Statesman* (2 May 1925), 72

Vande Moortele, Steven, *Two-Dimensional Sonata Form: Form and Cycle in Single-Movement Instrumental Works by Liszt, Strauss, Schoenberg, and Zemlinsky* (Leuven, 2009)

Vaughan Williams, Ralph, 'Good Taste', *The Vocalist* (May 1902), repr. in Ursula Vaughan Williams and Imogen Holst, eds, *Heirs and Rebels* (New York, 1974), 28

—*Letters of Ralph Vaughan Williams*, ed. Hugh Cobbe (Oxford and New York, 2008)

Vaughan Williams, Ursula, *R. V. W.: A Biography of Ralph Vaughan Williams* (Oxford, 1984)

Walker, Ernest, 'The Modern British Phantasy', *The Music Student*, 8 (1915): *Chamber Music Supplement*, 17, 17–27

Webber, Nicholas, 'Herbert Howells at 85', *Music and Musicians*, 26 (1977), 26

Wells, Robin, 'Howells's Unpublished Organ Works', *Musical Times*, 128 (1987), 455–9

Whittall, Arnold, 'British Music in the Modern World', in Stephen Banfield, *The Blackwell History of Music in Britain*, Vol. VI: *The Twentieth Century* (Oxford, 1995), 9–26

Winter, Jay, *Sites of Memory, Sites of Mourning: The Great War in European Cultural History* (Cambridge, 1995)

Index of Works by Herbert Howells

References in bold type indicate an illustration or music example on that page.

Antiphon (HH 347) 232–3, 237

Before Me Careless Lying (HH 84) 110
Behold, O God Our Defender (HH 267) 1–2
By the Waters of Babylon: A Rhapsody (HH 68) 69–72, **71**

Come, My Soul (HH 336) 234
Come, Sing and Dance (HH 164) 77–9
Concerto for Piano and Orchestra in C minor, Op. 4 (HH 31) 15, 17–18, 19, 118, 120, 121, 125, 170, 172–6
Concerto no. 2 for Piano and Orchestra, Op. 39 (HH 152) 134–5, 136, 162, 170, 175–84, 221, 283
Concerto for String Orchestra (HH 215) 123, 162, 171, 182, 278, 282, 291
Concerto for Violoncello and Orchestra (HH 205–7) 182, 274–84, **279**; *Fantasia* (HH 205) 157, 276–82; *Threnody* (HH 206) 278

Elegy, Op. 15 (HH 68) 70, 121, 123–4, **125**, 281, 282, 295, **297**, 300, 307n
English Mass, An (HH 276) 251, **255**, 268
Epilogue (HH 342) 257
Evening Service: *Chichester Service* (HH 317) 98, 227–9, **228**, 230, 232, 234, 236; *Collegium Regale* (HH 246) 23, 86–7, 91–6, **93**, **94**, **96**, 98, 103, 111, 112, 224, 228, 229n, 255, 256n; *Dallas Canticles* (HH 345) 95, 98, 226, 227, 228, 229–30, 233, 234, 235, 236; *Gloucester Service* (HH 249) 86, 87, 94–8, **95**, **97**, 224, 228, 231, 252, **256**; *Hereford Service* (HH 327) 98, 229n; In G major (HH 91) 90, **90**; *Magdalen College Service* (HH 330) 235; *St Augustine Service* (HH 320) 235; *St John's College Service* (HH 282) 98; *St Paul's Service* (HH 264) 98, 237; *Sarum Service* (HH 312) 98, 227n; *Winchester Service* (HH 319) 231; *Worcester Service* (HH 263) 226, 252–3; *York Service* (HH 340) 98, 230

Fantasia for Violoncello and Orchestra see Concerto for Violoncello and Orchestra
Fantasy String Quartet, Op. 25 (HH 71) 139, 185–6, 187n, **203**, **204**, **205**, **206**, **207**, 218, 219
Fear of the Lord, The (HH 349) 232, **234**, 235
Five Songs (HH 26) 64–6, 67–8; The Call 67; The Devotee 65, 67, **68**; The Sorrow of Love 66, 67, 68; The Twilight People 64, **65–6**; The Waves of Breffny 66, 67
Five Songs, Op. 10 (HH 67): Merry Margaret 75, **76**; Under the Greenwood Tree 74–5, **75**, 136; A Wanderer's Night Song 69, **70**, 71
Five Songs (HH 108): Gavotte 79
Flourish for a Bidding (HH 326) 257
Four Anthems (HH 230): Like as the Hart Desireth the Waterbrooks 23, 38, 224, 231, 235–6; O Pray for the Peace of Jerusalem 28, 38
Four French Chansons (arr. Howells), Op. 29 (HH 98) 63, 77
Four Songs, Op. 22 (HH 55) 75; The Widow Bird 75–7

Garland for de la Mare, A (HH 111) 62n, 79, 80n, 102, 103–9; Andy Battle 109, **109**; Before Dawn 101, 106–7, **107**, **108**; King David 72, 79–85, **82–4**, 102, 156, 250, **252**; The Lady Caroline 79, 102, 105–6, **105**, **106**, 107, **107**, 108, 292; The Old Stone House **108**, 109; The Three Cherry Trees 104, 108; Wanderers 103–5, **103**, **104**

House of the Mind, The (HH 274) 112–13, 231
Howells' Clavichord (HH 237) 22, 242n, 253, 259–64, 292; Dart's Saraband **241**, 261; Goff's Fireside 260–1, **263**, 271; Malcolm's Vision **241**, 260, 261, **264**; Rubbra's Soliloquy 261, **263**; Walton's Toye 292

Hymnus paradisi (HH 220) 23, 28, 38, 132, 133, 146, 154n, 159, 161, 222, 226, 231, 235, 236, 257, 268, 274, 276, 286–308, **298**

In Green Ways, Op. 43 (HH 172) 69, 69n, 74, 136, 182, 250, 276; The Goat Paths 69n, 72–4, **73**, 250–1, **253**
Intrata (no. 2) (HH 233) 259
In Youth Is Pleasure (HH 49) 110

Jubilate Deo (HH 316) 235, 292

King David (HH 102) *see A Garland for De la Mare*

Lady Audrey's Suite (HH 50) 139
Lambert's Clavichord, Op. 41 (HH 165) 42n, 63, 183, 243, 244, 275, 280n; H. H. His Fancy 22; Lambert's Fireside 243, **244**; My Lord Sandwich's Dreame 243, **245**, 252n, 271; Samuel's Air 245, **247**; Wortham's Grounde 244, **246**, 251
Little Boy Lost, The (HH 120) 156

Merry Eye *see* Two Pieces for Small Orchestra, Op. 20
Missa sabrinensis (HH 275) 146, 159, 160n, 224, 261, 268, 292
Missa sine nomine (*Mass in the Dorian Mode*), Op. 2 (HH 28) 40n, 110, 129–33, 223–4

O Garlands, Hanging by the Door (HH 121) 160
Old Man's Lullaby, An (HH 73) 77, **78**
Old Meg (HH 133) 109–10

Paradise Rondel (HH 159) 134, 135–6, **137**, 182, 221
Partita for Organ (HH 334) 181, 230–2, **231**, **241**, 257, 271, **272**
Pastoral Rhapsody, Op. 38 (HH 134) 133, 182, 221, 307
Peacock Pie set 1, Op. 33 (HH 104) 79–80, 102, 103; The Dunce 79; Miss T. 79; Mrs MacQueen 79
Penguinski (HH 193) 16
Piano Quartet *see* Quartet in A minor, Op. 21
Phantasy, Op. 29 No. 1 (HH 74) 212–13, **214, 215–16**, 217

Phantasy Ground Bass (HH 52) 212
Phantasy Minuet, Op. 27 (HH 105) 212, 214, 216
Phantasy String Quartet see Fantasy String Quartet
Prelude: 'De profundis' (HH 288) 259, **262**
Procession (HH 124) 125, 128–9, **132**, 176
Puck's Minuet *see* Two Pieces for Small Orchestra, Op. 20

Quartet in A minor, Op. 21 (HH 66) 118, 139, 150, 188

Requiem (HH 188) 274, 296–7, 298, **297**, 300
Restful Branches, The (HH 94) 77, **79**
Rhapsodic Quintet, Op. 31 (HH 107) 87, 139, 163, 187–8, 193, 195, **208, 209, 213**, 221, 235
Rhapsody for Organ no. 4 (HH 289) 257

Scribe, The (HH 285) 101–2
Sequence for St Michael, A (HH 299) 225, **225**, 226, 227, 286
Sine Nomine: a Phantasy, Op. 37 (HH 126) 40n, 129, 132, 133–4, **134**, 212, 218, 248n, 298–300, 304
Sir Patrick Spens, Op. 23 (HH 77) 126–8, **129**, 219, 224
Six Pieces for Organ (HH 226) 37–60, 231, 253, 259; Fugue, Chorale and Epilogue 22, 38, 39, 42–3, **43, 46**, 47, **49**, 52, 55–6, **56**, 57, 58–9, 255; Master Tallis's Testament 22, 38, 39, 42, 43, 44, **45**, 47, 49, 51, 52, **52**, 55, **55**, 58, 59, 255, **257**, 280n; Paean 42, 43, 45, 46, 47, **47, 48**, 49, 51, 52, 56, 57, 58, 59, 231; Preludio "sine nomine" 39–42, 43, 48, **50**, 51, **53**, 54, 59, 299n; Saraband (for the Morning of Easter) 38, 39, 40–2, 43, 44, **44, 45**, 46, 47, **49**, 51, 52, 53, **54**, 55, **56**, 58, 59, **241**, 257, 258–9, 268; Saraband (*in modo elegiaco*) 38, 40–2, 43, 46, 47, **47, 48**, 51, 52, 55, 58, 59, **241**, 258–9, **260**, 268, 271
Sonata for Clarinet and Piano (HH 251) 153, 154, 165–8, **166, 167**, 183, 292
Sonata for Oboe and Piano (HH 239) 153–65, **156, 157, 158, 159, 160, 161, 163**, 166, 167–8, 181, 183
Sonata in B minor for Violin and Piano (HH 24) 163, 173, 176

Sonata no. 1 in E major for Violin and Piano (HH78) 181, 187, 190, 196–8, **197**, **198**, **201**, 206, 211–12, 221
Sonata no. 2 for Violin and Piano, Op. 26 (HH 79) 147, 155n, 183, 195n, 275
Sonata no. 3 for Violin and Piano, Op. 38 (HH 136) 147, 157, 181
Sonatina for Piano (HH 333) **241**, 268, 270, **270**, 271
Songs for Low Voice, Op. 7 (HH 38) 66, 67, 69; By the Grey Stones 68; St Bride's Song 68; The Valley of Silence 67, 68; When the Dew is falling 67, 68; When there is Peace 67
Spotless Rose, A (HH 109) 1, 235
Stabat mater (HH 309) 11, 23, 222–8, 230, 232, 235–6, **241**, 249, 251, 252, 253, 261–5, **265**, **266**, **268**, **269**, 291, 292
String Quartet no. 3, *In Gloucestershire*, Op. 34 (HH 62) 139–51, **147**, **148**, **149**, **150**, **151**, **152**, 274
Suite for Orchestra, *The Bs*, Op. 13 (HH 42) 19, 120–1, **122**, **123**, 294, 307
Suite for String Orchestra (HH 80) 123
Sweetest of Sweets (HH 348) 232–3, **233**, 234, 235, 237
Symphony in D major (HH 97) **119**, 182

Take Him, Earth, for Cherishing (HH 307) 23–36, **25**, **26**, **28**, **29**, **31**, **32**, **33**, **34**, 225, 226, 229, 231, 236, 291

Te Deum 111–12, 226, 227, 292; and Benedictus for St George's Chapel, Windsor (HH 269) 111, **112**, **113**, 113, **114**; Exultate Deo (HH 316) 235; and Jubilate, Collegium Regale (HH 245) 87, 111; for St Mary Redcliffe, Bristol (HH 310) 111, 236; for Washington (HH 355) 227
Thee Will I Love (HH 332) 234
Three Dances, Op. 7 (HH 48) 19–20, 67, 122–3, 132, 162
Three Figures: Triptych for Brass Band (HH 297) 264; Iles's Interlude **241**, 242, 264–5, **267**
Three Psalm-Preludes, Op. 32 (set 1) (HH 56) 37, 280, 281
Three Psalm-Preludes (set 2) (HH 219) 253, 257, 278, **279**, 280, 281
Three Rhapsodies, Op. 17 (HH 57) 37, 70, 278
Three Rondeaux, Op. 12 (HH 59) 75, 136
Threnody for Violoncello and Orchestra *see* Concerto for Violoncello and Orchestra
Two Pieces for Small Orchestra, Op. 20 (HH 83); Merry-Eye 121, 126, 141n, 176; Puck's Minuet 87, 121, 124, 125–6, 129, 176
To Music Bent (HH 194) 251, **254**

Upon a Summer's Day (HH 81) 77, **80**

Whin, song set (HH 100): Blaweary 77

General Index

References in bold type indicate an illustration or music example on that page.

Aeolian Company, The 213
Allen, Sir Hugh 123, 128
Armstrong, Sir Thomas 178
Andrews, Herbert Kennedy 22, 277
Andrews, Paul 2, 20, 91, 92, 213n, 249n
Austin, Ernest: *Trio in One Movement* 220

Bach, Johan Sebastian 23, 245, 279, 282, 296
Bach Choir, The 224, 232, 261
Banfield, Stephen 72, 74, 79, 80, 105
Bantock, Sir Granville 128
Bartók, Belá 22, 171n, 242
Bauer, Harold 17
Bax, Sir Arnold 120, 164, 165; Walsinghame 131
Benjamin, Arthur 12, 17, 120–1, 128, 172, 180
Berg, Alban 172, 282
Birch, John 282
Bliss, Sir Arthur 12, 120, 131, 165, 173, 179–80, 277, 298, 306
Bowlby, John 289, 290
Borwick, Leonard 16
Brahms, Johannes 13, 15, 20, 62, 85, 174, 202
Brewer, Sir A. Herbert 11, 37, 124, 126, 172, 173, 293; *A Midsummer Phantasy* 212
Bridge, Frank: *Rhapsody Trio* 220
Britten, Benjamin 231, 236
Browne, Denis 105
Byrd, William 22, 85, 90n, 92, 164, 242–3, 244, 275, 280, 280n

Casella, Alfredo 213
catharsis 67, 77, 81, 85, 276
Celtic influence 20, 62, 64, 66, 219, 293
cenotaph 301–2, 304, 306, 307; The Cenotaph, Whitehall **301**, 302, 304, 306; *see also* memorial for World War I
Chosen, Hill at 118
chromaticism 20, 51, 65, 66, 95, 207, 211, 227, 232, 278, 307
church music, Victorian 88–9, 93
Cobbett, Walter Willson 142, 187, 220; competitions 175, 185–6, 188, 201
Cone, Edward 275, 281

Coronation: of King Edward VII 13; of Queen Elizabeth II 1
counterpoint 22, 23, 44, 224; fugue 22, 28, 42, 45, 52, 56–7; heterophony 27, 29, 30, 33; imitation 23, 29, 82; organum 26–7
critical response to Howells's music 37, 38, 40, 42, 43, 44, 56–7, 58, 60, 87, 106, 124, 127, 128, 129, 154–5, 160, 165, 174, 177, 178–9, 218, 228–30, 291–2, 297, 298, 300, 304, 306, 307

dance 78, 79, 105, 251; of death 268; minuet 79, 104; sarabande 109, 240, 242, 243–4, 245–6, 249, 250, 261, 266; siciliana 104, 108; *see also* Vaughan Williams, Ralph
Darke, Harold 88, 141, 282
Davies, Sir Walford 260n, 296–7
Dawe, Dorothy *see* Howells, Dorothy
Debussy, Claude 4, 5, 15, 130, 171, 173, 174, 179, 180, 246; *Le jardin sous la pluie* 213, **216**; *Pelléas et Mélisande* 68; *Première arabesque* 212–13, **215**; Sarabande (*Pour le piano*) **249**; Sirènes (Nocturnes) 130, 299–300; influence of 15, 68, 171, 179, 212–13, 298, 300
de la Mare, Walter 62, 79–81, 92, 100–2, 104–8, 156; *Peacock Pie: A Book of Rhymes* 79–81, 103, 109
Delius, Frederick 297, 307; *A Mass of Life* 67; *Song of the High Hills* 131; influence of 67, 297, 307
Diaghilev Ballet 120, 129, 180
diatonic dissonance 37, 46, 173, 220–1
diatonicism 65–6, 74, 205
Dickens, Charles 288, 307
Didion, Joan 287, 290, 293
Downes, Ralph 5
Dunhill, Thomas 13–14, 141, 294
Drakeford, Richard 144, 146
Duruflé, Maurice 40, 50
Dyson, Sir George 12–13, 14, 20; *The New Music* 14

Eggar, Katharine 5, 106, 128, 133, 135, 141, 175, 193, 195, 201, 206, 218, 219, 249
Elgar, Sir Edward 11, 15, 123–4, 129, 170, 173, 282, 291, 297, 298, 300; *The Dream*

of Gerontius, op. 38 297–8, **298**, 300; *The Spirit of England*, Op. 80 300; influence of 11, 15, 19, 123–4, 173, 297–8
Englishness *see* national style
enharmonic change 82, 197, 201, 211
Esty, Jed 165
Evans, Edwin 118, 121, 127, 136, 140, 142, 165, 172, 213
expression: ecstatic 1–2, 41, 54, 78, 94, 95, 97, 100, 103, 105–6, 107, 109, 112, 129–30, 132, 223, 297, 299; elegiac 41, 59, 70, 81, 121, 124, 151, 240, 242, 248, 252, 259, 268, 271, 299, 300; exultant 39, 41, 42, 53, 78, 257–8

Falkner, Sir Keith 284
false relation 75, 95, 228, 232, 242, 243, 244
fantasy (spirit of) 72, 100–1, 104, 212, 218–19
Fellowes, Edmund 88
Finzi, Gerald 4, 43, 56, 57, 100, 104, 160; *Let Us Garlands Bring* 100; *Lo, the Full Final Sacrifice* 100
folk-song influence 51n, 63, 127, 150, 155, 163, 164, 165, 202–5, 218, 219, 306–7
form 56, 155, 271, 278, 304; anagnorisis and peripeteia 64, 85; arch 39, 57, 160, 162, 163, 167, 218, 240, 244, 264; closure 55, 197–9, 205, 206, 211; double function 181, 190; episodic 166, 188, 211; experiment in 176, 179, 180–1, 182, 185–6, 187–8, 195–6, 218; rotational process 162, 166, 167, 188, 199, 213; single-movement 134, 185–6, 190, 195, 220, 221; phantasy 134, 185–6, 187n, 188, 190, 195, 216, 220; sonata 64–5, 85, 155, 160, 165, 175, 176, 179, 181, 183, 186, 187, 188, 190, 193, 195, 196, 199, 202, 206, 207, 213; thematic 64, 67, 70, 71, 80–1, 188, 190, 196, 198–9, 202, 206–8; through-composed 68, 69, 74, 75, 78, 190n, 250, 251; tripartite 42, 57, 85, 208
Forsyth, Cecil 17
Fuller Maitland, James Alexander 19, 186

Gibbons, Orlando 92, 242, 243; Galiardo 242, **243**
Gibson, Wilfrid Wilson 62, 77, 109
Gloucester 102, 289; Cathedral 11, 12, 37, 87, 94, 110, 130, 132, 136, 218, 281, 286, 293, 297

Gloucestershire as inspiration 118, 126, 135, 140, 141, 146, 165, 286, 288, 289, 306–8; *see also* place, sense of
Goossens, Sir Eugene 142, 180, 213, 298
Goossens, Leon 153, 154, 168, 294
Goethe, Johann Wolfgang von 69, 74
Gorer, Geoffrey 289–90
Grieg, Edvard 246; Holberg Suite 271n
Gurney, Ivor 10–11, 19, 64n, 69, 75, 107, 118, 120, 121, 141, 142, 146, 163–4, 173, 174, 285, 286
Guest, George 88

Hadley, Patrick 87
Hadow, Sir Henry 88
Handel, George Frideric 245
Hardwick, Peter 57
harmony 1, 23, 28, 30, 41, 44, 50, 58, 68, 74, 81, 161, 162, 177, 199; appoggiatura 25, 27, 28, 30, 33, 34, 35, 39, 44, 45, 51, 52, 54, 173, 204, 224–5, 232, 258; bitonal 29, 30, 33, 35, 95, 167, 280; chromatic 51, 95, 225, 240; dissonant 30, 96, 111, 227, 244, 259; 'Howells chord' 280; progressing by thirds 46, 47, 55, 65, 67, 75, 77
Harris, Roy: Third Symphony 4, 24, 26, 28, 29, 33, 35, 36
Harty, Sir Hamilton 124, 176, 177, 178, 182
hermeneutics 53, 198, 274; compositional voice 218–19, 274–5, 281; persona (frame of mind) 198, 206, 221
Hodgson, Peter 2, 141, 143, 258
Holst, Gustav 12, 63, 65, 90n, 92, 143, 236, 303n; *Hymn of Jesus* 272; *The Planets* 130, 171, 300; influence of 19, 164, 300
Housman, Alfred Edward 62, 295–6
Howells, Dorothy (wife) 64, 285, 286, 287, 288
Howells, Elizabeth (mother) 252
Howells, Herbert Norman 1–2, 38, 86, 87, 102, 103, 143, 175, 193–4; apprenticeship 10–11, 14, 17, 19, 20, 37, 64, 74, 79, 110, 120, 140, 172, 173, 174, 242; compositional restraint 58; conductor 69n, 126, 132, 136, 286; conservative 62, 183, 195; diary 102, 140, 141, 142, 144, 155, 187, 188, 193, 195n, 225, 235, 240, 252, 258, 259n, 261, 271, 275, 276, 277, 287; first performance 69, 141, 142, 172, 173–4, 176, 178, 286, 291n; loss of string quartet score 139, 140, 144, 145; Oxford

doctorate 136, 276, 277; personality 104, 281, 282, 284, 289, 292–3, 294–5, 304; reaction to criticism 135, 174; revision of works 143, 153, 274; suppression of works 138, 141, 146, 147, 170, 174, 177, 295n, 296, 297; as teacher 63; views on his music 5, 86, 115, 120, 121, 127, 133, 176, 182, 187, 188, 190, 193, 195, 196, 201, 206–7, 218, 220, 255n, 295; views on music 43, 46, 51, 74, 88, 102, 105, 110, 111, 125, 126, 135–6, 141, 154, 155, 160n, 163–4, 171–2, 173, 175, 180–1, 197–8, 214n, 219, 246, 248, 249, 272–3, 278, 279, 282; views on his life 10–11, 12, 14, 124, 126, 128–9, 145, 183
Howells, Michael (son) 259n, 276, 282, 285–7, 291, 296; influence of death of 23, 38, 41, 87, 102, 139, 146, 223, 225–6, 235, 258, 276, 277, 282–3, 286, 289, 292
Howells, Oliver (father) 103, 304
Howells, Ursula (daughter) 135, 259n, 276, 277, 282, 285, 286–7, 289, 291n, 292–3
Hutchings, Arthur 88

Ireland, John 179, 186; Second Piano Trio 220
impressionism 37, 38–9, 40, 48, 59, 69, 94, 132, 155, 160, 179
improvisation 38, 42, 43, 54, 72, 179, 204
influence: of modern style 19, 171; of Romantic style 11, 15, 19, 20, 40, 85, 170; of Tudor style 15, 22, 35, 38, 42, 44, 50, 61, 62, 85, 164, 242–3, 255, 280, 299; *see also* Debussy, Claude; Delius, Frederick; Elgar, Sir Edward; Holst, Gustav; Howells, Michael; Parry, Sir C. Hubert Hastings; Prokofiev, Sergei; Rachmaninoff, Sergei; Ravel, Maurice; Stravinsky, Igor; Vaughan Williams, Ralph; Wagner Richard
international style 165, 220

Joachim, Joseph 10, 19

Kennedy, John F. 23
Kerman, Joseph 281, 282
Klass, Dennis 283

Lambert, Constant 170
late style 222–3, 224, 226–7, 230, 231, 232–4, 236
Leighton, Kenneth 278–9

Lerner, Laurence 288, 307
Ligeti, György: Requiem 307
Liszt, Franz: Piano Sonata in B minor 185, 190
Littlejohn, Joan 182, 277, 282n
Lodge, Sir Oliver: *Raymond* 303
Lutyens, Sir Edwin 299, 300, 302–4, 306; *see also* cenotaph; memorial for World War I

Macleod, Fiona 66, 68
MacNamara, Hilary 240n, 268, 283
Malipiero, Gian Francesco 213
mannerism 43, 44, 51, 53, 55, 92, 232, 243
Matthews, Gillian 277
melancholy 80, 81, 240
melody 51, 52, 67, 204, 244; dissonance 24, 25, 280; 'knight's move' contour 24–5, 103–4
memorial for World War I 146, 247; Memorial to the Missing of the Somme at Thiepval 302, 304, **305**; *see also* cenotaph
Mendelssohn, Felix 13, 15, 89, 121, 186; *Elijah* 132
Milner-White, Eric 4, 87, 113
mode 51, 69, 161; Dorian 25, 30, 49, 50, 165, 216; Locrian 157, 158, 162, 167; Phrygian 27, 30, 43, 49, 50, 73–4, 166–7, 208, 261, 264
modernity 21, 22, 91, 133, 164, 165, 170, 175, 183, 206, 219, 221; Modernism 15, 170–1, 175, 183, 236, 299, 302, 304, 308; Romantic Modernism 170–1, 176, 183; *see also* influence
Moiseiwitsch, Benno 17
mood 39, 40, 41, 92–3, 111; complex 195–7, 202, 206–7, 212; unity of 38, 39, 56, 57, 64, 124, 196, 197–8, 202, 206–7
motivic organisation 24, 72–3, 78, 81, 84–5, 156–7, 158, 160, 162–3, 180, 183, 196, 202–4, 275
mysticality 86, 93, 115, 118, 133, 168, 206, 219, 247, 272

narrative 81, 85, 121, 206, 218, 274, 286, 287–9, 292, 296, 307
national style 164–5, 175, 219–21, 306–7

Oldridge, Diana 296
orchestration 18, 127, 136, 279
Ottaway, Hugh 154n, 297, 307

O'Sullivan, Seamus 62, 64
Owen, Wilfred 92, 295
Oxford Movement, The 88

Palgrave, Francis Turner 64
Palmer, Christopher 2, 37, 38, 58, 79, 94–95, 102, 120n, 123, 129, 143, 146, 153, 156, 174, 219, 226, 235, 257–8, 261, 271, 274, 277, 278, 280, 286, 288, 291, 293, 296, 298
Parker, Horatio 16
Parratt, Sir Walter 20, 37
Parry, Sir C. Hubert Hastings 11, 20, 62, 65, 67, 70, 87n, 170, 171, 173–4, 278; *Ode on the Nativity* 278; *English Suite* 246, **248**; influence of 173, 221, 246
pastoral 19, 29, 30, 63, 79, 164, 165, 306
pedal point 54, 65, 71, 77, 96, 109–10, 113, 173, 259
place, sense of 94–5, 110, 136, 141, 163–4, 164–5; *see also* Gloucestershire as inspiration
plainchant (plainsong) style 24, 51, 81, 92, 100, 132, 218, 230, 264, 299, 306
Plunket Greene, Harry 132, 141
Prokofiev, Sergei 171; influence of 19, 180
Purcell, Henry 244; Chacony in G minor **245**

Rachmaninoff, Sergei 4, 15–18; Piano Concerto no. 2 in C minor 15–16, 17–18, 172, 175; influence of 15, 17–18, 64, 172, 173–5
Rando, Theresa 290–1
Ratner, Leonard 195n
Ravel, Maurice 4, 5, 136, 183; *Bolero* 129; *Daphnis et Chloë* 130; *Jeux d'eau* 212–14; String Quartet 179; influence of 15, 171, 179, 212–14, 296n, 299
remoteness, sense of 106, 111, 133, 161, 219
rhapsodic quality 38, 70, 91, 148, 155, 161, 162, 272, 278
Ridley, Jane 302
Ridout, Alan 293, 294–5
Rosenthal, Moritz 16
Routley, Erik 91, 92, 98
Roy, Arundhati 290
Rutter, John 174

St Augustine 100
Salisbury Cathedral 87, 88, 175
Samuel, Harold 176, 177, 178
Sassoon, Siegfried 295

Saylor, Eric 306
Scholes, Percy 135
Scott, Anthony 296n
Scott, Marion 140, 141, 142, 144, 145, 148
semitonal shift 71, 72, 74, 157, 199, 202, 211
sensuality 93, 95, 96, 100, 104, 236, 293
Sibelius, Jean 275
Spicer, Paul 2, 4, 11, 15, 40, 44, 94, 132, 135, 154, 258, 274, 286, 287, 288, 291, 292–3, 294n, 299, 304
spirituality 87, 93, 100
spiritualism 303
Stainer, Sir John 17, 88, 89
Stanford, Sir Charles Villiers 10, 13, 89; Evening Service in C 89; Evening Service in G 89; *Flos campi* 131; *Fourth Irish Rhapsody* 19; *Musical Composition: A Short Treatise for Students* 14, 63; Piano Concerto no. 2 in C minor 15–16, 17; Service in B♭ 11, 13; *Suite for Violin*, Op. 32 19–20; Symphony no. 6 16; Symphony no. 7 13–14; conservative 10, 11, 13, 18, 21; influence of 17–18, 20, 62, 90–91, 127, 172, 173, 195; as teacher 10, 12–14, 17, 20, 63, 110, 175, 186; views 11, 12–14
Stephens, James 72
Stevens, Wallace 288–9
Stoeckel, Carl 16, 17
Straus, Joseph 222–3, 224
Strauss, Richard 11, 14, 233; Der Rosenkavalier 171
Stravinsky, Igor 5, 176, 213, 236; *Capriccio* 137; *Petrushka* 120, 129, 171, 220; *Pulcinella* 137; influence of 15, 120, 129, 136–7, 171, 179, 220, 296n
Street, Oscar 193
Sullivan, Sir Arthur 88

Tallis, Thomas 85, 90n, 255, 275, 280n
Terry, Sir Richard Runciman 15, 90, 110, 242n
thematic transformation 53, 156, 196, 204, 208; elemental transformation 53, 54, 55, 65
Three Choirs Festival 42n, 69, 126, 132, 135, 136, 172, 173, 175, 286, 297, 298
Thurston, Frederick 153
tonality: contrast with modality 49, 51; dynamic 156, 157, 159, 204–5; fluidity 65, 67, 69, 77, 199; focus 41, 44; resolution 95–6, 156, 159, 161, 180, 181, 196, 199, 201, 205, 211–12, 213, 218, 227, 228; structure

67, 68–72, 81, 162, 188, 196, 199, 205–6, 208–11, 212, 304; *see also* form, closure
Tovey, Sir Donald Francis 128
Trimble, Joan 277
Twigworth 276, 285, 289, 292, 293, 303, 306

Vaughan Williams, Ralph 10, 39, 59, 102, 127, 131, 155, 165, 178, 295, 303; *Pastoral Symphony* 110, 131, 134, 154, 163–4, 197, 247–8, **250**, 299, 300; *Dona nobis pacem* 23, 249, **251**; *Fantasia on a Theme by Thomas Tallis* 179, 255, 297; *Flos campi* 131; *Job, a Masque for Dancing* 248–9, **250**, 257, **258**; *The Lark Ascending* 123, 278; Oboe Concerto 154; *A Sea Symphony* 128, 182, 224; influence of 11, 15, 19, 27, 34, 39, 42, 69, 92, 110, 123–4, 128, 132, 150, 248–9, 255, 257, 275, 278, 296n, 297, 299; use of sarabande 247–9
Vierne, Louis 40

Waddell, Helen 23, 225, 291

Wagner, Richard 11, 12, 67, 69; Tristan und Isolde 65, 67, 68, 85; influence of 65, 66, 68, 85
Walker, Ernest 186
Walton, Sir William 168, 175, 182, 236
Warlock, Peter 164, 177; *The Curlew* 85
Warren, Francis Purcell 121, 123, 128, 281, 294, 294n, 296, 300, 304
Webber, Nicholas 277
Wells, Robin 60
Westminster Cathedral 87, 90, 110, 175, 231
Willcocks, Sir David 183, 232
Winter, Jay 302, 303, 306
Whittaker, George 122–3, 127
Whittall, Arnold 164
Wood, Charles 20, 69
Wood, Sir Henry 17, 125, 126, 129, 141
word setting 100, 105–7, 111, 113, 231, 249–53; melisma 96, 100, 103, 104, 106, 107, 108, 112–13, 270, 297
Wordsworth, William 281

www.ingramcontent.com/pod-product-compliance
Lightning Source LLC
Chambersburg PA
CBHW070409100426
42812CB00005B/1686